SEND
THE
LIGHT

C. H. G.

Chas. H. Gabriel

1. There's a call comes ring-ing o'er the rest-less wave, "Send the light!
2. We have heard the Mac-e-do-nian call to-day,
3. Let us pray that grace may ev-'ry-where a-bound,
4. Let me not grow wea-ry in the work of love,

Send the light!

Send the light!"

There are souls to res-cue, there are souls to save,
And a gold-en of-f'ring at the cross we lay,
And a Christ-like spir-it ev-'ry-where be found,
Send the light! Let us gath-er jew-els for a crown a-bove.

CHORUS

Send the light!
Send the light!

Send the light!
Send the light!

Send the light!
Send the light!

the
Send the light!

bless-ed gos-pel light; Let it shine from shore to
the bless-ed gos-pel light; Let it shine

shore! shine for-ev-er-more.
from shore to shore! Let it shine for-ev-er-more.

SEND
THE
LIGHT

LOTTIE MOON'S LETTERS
AND OTHER WRITINGS

EDITED BY
KEITH HARPER

MERCER UNIVERSITY PRESS
MMII

ISBN 0-86554-
MUP/

First Edition.

∞The paper used in this publication meets the minimum
requirements of American National Standard for Information
Sciences—Permanence of Paper for Printed Library Materials,
ANSI Z39.48-1992.

Library of Congress Cataloging-in-Publication Data

Moon, Lottie, 1840-1912.
  Send the light : Lottie Moon's letters and other writings / edited by
Keith Harper.—1st ed.
      p. cm.
Includes bibliographical references and index.
  ISBN 0-86554-744-0 (alk. paper)—ISBN 0-86554-820-X (pbk. : alk.
paper)
  1. Moon, Lottie, 1840-1912—Correspondence. 2. Missionaries—
China—Correspondence. 3. Missionaries—United States—
Correspondence. 4. Southern Baptist Convention—Missions—
China—History—Sources. I. Harper, Keith, 1957-
II. Title.
  BV3427.M55 A4 2002
  266'.61'092—dc21

                                                              2002004820

TABLE OF CONTENTS

ACKNOWLEDGMENTS

This project began innocently enough with three misplaced historians at a Southern Baptist archivist's meeting in Nashville, Tennessee. Someone, perhaps Steve McKinion, said words to the effect, "Wouldn't it be great to have Lottie Moon's letters available for everyone to read?" This collection grew from that simple suggestion. It has been great fun and I am honored to acknowledge my gratitude for those who assisted in its production.

Many students at Southeastern Baptist Theological Seminary, Wake Forest, North Carolina, volunteered their services once they learned that I was preparing Moon's letters for publication. Corey Tutor and Vaughn Benner assisted in the transcription process as did Laura "Bambi" Thompson and Stephanie "Scooter" Ritchey. Mardi Roberts helped me appreciate the changes that Lottie Moon experienced over her 39 year career and Alex Kinchen helped me understand how Moon's individual letters fit into a larger scheme.

My secretary, Mary Lou Stephens, deserves a tremendous amount of credit for the manuscript's completion. She did an outstanding job of preparing these letters for publication and grew to love Lottie Moon in the process. In a slightly different vein, our librarians, Shawn Madden and Theresa Jerose, were always helpful and I appreciate their many kindnesses. Likewise, Jim Lutzweiler, Poet Laureate of Schnappsburg and Southeastern's archivist (who should have been in the Nashville meeting, but wasn't) helped me decipher several important passages in Moon's letters. My sincerest thanks to each of you for jobs well done.

I am especially indebted to the International Mission Board of the Southern Baptist Convention. Jerry Rankin and Bill Bullington saw merit in this project and graciously granted me permission to use Moon's letters. Vicky Bleick helped me by reproducing the photographs and maps in this book. I truly appreciate their enthusiastic support. I am also pleased to thank the Southern Baptist Theological Seminary, especially their archivist, Sean Lucas, who granted me access to read and permission to use letters from their Lottie Moon Collection. Also, my friend Bill Sumners at the Southern Baptist Historical Library and Archives, Nashville, Tennessee, located an important letter from Jessie Pettigrew to Dr. James Gaston. He also gave me permission to use it.

Numerous friends and colleagues offered their encouragement and advice over the past several months. Among this entourage stands Rich Holl, Dan Lykins and George Ellenberg, the "Homer of the Cottonfields" for whom Faulkner searched. Brian Rolfe, Southeastern's "Microsoft Maven" solved all my computer problems with a smile on his face. Honest. Steve McKinion also helped me with computers, conceptualization and another "c" word that would have made this alliteration perfect, but I can't remember it right now. I also want to commend Emir Caner, Steve Prescott, and Jason Lee who would be highly offended if I mentioned McKinion without mentioning them. Additionally, my friend Jeff Ray encouraged me throughout this project with kind words and the persistent query, "Is it ready yet?"

I am especially privileged to acknowledge those closest to me, namely, my wife, Johnnie, and my son, David, for their unfailing support. Johnnie's close attention to detail and David's ability to keep his dear old dad from taking himself too seriously have made this project run smoothly. In another place I said that Johnnie and David were loving reminders that some things in life are infinitely more important than others – and they still are.

Marc Jolley, Marsha Luttrell, and the editorial staff at Mercer University Press have been helpful, not to mention patient. I should also add that Marc could have made this project much shorter but chose to give me a generous manuscript length that allowed for considerable editorial flexibility. Thanks, Marc.

Finally, it is my distinct pleasure to thank Edie Jeter, archivist for the International Mission Board of the Southern Baptist Convention and one of the original "Nashville Conspirators." Edie very quickly became indispensable in numerous ways, not the least of which was in procuring readable copies of Moon's letters. She also assembled a first-rate team of proofreaders in Dr. Helen Falls, Karen Holcomb and Gladys Smith. I am profoundly grateful to these ladies for the long hours they spent poring over various drafts of this manuscript. In addition to enlisting proofreaders, Edie located most of the *Foreign Mission Journal* articles that are used in this book. Through it all she remained calm, cheerful and encouraging. Edie Jeter's enthusiasm for Lottie Moon's ministry breathed life into this work and it is to these two women that this book is dedicated.

Keith Harper
Wake Forest, North Carolina
14 May 2001

BAPTISTS

HISTORY, LITERATURE, THEOLOGY, HYMNS

General Editor: Walter B. Shurden

This series explores Baptists in all facets of Baptist life and thought. Open-ended and inclusive, this series seeks to publish works that ad-vance understanding of where Baptists have been, where they are, and where they are tending. It will promote the exploration and investi-gation of Baptist history; publish classics of Baptist literature includ-ing letters, diaries, and other writings; offer analyses of Baptist the-ologies; and examine the role of Baptists in societies and cultures both in the US and abroad.

Walter B. Shurden is the Callaway Professor of Christianity in the Roberts Department of Christianity and Executive Director of the Center for Baptist Studies, Mercer University, Macon, Georgia.

Books in the series

Richard Groves (Wake Forest Baptist Church) ed., Roger Williams's *The Bloody Tenant of Persecution for Cause of Conscience*

Richard Groves, ed., Thomas Helwys's *A Short Declaration of the Mystery of Iniquity*

James P. Byrd, *The Challenges of Roger Williams: Religious Liberty, Violent Persecution, and the Bible*

Chester Raymond Young, ed., John Taylor's *Baptists on the American Frontier: A History of Ten Baptist Churches of Which the Author Has Been Alternately a Member*

James A. Rogers,† *Richard Furman: Life and Legacy*

Dedicated To

The Life And Memory Of

Charlotte Digges "Lottie" Moon

And

Edie Jeter

Who Labors Behind The Scenes

To Keep That Memory Alive

INTRODUCTION

In December 2000 the Wake Cross Roads Baptist Church, a Southern Baptist Church in Raleigh, North Carolina, was preparing for the holiday season and the annual Lottie Moon Christmas Offering for international missions. This Christmas season was somewhat different than the ones before because the church "saw" Lottie Moon in a unique light. On the first Sunday in the month Miss Caitlin Mallett entered the church's worship center just prior to the morning services. Wearing an authentic costume, she walked down the center aisle and read excerpts from Moon's letters until she at last climbed the platform, faced the congregation and quoted from one letter that echoed a recurrent theme throughout Moon's writings, namely, "When will Southern Baptists wake up to their responsibilities?" Although she was only 9 years old, Caitlin's 4 ft. 3 in. frame matched her historical counterpart to a tee and the visual impact was stunning. Caitlin Mallett brought Lottie Moon to life on that Sunday morning and the church surpassed its goal of $20,000 by receiving $25,510.30.[1]

Charlotte Digges "Lottie" Moon[2] continues to captivate the Southern Baptist imagination. Perhaps the most familiar of all Southern Baptists, Moon's life story is so well known that it has become a key component in the denominational lore that helps define Southern Baptist identity. Many local churches recount Moon's life story as part of receiving the offering that bears her name. Some use dramatic, visual presentations, as in Wake Cross Roads' case, while others simply describe Moon's life in a more story-like fashion.

Moon was born on December 12, 1840 in Albermarle County, Virginia. An exceptionally bright woman, Moon received her education from the Virginia Female Seminary and the Albemarle Female Institute from which she earned her Master of Arts degree in 1861. She became a Christian in December 1858 and her friends seemed to notice a remarkable change in her

---

[1] The Lottie Moon Christmas Offering is an annual and in many cases much anticipated aspect of life in Southern Baptist churches. This offering is used exclusively for international missions and missionaries. The International Mission Board of the Southern Baptist Convention uses no receipts from the Lottie Moon Offering for its own administrative overhead.

[2] Digges sometimes appears as "Diggs." According to Catherine B. Allen, however, Digges was a family name from Lottie's father's side and should be spelled with an "e."

demeanor. She taught school in Kentucky and Georgia before beginning her career as a missionary to China in 1873. She labored the remainder of her life in the province of Shantung (Shandong) and died en route to the United States on December 24, 1912.

This book's purpose is not to write Lottie Moon's life story. Interested readers who are looking for a biographical work would do well to consult Catherine Allen's *The New Lottie Moon Story*.[3] Rather, this work intends to present Moon in her own words with minimal editorial intrusion. Fortunately, Lottie Moon tells a fascinating story and her writings shed considerable light on the costs she and other turn-of-the-century missionaries paid in their service to God and humanity.

In *Taking Christianity to China: Alabama Missionaries in the Middle Kingdom, 1850-1950*, Wayne Flynt and Gerald Berkley studied Alabama missionaries in China over a 100 year period. They discovered that their missionaries almost always experienced "culture shock" upon arriving in China. This is scarcely surprising but neophyte missionaries were almost always stunned to learn that the Chinese looked upon them with contempt because they believed Caucasians were inferior to them. Too quickly, they also learned that direct, intentional evangelism did not yield the results they expected. Consequently, many missionaries began experimenting with innovative ways to propagate Christianity among the Chinese. Some tried to build schools; others built hospitals. Over time, however, nearly all missionaries came to identify more with the Chinese than their family and friends in America.[4]

Of course, Lottie Moon was not from Alabama but the patterns Flynt and Berkley found among Alabama missionaries have a familiar ring in her correspondence. Moon's letters to H. A. Tupper, Corresponding Secretary of the Foreign Mission Board of the Southern Baptist Convention from 1873-1893 and her personal friend, offer candid insights concerning her feelings about China, missionary life and Southern Baptists. Much like Flynt and Berkley's missionaries, Moon possessed a certain sense of superiority when she first went to China. Her various references to "John Chinaman" and "heathens" suggest that while she had a certain amount of love for the

---

[3] Catherine B. Allen, *The New Lottie Moon Story*, second edition, (Birmingham: Woman's Missionary Union, 1980).

[4] See Wayne Flynt and Gerald W. Berkley, *Taking Christianity to China: Alabama Missionaries in the Middle Kingdom, 1850-1950* (Tuscaloosa/London: The University of Alabama Press, 1997).

Chinese people, she could also be condescending in her attitudes toward them.

In the early 1880s Moon attempted to work among Chinese women by engaging in what she called "country work." She left her school work and ventured into nearby villages to spread Christianity to whomever would listen, especially women. It was difficult work and some of her letters even warned that her missionary methodology was not for the fainthearted. Even so, Moon delighted in her ability to adapt to her surroundings and her continued, personal association with her neighbors began the chip away at her prejudices. Over time she saw them endure the hardships of wars and revolutions. She saw them work to build better lives for themselves. She saw them endure famines and face death with courage and dignity. In short, she saw the Chinese people as human beings and resented "foreigners" who wanted to exploit them.

By the early 1900s "country work" had become too physically demanding and Moon began to see new evangelical opportunities in schools for Chinese girls. She always had loved children and thus had come full circle in her thinking. She had been in China long enough to shed the label "Devil woman" and be known as Miss Moon, the missionary. She was also known for being one of finest cookie makers in northern China.

If her letters and articles offer a unique window into Moon's psyche, they also reveal her attitudes about her work. She used the pages of the *Foreign Mission Journal* to tell people in America about China. It was an intriguing land, she observed, that was both beautiful and challenging. She told Southern Baptists about Chinese culture and folkways in a way that conveyed a message—China needs *you.* She also expressed her feelings when her constituents were slow to respond. In fact, the Lottie Moon Christmas Offering really grew from a challenge laid before Southern Baptist women. She noted that Southern Methodist women had organized themselves to conduct missionary work. Why, she pondered, could Southern Baptist women not do the same? Why, indeed. By 1888 Southern Baptist women had organized and helped collect $3,315.00 for Moon's much needed relief.

Besides exhortation, Moon also kept the Board informed regarding internal missionary issues. Her explanations regarding how missionaries conducted their business and how they responded to crisis merit close attention. For example, "Gospel Missionism," T. P. Crawford's plan to wrest control of Chinese missionary work from the Foreign Board sent shock waves through American Baptist churches and alienated Crawford from the Foreign Mission Board. Moon's letters on this issue are remarkably fair and even-handed, even though she was loyal to the Board and counted Martha Foster Crawford, T. P. Crawford's wife, among her closest friends.[5]

Taken together, these letters and articles chart the spiritual odyssey of a well-bred Virginia woman who spent most of her adult life becoming a missionary. By the end of her life Moon's feelings for the Chinese had gone from pity to empathy. Her writings chronicle numerous, subtle shifts in her thinking as she grew from novice to seasoned missionary. They also articulate her amazement, even frustration, that Southern Baptists in America never really grasped the enormity of China's needs.

Before examining these letters, readers should know something about them. Most of the letters and articles reprinted in this work came from two sources, namely, the archives of the International Mission Board of the Southern Baptist Convention and the Lottie Moon Collection at the Southern Baptist Theological Seminary, Louisville, Kentucky. The letters from Southern Seminary's Lottie Moon Collection are cited individually, as is one letter from the Southern Baptist Historical Library and Archives. This is not an exhaustive collection in that I did not use every letter available in these archives. However, it is a thorough collection (over 300 pieces) and representative of Moon's thought.

Moon had several stylistic idiosyncrasies that readers may find interesting. For example, Moon usually used an ampersand instead of spelling out the word "and." As we proofread the letters we double checked "and" if we saw it in written form. Occasionally, Moon used phonetic spellings for some English words. Hence, she sometimes wrote "wel" instead of "well," and words that ended with "ed" received a final "t," as with "reacht" instead of "reached." Her approach to phonetics also produced variant spellings for Chinese cities. For example, Tungchow, Tengchow, and Tung Chow all refer to the same place. The same is true for P'ingtu, Pengtu, and Pingtu, as well as Hwangshien which has several different spellings. For this book I wanted accuracy in transcription rather than superimposed uniformity. Also, finding Moon's paragraph structure could be an adventure at times. I did the best I could and I apologize if I am not right in every case.

Lottie Moon wrote in a beautiful, flowing script. She was an articulate woman who wrote forcefully and logically. Unfortunately, time has taken its toll on some letters and they are difficult to read in places. I chose to leave blanks where I found illegible words. In other places I transcribed words as

---

[5] See Keith E. Eitel, *Paradigm Wars: The Southern Baptist International Mission Board Faces the Third Millennium.* Foreword by L. Paige Patterson. Regnum Studies in Mission (Oxford: Regnam Books International, 2000).

best I could but used (?) to indicate that I was not absolutely certain about the transcription. This is especially true for the letters from the Southern Baptist Theological Seminary collection, nearly all of which have been type-scripted by an unidentified scribe.

Finally, Lottie Moon never signed her letters with her given name, "Charlotte." Instead, she wrote *L. Moon* and in nearly every case put a period after Moon. It is not at all surprising that a woman as meticulous and precise as Lottie Moon would include such a detail.

Lottie Moon, age about 30, missionary to China. (Courtesy of the International Mission Board.)

W. Harvey Clarke, 1907. (Courtesy of the International Mission Board.)

Lucille Daniel Clarke (Mrs. W. Harvey Clarke), 1907. (Courtesy of the International Mission Board.)

Tungchow. Missionary J. B. Hartwell, center; and Northern Presbyterians, Dr. Corbeth, left, and Dr. Mateer (pioneer missionaries in Shantung Province). Circa 1910. (Courtesy of the International Mission Board, given by Missionary Anna Hartwell.)

Dr. H. A. Tupper, executive secretary, Foreign Mission Board, Southern Baptist Convention, February, 1872, June 1893. (Courtesy of the International Mission Board.)

Robert J. Willingham. (Courtesy of the International Mission Board.)

J. B. Hartwell. (Courtesy of the International Mission Board.)

T. P. Crawford, October 1888(?).
(Courtesy of the International
Mission Board.)

Martha Foster Crawford
(Mrs. T. P. Crawford).
(Courtesy of the International
Mission Board.)

Lottie Moon, missionary to China, 1873-1912. Tunchow. Missionary Residence, "The Little Crossroads," yard. (Courtesy of the International Mission Board.)

Tungchow. Missionary residence, "The Little Crossroads," yard; Miss Lottie Moon, missionary, seated, Miss Ella Jeter, missionary (left), and Miss Jessie Pettigrew, missionary (right), circa 1905. (Courtesy of the International Mission Board.)

Chinese women with bound feet, measuring 3" in length. (Courtesy of the International Mission Board.)

Yuen Shi Kai, governor of Shantung (right) and secretary (governor during the "Boxer" rebellion in 1900, saved the lives of foreigners in Shantung Province). (Provided by Anna Hartwell; Courtesy of the International Mission Board.)

Chefoo. "Shanza," an early mode of transportation.
(Courtesy of the International Mission Board.)

Shantung Province. Curious villagers gathered around
American woman in rickshaw, circa 1910. Photograph by J.
Levering Evans. (Courtesy of the International Mission
Board.)

Shantung Province. Beggars along the road, including children and woman with bound feet, circa 1910. Photograph by J. Levering Evans. (Courtesy of the International Mission Board.)

Shantung Province. Buddhist temple; priest at altar, circa 1910. Photograph by J. Levering Evans. (Courtesy of the International Mission Board.)

Pingtu. Two men smoking opium in the village of Shui King. (Courtesy of the International Mission Board.)

Sun Hwo Chi. People in famine relief line. Hwangshien area. Famine relief program directed by Missionaries W. B. Glass and John Lowe, 1907. (Courtesy of the International Mission Board.)

Pingtu. Second home of Lottie Moon. (Courtesy of the
International Mission Board.)

Tengchow, China. Peng Lai Kwoa (temple), crowds on "first
moon and 16th day," circa 1921. (Courtesy of the
International Mission Board.)

Tengchow. A family cemetery, circa 1910. Furnished by
missionary Jane Lide. (Courtesy of the International Mission
Board.)

Shantung Province. Villagers in padded clothing, circa 1910.
Photograph by J. Levering Evans. (Courtesy of the
International Mission Board.)

Soldiers of the Emperor ready to fight the Japanese, 1894-1895.
Furnished by missionary Anna Hartwell. (Courtesy of the
International Mission Board.)

Chinese woman grinding millet. (Courtesy of the
International Mission Board.)

Pingtu. Marketplace. (Courtesy of the International Mission
Board.)

Two page sample of Lottie Moon's letter writing. (Courtesy
of the International Mission Board.)

Letter dated June 30, 1898 to Dr. Willingham. (Courtesy of the International Mission Board.)

Letter written by Lottie Moon. (Courtesy of the International Mission Board.)

THE LOTTIE MOON

CORRESPONDENCE

I. THE TUPPER YEARS

1873-1893

*"There are souls to rescue, there
are souls to save..."*

THE H. A. TUPPER LETTERS, 1873-1893

Henry Allen Tupper succeeded James Barnett Taylor as Corresponding Secretary of the Southern Baptist Foreign Mission Board in January 1872. Tupper had considerable ministerial experience, having served in Georgia and South Carolina pastorates. He had also established himself as an enthusiastic missions advocate. Tupper led the Foreign Mission Board until he retired in 1893. Under his leadership the number of missionaries increased from 18 to 94, while the number of countries in which they served increased from 3 to 6. Tupper also encouraged women to participate in missionary work, especially as educators.

Moon's letters to Tupper indicate that they shared a warm, personal friendship. In fact, some letters suggest a familiarity that was almost playful. In a letter dated September 8, 1879, Moon announced that she had adopted "fonetic" spelling and in her next letter dated September 21 asked, "Don't yu admir the nu spelling?" Although Tupper's exact words have been lost, he apparently did not approve because her letters quickly re-adopted near perfect traditional form. On the other hand, Moon's letters could also be incredibly forthright, even blunt. In a tersely worded epistle of June 27, 1885, she offered her immediate resignation over a misunderstanding regarding appropriate roles for women in missionary service. Tupper wisely declined Moon's hasty offer.

Moon's personal regard for Tupper as well as her own sense of propriety demanded that she keep him abreast of missionary life in China. Regardless of whether she was reminding him of the need for more missionaries in China or explaining the "unwritten law of missionaries" (see March 26, 1876), Moon kept Tupper well informed. Unfortunately, she also felt obligated to explain the problems facing his missionaries. Gospel Missionism, T. P. Crawford's suggested method for doing mission work that circumvented the Foreign Mission Board, briefly disrupted the work in China and Moon spared Tupper no details.

Considered as a unit, Moon's letters to Tupper capture the essence of both their professional relationship and their personal friendship. She admired his ability and respected his opinion. By the same token, Tupper trusted Moon and relied on her for accurate field information. Their mutual labors helped create a stable basis for Southern Baptist work in China.

————

Cartersville, Ga.,
Jan. 13, 1873
Rev. Dr. Tupper:
Dear Sir,

Letters received from China this morning place me in rather an embarrassing position. Some time since, I requested my sister, Miss Eddie Moon to put a question or two to Mrs. Crawford for me. It seems that they have jumped at the conclusion that I wish to join my sister as missionary, & I learn that Mr. Crawford has written you on the subject.

Years ago I very much desired to be a missionary but it was not then the policy of our Board to send out single ladies. The war came about the time I completed my education, & I could not have gone, even if there had been the change in views on the part of the board which has since taken place.

Meantime I have given a promise which I feel in honor bound to keep unless the lady will release me from it. It was a pledge to take care of her children in case of her death. About two years ago, I thought of offering myself to the F. M. B., but was restrained by this promise. I think of writing & asking a release from it.

I write you now to beg you not to let Mr. Crawford's letter become public. It would be very unpleasant to me to have the matter publicly discussed, & besides this it might injure my prospects here as a teacher, if it were known that I contemplate leaving.

I feel that I owe you an apology for this long trespass on your time & yet I could not well avoid it. Should I get released from the promise to which I have alluded above, I think it probable I shall communicate with you again. Regretting that the matter has been brought prematurely before you,

I remain
Very respectfully,
Lotte Moon.

Tung Chow, China,
Nov. 1, 1873
Rev. H. A. Tupper:
My dear Brother,

I herewith transmit you a report of my travelling expenses from Alabama to Tung Chow.

I arrived here about a week ago and have received a most hearty welcome from the missionaries stationed in Shan Tung. My first impressions of North China are of the most agreeable character. The climate so far has been exceptionally mild. The leaves are still green and flowers are yet blooming in the open air. Tung Chow has the reputation of being the cleanest city in all China. To one who has been sickened by offensive odors in merely passing through the streets of Shanghai, the contrast is the more marked & the more grateful. Here, in the heart of the city, we may have pure air and abundance of sunshine. I can not imagine how a foreigner could live in Shanghai in the native city.

At our very doors is the work we crave. The heathen are literally all around us. I have already had the pleasure of going with my sister on some of her visits to the native women. Much tact is necessary in dealing with these as the aversion to foreigners is still very strong. Some will not admit us at all; others listen coldly and with evident restraint; only a few hear the word gladly. Nevertheless we must "sow beside all waters." We *know* that God's word can not "return void." Of this we have strong proof in the recent tour of Mrs. Crawford & Mrs. Holmes in the country. In one of the villages, the women crowded eagerly to hear the words of life. The ladies could scarcely find time to take supper, so numerous were the hearers, & so eager the interest. They listened until a late hour, and begged their longer stay in the village. Circumstances were such, however, that the ladies thought it best to proceed on their tour. We are hoping that a revival may take place in this village such as has cheered & encouraged one of the Presbyterian missionaries in an out-station. There the interest is so great & the number of converts so large, that he has concluded to remain all the winter instead of returning to his home in Chefoo.

I wish you could see Mr. Crawford's beautiful new church, and better still could look upon the devout, orderly worshippers who assemble there. In Mr. Crawford's absence one of the native deacons conducted the services last Sabbath. The singing was very good, far better than I have usually heard in country churches at home. I am told that this is due to Mrs. Crawford's careful training. I wish some liberal hearted brother would reward her & encourage the church by the gift of a good organ. A bell is also needed. The present of the communion service, sent by the Young Ladies of the Richmond Institute, was both timely and acceptable. By the way, can you not stir up the hearts of our sisters in Richmond so that they shall build for my sister and myself? We need only about two thousand dollars for that purpose. In a heathen city each new mission house becomes a centre of influence. Thus the field of usefulness is largely widened and many more are brought under Christian influence. We are desirous as soon as possible of having a boarding school for girls. The greatest blessing we could bestow upon this people is the Christian education of the future wives and mothers. Now, their deformed feet and tottering walk but are a type of their narrow minds and degraded morals. It is considered very disgraceful here for women to go to church, and they are rarely seen on the street. The houses are enclosed by high walls. On entering the street door you pass into an open court around which are built the low rooms in which the Chinese women pass their days. The windows are small & admit very little light through the bars. The use of glass is unknown. The floors are the ground. The better class own two or more chairs: others sit on low stools or a dirty mat. All seem to smoke & they generously offer their pipe to the visitor. The beds are of brick & so constructed that a fire can be made underneath. This is their sole provision for warming. A more comfortless existence is hardly conceivable. Add to this their lack of cleanliness & their degrading superstitions and the spectacle is indeed pitiable.

The children interest me more than any other class, with their shining black eyes, solemn faces, & comic pig-tails. Yet that they can laugh as heartily as white children I have proved to my satisfaction when I have come upon a group and sought to learn a few Chinese phrases under their tuition. Their merriment was irresistibly contagious.

What we need in China is more workers. The harvest is *very* great, the laborers, oh! *so few*. Why does the Southern Baptist church lag behind in this great work? Our Presbyterian brethren are putting us to shame. Their missions, established since the war, are strong in young men in all the vigor of early manhood. We rejoice that these have taken a high stand in China and that they are doing a noble work; we are glad that others are expected to join them. But, when the veteran missionaries of our church shall fall at their posts after lives of unselfish devotion, where, we sadly ask, are their successors? Who shall take up the banner they have borne so bravely through weary years of gloom and discouragement?

I think your idea is correct, that a young man should ask himself not if it is his duty to go to the heathen, but if he may dare stay at home. The command is so plain: "Go."

With kind regards,

Very truly yrs.,

L. Moon.

Tung Chow, China,
April 27, 1874
Rev. H. A. Tupper:
My dear Brother,

Your kind letter, enclosing one from the Ladies of the 2nd Baptist church, Atlanta, was duly received, and the perusal of both communications afforded me no little pleasure. I wrote by return mail to the Ladies with regard to the work here, and especially of the house which it is proposed to build for my sister and myself. I have suggested that the Society in Atlanta correspond with the societies in Cartersville and Albany, and that whatever surplus funds are raised shall be used for this purpose. Of course it remains for the Ladies to decide whether they will so appropriate their funds. As they have voluntarily assumed my support, I am convinced that they will not be satisfied with merely having a missionary in the field, but that they will place at my command such facilities as are necessary for the work.

I had the pleasure of going last week with Mrs. Crawford on a two days' tour among the neighboring villages. We were accompanied by three native brethren & a native sister.

The first day we visited five villages. As we halted at one of them to take our dinner, Mrs. Crawford remarked that here probably no one would come near us as one of the brethren had had a difficulty with a man living here who had cheated and subsequently beaten him. The brother took the case to a Mandarin who promptly dealt out justice. The supposition was that the villagers had espoused the quarrel. However, we had scarcely begun our preparations for dinner before the people began to emerge from their houses in large numbers, and soon they were eagerly crowding around us. They watched us eat with infinite satisfaction; to see the foreigners use knives, forks & spoons, and to behold them drinking milk and eating butter,—these are sights of which the unsophisticated villagers never tire. When we were through with our meal, the brethren had an excellent opportunity for preaching. The scene was at once picturesque and inspiring. The audience, consisting of men, women, & children, sat on the green grass, beneath the trees which were waving gently in the wind, while above was that cloudless blue sky which seems peculiar to this region. The brethren were so much encouraged by the attention of the auditors, that they decided to have singing and prayer. I suppose this was the first time that anything even remotely resembling a regular service was ever held in that village.

We spent that night with the native sister to whom I have alluded as being in our company. The brethren held services at her house that night. The next day we returned to our home in the city, taking another route from that of the previous day and halting at a number of villages. In nearly all, we found audiences willing to listen, and Mrs. Crawford talked most earnestly to the women who eagerly flocked around her. The native sister gave valuable assistance in talking to the women. One of the brethren with us manifested a talent for preaching I had not imagined he possessed. His forte seems decidedly street-preaching. I was surprised at his skill in enchaining the attention of the crowd, and if he was not really eloquent, he certainly approached very near to that rare gift.

The ladies of our own & of the Presbyterian mission here have been accustomed for years to take longer or shorter tours, as the case might be, among the neighboring or more remote villages, with only the native christians for company and protection. Ladies could travel hundreds of miles under such circumstances & meet with no rudeness or insult. China is to-day perhaps more open to mission work than any other heathen country. The laws guarantee free admission to the missionary. Here, too, the priesthood is not a dominant caste. On the contrary, they are looked upon with contempt and are not allowed to enter the houses of respectable people. In the remote interior the opposition to foreigners is still very strong, but if the missionary will only content himself with itinerating in such sections for a few years and not settle there, the opposition is not likely to become organized and violent. Oh! that we had many active and zealous men who would go far and wide scattering books and tracts and preaching the word to the vast multitudes of this land. The Northern Presbyterian church has such men & so has the Scotch Pres. Church. Why does *our* church lag so slowly on? Where we send *one* man, other churches send scores. I understand that our Northern brethren sent *twenty* new missionaries to Burmah last year. I earnestly long for the time to come when the women of our Southern Baptist churches shall fully awaken to the great work of sending the gospel to heathen women. Oh! that Woman's Mission to Woman might take hold of the affections of our sisters at home and that *many* more representatives might be sent to China and elsewhere. In this city and in the hundreds of villages around, there is most urgent need for workers, and I believe that nowhere at home can a devoted woman accomplish more for God than here.

Mrs. Holmes, Landrum, & my sister, have gone on a trip to Shanghai, the former seeking health, the two latter for recreation. We are hoping they will all be greatly benefitted by the journey. In my sister's absence, I am teaching a few classes in her school.

Mr. Crawford proposes to go this week on a country tour, and expects to be absent about two weeks.

You speak of your desire to visit China. How gladly would we welcome you! Should a General Missionary Conference be held about three years hence—as is proposed, the Secretaries of all the Boards will be invited to attend. Can you not come? With kindest regards,

Sincerely yrs.,

L. Moon.

Tung Chow, China,
May 21, 1874
Rev. H. A. Tupper:
My dear Brother,

In writing you a short while ago, I neglected to mention the subject of salary. You announced that the Board had settled it at $600.00 to which one third was added, making eight hundred at home. I have consulted with my sister & she says she finds four hundred taels (400 Tls.) amply sufficient for her wants. Mr. Crawford says that this is equivalent to six hundred & fifty dollars. ($650.00) at home. I have decided to draw only that amount as salary. While we are boarding, we are at less expense than we would be if keeping house. In voluntarily relinquishing a portion of my salary, I feel confident that if future exigencies should require an increase, the Board will cheerfully listen to any reasonable request upon that subject.

My sister did not go to Shanghai after all. She only made a short visit to Yentai, and is again here at work. Her health is excellent. Mrs. Holmes is still in the South. While we fully recognized the necessity of her going, her departure leaves a serious gap in our very small circle. We are very glad to receive, through your recent letter to Mr. Crawford, the assurance of a speedy re-enforcement of this mission. Mr. C. continues in rather feeble health. Mrs. C. is laboring with her accustomed energy & efficiency. With kindest regards,

Yrs. sincerely,

L. Moon.

Tung Chow, China,
March 13, 1875
Rev. H. A. Tupper:
My dear Brother,

Early in January I was unexpectedly called away to accompany my sister to Shanghai, to which place she had been ordered by her physician. To face the dangers and discomforts of an ocean voyage is never pleasant, but when duty requires, there is no more to be said. Accordingly, in something over a week after the command to go, we found ourselves casting anchor in the river at Shanghai. Imagine yourself suddenly transported from a quiet country village to busy, bustling Broadway, and you can form an idea of the change from Tungchow to Shanghai. Here, we have no trade; business stagnates. Men fail to find employment and many of them seek it abroad. At Shanghai, it is far otherwise. First, there is the foreign settlement, English, French, & American, with an infusion of other nationalities. Where the Caucasian goes, he carries energy and an inferior race is aroused by the contact. In the foreign settlement, one sees large & handsome public buildings, while the private houses are not inferior to those in cities at home. Where the English are found, fine horses may be expected, & Shanghai is no exception to the rule. Go out after five o'c'k in the evening & you will see handsome carriages drawn by well-kept horses, and gallant horsemen, dashing past, on their way to the paper hunt, or perhaps simply riding for recreation. The Chinese are imitative & now & then you see a trap full of Celestials driving usually at a more sober pace than foreign affect. The Chinese likewise use the wheel-barrow, an awkward, ugly concern with the wheel *under* the barrow, and the jinricksha, which they have introduced from Japan. Such are the sights of the foreign settlement where many Chinese live, willingly paying the additional tax which secures them a home within the concession with its better government & greater privileges.

To the native city with its narrow, dark, crowded, filthy streets, its odors, its sounds, no words could do justice. It would doubtless be fatal to a foreigner to reside in this native city.

After a stay of nearly two weeks in Shanghai, we set out for Soochow to visit some friends, of the Southern Pres. Mission. After my experience of Chinese travelling in the North, I was surprised and delighted to see how comfortable we could make ourselves on a native boat. The day was beautiful & we indulged our love of exercise by rapid walking along the banks of the canal.

We had but one adventure, which, without being dangerous had at least the zest of novelty. About two o'clock in the night, our boat came into collision with another boat. One of our men, to make sure of recovering damages, at once boarded the enemy's vessel, and seized upon some property belonging, as it turned out, to a passenger on that boat. The intruder was instantly set upon and he seemed in danger of being pulled to pieces between his captors, and his friends who were seeking to rescue him. Then followed that fierce quarreling which is so characteristic of the Chinese, but which means nothing. We ladies would have been alarmed, but our kind and thoughtful escort, Rev. Mr. Dubose, assured us there was no danger, and we heard the altercation with no little amusement. Finally, a compromise was effected & we proceeded on our way.

Time would fail to tell of the wonders of Soochow, the great pagoda, the ink pagoda, the twin pagodas, the great Confucian temple, the rockeries, the temple of five hundred gods, the bridge of ten thousand ages, the handsome shops, the immense crowds of people. Here, at last, I felt, was the China of one's youthful dreams, the China which artists have sketched & of which travelers have told glowing tales. The people too, with their lively manners & soft Southern tongue, are different from those of North China. But for all that, I should not like to live in Soochow. The city is intersected with canals which are receptacles of filth. Then there are many stagnant pools from which fatal miasms must arise. The climate, too, even in winter, is very debilitating as compared with the bracing air of Shangtung. There are four missions in Soochow, the So. Presbyterian, Northern Pres., London Mission, & So. Methodist Mission, comprising in all twelve foreigners and a number of native assistants. As yet the work is in its infancy. The missionaries there, as a body, are young, cheerful, & hopeful.

Speaking of the great pagoda, it may not be out of place to relate a superstition connected therewith. Dr. Yates is my authority and he had it from a Chinaman. The city, says this story, is built in the shape of a tortoise. As there is water all around the city, the sage inhabitants feared the tortoise would some day walk off into the water. The pagoda was therefore erected to keep him in his place. There is also a story of the twin pagodas & the ink pagoda. The twin pagodas having been built, the luck was not good. The fortune-tellers were consulted, & they said that the two towers were like pens. What was the use of pens, without ink? Hence, they must build a pagoda making it black & the luck would then all be right. Hence arose the ink pagoda.

While we were absent in Soochow, the Sabbath of the Chinese New Year, Dr. Yates had the satisfaction of dedicating his new church, which he has re-modelled at a heavy expense, the larger portion of which he has borne himself. And this leads me to say that such is the modesty of the Doctor that he will not write of his sacrifices for the cause, nor tell how nobly & successfully he has worked to build up a true Christian church. Where other men have sounded loud trumpets and announced wonderful achievements which existed largely in their own imaginations, (I do not refer here to any missionary of our Board,) the Doctor has worked on quietly & faithfully, sending now & then only a brief, cautious, modest report. While many have yielded to the temptation to overestimate the value of their work in the accounts sent home for publication, I rather think that our missionary in Shanghai, in his scorn of humbug, has erred in the other extreme. He has been inclined to make too light of what he has accomplished. The new church is perhaps the most complete in its appliances of any in China. The provision for ventilation, & for lighting it at night, is equal to that of any city church at home. Then the baptistry is all that could be desired. It is in the rear of the pulpit, shut out from it by folding doors. Leading into the baptistry, on either side are dressing-rooms, also supplied with gas-burners. Within each dressing-room are steps leading down into the baptistry, so that the candidate is in the water before he is seen by the congregation & emerges therefrom entirely out of view. The church formerly fronted away from the street, but this has now been remedied. A valuable bell has been presented to Dr. Yates for his church. This Chinese church is far ahead of the majority at home in its adjuncts: there is a parsonage and a school on the same lot. One cannot but be filled with admiration at the wonderful economy of space here manifested. There was only a given amount of land: no more could be secured. The problem was to make the most of this, & it has been done. Every foot has been made to tell for some useful purpose. In the pastor's house, is a room intended to be used for the assembly of the brethren one night during the week. Dr. Yates' design is that the church shall form itself thus into a sort of school of which the native pastor shall be teacher, that so they may grow more & more familiar with the Scriptures. The pastor is a valuable man. Unfortunately he is so popular with missionaries of other denominations, that they are perpetually drawing him away from his legitimate duties to engage in some union meeting, or to give advice on some matter in which he has properly no concern. This is very provoking, but Dr. Yates has borne it with a patience that is simply admirable. How one missionary can have the conscience to interfere with the work of another in this way, passes belief, but nevertheless such things *do* take place.

The arrangements for the school are worthy of all commendation. The school-room is on the ground floor. Upstairs is the teacher's room which opens out into a small veranda. Below stairs is a tiny kitchen, large enough, however, for the purpose. The teacher is a widow, with a sweet, pleasant face. She has recently united with the church. Mrs. Yates writes me that she has four little girls as pupils. This is certainly a good beginning, & doubtless the school will grow into wide usefulness. I had the pleasure of attending only one service in the new church. It was the Thursday evening lecture. Of course I could not understand the Shanghai dialect, but Dr. Yates said it was a very good address. Among other things, the speaker observed that the good news of salvation had always been communicated by men going from place to place. Thus it had been carried to the foreign country, & now it had come to China. Formerly, said he, one heard much of the wonders wrought by idols. Now, since the Bible had come to China, we heard no more stories of the power of idols.

Five new members had lately been received. The most gratifying fact about accessions to the church is that they are mostly relatives or friends of those already Christians. Thus the growth is natural & healthy. Dr. Yates is seeking to impress on the church that now is the time, as it were, for a "new departure." With their new church, parsonage, and school, they should feel that all has been done for them that they could possibly ask, and that henceforth, they must put their own shoulders to the wheel, support their pastor, & work individually for the conversion of sinners. Dr. Yates seems greatly encouraged in his work. "No," he said, in reply to a remark that Mr.------ considered missions a failure, "No, they are not a failure. Here is my church in a retired part of the city, yet every Sunday we have a full house. People come from a distance to attend church. Even during the week, at night, we have a respectable congregation. Why, when we first came," added he, "the Chinese used to run from us in affright. Now, all that has changed."

The truth is, to a new-comer on the mission-field, the matter of astonishment is that so much has been done. Formerly there were no books from which to learn Chinese. There was no means of communicating even with one's teacher except by signs. If you wanted to know the word for water or bread, for instance, you must show these to your teacher. Did you want to know how to say walk or run, you must go through with those motions, & so on *ad infinitum*. The New Testament was not translated & there were no hymns. Imagine a worship without hymns, & where only the preacher prayed, while all around was confused talking & people continually going out or coming in. Then–as to schools, there were no religious or scientific books such as the new missionary now finds ready to his hand in abundance, as soon as he is able to use them. Better still, he may sometimes find Christian teachers to put in charge of schools, where formerly none could be procured but heathen.

The more I see of mission life, the more impressed I am with the amount of hard work, real drudgery one might call it, of those noble veterans, the pioneers of missions in China, many of whom are now gone to their reward above, others of whom are still toiling at their posts with all the ardor of their early days, & yet with the added experience of years of active service.

I saw *Quang san*, Dr. Yates' out station, only in the distance. The city is built on a mountain, the summit of which seems crowned by a pagoda. Here are a few Christians over whom is a native pastor. Dr. Yates speaks of him in the highest terms. Recently this pastor was in Shanghai & on Sunday night he was to preach. When he rose, standing there in the brilliant gas-light, with the crowd of expectant faces turning up to him, his ideas seemed all to dissert him. It was certainly a trying situation to one accustomed to speak only to a few brethren in a plain Chinese house. Dr. Yates kindly told him that he understood it all, he himself had been through a similar experience. The result was that the man concluded that he would stay awhile in Shanghai & learn to preach to a large audience. This shows that he has pluck.

As to the cost of altering and improving the church, some seven hundred dollars were contributed by the churches at home. The Chinese gave about forty-two dollars. Of this, two dollars were brought voluntarily by an aged sister, very deaf, who said she wanted to have some share in building the Lord's house. The Chinese workmen, heathen though they were, gave about twenty dollars. It seems hard that when a man has given his whole life to building a spiritual church, he should also have to furnish the means to construct the material one.

Here in Tungchow, schools, not only in our mission but in the Presbyterian, have opened with hopeful prospects. Mrs. Holmes has seventeen or eighteen girls & women. My sister's school has gone up to fourteen. Mrs. Crawford has more applicants than she can receive.

We are much pleased at learning from a recent number of the *Journal*, that Mrs. Lewellyn will perhaps join us in Tungchow. There is a plenty of work for her & for as many more as will come. We long to see other large cities in this province occupied by faithful men & women. If you should send us too many workers for Tungchow (!) there is *Hwang hsien*, a city twenty miles from here, where there is not a single missionary. There are villages by the hundred where the gospel is heard only at long intervals, & very many in which it has never been proclaimed. "Pray therefore the Lord of the harvest, that he will send forth labors into his harvest."

Yours truly,

L. Moon.

Tung Chow,
China
Nov. 2, 1875
Rev. Dr. H. A. Tupper:
My dear Brother,

I have heard it intimated that a project is on foot among the brethren of the North Street Church to send a petition to the Board to this effect, viz.: to build a church for them, to support a school for them, & to continue the salary of the native assistants, in short, proposing to put themselves in direct communication with the Board. Believing that if such a policy should be adopted by the Board, it would be fraught with the most disastrous consequences. I beg leave most respectfully, to make a few statements. I honestly believe, in common with other missionaries older & wiser than myself, that the *curse* of missions is *foreign money*. It corrupts the very foundation of all attempts to do good. It attracts around us needy adventurers whose *sole* aim is "a place." I will give you an instance. There is a mission in Chefoo with which is connected a large hospital. A number of the patients plotted to join the church, the native assistant assuring them of "places" & instructing them *how to answer* when they should come before the session. They made a joke of it among themselves. One of Mrs. Crawford's schoolboys was then under treatment in the hospital, & on his return, he told of it, expressing his disgust & astonishment. Some months later, that assistant was dismissed in disgrace, his employer having at last discovered his true character.

I am very far indeed from wishing to intimate that all native assistants are such characters. I am fully convinced that the pastor of the North Street church is a true Christian man, in spite of his narrow & illiberal spirit towards foreigners. I have no word to say against the right of *any missionary on the ground* to employ native assistants where his Board sanctions it, but I do deprecate most earnestly any action which will place money at the disposal of the Chinaman without a constant present check.

The policy of our mission has been to pay *no one* to preach the gospel. Every member of the church, male & female, is expected to preach as opportunity offers, whether in their home, visiting their neighbors, or journeying by the wayside. I think I may say truthfully that we have a *live*, working church. They preach because they love it, & esteem it an honor.

But human nature is the same in China as elsewhere. Suppose they should see the leading members of another church paid by the Board to do what *they* do for nothing. Straightaway will arise dissatisfaction, & the injury will be incalculable.

I am fully convinced that the time has not come for Chinese churches to walk alone. They have, I believe, neither the grace nor the knowledge to do this. In Shanghai, good old *Wang* is constantly under the supervision & direction of Dr. Yates. Should Pastor *Woo* be set up here as an independent agent of the Board, it will only foster in him & in his leading church members that spirit of arrogant self-conceit & superiority which has culminated in the rude letter they requested Dr. Yates to communicate to the Board.

With the members of the North Street church, I have had none but the most amicable relations. Since we have moved to Mr. Hartwell's house, I have received frequent visits from Pastor *Woo*. Knowing the strong anti-foreign spirit of the church, I have felt some embarrassment as to how to serve them. While most anxious, in every way, to promote the welfare of their church, I have feared they would regard me as intrusive. Still, I had hoped, indirectly, to be of benefit to them.

My motive in writing has not been to injure these brethren whom I love as fellow Christians, but simply to inform the Board of facts which they, at a distance, cannot be supposed to know.

Requesting the Secretary to communicate this letter to the Board, should the petition referred to have been sent, I remain,

Very truly,

L. Moon.

Tung Chow,
China
Nov. 4, 1875
My dear Dr. Tupper,

I wrote, a day or two since, a letter which I desired you to read to the Board, should a certain petition be sent you from the North Street brethren of this city. The letter contained a moderate estimate of facts with facts which I thought you should be made acquainted.

I write today moved by feelings which come over me constantly when I go out on country trips. "The harvest is plenteous, the laborers are few." Yesterday, Mrs. Holmes, Mrs. Crawford & I went out for the day. We visited nine villages & in some of them we had a crowd to hear us. The people are very friendly & receive us most kindly in some places. As we were passing on the outskirts of a village which we visited last week, & which we did not mean to stop at yesterday, we saw the main street full of people. Mrs. Holmes said, "This is too tempting: let's go & give them a little talk." On approaching, we found that they had assembled expressly, to hear us, on learning that we were in a neighboring village. What we find missionaries can do in the way of preaching the gospel even in the immediate neighborhood of this city, is but as the thousandth part of a drop in the bucket compared with what should be done. I do not pretend to aver that there is any spiritual interest among the people. They literally "sit in darkness & in the shadow of death." The burden of our words to them is the folly & sin of idol worship. We are but doing pioneer work, but breaking up the soil in which we believe others shall sow a bountiful crop. But, as in the natural soil, four or five laborers cannot possibly cultivate a radius of twenty miles, so cannot we, a mission of five people, do more than make a beginning of what should be done.

I know that the Board cannot send men & women until the churches furnish the money, & I fully agree with Dr. Yates that more should not be sent until the churches meet promptly their obligations to those already in the field. But is there no way to arouse the churches on this subject? We missionaries find it in our hearts to say to them in all humility, "Now then we are ambassadors for Christ; as though God did beseech you by us, we pray you, in Christ's stead," to remember the heathen. We implore you to send us help. Let not these heathen sink down into eternal death without one opportunity to hear that blessed Gospel which is to you the source of all joy & comfort. The work that constantly presses upon us is greater than time or strength permit us to do. In a little over two years, Mrs. Holmes *must* go home on Landrum's account. Who is to take her place unless Mrs. Llewellyn comes at once? Mr. Crawford, that old & faithful missionary of the Board, needs help in his manifold & pressing duties. He is doing the work of two or three men, some of which work *should* fall on younger shoulders. Mrs. Crawford & Mrs. Holmes have their hands full with their respective schools, yet they continue to do a great deal of country work & some city visiting besides. My sister has been compelled to give up country work on account of her throat, but she does city work as health permits & expects to begin a boarding school for girls at the Chinese New Year. My own time is divided between city visiting & country work. There is a greater call for both than I can possibly meet with the time & strength at the disposal of one person.

Thus, you see, my dear Brother, that we do most imperatively need help. I know that the Board would gladly reinforce at once, but that they are powerless without the hearty cooperation of the churches.

I have the most abounding confidence in the Southern Baptist churches if they only *see* their duty. The question is *how* to make them see it. I confess I know not how to answer that question.

We have planned another country trip tomorrow & I shall feel more comfortable for having written this letter. Would I might hope it would have effect in bringing us the help we so sorely need! We looked for Mrs. Lewellyn in August, as she wrote that she expected to leave in June. There is abundance of work ready for her, & as many more as you can send, so soon as they can acquire enough of the language to do it. All who come must expect to "endure hardness," but the joy of the work more than repays all that.

With sincere Christian affection,
Yrs truly,
L. Moon.

Tung Chow, China
Feb. 25, 1876
My dear Dr. Tupper:
Per last mail before close of winter navigation, I rec'd an order for £231.3.1, sent from New York at the request of the Treasurer of F.M.B. I wrote to him to-day to acknowledge its receipt. Our mission decided that the money had better be placed in Dr. Yates' hands for investment until we hear definitely of Mr. Hartwell's plans. If he intends returning to Tungchow to settle, of course we give up his house to him any day he wishes. If, however,

he settles elsewhere, it seems wisest for us to remain where we are instead of building a new house. A great deal of money has been spent on this place, & it is admirably adapted for mission purposes. As a dwelling, its situation is exceedingly desirable, being right at the North city gate & so affording egress to the country for air & exercise, not to speak of the city wall with its beautiful view of the sea. In the bathing season, a short ride will take us to the sea. For mission work, the location is also desirable, being nearer than any other mission residence to the Northern suburb & to what is known as the water city. While the house is not as comfortable a winter residence as we could wish, still, its other advantages are so great that we would prefer to remain here if Mr. Hartwell does not return. If he does, we must look out another location. My sister has commenced her school. She has four pupils. I am truly thankful she has this work as she is not strong enough for city visiting or country trips. Enforced idleness is exceedingly discouraging to a missionary. Her throat was so bad from overwork that for months she could do no mission work. It hurt her to talk much even in English, & Chinese is especially trying on the throat.

Mrs. Crawford & Mrs. Holmes have re-opened school. Mrs. C. has far more applications than she can receive.

My own time is devoted to city visiting & country trips. It is my purpose when in the city to go out twice a day. Sometimes I make several visits each time of going out, sometimes only one. It depends mainly on the length of time to which I find it profitable to extend my visits. Yesterday afternoon I set out to visit an old woman in the North suburb. As I neared the place, some children called out, "Where are you going?" the usual polite question. "I have come here to make a visit," I answered. A woman whom I did not know was standing in the door as I reached it. I asked if I could go in. She said there was no one at home. Not believing this, I persisted in my wish to enter. She then said a fight was going on. I passed her & walked in. At first it seemed very doubtful whether I should be able to make a visit, but an elderly woman came out & bade the woman I had seen at the door to ask me in. At last, I found the old woman I was seeking seated on a "*kong*" in an inner room. She received me very kindly & a crowd of women & children gathered around. I had a really delightful time teaching the children, both boys & girls, out of the catechism. Then I made them repeat after me the first stanza of "Happy Land" & sung it over with them several times. I also talked to them all about the foolishness & sin of idol worship. On leaving the house, I was greeted by a crowd of soldiers & soldiers' hostlers. "Where have you been Miss Moon?" they asked politely. Immediately, against my will, I was surrounded by these rough fellows, begging for books & asking me to "giang shu"—literally "explain books." I had none to give them, but I said a few words to them about the idols. In the morning I had a similar experience in another part of the city, the soldiers crowding around & begging books. Unfortunately I had only one to give them. Next time I pass that quarter, I will take a number for distribution. Of course it is unpleasant to a lady to be surrounded by these rough soldiers, but certainly it is far more agreeable to be kindly treated by them than to have them call me "foreign devil" & threaten to kill me, as they used to do at first. We had either to make friends with them or to be greatly annoyed by them, so my sister & I early adopted the plan of talking kindly with them whenever they addressed us. I think you would be amused if you could take a walk or ride with me sometimes to hear these soldiers calling out in the most friendly tones, "Where have you been, Miss Moon?" or "Where are you going?" & then perhaps three or four will follow some distance to have a conversation. I find now that if any are disposed to be rude, that the public sentiment of the others puts them down, so I have nothing to complain of. This is true only of those with whom we are brought in frequent contact in passing to & fro. Out west is a large body of soldiers in the Fort. When we pass there, which is very rarely, there are usually an abundance of complimentary epithets showered on us.

Now that mild weather is again at hand, we are resuming country work under most pleasant auspices. We were out two days this week & visited twelve villages. We return to the city at night. The first day, Mrs. Holmes & I went out alone, walking, & taking our lunch in our pocket. We were first greeted by two men working in a field. We sat down on a low stone fence to rest & to talk & pretty soon a dozen or more men & boys & two or three girls were around us having seen us from the neighboring villages. We talked with them a good while finding them simple hearted & kindly. They received gladly the books we gave them. That day we went to six villages & met with nothing but kindness. It is really astounding, the freedom to which we can go about among these villages, & the cordiality & respect that are manifested. The second day, Mrs. Crawford went with us. Although we went farther that day, it was not such hard work as we were riding & there were three to do the work. That day likewise we found large audiences & had our hands full. Mr. Crawford wished he could go but was too busy preparing for his theological class & c. to spare the time. If the present good temper of the people lasts, we will have our hands filled to overflowing with work. We are trying to sow the seed far & wide. In God's own good time, it will bring forth a rich harvest. Meantime we are content to wait.

Yours with Christian affection,
L. Moon.

Tung Chow, China,
March 24, 1876
Rev. H. A. Tupper, D. D.:—
My dear Brother,

Your letter of Jan. 18th came to hand last week. I have also read the resolutions of the Board in regard to affairs in Tung Chow.

There is an unwritten law of honor among missionaries which forbids their bringing each other's affairs before the Board. The Board will therefore understand why I have scrupulously refrained from giving any hint of the difficulties in Shantung. Now that I know the affair has been brought before the Board, the restriction under which I have been withheld from speaking is removed. I can now speak out on matters in which the Board are deeply concerned. Before doing this, however, simple justice to myself demands that I should make some statement of my reasons for coming to live on the North St. premises, & of my feelings toward the North Street church.

A letter of instruction from the Board to Mr. Crawford, bearing date July 7, 1875, contains the following passage: "Will you take all the property at Tung Chow in which the Board are interested, including chapel & the House of the North street church, as your absolute possession" & c. We all thought that "the house of the North St. church" was the dwelling house, with rear & front buildings. *Woo shen sung* said that the boys' school buildings were Mr. Hartwell's personal property. If this were so, & we had no cause to doubt the fact of his being correctly informed, then the natural conclusion was that the letter of the Board referred to the North St. dwelling house in which it has money invested. Mr. Crawford declined to accede to the proposition of the Board. Believing that the valuable mission property would be lost to the Board unless someone stepped in & become responsible to the native owner for the rent, my sister & I determined to move over & thus preserve the property for the Board. In doing this, we would at the same time preserve a chapel for the North St. church free of rent to them. In addition to this, my sister, who had for two or three years planned the opening of a girls' school, could now carry out her long cherished design.

The kindly feelings I have had towards the North Street brethren may perhaps be best shown by the following extract from a letter which I wrote Mr. Hartwell under date March 4.

Extract. "*Woo shen sung* keeps the chapel keys & has entire control of it. My sister's school teacher was a former pupil of Mrs. Hartwell & attends the North street church with the pupils. When persons have called here to ask for books, I have invariably when inviting them to attend church, ask them to come *here* & hear the native *shen sung*, & have taken pains to inform them what day would be Sunday. My sister tells me that in visiting in this neighborhood she has invariably invited the women to come to church here. I have visited on North street, in the Northern suburb, in the water city. If I had invited the women anywhere to church, it would have been to come here, but it is my habit only to invite them to see me. I do not invite the women to church twice during the year, I suppose, for the reason I think they would not come.

"When I proposed to come here, & the proposition originated with me, it was with the honest wish to do all in my power to build up the North St. church. I was all the more anxious to do this after Dr. Yates visit had resulted in the reestablishment of fraternal relations between the two churches. *****
As a member of the Monument street church, I am bound to attend its services. In every other way, I am as ready to serve one church as the other."

The Board will see from the above extract that I have the most cordial good wishes for the North street church. Common honesty compels me to qualify this assertion by saying that it does not include *three members of that church* who live in Chefoo, & who have been notoriously guilty of crimes of the deepest dye. Those men I can only regard with a feeling of unmitigated horror.

With this preliminary statement, I beg leave to submit to the Board the following facts.

1. From the ground plan of the buildings which my sister will enclose in her letter, it will be seen that the North street mission premises on which we live consist of three rows of buildings.

The first now contains one large room which is used as chapel, & a very small room which serves in the day for my teacher to sit in & at night for a servant to sleep in.

The second row is the *mission dwelling house* & contains five rooms. Connected with this row is a kitchen, pantry, wash room, & coal house on one side, & on the other is a small stable with shed adjoining.

The third row contains the school buildings. It was used by the late Mrs. Hartwell for a girls' school & more recently a part of it was used by *Woo shen sung* as a dwelling.

— —

The school buildings for the boys are not on this lot, but are some doors to the North of it. *Woo shen sung* on hearing that we proposed to move here, said at once, "Good! What do I want with this big house?" & cheerfully exchanged his quarters in the rear for rooms on the boys' school lot, rooms more eligible than those he was occupying.

--

The second row, the mission dwelling house, has been locked since 1871 with the exception of the few months Mr. Hartwell & his family spent here after his return from America, & previous to their removal to Chefoo. Looked at from an economical point of view, with financial embarrassment constantly pressing the Board, it hardly seemed to us wise to build a new mission house when the Board had about a thousand taels invested in a mission dwelling house which is admirably located for mission work, besides being a most desirable locality for health from the ready egress into the country, & its proximity to the sea.

Among the unwritten laws of missionary life is this, that so long as a missionary occupies a house it is his to do with as he pleases just as if he absolutely owned it by purchase with his own money. As soon as he vacates that house, then it is understood to revert to the Board & any missionary of the Board may occupy it.

Rev. J. B. Hartwell wrote to the Board as follows (See Proceedings of the Eighteenth Meeting of the Southern Baptist Convention—1873 Appendix, P. 41—Heading, Chefoo):

"A number of our members are here. I therefore earnestly request the Board to appropriate $4000 for a dwelling house & $4000 for a chapel in Chefoo." It seems scarcely credible that a missionary should propose to live in Chefoo & yet continue to rent & lock up a large, roomy, & commodious dwelling house in Tung Chow, a dwelling house to which are attached all necessary out houses, & rooms that have heretofore served for a girls' school. True, the girl's schoolrooms, *from the beginning of 1874*, were occupied by the native pastor. Any one who knows China is aware that an outlay of twenty five thousand cash *per annum* (about twenty five dollars, greenbacks) would furnish Pastor *Woo* with a *very nice dwelling*. From an economic point of view, it seems cheaper for missionaries to occupy the hitherto locked up second row of buildings, even if another house should have to be rented for Pastor *Woo*. The question is fairly this: Is it better to spend from two to three thousand dollars to put up a new house, with proper out houses & school buildings, or to spend twenty five dollars a year to rent a suitable house for Pastor *Woo*? This goes on the supposition that he cannot live on the school lot where at present his presence is most desirable since the teacher he has engaged is a heathen. What Christian influence *can* be thrown constantly around the boys if they are to have *only* the heathen teacher constantly with them? (Note. The heathen teacher is only engaged for six months. At the end of that time, the deacon of the North Street church will be free, it is hoped, from existing engagements, & is to take charge.)

2. The dwelling house on the North Street premises has been fitted up in foreign style at an expense of about Tls. 1000. No Chinaman could be induced to live in this house as it now stands. It has large glass windows & plank floors, & there is not a *kong* (brick stove bed) in it. I have visited in a good many wealthy families in Tung Chow & have always noticed brick floors. As to windows, I have never known a case in which they have gone beyond a single pane of glass fastened in the center of the thin paper window.

The mission dwelling house so long as it was in the hands of the Chinese owner was a pawn shop. With its lofty ceilings, & foreign improvements of plank floors, glass windows, foreign doors, locks & c. it would be anything but a comfortable dwelling for a Chinaman. He would inevitably retire to the third row in the rear where there are *kongs* & places for cooking according to Chinese style. Thus this valuable property in the second row must continue indefinitely under lock & key unless occupied by foreigners.

3. The Board seems to labor under the misapprehension that the North street premises are *only* rented property & therefore not subject to sale by the Board. The ground & simply the shell of the house belong to a Chinaman, but I would respectfully state that the improvements are the property of the Board & as such can be disposed of when there is a purchaser. To illustrate, Mrs. Holmes, on leaving Chefoo, sold to the Presbyterians the Board's interest in a Chinese rented house for Tls. 100, which sum she paid into the mission treasury. Mrs. Holmes lived for a time in a house on North Street in this city. Subsequently she removed to her present dwelling, & the windows, doors, floors, & c. of the other dwelling were taken away when the house was restored to the owner & the rent ceased. The North Street premises are secured to the Board forever, by deed, on payment yearly of $140.00 (green backs). No matter how much property may rise in value, no more than 140.000 cash ($140.00) can be demanded as rent. Neither could the Chinese owner rent it to any one in preference to the representative of Our Board.

4. It is another unwritten law of missionaries that when a missionary changes his station, the work he leaves comes under the supervision of the

missionaries of the same Board who continue to live in that place. For instances, no missionary in Shantung would dream of attempting to control mission work or mission property in Shanghai. After they left Shanghai, all mission affairs there, & all mission property, including two dwelling houses & two churches, passed in to the hands of the resident missionaries. According to this rule, mission matters in Tung Chow city came properly under the supervision of the Board's accredited missionaries who live in that city.

To show that this rule is not confined to our mission, I will state that formerly Dr. & Mrs. Nevins & Mr. & Mrs. Corbett of the Presbyterian mission lived in Tung Chow. When they removed to Chefoo where they have established themselves permanently, they relinquished Tung Chow city entirely to the missionaries of their Board residing there.

5. I append a list of the members of the North Street church now living in Tung Chow city. They are as follows:

Men	Women
Pastor Woo	Mrs. Gwoa
Mr. Sun	Mrs. Ju
Mr. Ku	Mrs. Soong
Mr. Jiang (occasional resident)	Mrs. Wang (teacher in my sister's school)
Mr. Soong	
Jeow feng whâ	
(servant in Mr. Crawford's family)	

Within ten *li* (about 3 1/3 miles) there are Mr. *Leo* & his daughter-in-law. He comes in to church frequently, she very rarely. The members living in Tung Chow except the Pastor are *not* the leaders of the church. Their social standing is not high, & their Christian influence, so far as I know, is very slight. Only two of the women habitually attend church, viz.: my sister's teacher & Mrs. *Ju.* The latter has attended regularly since the school opened: before that she was frequently absent. Indeed some days *not a single woman* attended the services. My sister's teacher is the daughter of Mr. *Leo* mentioned above, & before opening school lived in the country & rarely attended church.

I regret to say that *Woo shen sung's* congregations are very small. Besides the boys' school & my sister's little school I think he has usually most of the male members who live in the city, two women in our employ, & a few outsiders who stand mostly about the door & come & go as they like. The majority of the members live at a great distance from Tung Chow: a few of these come up occasionally to bi-monthly communion. "A number," says Mr. Hartwell, "are" in Chefoo. Fifteen or sixteen are at *Chau Yuen*, distance 66 2/3 miles (200 *li*). Not knowing the exact number in Chefoo, I can not state positively, but my impression is that of the three stations, *Chau Yuen, Chefoo* & *Tung Chow city* the number of resident members is fewer in the latter than in either of the other two. *Woo shen sung*'s own home is about 8 or 10 English miles from Chefoo & about 46 or 48 English miles from Tung Chow.

(Note. I have included the boys' school in the congregation because it will be re-opened next week. It was dismissed last fall by *Woo shen sung* on his own responsibility & authority because he did not receive a remittance from Mr. Hartwell as soon as he anticipated. As many of the boys as could be accommodated were received by request of their parents, into Mrs. Crawford's school, & Mrs. Holmes took charge of two of them whom she placed in her day school.

I may also mention in passing that *Woo shen sung* also closed up the Yentai (Chefoo) station & dismissed the assistants for lack of funds. I heard that the Presbyterians rented the Chefoo (Yentai) chapel, but know nothing about it further than that *Woo shen sung* controlled the matter entirely, acting on his own responsibility.)

6. A "self supporting church" sounds beautifully in Richmond, & reads prettily on paper, but to us who live in Tung Chow there is a spice of the ludicrous in the phrase when we see it applied to a church which receives from the Board its chapel, & its pastor's residence, & buildings for boys' school, & four hundred dollars for the support of a school, & a chapel in Chefoo, & salaries for three assistants (Messrs. *Wang, Liang,* & *Sun,* until recently paid assistants)—not to speak of the fact that a missionary & his family are also maintained in connection with that church. The church itself is pledged to pay $144.00 (greenbacks) a year: I do not know how many thousands the Board disburses annually for that church.

A little modesty from a church which receives so much would be truly refreshing, especially when we remember that it commenced its independent existence a few years ago with the boast publicly uttered—"Now you will see what we Chinamen can do." "Now we have a church without foreigners"— and that last year it sent to the Board its defiant Declaration of Independence, asking "What have you done for us in the past? What do you propose to do for us now?"

The church in Shanghai pays its pastor $15.00 pr month, yet we hear no such boasting from it.

7. Mr. & Mrs. Hartwell arrived in Tung Chow two & a half years before Mr. & Mrs. Crawford. On the other hand, the latter have labored in this city six years longer than the former. In addition, Mrs. Holmes has labored here in all eleven years. Miss E. Moon nearly four years & myself, two years & a half. This makes an aggregate of additional work = 17 _ years. Again, two years of Mr. & Mrs. Crawford's labor & four years of Mrs. Holmes' labor were devoted to building up the North street church.

— —

Referring to the resolutions of the Board, I note that No. 1 says, "That the house of worship heretofore occupied by the North Street church be continued in its possession & that the Misses Moon be requested to vacate it" &c.

I am happy to state that the wishes of the Board were anticipated from the first & that the exclusive control of "the house of worship" has been all along in Pastor Woo's hands.

Resolution 5 says, "That the funds remitted for the Misses Moon *** should as soon as it is practicable & wise be vested in a house."

While the wishes of the Board are to us a law we have deemed it "wise" not to invest the money in a house until the Board should have the above facts laid before them. Having fulfilled the obligations of honor to a brother missionary in remaining silent up to the present time, & now having done my duty to the Board in placing these facts before them, if, after a full acquaintance with these facts the Board still wishes us to "vest the money in a house," we will gladly do so.

In the preamble to the resolutions, the Board suggests that the two brethren make it a subject of prayerful inquiry whether they shall not, one of both of them, leave Tung Chow. If Mr. and Mrs. Crawford should decide it to be their duty to seek another field, the rest of our mission are a unit in the wish to be transferred with them, & this, not only from warm personal attachment to these dear friends with whom we have labored harmoniously & happily, but because we are unanimous in our views of mission policy.

Requesting that this letter be submitted to the Board, I remain,

Yours truly,

L. Moon.

Tung Chow, China,
March 24, 1876

My dear Dr. Tupper,

I am sure you are much grieved at the unfortunate alienation between the two brethren. May I remind you, if it be any comfort, that it is said of Paul & Barnabas that "the contention was so sharp between them that they departed asunder one from the other"? In China, alas! such things are not confined to missionaries of any one Board. The late lamented Dr. Knowlton had a difference with Dr. Lord of a most serious nature, lasting many years, but it shook nobody's confidence in either. In Shanghai, two missionaries of the London Mission had such variances that one of them resigned & went home, universally regretted by those who knew him as a number one missionary. By a late English steamer he has returned to China & and is to live in Peking. Thus the Mission loses the services of neither. Cases of incompatibility are of constant occurrence on the mission field & are usually settled by one of the parties removing elsewhere. Such differences frequently are settled by the quiet withdrawal of one of the parties. You hear it reported, "Mr. so & so has moved to such a place; he could not get on with Mr. so & so." Nobody thinks less of either party unless it is well known that one of them quarrels habitually with other people then he is set down as queer or hard to get on with. People out here are very tolerant. I suppose we must make allowances for troubles between missionaries by remembering that the very strength of character which impels them to the mission work is apt to manifest itself in sharp angles.

I have sold the two drafts on London to Messrs. Wilson & Cornabe of Chefoo with whom the money is to remain on deposit until needed.

With Christian affection

Yours truly,

L. Moon.

Tung Chow, China,
April 14, 1876
Rev. H. A. Tupper:--
My dear Brother,

Mrs. Holmes & I returned yesterday from a country trip, some of the incidents of which I thought might interest you. Several weeks ago, we were invited by a native preacher, Mr. Dzoong, to visit him, & he added that he would go around with us among the neighboring villages. We gladly accepted the invitation, though we could not then say when we could go. Mr. Dzoong lives seventy-five *li* from Tung Chow (25 miles). He is a most excellent man, full of humility & self-denial, & ready for every good word & work. I have never met any one who seemed more fully to realize in his character the words, he "had been with Jesus & learned of him." His pious & sensible wife is to him, in the truest sense, "an help meet." The well ordered household reminded me of Christian homes in Christian lands. This brother is supported by the native Christians at a salary of five thousand cash a month (about $60. greenbacks a year). He has a small, neat church, reminding me very much of country churches at home. Towards building this church, the native Christians contributed forty thousand cash ($40.). The remainder was collected in Chefoo by subscription among foreign residents. The church has a dirt floor, a thing I was glad to see because in accordance with Chinese ideas. The heathen will naturally feel more at home sitting or standing in such a house than if it had a plank floor. The windows are small, but of glass & open so as to afford perfect ventilation. The baptistry is a large wooden box, not handsome certainly, but useful. The benches are the plain, narrow wooden ones that are universally in use in well-to-do & even wealthy families. Good sense & economy seem to have combined in making this a model edifice. As you will see, I was very much delighted with this church, but when I came to mingle with the native Christians my heart was filled with joy. They received Mrs. Holmes & myself with the most grateful affection. We were to them beloved for our work's sake. Instead of regarding us as foreigners of whose influence they were to be jealous, they received us with all the warmer affection because we had come from afar for their sakes, and this feeling they constantly sought to awaken in their heathen acquaintances & friends. The consequence was that we met with cordial kindness even among the latter. It is proper to state that the Christians in that section are all connected with the English Baptist mission, under the supervision of Rev. Mr. Richard who resides at *Chingchowfu*, 200 miles in the interior. Thus much by way of introduction.

About ten days ago, had you been in Tung Chow, you would or might have seen a donkey & a pony each carrying a lady's saddle & another donkey loaded with bedding, baskets of food, &c. When the time for departure came, we walked ahead leaving our animals to overtake us outside the city. Once fairly mounted, we proceeded on our way in high spirits for we always enjoy a country trip in spite of physical hardships. Before sunset we reached *Woo she li p'u* (fifty li station, 16 2/3 miles). We had meant to spend several days there as we knew of an unusually clean inn, the landlord of which is so cross that the Chinese won't go there if they can avoid it. The cleanness attracts foreigners who only laugh at the surliness of "mine host." The landlord was in dismay when he learned our intention. He said if he let us have the rooms, he would have no place to put the students who were returning now in large numbers from the examinations. He asserted that he would lose money by us. We felt disposed to make quite light of this, because we knew the Chinese wouldn't lodge with him if they could help it, & there are two other large inns & several small ones in the place. The landlord insisted we should only spend a night & leave next morning. Ne'er a word did Mrs. Holmes answer, but we stayed on, saying to each other we would wait & see. On the evening of our arrival, we went out & made a visit. About thirty women & girls soon collected & we had a good time talking to them & teaching them. Returning to the inn, pretty soon the village school boys came in. We soon had them vigorously at work learning the catechism by heart, & all through our stay they seized every opportunity to come in & learn. We gave books to several as a reward, but not having books enough I gave a few of those pretty cards sent from Savannah which delighted them greatly. We promised them that if they could recite the whole catechism when we go back next fall, we would give each a foreign picture. They seemed more than pleased with the idea & said they would take the books to school & learn them. Meantime women & girls came to call on us & we used the opportunity to impart Christian truth. All next day our hands were full. There were visitors, or women & girls coming to show us the way to their homes & whenever we visited we found ready occasion for mission work. A few women & girls learned the catechism & to these I gave illuminated cards. (I find them very useful. I wish you would stir up (privately) the Sunday School children of your acquaintance to send me some. The less English on them the better, though an illuminated text is as good as a picture.) To return to my subject. Feeling very tired, we thought it best to get out of doors, so we walked over to a neighboring village. The women were at first uncertain whether we were women or men, but on being informed that we also were women, they crowded around. We talked to them some time & then went back to dinner. At dinner time, large crowds of school boys, to whom I attempted to teach a hymn. The house was so full of people, I had to take the boys into the yard. After dinner, I made another visit, & then we walked over to another village, where we had even more auditors than in the morning. At night, school boys again. The landlord came in with a piteous appeal for us to go, & thinking that after all we might be injuring him, we decided to go next day. We paid him a good price for his lodgings. Chinese pay for food, *not* lodging. As we took our own food, we paid for the use of the house.

Having worked so hard indoors, we were glad to be again in the open air, & we rode forward in high good humor, turning aside to visit five villages, ere we reached the home of our friend, Mr. Dzoong. Once there, we had a great many visitors, mostly women & children. A few men came in at night when their day's work was over. Next day we visited six villages escorted by Mr. Dzoong. We were delighted to see the cordial regard entertained for him by his heathen neighbors. In several villages he has a hall freely at his service, the ancestral hall of a heathen household, or, if the family be not rich, access to some small room where he can teach or preach. We, who are so used to sitting on door steps or standing in the street to talk to the women, were equally surprised & delighted at being invited into the guest hall of a native gentlemen, served with tea, the women urged to come in, & full liberty given us to talk to them as long as we pleased. It is much easier on the throat to talk in a room than in the open air.

Next day was Sunday & we of course stayed at home and worshiped with the Christians. The church was well filled, mostly with women & children. In the afternoon, at Mrs. H's suggestion, we had Sunday School. She took the women, Mr. Dzoong the men, & the children, as usual, at my request, fell to me. I had about sixteen in the class ranging in age from six or eight to twelve. Having taught them a good deal before, they could answer very well, & there were several children in the class whose Christian parents had long instructed them. We enjoyed it very much.

Mr. Dzoong insisted that we should prolong our stay as he wanted to take us to visit some women who had been long among the undecided & over whom he hoped we might exert a good influence. He was likewise desirous of introducing us to the native Christians in the region he proposed to visit.

Monday morning found us again in the saddle, & after stopping at several villages we reached the home of a native Christian, Mr. Jeo. His wife gave us a cordial greeting & we felt at home at once. Our quarters were very pleasant, being a new house, dirt floor of course, but we are used to that. Two rooms were pretty full of hay, but the third was clean & comfortable. We had visitors or visited incessantly. The one Christian woman & the inquirers recited to us what they had learned in the catechism & hymn book & we sung with them. (At night Mr. Dzoong holds general service.) It did my heart good to see the work this good humble man is accomplishing. He has ready access into the families of many of the heathen, going into the apartment of the women, teaching them & their husbands together. What most surprised & pleased me was to see young married people united in learning the gospel, instead of one or the other opposing & scorning. Mr. Dzoong seems to labor to build up Christian households. I heard him exhorting a husband & wife to pray together daily. The people in that region are well-to-do farmers. We spent a night & most of the next day among this warm hearted, hospitable people, & left with pressing invitations to go back. In the morning, a gentleman from the neighboring village had come over to invite us to spend the night at his house. In the evening, he came again to escort us. There was a large crowd pretty soon in attendance, so many that the hall would not hold them & they adjourned to the yard. I hope you won't think me desperately unfeminine, but I spoke to them all, men, women, & children, pleading with them to turn from their idolatry to the True & Living God. I should not have dared to remain silent with so many souls before me sunk in heathen darkness. Mr. Dzoong followed, & Mrs. Holmes spoke last. The people were then told to go home & return for preaching at night. Mrs. Holmes & I, with Mr. Dzoong, then walked over to a neighboring village.

After supper, Mr. Dzoong held services in the hall, the women who came sitting with Mrs. Holmes & myself on the *kongs* in the inner room where we could hear all & take part in the singing. Services over, we retired with inward groans to our sleeping apartment. I can never forget that night. The smoke blackened walls, the window that would not open, the stifling atmosphere, the living creatures that crawled over us (insects!)—such a night I never passed. We could not but laugh at the situation, but we wished no less for morning. At the first dawn, you may be sure, we were up and out, for we knew that when they commenced to cook in the next room our apartment would be filled with smoke. On our return from a walk, our host took us to visit a relative of his to whom he wanted us to talk. We found them at breakfast. Returning we had our own breakfast, after which Mrs. Holmes saw some inquirers & I taught some boys. Then followed a general service by Mr. Dzoong. We welcomed the time of departure for Mrs. Holmes & I were exhausted. Our throats were sore & tired, imperatively demanding rest. The strain of teaching, teaching, talking, talking, right through, all day long from before breakfast frequently, nearly always till after supper, was beginning to tell on us. Our courteous host, who, by the way, is to be baptized soon, escorted us out of the village. We were too tired to do any talking at villages on the way & how glad we were to get back to our clean, comfortable quarters at Mr. Dzoong's! He sent away visitors that we might have a good rest. After dinner, I taught the children catechism. At night Mr. Dzoong had family prayers and a good many neighbors were in.

When the last hymn was sung, my poor throat felt itself very ill-used, & I knew if I did not rest it you would have another missionary on the retired list before long. We had agreed to go home next day, & Mrs. H. planned that we should stop at a village and take our dinner, which would give us an opportunity to talk to the women. "No," I said most decidedly, "not one word do I mean to say tomorrow." Next morning Mrs. Holmes had come to the same conclusion, her throat being even worse than mine. We set out early on our return journey. The best part of it all was that we had two little girls coming back with us to Mrs. Holmes' school. The little creatures were so merry! so full of happiness at the prospect of the journey! They were quite heroines in the eyes of their playmates who came to see them off. I hope we have in that village a rich mine which will yet fill our girls' schools full to overflowing. Chinese children travel frequently in baskets slung across a donkey's back. Accordingly, the two little girls were stowed cosily in baskets & lifted onto a donkey. How gayly they chattered! Mrs. Holmes intends to have our return cavalcade painted by a native artist & send it to you. If not sent with this letter, it will go before long. We were very happy to carry back this tangible result of our labor. The little girls are children of church members. Mrs. Holmes has the promise of another pupil from there next month or next year, & one was promised me for my sister's school who is to come next month. They might have come at once, but for want of clothing. (We require their parents to clothe them.)

We had twenty-five miles before us, but we passed over it rapidly & were at home by four o'clock, resting about noon for dinner at an inn. The pleasures of cleanliness, quiet, & comfort, after such a journey is better imagined than described.

Mrs. Holmes & I have another journey planned for some ten days hence. Then I am to go with Mr. Crawford to visit the islands some twelve miles across from our city, after which I have promised to go out with Mrs. Mateer on the Chefoo road. This will take us partly in the region Mrs. H. & I have lately visited, only, leaving the Dzoong village to our left, we will go a day's journey nearer Chefoo. –

I have deposited the money you sent me with Messrs. Wilson, Cornabe & Co. until I hear the final decision on the matter. If Mr. Hartwell accepts our proposition to take the most of that money (see my sister's letter to you), all I will have to do will be to give him an order on the above House. The Ladies will thus have provided us a Home & school quarters as really as if we built a new house, & certainly far more economically to the Board. Hoping to hear from you soon, I remain,

Yrs truly,
L. Moon.

Tung Chow, China,
April 22, 1876
My dear Dr. Tupper,

Enclosed please find the picture by native artist which Mrs. Holmes wished me to enclose. I mentioned it in my last letter to you. Mrs. Holmes leads the procession on her donkey. I follow on my pony but pray *don't* think I hold the bridle in my right hand & whip in the left, for the reverse is true. Of course, John Chinaman *must* make a caricature. The little girls in the baskets are the two pupils coming up to school. The woman following is mother of one of the children. The baggage brings up the rear.

Mrs. Crawford & I returned yesterday from a country trip. We visited twenty-four villages.

Mrs. Holmes & I contemplate a trip next week & another probably the week after. I was nearly *cooked* on my last trip, having to sleep on a hot *kong* connected with *gwoa* (brick cooking stove), where cooking had been going on all day. As we were staying in a private family, & they had given up their best room to us, there was nothing to do but endure it.

My sister's health continues to give me great uneasiness. I do not think it will do for her to spend next winter here. She must seek a warmer climate until her lungs get healed. She wishes to try Japan next winter. I don't think she would have been in this condition but for country trips. The exposure & hardships are too much for most women. With her example before me, I hope to make these trips with impunity by stopping short in time. Mrs. Holmes' break-down two years ago was from cold taken on a country trip. She spent some time in the south & has been comparatively well since. Mrs. Crawford never stays longer than four days, that being the limit of her powers of endurance. I have made up my mind that six days are the utmost that I intend to spend in one trip.

I wonder if all this interests you! If not, pray excuse it on the score that much mingling with the heathen makes one stupid.

With kindest regards,
Yours truly,
L. Moon.

(appended to the same letter)

April 24
Dear Dr. Tupper,

Please don't put me in the *Herald*! I quite shrink from the idea. I thought you were only going to write about the missionaries who are gone from this world, or those older ones who have "borne the heat & burden" these ten or twenty years. But I see from a late *Herald* that your plan embraces us who have hardly had time to *begin* our life work. *Please don't put me in*! Perhaps it is a foolish sensitiveness, but I had rather not appear before even the Baptist public in that way.

Yours sincerely,
L. Moon.

Tung Chow, China,
May 6, 1876
Rev. H. A. Tupper: -
My dear Brother,

I write on a subject in which we of Tung Chow feel much concerned as the welfare of our mission will be deeply affected by its decision. Our hope of a lady to come out in time to learn enough in order to take charge of Mrs. Holmes' school when she shall go home, has faded into nothingness. Mrs. Llewellyn is married, & even if there were another lady applying to be sent, there are no funds to send her. The question comes up, What is to be done? Shall the school be disbanded? *That* is out of the question. A school of nineteen girls & women is too precious to be lightly sacrificed. Shall I take charge? That could be done, but as it is by no means absolutely certain that my sister can live in Shantung, I may yet have to take charge of her school. *Two* boarding schools & a day school would be too much for one person to undertake, & yet I should have to assume that burden if Mrs. Holmes goes away & my sister's health does not permit her to live in Shantung. In this case, my own chosen work of city visiting & country trips would have to be almost entirely laid aside. Worse still, it would be impossible to conduct *two* boarding schools with proper efficiency, for I could only give partial supervision to each & a school not constantly under the missionary's eye very soon degenerates—I had almost said into a curse instead of a blessing. Thus you see our prosperity as a church & mission is largely at stake.

Mrs. Holmes has taken the subject into very serious consideration. There can be no question that her first duty is to her fatherless boy & yet when God blesses her work with such great prosperity, the indications of

Providence seem plain that she should not abandon that work. How shall these duties be reconciled, her duty to the child God has given her, & her duty to these poor heathen to whom He has sent her? With an almost breaking heart, she decides that if proper arrangements can be made, Landrum must go to America for his education without her. You may readily imagine the anguish with which a widowed mother contemplates the idea of giving up her only child for many years. The question comes up, to whom shall she confide this child of many prayers & many hopes. His father's relatives are Methodists, & are Northern in political sentiment. The same is true of Mrs. H's own brothers. She is not willing to subject her boy to influences, religious & political, of which she does not approve. It has been her plan to educate him at Richmond College, & she had intended to live in Richmond for a few years, at any rate until he was well started in his studies & the feeling of strangeness had worn off.

I have suggested to her that it was probable you & Mrs. Tupper would be willing to receive Landrum into your family. I am sure that in asking that of you, I need not plead the interests of the mission, or your desire to oblige Mrs. Holmes. Your own heart will suggest the debt we owe to him who fills a martyr's grave in Chefoo, & I am sure you will feel, as we do, a peculiar tenderness for his boy, deprived so ruthlessly of a father's care. I have every confidence that if you can do so, you will grant our wish.

Mr. & Mrs. Mateer are to leave for America in about a year from this time. They have cordially consented to take charge of Landrum & it only remains for you to say whether you can receive him. If you cannot, then we must look to the loss of Mrs. Holmes to the mission for some years, a loss which we on the field, who know her work, regard as irreparable.

I should have mentioned that Landrum will be fourteen years of age next June.

Hoping to hear from you favorably, I remain,

Yours truly,

L. Moon.

Tung Chow, China,
May 29, 1876
Rev. H. A. Tupper, D.D.:-
My dear Brother,

I always like to write you when I have something pleasant to tell. The good news is that four have applied for baptism, two women, one girl & a boy. The three former are in Mrs. Holmes' school, & the latter in Mrs. Crawford's. Others in both schools are serious. Our congregations continue to increase in numbers & are remarkably orderly. My Infant Class in Sunday School yesterday numbered fourteen, twelve of whom I hope are permanent. Mrs. Holmes had seventeen women in her class, which has been steadily increasing for some time. Her school now numbers twenty-one. My sister had two new pupils last week, so she now has five. Occasionally a day scholar drops in for a day or two.

I wrote you some time ago of my pleasant visit with Mrs. Holmes among the native Christians twenty-five or thirty miles from here. Some of them had been planning a trip to Tung Chow, having heard, they said, that the church was prospering here & the brethren warm hearted (zealous). Accordingly about eight of the brethren, including *Jing shen sung*, the pastor at Chefoo, came & spent two or three days, remaining over to our Thursday evening prayer meeting. They told us then that some of the women were coming up at the end of the Chinese month. Last week three women came, two of them bringing each a daughter to my sister's school. One of them already had a daughter in Mrs. Holmes' school. Two of these women are now making me a visit. I never saw anything like the way they apply themselves to study. They seem to realize the preciousness of time. This morning they have worked steadily at the hymn book for about three hours. After dinner they will study the catechism & again after supper, one of them is almost sure to come in to read the hymn book. Neither of them are church members, though I feel convinced that one of them is a Christian.

I have had five visitors this morning, three girls & two boys. I took two of the girls to the school room, & one of them, a very bright girl who is anxious to learn, is staying all day. All of the five recited some of the catechism to me & I taught some of them part of a hymn. We have had more visitors in the last few weeks than in all of the previous months since our coming to North Street to live. I ascribe our increase of visitors to three causes: 1st. The soldiers stationed near us have been ordered to another place. 2nd. We have been here long enough to convince our neighbors that we are decent people. (It takes a long time to get the confidence of the people.) 3rd.

People generally are beginning to learn that the mission house on North Street is again open. (You know it had been closed about two years & a half.)

We have been visited by some very nice people, our near neighbors. My time has been so occupied lately with teaching visitors that I have had no time to go out visiting. When I do go, I am usually very kindly received. We notice a general softening among the people. The fear of the soldiers, that almost paralyzed our city work for a time, seems to have passed away.

I think the usefulness of my sister & myself has been increased very greatly by having an establishment of our own. A girls' school becomes a nucleus around which to gather women & girls.

Woo shen sung had one addition to the *Chan yuen* membership during his visit out there. Yesterday was the communion day of the North Street church. One of the former Mrs. Hartwell's pupils, a Mrs. *Gow*, came up to communion & spent the night here with the teacher of my sister's school, an old school mate of hers (the teacher). Mrs. *Gow* is a very nice woman. I invited *Woo shen sung* to bring his country church members (women) whenever they *came* up to communion. I should be glad to entertain them always when they come. Since the soldiers left, *Woo shen sung* has decided to open the chapel on market days. He very considerately came in to consult me about it, not knowing, he said, whether it would be pleasant to us to have it open. I highly approved the plan, telling him that men often came here & asked me for books & it would be just so much gain if he were in the chapel to receive them. I also offered to provide him suitable books for distribution when the box we have ordered from Shanghai arrives.

So you see whatever our past trouble may have been, we are now moving harmoniously on a harmony which will probably continue if the two brethren who are at variance could only be reconciled. With kindest regards,

Yours truly,

L. Moon.

(marginal note)

The two drafts realized Tls. 1,283.10 (Taels twelve hundred and eighty-three, & ten tael cents). This is in Chefoo taels. In Shanghai taels it is over thirteen hundred. The money is on deposit with Messrs. Wilson Cornabe & Co. of Chefoo, & I only await the Board's decision as to its disposition. If they decide to lock up the North Street mission house permanently for the sake of keeping up two conflicting interests in Tungchow, I can buy the property almost any day. But I hate to see the Board's money wasted.

Please ask somebody, everybody, to send me pictures. No matter if they are old. Ask them to send by *San Francisco*, else postage is enormous.

Tung Chow, China,
Aug. 9, 1876
Rev. H. A. Tupper, D..D.:-
My dear Brother,

Your very kind & welcome letter of June 8th came to hand two days since.

You will perhaps be surprised to learn that Mr. & Mrs. Crawford are on their way to Japan. Both were much worn down even more mentally than physically, by their long & arduous labors. A change was imperatively needed. They have been gone two weeks, & were to leave Chefoo tomorrow or next day per steamer direct to Japan. By the way, the next missionary who comes to North China would do well to "make a note" of the fact that a monthly steamer now plies between Japan & China. It is Japanese, & is said to be large & clean. By coming direct, the traveler avoids the tedious & often dangerous journey to Shanghai, & the expense, I doubt not, is less. Mrs. Crawford expected to be absence about two months. Mr. C spoke of staying away four.

As I write, I hear the gong sounding in the streets, followed by yells—the people are praying for rain. Meantime the rain has been coming down steadily for perhaps half an hour, not to speak of a glorious rain at dinnertime. These poor souls take care to pray for rain most earnestly when everything gives promise that the rain is at hand. In truth, I have felt deep anxiety & pity for them in the long droughts that have prevailed. Thank God! the prospect is more hopeful now. Last Sunday one of the deacons told me if there was not rain within ten days there would be no hope. The spring was very dry & the wheat crop a failure. The most gloomy apprehensions prevailed. Then the rainy season seemed to set in favorably in July, the people ploughed in hope; & our hearts were filled with gladness. To these very abundant rains, succeeded a season of most intensely hot, dry weather, lasting some weeks. How anxiously we have watched the skies for some token of rain! At last God has very graciously heard our prayers & we can not but hope that the horrors of famine will be adverted. Already we are drawing on our private means to aid the many who call for help. Had the anticipated famine come, God only knows the horrors we should be called on to witness with power to do so very little in aid! What are the private means of a few missionaries to relieve the starvation of thousands & tens of thousands? Mr. Richard, English Baptist missionary at *Ching Chow*, west of here perhaps half way on the *Che nan fu* road writes the most touching account of the famine there & tells of his own efforts to relieve want until he was reduced almost beggary himself. Then he went to *Che nan fu*, the capitol, to present the Governor a scheme for the relief of the poor starving people. Mr. Dzoong, the native preacher of whom I wrote you, left here today. He says this withholding of rain has made the people more willing to hear the gospel, showing them the falseness of the gods to whom they are praying. He is the same good, earnest Christian & I love him warmly. He came to bring his two sons to school and to consult about two more girls entering my sister's school. He brought her two last session, of whom I believe I wrote you.

All this is a digression, however, for I set out to tell you about the departure of Mr. & Mrs. Crawford. I volunteered to take the oversight of the school in her absence & she gladly accepted. So here I am living all alone, while my sister is in the same condition on North Street. The school has been under such strict discipline that I do not anticipate any particular trouble in its management. My only anxiety now is about a sick boy whom I have to doctor myself as we have no physician here. I gave strict orders yesterday about his diet, & the first thing this morning I learned he had himself gone on the street & purchased some mutton & eaten it. I had ordered him to remain very quiet, motion being injurious to him. So here was a double disobedience. I should not like you to have seen me scold him, for I was "terribly in earnest." He came on my hands sick at the close of the vacation, & the case is really serious. I have been using energetic measures today, however & I hope he is better. I think he will not venture to disobey again. At any rate, he has promised not, and as he is, I believe a real Christian, I believe him.

My sister is getting over a bad attack of cold. Her health has given me great uneasiness for some time past. She expects to go to Japan in Oct. or Nov. Sometimes she talks hopefully of a return to her work here. Again, she seems to think she cannot stand the climate. I will take charge of the school during her absence. So you see, I can fill up gaps in other folks' work if nothing else.

Since writing the above I have had a visit from two women who came to ask medicine for a sick man. We have many such calls. I suppose scarcely a day passes that medicine is not dispensed at one or two of the three mission houses, & often at all three. It pays by conciliating opposition, not to speak of the pleasure of relieving suffering.

My sick boy reports himself better.

You will be glad to hear that the native brethren have been stirred up by Mr. Crawford's absence to more earnest work. They keep up three services on Sunday, & the weekly prayer meeting is more spirited than when Mr. C. is present. I wrote him I thought his temporary absence would be a real benefit to the church, teaching them self-dependence.

Stepping out of my street door last Sunday evening, the name of Jesus caught my ear when I had expected to hear only the rude sounds of traffic. One of the North Street brethren was seated on the door step, with a small book in his hand & mostly talking of the great salvation to a man who seemed to listen with interest. You may imagine how it warmed my heart. The three churches here have passed a resolution that each member shall spend one hour every Sabbath in work for the Master. Mr. Crawford proposed & urged the plan. *Woo shen sung* took it up enthusiastically & set it to work in his church before any formal action was taken, after hearing Mr. Crawford tell the Union Prayer Meeting of Oncken's work in Germany.

With kindest regards & Christian affⁿ.

L. Moon.

Notes:

The boys from Woo shen sung's school come over twice a week to sing with our boys. Mrs. Crawford is an excellent teacher of singing.

Three very bright girls came in a few days ago to enter Mrs. Holmes' school. One is daughter of a church member, the other two are not. Mrs. H. has over twenty pupils.

Letters passing through Shanghai require but five cents—south of that port ten cents.

Tung Chow, China,
August 11, 1876
My dear Brother,

You asked Mr. Crawford, in a letter he has sent me, if "the Misses Moon were charged with $25.00 & $125.00." Fearing Mr. C. may forget in the hurry of travel to answer your question, I submit below an extract from my mission account of last year.

---------   ----------

Mission		Dr.
To Teachers' pay for 1 yr. at 4000 cash		
Per month		48000 cash
To Country trips from		
Dec. 2nd 1874 to Oct 7, 1876		4550 "
Repairs at North St.		2930 "
" " " "		300 "
		55780 "
By credit $25.00 pd. In		
Richmond	=	25000 cash tls. 18.10

—

1700	30780
	1700
	13780
	13600
	1800
	1700
	1000

We pay mission running expenses out of our own salaries. At the final settlement of the year, or at the beginning of the last quarter, we bring in our accounts against the Mission. The above is my account for last year against the Mission up to last date* (Oct.), & the $25.00 is deducted, being valued at 25000 cash. The balance 30/80 cash equals Tls. 18.10. Mr. Crawford paid me, and I dare say *only* that balance appears in his books. I regret that I cannot find the books to verify the statement. Mr. Crawford positively declines to make his accounts except in Tls., which will account for the non-appearance of the credit to the Mission in the account sent the Board. (Of course the credit was there only not in dollars, or rather, the credit was neutralized by the debt, leaving balance in my form.)

Thanking you for having paid the $25.00, which was to aid the struggling church in Scottsville, Va., I remain,

With Christian affection,

Yrs. truly,

L. Moon

*This includes teacher's salary to Jan. 1, 1876.

Tung Chow,
China,
Sept. 16, 1876
My dear Dr. Tupper,

Your letter of July 15 came to hand yesterday, also a letter to Mr. Crawford enclosing Resolutions of the Board. Mr. & Mrs. Crawford are still in Japan, but by permission previously given, I opened Mr. C's letter to read the Resolutions. I cannot but congratulate the Board on the decision which seems to me just, & wise, & which, if adhered to in practice, will free us from future occasions of misunderstanding between the two churches here. There has been harmony & kindness between us for about a year. You may feel assured we will do our utmost to cherish & increase mutual regard & affection.

Thank you very much for your kind interest in Landrum. I see it would be clearly impossible for you to receive him into your family, & perhaps not quite desirable if you live so far from College. Mrs. Holmes is very much pleased at the idea of committing him into Dr. Dickinson's hands. There is no one in the world to whom she would more willingly confide him. It is proper to state that she wishes to pay his board out of her own private funds. While cordially acknowledging the kindness of friends who would wish to do this, since there is no necessity for it, she prefers to pay his board herself. You may take my private assurance that she is able to do this from her own property without its being any heavy burden.

We had letters from Mrs. Crawford last night. Though sorely longing to be home again, they have decided to remain a month longer, hoping by this long holiday to obviate the necessity of going to America. They were both when they left here imperatively in need of rest & change.

My sister does not improve. Sometimes the feeling steals over me that she cannot live in Tung Chow anymore. The climate is very severe & her throat & lungs are weak. She will leave in two or three weeks.

Affairs are still in a very unsettled state. The great men in Chefoo, English Ambassador & Chinese Grand Secretary are trying to come to terms of agreement. Meantime trade becomes more depressed. Add to this, scarcity & high price of food, low price of silver, famines in the West, the wildest delusions in Soochow & neighborhood, the murder of Catholics,—& you have a state of affairs grave in the extreme. We can compare the Soochow delusions only to the witchcraft mania in Massachusetts. The people state that paper men are sent out to cut off their "pig-tails." These paper men are sent out by the missionaries & the Catholics. Another delusion is that a certain something, say the size of a gnat, hovers over a sleeper, growing until as large as a horse or cow & crushing him to death. The frantic populace herd together beating gongs all night to scare off the demons, & sleeping by day forty or fifty together. The delusion is said to be going on to Hang Chow, & will possibly reach us in time. The hatred seems especially against the Catholics & many, some say, hundreds, have sealed their testimony with their blood. As the Chinese do not & can not distinguish between Protestants & Catholics, we may expect some of the former to fall victims—as indeed I have read of the murder of a native assistant connected the English Mission at Soochow.

With kindest regards,
Yrs. truly,
L. Moon.

I forgot to say that Pastor Woo's letter will be delivered to him. Mrs. Holmes has kindly consented to translate it & the Resolutions of the Board & communicate them to him. I feel assured that he is very desirous of harmony—& I believe him to be a good man & sincere Christian. He officiated for us at the funeral services of one of our members, doing it of his own accord. This member died since Mr. Crawford has been away.

Tung Chow,
China
Oct. 20, 1876
Rev. H. A. Tupper, D.D.
My dear Brother,

I send you herewith, for the mission rooms, a copy by hand of an ancient Chinese book of prophecy. It was composed, so the story goes, by two brothers, one of whom drew the pictures, and the other wrote the poetry. They sat with their backs to each other and as one wrote, the other drew the accompanying picture in illustration. Many of the prophecies are believed to have been fulfilled! As one relates to the fall of the reigning dynasty in China, the book is interdicted. Yet most literary men of any pretensions have a copy.

You will observe in one picture a yellow ox, with a duck on its back. Mr. Crawford says, I don't know on what authority, that this represents China and England: yellow is the imperial color here, and the ox is almost a sacred animal. That much may well be, but why the duck is England, I don't see, unless its resting securely on the back of the ox represents England's superior attitude to China, and the enforcement of her demands upon that nation. Accompanying this picture, on the next page, is a prophecy which has been said to relate to the introduction of Christianity. It speaks of the coming in of the "Heavenly doctrine" & says that bells (jury church bells?) shall ring all over the empire.

I thought the book would interest you, and perhaps some visitors to the mission rooms.

Mr. & Mrs. Crawford reached home day before yesterday. We are delighted to have them back. Both are much improved by the trip. It was very much needed, and I think both would have broken down without this rest and recreation. As it is, they are ready again for hard work.

I am at home again, in charge of my sister's school. There are twelve girls, which I consider very good success indeed. It took Mrs. Holmes about four years to reach that number. There are two reasons why my sister has been this successful. The first is, that, Mrs. Holmes' school has been in operation long enough for some of the girls to grow up, and to be married. This proves that we don't mean to carry them off to the "foreign country." Hence, we are gaining the confidence of many who doubted. The second reason is that times are very hard and people are glad to put their daughters where they will be fed without expense to themselves. *We do not furnish clothes*, either in the boys' or girls' schools. We think it has a demoralizing effect upon them to make them so dependent on the foreigner as they would be if we furnished them clothes. Those who adopt that plan, have a hard time, they say. The pupils are careless of their clothes, & very often dissatisfied with the quality. They have been known even to steal and pawn their own clothes, looking to the foreigner to give them more.

My sister is now probably in Shanghai.

With kind regards,

Yrs. truly,

L. Moon.

P.S. Pastor Woo went to Mrs. Holmes to translate your letter for him. He has lately returned from a trip, and has called twice. I hear that Mrs. Hartwell has sent him 100 tls.

October 23, 1876

One of the members of the North Street church who treated Mr. Crawford so badly, has died in Japan. His name was *Liang*, & he was formerly a preacher in Mr. Hartwell's employ. His widow came up to the communion which was held yesterday in the North Street chapel. She came to call on me Saturday, and as I do not propose to hold her responsible for her husband's crimes, I invited her to stay a day or two. So she spent the night & yesterday here. She seems to be quite a nice woman, & very friendly. She said her mother-in-law was coming up to church before very long, & I sent her an invitation to come here. So you see I am doing what little I can to promote harmony & kindly feeling.

Liang was a perjured man, & he attempted to black-mail Mr. Crawford, threatening to mob him in order to extort money on false pretenses &c. Mr. Crawford stood firm. Then Mr. Crawford was summoned to Chefoo to defend himself in a lawsuit brought by a man named *Gow ku san*, who swore that Mr. C. owed him Tls. 3000. Liang also perjured himself in this suit. The papers and evidence showed conclusively that *Gow* owed Mr. Crawford that sum, & was trying to elude its payment. Baffled in this, & maddened by defeat, *Gow* came to Tung Chow to murder Mr. Crawford & commit suicide. Mr. Hartwell, finding he had left Chefoo, wrote up warning Mr. Crawford, & urging Pastor *Woo* to look up *Gow*. The latter was found at an inn in the suburbs. He was induced to come into the city & a strict watch kept on him. He confessed to Mr. Corbett, who was then visiting Tung Chow, that he had come here for the purposes of murder & suicide. (The latter is the chinaman's usual resort in trouble.) Gow was finally persuaded to leave Tung Chow & return home. Meanwhile, at Mr. Hartwell's urgent request, Mr. Richard of the English Baptist mission, had started from Chefoo in hot haste to warn Mr. Crawford. He met *Gow* returning with Mr. Corbett.

When the danger was all over, mark you!—it was imputed to Mr. Crawford's *nervousness*!!! & when he wrote to the consul in Chefoo to arrest the would-be assassin & bind him over to keep the peace, the consul was advised just to let the matter drop—which he did. As Mr. Mateer told the consul afterwards, he had committed a breach of the law in declining to arrest this man & bind him over to keep the peace, which in America would be regarded as a very grave offense indeed in an official.

Afterwards, Mr. Crawford made formal charges before the North St. church against these men (there were three of them—one, *Gow's* son-in-law, a weak fellow, hardly responsible.) They were not even suspended from communion. There may possibly have been a slight censure, but I am not certain. If there was, it amounted to nothing.

Meantime Pastor *Woo* had picked a quarrel with Mr. Crawford about an exceedingly trivial matter. Mr. Hartwell wrote to Mr. Crawford, & in the letter referred him to a letter he had written Pastor *Woo*, for further information. Mr. Crawford went to Mr. *Woo*'s house, but found him absent. The letter had come. Mr. C. told Mrs. *Woo* the circumstances, & asked her to open the letter & allow him to read it. This she did. When Pastor *Woo* returned, Mr. C. went around to tell him that he had gotten Mrs. *Woo* to open the letter. He was grossly insulted for his pains. More than that, Pastor *Woo* brought the matter up before the North Street church in church meeting, & asked their advice. They censured Mr. Crawford, (the pastor of another church!) but advised their own Pastor to forgive him! Now, in Chinese eyes, the opening of another man's letter is *no offense at all.* It is done any day. When *Woo* apologized to Mr. Crawford, he said it was not the opening of the letter that made him angry, but that Mr. Crawford had gone on & acted in the matter without waiting to consult him. To put it mildly, he was angry because a man whose life had been in danger, ventured to take measures for self protection without waiting until his return, when it *might be* too late.

I have entered on this very disagreeable subject, because it naturally came up in speaking of the death of Liang. I think too you have never heard the story except as it came out incidentally in our letters to the Board.

Yrs. &c.,

L. Moon.

Yokohama, Japan,
Nov. 14, 1876
Rev. H. A. Tupper, D. D.:—
My dear Brother,

Dr. Yates' letter will inform you why I am here, but I desire to write you more fully on the subject myself. I will begin by copying from a letter I wrote you last April on the subject of my sister's health—a letter she would not allow me to send.

"About three years ago she sustained a serious injury while riding, when on a country trip. In addition to this, she contracted a violent cold during the same trip, & on her return was so seriously ill that Dr. Brown was summoned from Chefoo. Most of the following summer she was sick with the diseases incident to the season. When I arrived, I found her weak & unable to sit up all day. As cold weather advanced, she seemed to get better. Unfortunately, in Feb., she was induced to go on a country trip. The day we returned was one of the most intensely cold I ever experienced. A slight snow had fallen the night before & the North wind blew fiercely. That day my sister was far from well & the disease proved to be pneumonia. Since that time she has never been free from sore throat. Her health growing constantly worse, she went to Chefoo in the fall of 1874 to be under medical treatment. Her physician, thinking the sore throat might be aggravated by bad teeth, ordered her to Shanghai where there is a good dentist. The teeth were extracted, but she continued sick enough to require medical advice. After she got better, we went to Soochow & spent three weeks during which her health seemed to improve a little. We returned home in March 1875, hoping for a permanent cure, though the throat trouble remained, resisting every remedy. It grew so bad that I took the boys' school off her hands in order that she might have perfect rest. (Note. She took her last country trip in the spring of 1875 & came back much worse from it.) She did not resume regular work until the middle of Feb. 1876, & all the time she has grown worse. Not only is the throat no better, but she has almost constant pain in her lungs, & is not strong enough for work. She takes cold at the slightest change of weather & sometimes without any apparent change or any assignable reason.

She has planned to spend next winter in Japan, with the intention of returning to Tung Chow next year if she is better; if not better, she must ultimately go home. I am convinced that the wisest thing for her to do is to go home at once. Two years at home would probably effect a thorough cure. The irritated throat & lungs would doubtless heal before the disease is fastened permanently on them. One thing is certain, *she must not remain here next winter.* Much as we deprecate the expense, I write to ask the Board to authorize her immediate return home & to make the necessary appropriation for it. I believe she can stand this climate if once cured, provided she gives up country trips forever, & this she is prepared to do. I propose to take charge of her school during her absence. When she returns school work & city visiting will afford her ample employment, & I will be freed from the confinement of the school room and able to devote myself to country work for which I have "the necessary strength."

In accordance with the plan of spending the winter in Japan, my sister left Tung Chow Oct. 2nd. After some stay in Chefoo, she took steamer for Shanghai in company with Miss Safford. On Oct. 24th, I was much alarmed & distressed by receiving a telegram sent by Mrs. Yates from Nagasaki, Japan, to Shanghai, & forwarded by Dr. Yates. It said, "Eddie much worse. Send her sister to Japan immediately." With this telegram came a letter from Dr. Yates. He said, "Your sister arrived on Saturday last in very low spirits. She remained in bed from Saturday till Wednesday...We did all we could to divert her thoughts from the subject that causes her so much mortal agony." (The thought that so much mission money has been spent on her & now she must go home, for it seems she has come to the conclusion that this was necessary.) Dr. Yates continues, "This morning I received the enclosed telegram that will speak for itself. Sad as it is, it requires *immediate attention!* Come at once & prepared to go to the States if necessary, and I fear it will become *absolutely* necessary."

There was much more than this, but I quote just enough to show you I was *obliged* to leave my post. There was no choice in the matter. With a most heavy heart, I made my preparations, & in four hours from the reception of the telegram, I started on my sad and lonely journey. I reached Shanghai in due course of time & there found a letter from Mrs. Yates to Dr. Yates which wrung my heart with anguish. The letter was of the same date as the telegram. I cannot tell you the torture of suspense I endured. When I reached Kobe, Japan, I had good news. I reached here last Thursday & found my sister better. I had duly made up my mind that it was my duty to go home with her. I had to persuade her that it was the right thing to do & I succeeded. I think it would nearly have broken my heart to have seen her go off with only strangers to care for her. I thought too, Mr. Hartwell went home with his wife & so did Mr. Williams. My sister has as much need of me as these ladies had of their husbands. She is very dependent on men, very unhappy away from me.

While in Chefoo, I received a letter from Mr. Crawford in which he says, "In my opinion Miss Eddie has done all she could (perhaps more than she ought) to remain at her post, that her throat & lungs are not able to bear the strain of life & missionary labors in this land, & that she may return home with *honor* under providential necessity which she is wholly unable to control, & will be entitled to the kindest sympathy of the Board & the churches. I am also authorized to say that such are the sentiments of all associated with me. Tell the Board & the sisters at home to trust in God & not to allow this misfortune to discourage them. The stroke falls very much more heavily on us as than on them, & if we bow properly to the will of our Heavenly Father—a blessing will follow."

For expenses Mr. Crawford gave me an order for 500 tls. This realized Dr. Yates arranged for me to draw in Yokohama

$666.28

274.00

$240.28

Please keep my sister's health in prayer. The mo. before leaving Chefoo, we will keep an account of this & send it to you.

I should grieve very much at leaving my work only it seems to me that the will of God has so plainly called me away that it would not be right to be distressed.

With kind regards,
Yours truly,
L. Moon.

View Mont
Alb. Co., Va.
Jan. 6, 1877
Rev. H. A. Tupper:—
My dear Brother,

Both your letters came to hand in due time. I was disappointed you did not come, but it has been so very cold that I think it was wise in you to delay, not to speak of the roads which have been snow-covered. By deferring your visit till the weather is warmer, my sister will be in better condition to enjoy it. Thus far, she has been confined to her room. There is not much hope of her recovering strength before spring. She still thinks she will not be able to return to China.

I had a letter to-day from Mrs. Crawford in which she urges my return as soon as I recover from the fatigues of the trip. She is so kind as to add, "We shall miss you in every department of our missionary work as well as in our social circle." These letters from China have made me home-sick. I fear there is not money in the mission treasury to send me back, but if there is or should be, I am very anxious to return to China by the very first available opportunity. There are missionaries going over nearly every month, & by correspondence with various boards some arrangement might be made by which I could get company. When do Mr. and Mrs. Simmons go back? Once in Japan, I should have no trouble. I have friends there, from one of whom, Dr. Nathan Brown, I had a letter to-day.

I have been keeping the enclosed account to hand you when I should see you, but as you have not come, I think it best not to delay sending it any longer. The $40.23 still in my hands are subject to your directions.

Reciprocating the wish of a "Happy New Year," I remain
Yrs. Sncly,
L. Moon.

P.S.

I had a letter from Dr. Yates this morning bearing date Nov. 14th. He was looking remarkably well when I saw him & he was in fine spirits, especially about his church. I was delighted with the congregation that assembled to the ringing of the bells. If our Board never does any thing more, it has done a good work in establishing that Shanghai church.

Yrs. & c.,

L.M.

View Mont, Alb. Co. Va.

Jan. 20, 1877

Rev. H. A. Tupper:—

My dear Brother,

Your letter of Jan. 12th is to hand. It seems to me that the simplest way about the Boarding School fund is to let it be a personal transaction between Mr. Hartwell & my sister & myself, of which we ask the approbation of the Ladies rather as a matter of courtesy than anything else. Their object has been to give us the means to open a girls' boarding school. It does not concern them in the least whether we buy or build. The only question is, Has the money been used as intended? We arrange with Mr. Hartwell, with the consent & approbation of the Board, to use the premises formerly occupied by Mrs. Hartwell for a girls' boarding school, & not by way of purchase, but simply of kindly cordial Christian feeling we transfer any rights we have in the money in exchange for any rights he had in the house. My Sister does not expect to return to China. If she ever should, it will be time enough then to speak of the necessity of her having a room upstairs. She would need purer air & a drier room than is to be found in the premises as they now stand. As she does not expect to return, it would not be worthwhile to retain any of this fund to put up a room for my sister, as we once thought might be best, & the whole amount Tl. 1283.10 might be transferred to Mr. Hartwell. It is now lying with Messrs. Wilson, Cornabe & Co. to my credit in Chefoo, & I could send Mr. Hartwell through you an order for it. My only fear is, & I say it to you in confidence, that he means to keep up the fight in Tung Chow. His implacable spirit has embittered the lives of two "of whom the world is not worthy." They are deeply ashamed of the quarrel & would so have rejoiced in a full reconciliation. While the one party has bruted it in correspondence from one end of China to the other, a dignified silence has been preserved by the other party. While the one, by a shrug or a sneer, has given the cue of scorn & contempt to the native christians of one church, the other has remained absolutely silent or has resolutely upheld the christian character of his opponent.

I assure you that we in Tung Chow are too thoroughly ashamed of the quarrel ever to hint it on any of our letters whether to persons in China or America. What *could* be more disgraceful?

My sister is not well enough to write to you & the Ladies, but hopes to do so ere long. If you approve the style of letter indicated on the first page, I will write such to the Ladies of 2nd Baptist church Atlanta, & forward to you for perusal.

Thank you very much for your invitation to Richmond. Perhaps it will be in my power to accept it at some future day. My brother-in-law, Dr. Shepherd, with his little motherless girl, is visiting us now.

My sister does not regain her strength though she seems better.

I understand the difficulties of your position & sympathize in the annoyances & perplexities that Tung Chow affairs have brought upon you. Hoping they may be wisely adjusted, I remain

Yours truly,

L. Moon.

View Mont
Alb. Co., Va.
Jan. 29, 1877
Rev. H. A. Tupper, D.D.:—
My dear Brother,

I am so astonished to learn from your letter of Jan. 25th that Mr. Crawford's private business affairs have been reported to you & as I infer, are to be brought before the Board, that I cannot refrain from writing to express my surprise. I am not informed on the subject upon which you ask information. I heard of Kao's imprisonment, but feeling no interest in the subject & knowing him to be a bad character, I made no inquiries. Dr. Yates, however, told my sister that the imprisonment was on account of "something back of" Mr. Crawford's affair. This I do know, that he was arrested three or four years ago in Shanghai & thrown into prison for an old debt due some parties in Shanghai for a steamer he bought & failed to pay for. The parties in that suit are Chinese, I think, but I dare not say positively.

It is my impression that the recent imprisonment was at the instance of those parties.

I *know* that Mr. Crawford will never defend himself before the Board on matters over which they have no jurisdiction.

If his ministerial character is impeached, according to printed "Regulations" of the Board, this should be done in writing over the signature of the one making the impeachment & a copy should be forwarded Mr. Crawford that his defense may be laid before the Board at the same time as the charges. Otherwise, the decision will simply be, "Judgement for plaintiff without hearing defendant."

It is exceedingly disagreeable to me to be drawn into this unfortunate affair, but a sense of justice to those who are too far away to defend themselves, compels me to speak out.

I only wish you could have an hour's talk with Dr. Yates. With his thirty years' experience in Chinese affairs, & above all his keen insight into Chinese character, he would cast a flood of light on this whole affair. Could you possibly go to China & investigate matters for yourself? The Missionary Conference meets in Shanghai in May. The pleasure of attending that would be something to look back to the remainder of your days. You would meet there with Mr. and Mrs. Crawford & could afterwards visit Shantung if you thought proper.

You will be glad to hear that my sister is much better. Dr. Shepherd has put her on cod liver oil & whiskey three times a day, & her improvement is delightful to witness. She is so much better that she is going this week to visit my brother. I also shall be visiting in that neighborhood & must ask you to direct your reply to Glendower, Alb. Co. The weather is so beautiful now (though the roads are frightful still!) that I feel inclined to ask you to make us that promised visit. You would find us at Church Hill, my brother's place of residence. I am sure that he would be delighted to see you. You would have to take the cars to North Garden in this county. Three days in the week a hack runs from there passing by Glendower P. O., & at the latter place my brother would meet you, or send some one to meet you. The three days are Monday, Wednesday & Friday. It would be better if you would write of your coming several days in advance, on account of the uncertainty of county mails. If you cannot make us a visit, I am now free to accept your invitation to Richmond. Dr. Shepherd has left us & I could forego for the present a number of visits I have planned among my relatives. I confess I would *rather* have a visit from you for two reasons. First, I want you to see my sister, & 2nd, I shrink (foolishly perhaps) from meeting the Woman's Society. I had rather talk to Chinese women than American ladies! My sister joins me in kind regards.

Yours truly,

L. Moon.

View Mont,

Albemarle Co., Va.

May 15, 1877

My dear Dr. Tupper,

I enclose for your perusal a recent letter from Mrs. Crawford. I have notes from Mr. and Mrs. C. of as late date as March 27th. Mr. C. writes that he has been put in possession of the houses & adds, "all quiet." Mrs. Crawford says they are to have the two children from Japan they wanted to adopt. They are brother & sister. The girl is fourteen, & a lovely character–a future missionary, I doubt not. She has already been teaching in the orphan's home at Yokohama. The boy is seven. They will be a great comfort & pleasure to their adopted parents. They are English children.

I almost fear to hear from the Convention, having had an intimation of the trouble likely to arise. God grant it may have been averted, & that no damage may result to the cause we love.

My sister is better. Our dear little Mamie is the source of unceasing happiness to her.

My sister of whom I told you as being in the Treasury Dept. at Washington, returned home about three weeks ago & I have been enjoying her society extremely. She is very vivacious & her accounts of Washington life are amusing. She is to me very much what the dear sister who died was to Eddie. You can imagine then what a pleasure it is to us both to be together again.

Miss Downing of Chefoo writes that she could get fifty pupils if she had the means of support. Mr. Richard of Eng. Baptist Mission has plunged, like the noble man he is, into the heart of the famine district. He is reported to have four hundred orphans under his care. There is something terrible to me, as well as heroic, in the idea of thus contending alone & single handed against this grim famine frenzy, yet Mr. R. is doing it with no thought of glory or reward—only intent to follow in his Master's footsteps.

Hoping to hear from you soon, I am, With kindest regards

Yours sincerely,

L. Moon.

Mt. Ayr,
Albemarle Co., Va.,
June 11, 1877
Rev. Dr. H. A. Tupper:—
My dear Brother,

I enclose my last letter from Mrs. Crawford.

I am not able to answer your inquiries. My impression is that Mr. Simmons would be acceptable to all in Tung Chow. There is one difficulty. He, of course, shares the usual view about employing native assistants. Our mission oppose it from principle. We think there is more evil than good in the practice. To have two missionaries of the same Board in the same city carrying out antagonistic policies would be very detrimental to the best interests of both. All we ask for our side of the question, is a fair field to work it out. We do not ask to interfere with the working of any other mission. Now, if Mr. Simmons *could not* refrain from employing native assistants, I do not hesitate to say that his presence, much as we desire help, would embarrass more than it would benefit us. I dare say Dr. H. would expect him to go on in the old way employing Messrs. *Wong* & *Sun*. The only effectual way to settle the matter is for the Board to say we have two plans of conducting missions. We will give both plans fair play. Let Tung Chow & the vicinity be the field of one experiment—other parts of China, of the other, but please don't send us any body who *must* have native assistants. Of course a man must hire his personal teacher, & he may get all the preaching he can out of that man, but let it be understood that foreign money does not go to pay men for preaching.

With kindest regards,
L. Moon.
Please address yr.
next to Glendower, Alb. Co., Va.

View Mont., Albemarle Co., Va.,
July 3, 1877
Rev. Dr. H. A. Tupper:—
My dear Brother,

Your letter of June 29th was rec'd yesterday.

I think your decision about Miss Lightfoot imminently wise. If the Mission brethren & sisters will prepay the expense, of the journey & one year's salary, then it would be very good to appoint her. If, however, they only promise, & raise, say a few hundred, then it would scarcely be justice to the lady to appoint her. She will be in China among strangers, & she should have the power to draw her salary promptly in advance that she may meet her own current expenses. To have to borrow from strangers (even though they be brother missionaries) is mortifying, to say the least, & the lady should not be subjected to any such probability. It should be placed sharply & distinctly before these good people who want her appointed that they are incurring a very serious obligation if they profess to undertake her support. If her salary comes behind time, she is annoyed & harassed in a way that may, I do not say it would, impair her usefulness.

If she is appointed, she could live either with Mrs. Holmes or myself. If with Mrs. Holmes, she could give herself to city visiting & could take charge of the school when Mrs. H. is absent, as frequently occurs, on country trips. It is my opinion that Mrs. Holmes will not be able to bare the separation from her only son. Though a missionary, she is only human. I very greatly fear she will break down under the trial. Landrum is her all. If this lady were with her, she could be preparing as her successor, & I do not know any one superior to Mrs. Holmes in training a newcomer, for work.

If, for any cause, it should be thought best for her to live with me, she could do city work & teach some classes in the school. I do not think she should undertake much country work. I do not honestly believe that many women should undertake to rough it as Mrs. Holmes and I are accustomed to do. My sister's failure of health was due, I feel sure, to the hardships of country work. Of course the lady would have to decide that matter for herself, only I should feel it a duty to warn her that Mrs. Holmes, in her enthusiasm, will push her beyond the bounds of reason, unless she has the firmness to stop short when she should do no more.

If Miss Lightfoot is appointed, I should be glad to have her address, & will write & welcome her to our mission circle. She could be very useful in Tung Chow. I know that Mrs. Holmes was delighted at the thought of having Mrs. Llewellyn with her. Now that she will be alone, I think she would be doubly glad to have someone. For myself, I have no dread of living alone. Please assure Miss Lightfoot of the most cordial & hearty welcome from the Tung Chow foreign community. She will feel herself from the first among warm & loving hearts & we will do our best to make her happy.

With kindest regards,
Yours sincerely,
L. Moon

Carter's Bridge P.O.
Albemarle, Co.,
Va.,
Sept. 15, 1877
Rev. Dr. H. A. Tupper:-
My dear Brother,
    Your letter of the 10th Inst. reached me to-day. I know of two ladies, Miss Pitman & Miss Nelson of Charlottesville, who are to leave about the middle of Oct. for Japan. Once in Japan, I would be all right. I think these ladies will take the Nov. steamer at San Fran. I could find out by writing Miss Pitman who is now in Delaware. She has been anxious for me to go with them. A young lady of the Northern Pres. Board was to go out this fall to Chefoo & a friend of mine & hers wrote with regard to our going out together. I do not know whether she has gone or not. My decided preference would be to go with Mr. & Mrs. Simmons, & if it is at all certain that they will get off by December, I would prefer to wait & go with them. If I should go by Nov. steamer, I would reach Tung Chow about Christmas. This is with us the least busy time of the year. The schools close a little later, it is too cold for country trips, & the city people do not want visits so near the New Year. So you see there is comparatively little to do. If we could go by Dec. steamer, we would reach Tung Chow just after the Chinese New Year, when the schools open, our city visiting begins, & soon after we make country trips. It would not do to wait as late as Jan. to leave here, because the railroad is likely to be blocked up by snow during that month & Feb. Still if the Board *can not* send Mr. & Mrs. Simmons as early as Dec., my preference would be to go with Miss Pitman in Oct. I do not care to be in Tung Chow now before the Chinese New Year, but I shall be sorry to get there much later. I shall be inexpressibly happy to get back, though very sorry to leave my relatives & friends.
    I should like to meet the Ladies' Miss Soc. of Richmond if it could be arranged before I go. I want to ask their continued support of my sister's school which I hope to resume & carry on.
    With kindest regard,
    Yrs. truly,
    L. Moon.

Carter's Bridge P.O.
Albemarle Co., Virginia
Oct. 10, 1877
My dear Brother,

Your letter of the 8th Inst. is just to hand. I shall be delighted if you can arrange for me to go with the party leaving N.Y. Oct. 20th or 22nd. Any day you name after this week, I should be most happy to be your guest. I suspect it would be better to take Richmond en route for New York. It would save time and expense.

I have not a doubt that the Ga. ladies intend to support me in the future as in the past. It would give me pain to sever my former very pleasant connection with them. What I would ask of the Richmond ladies is that they continue their support of my sister's school. That has always been their work and I hope they would not willingly abandon it. I shall try at once to resume it on my return & I hope that in a few years it will be large & flourishing. I should expect to keep the ladies posted as to its affairs and I hope their prayers and sympathies would be with the school. Hoping to hear from you soon, I remain

Yours sincerely,
L. Moon.
P.S.

Of course I shall not object to the Va. ladies sending me back to China. It is no matter where the money comes from, so I go, but I have a love for the Ga. ladies that would make me feel badly if they give me up.

L. M.

Viewmont
Albemarle Co., Virginia
Oct. 12, 1877
Rev. Dr. H.A. Tupper
My dear Brother,

Your letter of Oct. 10th is just to hand. You may expect me in Richmond on Tuesday, Oct. 16th & I shall be happy to be Mrs. Tupper's guest. I have written Miss Pitman that I will be in New York on Friday night. I could meet the Woman's Missionary Society on Wednesday or Thursday as most convenient.

By referring to my account book, I find that my expenses to America were about five hundred & forty dollars ($540.00). Since then, there has been an advance on fare from Yokohama to Shanghai, putting it back at the old rates. I should not like to start with less than seven hundred dollars ($700.00), which will be ample allowance, I think, for exchange. Whatever is left, I will pay over to the Mission Treasurer in Tung Chow.

I am delighted at the thought of so soon being back in China. I am only sorry that Mr. & Mrs. Simmons can not go yet. Hoping to see you soon. I am

Yrs. sincerely,

L. Moon.

P.S.

I do not know what route the party will take to San Francisco, probably by Chicago.

New York
Oct. 20, 1877
Rev. Dr. H. A. Tupper
My dear Brother,

I should have sent you a postal ere this, but I have been waiting, thinking I would write more at length. I have been persuaded to remain until tomorrow night. I should gain nothing by going earlier, for the party does not leave Chicago until Tuesday, two hours after I am due there. I had the pleasure this evening of seeing some missionaries off for India. They go to England by one of the Anchor Line steamers. The lady with whom I went to the steamer, Miss Robinson, of the Woman's Miss. Board, has been very kind to me. She went with me this evening to get my ticket & secured for me special rates, saving to our Board $25.00 in gold, on the passage to Shanghai. She has shown me many pleasant attentions besides. Other ladies have also been very kind. Miss Doremus, of the Woman's Board, is to take charge of me tomorrow. So you see I am well cared for. I am hoping Dr. Shepherd will reach the city tomorrow, two or three hours before I leave.

I had some trouble about cashing my check, as there was no one to prove my identity. If Dr. Cutting had been in the city, there would have been no trouble, I think. However, the subordinates of the Home Mission rooms kindly took the responsibility, with permission of a member of the finance committee & exchanged checks with me. Then one of them went to the bank & got the money & I was all right. Please, when you write to any of them, thank them cordially for this courtesy & kindness. If you could find time to send them a few special lines of thanks, I should be glad.

I had a pleasant trip from Richmond. Mr. & Mrs. Wilson were socially inclined, the latter particularly. I liked her very much.

I hope you have heard ere this that your little grandchild is better. I think often of you all. Please present my most cordial regard to all the family. I never enjoyed a visit more. It will be one of the sunniest memories of my life. You & Mrs. Tupper must return my visit & I will do my best to make you enjoy yourselves! I only wish there were some hope of your coming. Our steamer does not sail until Nov. 3rd. With kindest regards,

Yrs truly,

L. Moon.

San Fran., Cal.

Oct. 31, 1877

My dear Brother,

I telegraphed you today that I had drawn $350.00 (three hundred & fifty dollars) on the Bank of Cal., & that the children would be cared for. I left your letter to Mrs. Nevin at the Bank, & the money is deposited there to her credit. Rev. Dr. Francis, who kindly identified me at the bank, will likewise identify Mrs. Nevin & she will have no trouble. I will leave a letter of my own for Mrs. Nevin with Rev. Dr. Kerr, Missy to Chinese, & he promises to deliver it. Assure Dr. Hartwell that every care will be taken of the children. He need not feel the slightest uneasiness about them. Dr. Francis will be on the look out for the steamers & will meet them. If they arrive before I leave, I hope to see them. Dr. Francis suggested that if Dr. Hartwell is coming here to live, the children might as well stay here, & said he would take them into his own family. Of course if that is the decision, you had better telegraph him at once for I have arranged for the children to go with Mrs. Nevin to Baltimore, provided she shall be willing to take them. The rail road agent agreed to take the children at rate for two. Then, we allowed for sleeping car fares & for food, and Dr. F., the Bank Officer, & I concluded that three hundred and fifty was the right amount. The Bank official was very kind & polite, shook hands at parting, & wished me a safe voyage—I could not but think today of the passage of Scripture, "Cast thy bread upon the waters and thou shalt find it after many days." About twenty years ago this Dr. Francis was a sort of travelling missionary, or agent of some sort in Virginia. He & his nephew came to my mother's & remained there perhaps a week or ten days, & were treated with all the old fashioned hospitality of those times. Hearing through Dr. Kerr of my being here, he called yesterday, & at once took the affair of the children into his own hands. Dr. Graves had previously written him about them. To-day he came around & escorted me to the Bank of Cal. where he transacts his own business. After settling about the children, I bought an order in Shanghai for Mexican dollars, so all my business affairs are now settled & I have nothing to do but enjoy myself till the steamer sails, Saturday, Nov. 3rd. Speaking of business, I must mention that I had to lend twenty-five dollars to Miss Nelson, Missionary of the Woman's Miss. Union. Some unexpected expenses made her funds run low and I offered to lend, knowing you would approve. When I was in New York, the Ladies of the W. Miss. Union treated me not only with the greatest attention, but with the utmost kindness. My own sisters could not have done more for me than they did, and I was very glad to have it in my power to return a little of their great kindness.

I have had a very pleasant time here—a number of calls and several invitations out. Yesterday we spent the day with an old school-mate of a cousin of mine. She saw my name in the list of arrivals & called promptly. It is an Alabama family, & we had a delightful day. The lady was once a student at R. F. Ins., in Dr. Manly's time I think. They told us marvels about this land, the extravagance of its magnates, the size of its vegetables & fruits, &c., but I have not time to repeat it. We had a very pleasant overland journey. I never enjoyed the trip as much before. From Chicago, nearly to Omaha, we had the very pleasant addition to our party of Rev. Dr. Humphreys, Dist. Sec. of the American Board. As I know a number of missionaries of that board in Japan and China, we were soon on the easy footing of old acquaintances. He was introduced to us by Mrs. Avery of Chicago. Mrs. A. inquired very particularly about Mrs. Crawford & wondered that Mrs. C. had not requested me to stop in Chicago to see Mrs. Buckingham who used to contribute annually one hundred dollars for the support of two Chinese girls in Mrs. H's school, Martha and Lucy. Mrs. Avery asked very particularly about the girls and said she would tell Mrs. Buckingham.

I don't know Dr. Francis' address as he lives in Oakland, but a telegram to him, care of Dr. Kerr, No. 800, Corner of Sacramento & Stockton, would reach him immediately, I am confident. I am very glad to have attended to the matter for Dr. Hartwell. I fear that you & he will have had anxiety on the subject. Love to Mrs. Tupper, please. I remember my delightful visit to you with much pleasure.

We are invited to go out tomorrow to Brooklyn, about nine miles from the city & stay until Saturday, going thence to the steamer. Miss Pitman, who has already been out there says, if there is a paradise on earth it is that spot. I hope to hear from you soon after reaching China.

Yrs. Truly,

L. Moon.

There will be eleven missionaries on the steamer. By last steamer seventeen went out.

San Francisco, Cal.

Nov. 2, 1877

My dear Dr. Tupper,

The steamer *Gaelic* has arrived & Mrs. Nevin's name is not in the list of passengers. I telegraphed you, and afterwards wrote fully on the subject. I have written a letter to Mrs. Nevin in which I have said all the polite & proper things necessary—cordial thanks for her care of the children &c. Do not feel the slightest uneasiness about them. If Mrs. Nevin can not take them, Dr. Francis will look after their comfort.

I mentioned that I had lent Miss Nelson $25.00. She has now returned it, so there is no use to make any record of the matter.

Our steamer is advertized to sail tomorrow at noon. I think I may say that I go in fine health and high spirits. I have never enjoyed a trip so much as the overland journey this time. We had the merriest party. I anticipate the sea voyage with real pleasure. Hoping I hear from you soon, remain, with love to Mrs. Tupper,

Yrs. sincerely,

L. Moon.

Yokohama

Japan

Nov. 24, 1877

My dear Dr. Tupper,

We had the best possible voyage over the water—good weather, no headwinds, scarcely any rolling or pitching—in short, all that reasonable people could ask. Here, I am staying in the family of Rev. Dr. Brown, of the Northern Baptist Board. They are very kind and cordial. Mr. Crawford had written them in September to look for me, and they had been on two previous steamers to meet me. Dr. Brown and his daughter were just starting yesterday for the steamer when I walked in having come ashore with some friends. I spent a week here last fall and of course feel very natural to be here again. I do so love the East and eastern life! Japan fascinated my heart and fancy four years ago, but now I honestly believe I love China the best, and actually, which is stranger still, like the *Chinese* best.

We had fourteen missionaries on our steamer. The majority were for this favored land, two for Siam, & four for China.

I leave for Shanghai two days from this time. I am anticipating with pleasure the passage through that lovely Inland Sea. It seems like fairy land. I hope to reach Tung Chow by the middle of Dec., & to begin the New Year in my dearly loved home.

Please give kindest remembrance to your family. I hope Mrs. Hamilton's child recovered. Hoping to hear from you soon, I remain, with kindest regards,

Yours truly,

L. Moon.

Shanghai, China
Dec. 13, 1877
My dear Dr. Tupper:

After Dr. Yates' inquiring of the Agent & learning that the steamer for Chefoo would leave about the middle of this month or later, I determined to visit my friend Miss Safford in Soochow. To my dismay, my steamer went off two days ago without me. So here I am waiting and hoping for another. People say there will probably be one about Christmas & I still hope to be settled & ready for work by Jan. 1st.

I had a delightful visit to Soochow. Miss Safford had come down to Shanghai to meet me and I returned with her. It is almost worth while to go away from China for awhile, to get the hearty welcome one receives on returning. I sometimes think that missionaries are the warmest-hearted people in the world. At Soochow, you might have thought I was a near & dear relative instead of a comparative stranger. Such overflowing cordiality & hospitality! I had but two days there and came away very reluctantly, reaching here to find that my steamer had left the day before. I do not worry about it because I could not do much in Tung Chow anyway until after Chinese New Year. The schools close in a few weeks & according to Chinese etiquette one must not visit for some time before the New Year. People are too busy to have company.

I am enjoying the very kind and cordial hospitality of my dear friends, Dr. & Mrs. Yates. They make me feel perfectly at home & are just as good to me as friends could be. I have been distressed to see that Dr. Yates' health has very seriously failed. He has determined to run over to San Francisco for a change. I am very glad indeed that he has so decided, for heretofore he has always been restored by a sea voyage. He does not propose to go east, but I sincerely hope the Board will give him an urgent invitation to visit Richmond. I am sure that his presence & conversation will arouse a new interest in the cause of missions. This veteran of thirty years' service—how nobly he has toiled—how generously he has given to that work to which he consecrated his life! It seems to me that the coldest heart would be stirred by his presence. There is not a man in China who could give you more valuable information as to the past history & present status of missions in this land. In short, you & the Baptists of Richmond would alike enjoy a feast if you could induce him to visit you. I must beg you, however, to spare our friend & not let him work too hard. When he was in Richmond before, he had to go through with *four* services one Sunday & it about used him up, but I know that *you* would not allow anything of that kind.

Mrs. Yates sends a large bundle of kind regards. She was so pleased with your last letter.

I hope Dr. Hartwell's children reached Baltimore all right.

With kindest regards, I remain

Yours sincerely,

L. Moon.

Tung Chow, China
Dec. 24, 1877
My dear Dr. Tupper,

I write merely to announce my safe arrival here. We had head winds and so took four days instead of two from Shanghai, and I landed at Chefoo in a snowstorm. One of the native brethren had been sent down to meet me. Under his escort, I made the short overland journey very pleasantly. Mrs. Nevins bundled me up so thoroughly that it was impossible to suffer from the cold. I feel like a Chinese mandarin with so many clothes on, & some of them wadded.

I found my dear friends here well and cheerful. Of course we have done little but talk the two days I have been here. There is so much to hear & tell on both sides.

I hope to write you a long letter next time. Do make Dr. Yates go east. His visit would be worth more than the money it would cost. He will not go unless urgently invited. He bears his own expenses as far as San Francisco.

Yrs. Sincerely,

L. Moon.

P.S.

I think the Board will receive a petition ere long from our mission to send Mr. Simmons to Tung Chow *at once.* Mr. Crawford *must* have rest and change. He desires to shift the pastorate on to younger shoulders. Whether any one comes or not, he will go away. He needs it very much. Dr. Nevins told me to say to the Board from him that you should send Mr. Simmons immediately to Tung Chow. He says you will wake up some day & find yourselves without a man in Tung Chow & in Shanghai, & that it will take you years to regain what you will have lost by the failure to have men here growing into the places that *must* be left vacant sooner or later. All this he volunteered as a message to our Board and I promised to deliver it. I heartily endorse every word of the message.

L. M.

Account of Travelling Expenses
Tung Chow, China
Dec. 31, 1877

Account of Travelling Expenses from Charlottesville, Va. to Tung Chow, China

Ticket from Charlottesville to Richmond	$ 4. 25
" " Richmond to New York	12.85
Sleeping Berth	2.00
Carriage & luggage to depot	1.00
New York transfer coach	.50
Returned Episcopal Board for telegrams	.80
Hotel Bill in New York	9.30
Coach Ticket	.75
Luggage to Erie RR	.80
Ticket to San Francisco	130.00
" " Shanghai	284.00
Sleeping Car to Chicago	5.00
Breakfast, Oct. 22	.90
Dinner, " "	.85

Supper, " "	.65
To porter at Chicago	.25
Breakfast, Oct. 23	1.00
Dinner, " "	.75
Supper, " "	.75
Sleeping Car to Omaha	3.00
Breakfast, Oct. 24	.75
	$460.15

Brought over	$460.15
To porter at Omaha	.25
Sleeping car to Ogden	8.00
Lunch, Oct. 24	.50
Telegram to San Fran.	.70
Extra baggage	5.50
Breakfast, Oct. 25	1.00
Lunch, " "	.30
Breakfast, Oct. 26	1.00
Lunch, " "	. 40
Supper, " "	1.00
To porter at Ogden	.25
Sleeping car from Ogden to San Fran.	$ 6.00
Breakfast, Oct. 27	1.00
Dinner, " "	1.00
Supper, " "	1.00
Breakfast, Oct. 28	.75
Dinner, " "	.50
Coach to Hotel in San Fran.	.50
	$489.80
Paid premium for gold	3.85
	$493.65
Telegram to Richmond	2.00
Bill at Hotel San Fran.	19.50
	$514.15
Coach & trunks to steamer	1.83
Wine for sea-sickness	1.50
Luggage ashore at Yokohama	.65
Board in Yokohama	5.00
Telegram to Dr. Yates	2.40

Ticket to Chefoo	_27.28_
	$552.81
Chefoo to Tungchow	_7.00_
	$559.81

Gained $2.00 in San Fran.
in buying check on Shanghai
for Mexican dollars   _2.00_

Total $557.81

Rec'd from
Dr. Tupper $700.00
Total trav. Exp.   _557.81_
             $142.19   Thrown into House Fund.

Note: This journey was more expensive than it should have been because we started too early in Oct. As the steamer did not sail till Nov. 3rd, we should have left Va. about Oct. 25th. This would have given plenty of time & saved hotel bills.

L. Moon.

Tung Chow, China,
Jan. 7, 1878
My dear Dr. Tupper,

Enclosed please find postage stamps for one year's subscription to the *Foreign Journal*, with postage, seventy-six cents.

The owner of this place positively refuses to sell. He snubbed our "go-between" decidedly. Indeed, according to Chinese usage it is an insult to offer to buy a man's property. He has a right to snub you. The owner of property may propose to sell, but he is offended if the proposition to buy comes first. No one is supposed to sell property unless he is in embarrassed circumstances. We think now of trying to get a reduction of rent. I hope he will negotiate on those terms. If so, I will have a new paper drawn up in my own name. The old one is in Mr. Hartwell's name. I have a right to decline to be bound by that, & to demand more suitable terms. I do not mean to intimate that those terms were formerly unsuitable. Under the then existing circumstances, Mr. Hartwell did wonders to get the plan at all. But now things have changed & fences have fallen.

We are having an exceedingly cold winter. I can but rejoice that my sister is spared it. All the mission are in usual health. With kindest regards,

Yours truly,

L. Moon.

P. S. Please do not publish my letter unless marked for *Foreign Journal*—otherwise I can not write freely to you as I wish.

L. Moon.

Tung Chow,
China.
Feb. 13, 1878
My dear Brother,

I have done my best to buy the North St. property & the man will not hear of selling. Thus far, he has not even consented to reduce the rent. I shall try again to get a reduction, but have very little hope of success. What shall I do? Is it unreasonable to go on paying the same rent now that the house is occupied as was paid during the long time it stood locked up? True, we are paying for our own improvements, but does it pay, on the other hand, to pull up and leave most of those improvements behind us? In a word, shall we throw away about Teals 1,000 now invested on improvements in order to invest Teals 1,300 (about) in property elsewhere? It seems to me unwise. There is much to be said, besides, in favor of this place as a permanent location. We have had it already seventeen years. It is the natural rallying point of the North St. church members. I have tried to make it so since I have lived here. Such of them as live in the city are in this neighborhood. There is no other missionary on this street. I am the only one of our mission in this section of the city. Hence, I have a field all to myself. My neighbors are mostly of the better class & some of them are disposed to be friendly. The house is near the North gate & so I have the best opportunity for recreation & exercise. A walk of five minutes takes me outside the city & ten more to the seashore. These are important matters for health. Lastly, I like this part of the city better than any other. I am attached to the places & should leave it with real reluctance. I have a home feeling here that I should not have elsewhere. Besides I do not want the worry of building a new house or of getting rid of the old one.

Please tell Mrs. Wortham that I have written her by this mail. I feel she might not get the letter, as I am not certain about her initials. It is a letter to the W. M. Society & I should like to have her input.

L. M.

Tung Chow, China,
March 8, 1878
My dear Dr. Tupper,

I sent you a short letter last week conveying the intelligence that the long desired union of the Baptist churches in this city has been effected. It is now no longer proper to speak of the North St. church or of the Monument St. church: the two have been merged into the "Tung Chow Baptist church."

Some months ago, called into the far interior by imperative duties to the famine sufferers, Rev. Mr. Richard of the English Baptist mission transferred to Mr. Crawford all his work in this region. Mr. R. had members scattered over a wide extent of country, with headquarters at Chefoo. Pastor *Woo* of the North St. church had resigned his charge here and returned to his home near Chefoo. Under these circumstances, a reorganization of the three churches seemed absolutely necessary. Invitations were sent out to the brethren to meet in this city for consultation. At the time appointed, the choice spirits of all three assembled, full of zeal and anxious to do whatever should be for the glory of God. The conference was opened on Sunday by some wise and weighty words from our beloved and honored pastor, from the text, "Whether therefore ye eat, or drink, or whatever ye do, do all to the glory of God." After the sermon, two applicants for baptism came before the church. After a satisfactory evaluation they were received. In the afternoon, at the close of Sunday school, they were baptized. At night we had a sermon from Pastor *Woo*.

Next day, after prayer by Mr. Crawford, Pastor Woo, and one of the *Chan yuen* brethren, the business meetings commenced. A deeply solemn spirit pervaded the assembly. Mr. Crawford as moderator requested of the brethren a full and free expression of opinion. They were asked to state their views without fear no matter what those views might be. One after another arose, the speakers all favoring the idea of union, but two difficulties were suggested. In one of the churches, the brethren had not been able to come to an agreement about certain funds that were in their hands: until they had decided this question, how could they go into another organization? A member of the Chefoo church inquired, "Suppose Mr. Richard comes back and wants us again, what then? Is there any power to transfer us again to his pastoral oversight?" These difficulties being satisfactorily met or put aside, one of the North St. brethren addressed the Moderator, "Why," he said, "should there be a North St. church or a Monument St. church? Why not have the *Tung Chow Baptist Church*?" The proposition was received with enthusiasm. The vote was put and carried unanimously that the three churches should unite under the name proposed. It was then voted that the deacons of the North St. and Chefoo churches should retain their office as deacons of the new organization, and that one of the deacons-elect of the Monument St. church should be set apart to that office. (The other deacon-elect had been on trial for the office two or three years and had shown himself not worthy.) It was afterwards proposed that the united church should have two pastors, Rev. Mr. Crawford and Rev. Mr. *Woo*. This was also unanimously carried. These business matters took up a morning and afternoon session. At night we had a Union prayer meeting. The house was well filled with Presbyterians and Baptists. The pastor of the Presbyterian church, Rev. Mr. Mills, gave us a talk on the requisites for a continuation of church fellowship, stating various points which should be held as valid reasons for exclusion. Mr. Mateer followed with an earnest, manly appeal for a higher standard of Christian living.

Next day we had a short business session for settling some minor details after which the conference was declared adjourned. An informal meeting was then held at which Pastor *Woo* presided, in aid of the famine sufferers. I believe thirty-two dollars were subscribed.

I would like to speak of the excellent spirit manifested by the brethren, of their zeal and earnestness, of their promptness in transacting church business, but I remember the contracted space of the *Journal*, and I forbear.

Yours sincerely,

L. Moon.

Tung Chow,
China
March 17, 1878
My dear Brother,

I have written you several times recently, & now write mainly to acknowledge the receipt of your welcome letter of Jan. 10th. I wrote you twice of the so happily effected union of the three churches, two of this place & one of Chefoo. The best feeling seems to prevail. I have not heard of any disaffection & the North St. members come about us freely & naturally. I believe they are glad they belong to us!

But I took up my pen to speak of a business matter. I have bought some very desirable property in another part of the city. The papers (deed) have gone to Chefoo to the proper official. When the document has been properly stamped, the property will belong to the Board. The unseen obstacle to which I refer is whether the woman who makes out the deed has a right to sell. It is the business of the Chinese official to settle that question. If the purchase is effected "What is to be done with the North St. property?" It can be kept at a slightly reduced rent. I hate to see it go out of our hands. It is a good missionary house & I do not like to see it torn up. If you decide to give it up, I will take away windows, doors, floors, &c. &c. If you mean to send another, it would seem a waste to throw away the house.

Please send me definite instructions. I will not begin to pull up until I hear from you.

Yrs. sincerely,
L. Moon.

Tung Chow, China
May 27, 1878
My dear Dr. Tupper,

I wrote you I thought I had bought a house. The Mandarin decided that the woman had no right to sell. I am still in a state of uncertainty. The house money is in a Shanghai Bank and draws four pr. cent interest. If deposited for a year, the rate is five pr. cent. Until recently, it has been with Cornabi & Co. of Chefoo, through no fault of mine, but simply because the time of purchasing a house has been so uncertain. When the money first came, I requested Dr. Yates to deposit it in Shanghai. He was willing, but wrote back, "The Board says you must buy a house." I enter into this explanation to show why the money has not been on interest before. Cornabi & Co. keep our mission money and are very obliging, but they pay no interest.

My school has now up to thirteen. The girls manifest a most studious spirit and are worthy of much praise. If the ladies could see the school, they would feel that their money is well expended. I have wanted to name one of the girls for Mrs. Jeter and one for Mrs. Wortham, but I do not know Mrs. J's given name. I named one who came in yesterday for Miss Jennie Clayton whom you know, I believe. These names are "school names." They all have "little names" when they come.

I end here with a sketch of Mrs. Holmes written at her request. The book I sent to Mrs. Yates, asking her to forward to Dr. Graves, & wrote him that you wanted it in August. (I *think* I wrote him this, but am not quite certain.) Please do not publish this note and oblige.

Yours sincerely,
L. Moon.

Tung Chow
July 3, 1878
My dear Dr. Tupper:

We send a formal mission letter for the Board with a full statement of our present difficulties. We think it best to mention a few facts to you privately. Mary was requested soon after she came here by Mr. *Chiang* to write to the Board in behalf of the North St. Church. (You know there is no North St Church in existence.) She declined writing to the Board, but said she would write to Mr. Hartwell. She wrote retailing Mr. *Chiang's* conversation. He said that when they established a native church, the Board had said they would stand by them & help them. Instead of doing this, the Board not only broke its promise to build them a church, but it also does not furnish them a house of worship, & told them to go & join another church. (Note. They have *always* had the North St. mission chapel until they voluntarily gave it up on Pastor Woo's leaving.) *Chiang* said *he* wouldn't submit to such treatment, that they meant to have a native church. Unfortunately Mary wrote this stuff to Mr. Hartwell. He doubtless will communicate it to the Board & make much of it. Now, is it too much for us ladies to ask that the Board will quietly notify Mr. Hartwell that he can not be allowed to have any say in Tung Chow affairs, that they are discussed only between the Board & the Tung Chow Baptist mission?

I have told Mary that I am very sorry she sent such a letter without telling me. I had previously warned her that Mr. Crawford being one of my best friends I could have nobody here who should do anything against him, but it had not occurred to me to warn her about her correspondence. That letter to Mr. Hartwell went, she tells me, last week. Last night letters were brought her & delivered her in my presence with the request that they be forwarded immediately. The letters were to Mr. Hartwell, the Board, the Canton church, & the Shanghai church. Considering that the mail to Chefoo is an entirely private affair for which the foreign community here pays, & that Mary's own letters go simply because she is under my roof & I pay a monthly proportion of the mail messenger's hire, it was altogether the coolest thing I have known of in a long time. Still as a matter of Christian courtesy I did not hint this or express the least objection to the letter's being sent. This morning the same man brought a letter to Pastor Woo to Mary to be forwarded by our messenger. I invited him in, courteously chatted with him about mail matters in general & added, "Whenever you have any letters to send, you can bring them here."

It seems a pity that when we have been actuated simply by compassion in bringing Mary here at our own expense & have tried to make her comfortable & happy since she has been here, that she should have allowed herself to be used as the tool of designing men to stir up strife in America. We heard of her as being ill & needing medical treatment which could only be had in Shanghai & I wrote to Dr. Graves asking that arrangements be made to send her. Mrs. Holmes, thinking the Canton climate did not agree with her offered her a home. The Shanghai doctors ordered her North & Mrs. Mills of the Pres. Mission kindly took charge of her from Shanghai to this little place. She is now with me. She is a good, conscientious girl, but in the case of write to Mr. Hartwell as mentioned above, she has acted foolishly. She tells me Mr. Hartwell sent her $130.00 in Jan. from the Welsh Neck Association, S.C. You told me the Board would do no more for her. She asserts that the money does not come from the Board at all but from the Welsh Neck Association! She has written to thank them & expects to hear from them in October. Of course, if she is to be supported in this way, she ought not to remain in Tungchow because our steadfast opposition to native assistants paid with mission money extends also to "Bible women" so called. Bun & Wang were both paid assistants in their day. By the way, why are they & Liang who is said to have had himself falsely reported as having died in Japan, & whose flaming obituary appeared long since in the "Western Recorder," still put down in the Journal as "three native assistants" at Tungchow? The native pastor is also not here but near Chefoo. None of them are in mission employ.

If the work here is to be kept from going to destruction, we must be backed most powerfully by the whole moral weight of the Board. If these men can set up a church & be recognized as such, ten men or five men, or anybody that likes can withdraw any time he likes & set up a church & appeal to the Board for moral & pecuniary support, & we are powerless.

Mr. Mateer called in tonight on business. I told him of the events of Sunday night & yesterday. He said emphatically, "They will not get one bit of countenance from anybody," but added hesitatingly, "except perhaps Mr. Hartwell, & I should not think he would do it if he had the good of his brethren at heart." Mr. Mateer further said that the new organization would be a sort of catch-place for all discontented members & would give us trouble in that way, but he says, "all they want is money. If your Board doesn't give them that the affair will soon fall through." Then with his usual shrewd practical sense, he said, "If it were my affair, I should say kindly to the really good ones who may be led off, 'We won't take your names off the church book. You'll be sure to come back in time.'" He says all will probably come back but the leaders.

My house matter is settled & I am to keep the place as long as I like at $100.00 rent. I do not pledge myself to keep it longer than to the close of the year, as they decline to open a room I want. I do pledge myself, however, not to deliver over the house to any one else but to give it up to them when I leave it. They profess to think hard of it that Mr. Hartwell did not deliver it back to them. This is the only condition they have made in reducing the rent about one third, & I thought it right to accede to the demand.

Don't think that we ladies are unduly troubled or discouraged. Far from it! This is only a temporary annoyance which time will settle. I don't know that they will venture to ask for the North St. chapel, but if they do I shall not hesitate to decline to let them use it. If they had gone out decently, I would have felt bound on application to open to them the North St. chapel, but I should have done it unwillingly because I should have been in a troublesome dilemma. With a Baptist church at my door, in my yard, how could I take the girls a mile to church twice a day? Wherever my girls go, there I go. I do not trust them out of my sight during public worship. Should I take them with me, then, to our church, or should I stay with them here? I knew it would be as gall & worm wood to these men to have a foreigner, most of all a foreign woman (they———————!) at their meetings every Sunday. Moreover I dreaded their influence on my girls. I would not have dared to risk it without being constantly present. As they have chosen to go off as a clique of schismatics, I shall not hesitate to decline to let them have the chapel if they ask it.

I promised Mary to state to you that she is ending the letters mentioned above with my full approbation & consent.

Yours sincerely,

L. Moon.

Tung Chow,
July 8, 1878
My dear Dr. Tupper,

Things look far more hopeful than when I last wrote you. We have taken energetic measures to stop the schism, & except one of the leaders who lives in the city, I know of but one church member in the city or vicinity who is even undecided. All the others stand by the "Tung Chow Baptist Church." We will not let the *Chan yuen* brethren be led off without strong efforts to show them the right way. As far as this city & vicinity is concerned, I think you may dismiss anxiety. The four leaders, whose motives are bad, will end by ceasing to be known as Christians. They will pocket the money they owe the church & that will end the matter with them.

I have let it be distinctly known that I will not allow either chapel or school room to be used as a place of meeting by those people, nor shall they have bench, book, lamp, in fact anything owned by the Board. If they had had sense enough to withdraw regularly as the former North St. church, of course I would have given up whatever was in my hands. But they say falsely that they never united, decline to vote a division, and go off in this disorderly manner. The mission declared its purpose to regard them as schismatics & not to countenance them in any way. I thought it best to tell them that the Board had placed all affairs in Tung Chow in the hands of the missionaries living in Tung Chow & that Mr. Hartwell had been requested not to communicate with them. I said this to one of the leaders. I reminded him that the letter to the Board about *Ku San* had never been answered. He at once jumped to the conclusion that the letters lately sent would get no answer. I told him the Board certainly would not write to them.

Mary fully understands the case now and declares herself a member of the "Tung Chow Baptist Church." Those men flattered her, and truly it was tempting to any Chinese girl to undertake to play the part of foreign pastor, to communicate with the Board, draw money etc. No wonder her head was turned at the idea. Mrs. Holmes and I told her very plainly her true status here, and the real facts of the case, and now she gives no trouble. She is getting well fast.

I think her an excellent Christian girl, very amiable and truly pious. How about the $130.00 she gets from S.C.? Our teachers get only 4000 or 5000 cash a month ($4.00 or $5.00), the very highest, 6000 cash. The native churches pay 5000 cash a month to their pastors. Missionaries in this region are much opposed to that sum being exceeded because they want the churches to become self-supporting. Fancy the dissatisfaction! Here is a girl whose Chinese education is exceedingly defective—any of those teachers could instruct her for years—and Mr. Hartwell sends her irresponsibly $130.* [*She says $130. Dr. Graves wrote me that $100 were sent for her & all spent on medicine.] We brought her here out of sheer pity to save her life, but her coming has wrought harm & given us no little embarrassment. Still we *could not* have done otherwise. It seemed that her life depended on her getting away from Canton.

My house matter is settled. I am to stay here as long as I please without any conditions, and the Board has all its old claims here, only at the reduced rate of $100 instead of $120. Mr. Crawford planned the affair of getting the rent reduced, but Mr. Mateer succeeded in putting it through. It took just six months to work it & no little trouble.

I have gone through an amount of annoyance & worry such as has not been good for my usefulness or happiness.

I think therefore that it is not wrong for me to ask the Board that the matter of residence be now considered definitely settled for me, no matter who shall be sent to Tung Chow in future. I have been three years unsettled & I want to feel that this arrangement is permanent. The money is now in Shanghai at four pr. cent for six months. For a year, the rate is 5 pr. cent. I have an offer from Mr. Mateer to take it at 8 pr. cent. If Mr. Crawford agrees, I will do so. At eight pr. cent, the interest would be about one hundred and thirty dollars. Please mention these facts to the Ladies of the Soc., with my love. My school is doing well.

Yrs. sc.,
L. Moon.

Tungchow, China
July 27, 1878
My dear Dr. Tupper,

The stamps and ear ring were duly rec'd. The stamps will be appropriated to the needy. I don't know what to do with the ear-ring. If there had been a pair, I suppose somebody might wear them, but one is rather embarrassing. I enclose a letter from Mrs. Yates on a subject of which I wrote you. You will see that her opinion co-incides with mine.

About the church troubles, the *Chan Yuen* brethren are "on the fence." It has been strongly represented to them that they were acting disloyally in giving up the North St. church. They say that if Mr. H. comes back, they will follow him. If not, & the Board sends another man to keep up the former North St. church, they will follow him. Otherwise, they will adhere to the action taken at the Feb. meeting. Dr. Yates writes us, "Your letter filled me with sorrow upon sorrow. There must be *some wicked men* among the disaffected. I rec'd a letter from the 'Holy Baptist Church' to which I shall make no reply. I enclose a letter in Chinese to the Tungchow Baptist church & a copy for the schismatics in order, if possible to impress the disaffected with the idea that they will get no sympathy here or in Richmond. You can look over the letter & do as you think best about delivering it." He further adds, "The leaders are schismatics & are now ecclesiastically in a position to be dealt with for the sin of schism by the Tungchow Baptist church whenever it is deemed prudent so to do."

I think the result will be the loss of the four leaders, & possibly a few others,—no serious moral loss. We want not Confucianists but Christians in the church.

I hope ere this you have the money for the Rome chapel. Allow me to congratulate you on your successful trip through the South. I trust the dawn of a better day is at hand.

We are in usual health, though the excessive heat is trying. With kindest regards,

Yrs. truly,
L. Moon.

Tungchow, China
Oct. 10, 1878
My dear Dr. Tupper:

The money you sent me, five dollars and fifty cents, from some lady for the "hungry Chinese" was disposed of as follows: I sent five dollars to Rev. Mr. Richard who has been distributing food to the famine sufferers the past two years. The remaining fifty cents I gave to famine refugees here. We consider the famine about over now, though there is much destitution & suffering still in parts of the country, & a number of missionaries are still engaged in the work of distribution. In our section, crops have been fine, the price of food has gone down, and the value of silver has risen somewhat. Still, one can't help looking a little longingly back to the days when a tael brought seventeen hundred & forty cash while now it brings only about fourteen hundred and forty.

I wrote you some time ago that my house matter had been satisfactorily settled. The rent is now reduced to one hundred dollars. The money is in the Shanghai bank. The yearly rate is five pr. cent. At private investment twelve pr. cent could be had, but the bank seemed safest. I hope the house question is now definitely settled, for a state of doubt as to one's "local habitation" is conducive neither to usefulness nor happiness.

I have a special request to make of the Board. It is that they pass a vote of thanks to Rev. C. W. Mateer. Since Mr. Crawford has been away, Mr. Mateer has preached for us twice every month, & will continue to do so until he himself leaves for America, probably during the winter. One would have to be in China to understand the very great advantage it is in keeping a church together to have preaching, if only twice a month, by a foreigner.

Then, too, no Chinaman can attract & hold a heathen audience as a foreigner can. We feel under very great obligations indeed to Mr. Mateer for his great kindness, & we would be very glad if the Board would give some official expression of thanks.

The mission are in usual health. The schools are prospering. The church remains *in status quo*. With no one to administer the communion, or the ordinance of baptism, it would require large faith to expect a great revival. It is odd that the million (is it a million?) Baptists of the South can only furnish three men for China! Odd that with five hundred Baptist preachers in the state of Virginia we must rely on a Presbyterian minister to fill a Baptist pulpit. I wonder how these things look in Heaven: they certainly look very queer in China. But then we Baptists are a great people as we never tire of saying at our associations and Conventions, & possibly our way of doing things is the best!

With kindest regards,
Yrs. sincerely,
L. Moon.

Tungchow, China,
Nov. 11, 1878
My dear Dr. Tupper:
I returned two days ago from a country tour with Mrs. Holmes & while it is fresh in mind I will give you some of the particulars.

The morning of our intended departure dawned cold, windy & disagreeable. It seemed to me the part of wisdom to stay in-doors. To my pencilled query "to go or not to go," came back the emphatic monosyllable, "Go." There was nothing to be done but to get into one's chair and depart. About twenty *li* from the city are a row of villages known as the "An hing" villages; we meant to take these on our way & spend the night at the thirty *li* station. However, we gave general directions to our chair-bearers to take us to as many villages as possible. They following our commands literally, the afternoon found us still within twelve li of the city. Upon consultation we decided that as the weather was still cold & cloudy we had better, after taking two more villages, return to the city. At the last village the children crowded eagerly close about my chair & answered promptly from the catechism what had been taught them more than two years before. We had been all along pleased with the spirit with which we had been received but here we were delighted.

Our chair-bearers, who had set out for a good job & did not feel disposed to lose it, were disconcerted at the idea of returning to the city that day. They respectfully assured us that there was no fear of bad weather next day, but what was to be done? There was no inn nearer than the destination for which we had set out in the morning & it was now too late to go there. Seeing our willingness to stay, two of the chair-bearers set off to seek quarters in the village & in a little time returned with the agreeable intelligence that a gentleman had consented to open his house to receive us. We have sometimes found difficulty in making good our right to stay at inns, but to be received into a private family in a village where all are heathen was a most unexpected piece of good fortune. We took immediate possession of our room & it was at once filled with an eager, excited crowd of boys, girls & women. Mrs. H. & I undertook to teach them but the space was too small & the confusion too great for any success to attend our efforts. Pretty soon she withdrew to the yard carrying off the boys with her & I could hear her putting them through on the catechism in her usual vigorous style. I wish I could convey to you some of the delight I had in teaching those who stayed in the room. In especial there were three young girls whom I taught with a keen pleasure. They begged earnestly for books, a rare request from girls, for they usually think themselves too stupid to learn.

Our host, while never obtrusive, was very kind & polite. He asked for a New Testament & I was sorry to have none with me. I, however, gave him a copy of St. Mark's Gospel.

Next morning we had visitors till the time of departure. We had now changed our plans & concluded to leave the "An hing" villages for the last day of our tour, & had decided, on this the second day, to take a line of villages known as *Wan esz k'o*. We knew that whenever we took them it would be a hard day's work, for they are many, some of them are large, & the people are inclined to be disorderly. We meant after taking them all, to push on to the thirty *li* station that night. They were out of our direct course, but we hoped, by losing no time, to carry out the plan. The sun was nearing its setting when we found ourselves at the eleventh village for that day with many, many *li* between us & our intended sleeping place. I had said to Mrs. H. very decidedly at the tenth village that, I should do no more missionary work that day, but no sooner had our chairs been set down than the people came crowding about us & it was impossible to keep silence. We have "the words of eternal life" & we *must* speak them to this people spite of all weariness. While we were talking our chair-bearers had not been idle. They had no fancy for the long pull before them & they bestirred themselves to find quarters. Receiving a premature report of non-success, we started off, but had scarcely left the village before we were recalled by the joyful intelligence that a place for the night had been secured. We were prepared to put up with anything, & we expressed our pleasure to "mine host" when he had conducted us to our quarters. Fancy a low pitched room, nine feet by nine, with smoke-blackened walls & rafters, a dirt floor, a mud bed covered with matting, a dust covered table & one bench. There was a small paper window which could not be opened, & a door way with no door. This doorway opened into a room which our chair-bearers used as an eating room, & this led in turn into their sleeping apartment. We were scarcely seated on the mud bed according to Chinese style, before the room was filled with a crowd & as usual, we found it best to divide our forces, Mrs. H. teaching in the yard & I in the house.

Of course the crowd watched us eat supper with the usual eager interest. Sometime after supper we were invited to visit a family living in the same enclosure. We willingly accepted the invitation, but scarcely were we seated before the room instantly filled almost to its capacity. The Chinese know nothing of ventilation. Their windows are never opened in winter. We found the room stifling, between the heat, the crowd & the tobacco smoke. I was so weary I could scarcely sit up, but Mrs. H. chatted as if she were fresh. I was a little amused at a question they often put to us, "In your country, do the women rule?" Mrs. H. explained that, as in our country the women are educated, the men respect their opinion & consult with them, but that if, after consultation there is irreconcilable difference of opinion, the right of final decision lies with the man. "Ah!" said the questioner, "just as it is here; they consult together & the man decides." Our wearisome visit came at last to an end, but our new friends escorted us back to our room & made a short visit. Right glad were we to hang a shawl before the door & prepare for slumber. One might think that to people brought up in a civilized land slumber on a mud bed would be out of the question. Such, however, was not our experience; we rather congratulated ourselves next morning on the pleasant night's rest we had enjoyed. No sooner was our elegant apartment thrown open than we had a swarm of visitors. As we sat on the "kong" eating breakfast, Mrs. H. counted over thirty spectators in the room, two in the door way, & behind these there were I don't know how many trying to peer in. Four boys stood on the table for a better view. On the outside, some enterprising youths were tearing holes in the paper window that they too might have a glimpse of the wonderful scene. Did you ever, my dear Dr. Tupper, feel the torture of human eyes bent upon you, scanning every feature, every look, every gesture? I felt it keenly for a moment & then went on chatting with an old lady. "Do you know what I have been doing?" I asked her. "I have been counting the number of persons in this room." For a moment she looked disconcerted, then she said apologetically, "We have never seen any Heavenly people before" (!) After such a magnificent compliment, what could one do but redouble one's effort to be gracious?

It was at this place that one of Mrs. H.'s chair-bearers received a serious hurt. Striking his head against a hallow that hung from the wall or low-pitched roof, he skull was at first reported broken, but, having gotten it bound up, with a Chinaman's usual nonchalance he declared himself ready to travel. On this day villages were not so thick & the work was consequently less. We turned aside to see a national curiosity of which the people told us, a lofty cliff close beside the sea, from which for a space of about fifty yards, there trickled countless streams of clear, pure fresh water, delightful to the taste. At the base were spots of beautiful green moss. They say there is an underground outlet into the sea. We felt amply repaid for going out of our way. There were boats drawn up on the beach, & the rough looking fishermen crowded around Mrs. H. begging for eye medicine.

About sunset we found ourselves at *San she pu*, the thirty *li* station. Here at the inn they are old acquaintances & treat us with kindness & cordiality. We have free access to the family quarters & go in and out at our pleasure. Spending the night here, we started as early as we could get off, and near sunset reached the eleventh village. Across a narrow stream there was another village & a little farther on still another. When we had finished at the eleventh village Mrs. H. said, "What now?" I had been gathering all my courage to say "No more work to-day," so I answered resolutely, "I am going right on to *San she pu*." "I am going to the village across the creek," said Mrs. H., but added in excuse of my desertion, "the sun will be down when you get to *San she pu*." We parted company then & I proceeded to the inn. Going to the family quarters on my arrival, the landlady invited me to sit on her "kong," and get warm. I was immediately surrounded by two or three boys & two young women eager to be taught. I questioned them from the catechism until summoned to supper. That meal being over, I resumed the lesson. Pretty soon they were called off to their own supper. "Don't go to sleep," was their parting injunction; "we are coming back to learn again," which they did afterwards with a good will. While they were gone, I taught a man & boy, while another man looked on. By time they were all gone for the night, I was too weary even to speak without an effort.

Next morning we woke up to find a high wind blowing & some snow on the ground, while it still snowed at intervals. The question was, since it was Saturday, whether to spend two days in a Chinese inn, or to travel ten miles in an open chair in a N.W. wind with snow. To one who knows the manifold discomforts of a Chinese inn, it would be no wonder that we decided in favor of the latter alternative. Contrary to expectation, however, after we started the wind abated, the snow ceased, & we made the journey in comparative comfort. It was good, though the wind blew sharply as we ascended the plateau overlooking the city, to catch a view of the grim old walls with their massive gate-way. We knew that within them we should find warmth & comfort. Pleasant too was the welcome home from teacher & pupils. Pleasant also the coming in after dinner of my opposite neighbor with her two little girls to welcome me back. The latter recited from the catechism & sung a stanza or two they have learned from the hymn book.

Possibly you may have noticed throughout this letter that I have made frequent illusions to physical discomforts & to weariness of mind & body. I have always been ashamed in writing of missionary work to dwell upon physical hardships, & then too we get so accustomed to take them as a matter of course that it does not occur to us to speak of them save in a general way. In this letter I have purposely departed from my usual reticence upon such matters because I know that there are some who, in their pleasant homes in America, without any real knowledge of the facts, declare that the days of missionary hardships are over. To speak in the open air, in a foreign tongue, from six to eleven times a day, is no trifle. The fatigue of travel is something. The inns are simply the acme of discomfort. If anyone fancies that sleeping on brick beds, in rooms with dirt floor, with walls blackened by the smoke of generations,—the yard to these quarters being also the stable yard, & the stable itself being in three feet of the door of your apartment,—if anyone thinks all this agreeable, then I wish to declare most emphatically that as a matter of taste I differ. If anyone thinks he would like this constant contact with what an English writer has called the "Great Unwashed," I must still say that from experience I find it unpleasant. If anyone thinks that constant exposure to the risk of small-pox & other contagious diseases against which the Chinese take no precautions whatever, is just the most charming thing in life, I must still beg leave to say that I shall continue to differ in opinion. In a word, let him come out & try it. A few days roughing it as we ladies do habitually will convince the most skeptical. There is a passage from Farrar's "Life of Christ," which recurred forcibly to my mind during this recent country tour. "From early dawn ... to late evening in whatever house He had selected for His nightly rest, the multitude came crowding about him, not respecting his privacy, not allowing for his weariness, eager to see Him ... There was no time even to eat bread. Such a life is not only to the last degree trying & fatiguing, but to a refined & high-strung nature ... This incessant publicity, this apparently illimitable toil becomes simply maddening unless the spirit be sustained by boundless sympathy & love. But the heart of the Savior *was* so sustained." He was the Son of God but we missionaries, we are only trying in a very poor way to walk in His footsteps & this "boundless sympathy & love" is of the divine & not the human.

A few words more & I have done. We are astonished at the wide door opened us for work. We have such access to the people, to their hearts & homes as we could not have dared to hope two years ago. Instead of regarding us with the former hatred & cold distrust, they receive us with cordiality & kindness. We feel that we should press this country work to the limit of our ability. But how inadequate our force! Here is a province of thirty million souls & Southern Baptists can only send one man & three women to tell them the story of redeeming love. Oh! that my words could be as a trumpet call stirring the hearts of my brethren & sisters to pray, to labor, to give themselves to this people. "But," some will say, "we must have results, else interest flags." I have seen the husbandman go forth in the autumn to plow the fields; later, I have seen him scatter the seed broadcast; anon, the tiny green shoots came up scarcely visible at first; then the snows of winter fell concealing them for weeks; spring brought its fructifying rains, its genial sunshine, & lo! in June the golden harvest. We are now, a very, very few feeble workers, scattering the grain broadcast according as time & strength permit. God will give the harvest; doubt it not. But the laborers are so few. Where we have four, we should have not less than one hundred. Are these wild words? They would not seem so were the church of God awake to her high privileges & her weighty responsibilities.

Yours sincerely,

L. Moon.

Tungchow, China,
Nov. 11, 1878
My dear Dr. Tupper,

Mr. Crawford wrote & advised that a resolution should be introduced allowing the members of the former North St. church to withdraw & reconstitute themselves into a church. We had done our very best to prevent the bad men from leading others astray, but failed of success, save very partial. We therefore yielded gracefully to the force of circumstances, & had the resolution introduced & passed. Pastor Woo was here two Sundays ago & I placed the chapel on this lot at his disposal. He preached there and I attended with my girls. Pastor W. says he is still a member of Tungchow Baptist church (!). In short, since we let them go freely, they say they are still in!!! They wanted a distinct pledge from us missionaries & from native members of the former Monument St. Church with regard to certain moneys now in the hands of members of the former North St. church. As a mission we said kindly but firmly, "The only question now is for you brethren to decide where you stand. If you are in the Tungchow Baptist church, all questions must come up regularly at church meeting & be decided by vote of the whole church. We think the best thing for you to do is to reorganize the North St. church. I pledged them personally all the help I could give if they decide on this last.

The union with the Chefoo church has also developed into a muddle. Mr. Richard & Mr. Jones with their open communion notions & with the usual English loose idea of order, without waiting for any action from our church, of which they are still members, & without previously informing us, advised them to join the Presbyterians. The Chinese objected, not from principle but because they want to hold on to some property that would go to any organization they join, so our English brethren resumed control of them, notifying us by last mail that they had done so. We are absolutely certain that they meant no discourtesy, & we know that they were greatly hurried, & are overwhelmed with work in the remote interior to which they have now gone. Still their action has been very disorderly. How are we ever to teach the Chinese the first principles of church government if missionaries depart so from all established rules? We think the best thing under the circumstances is to pass a resolution with preamble about as follows:

Whereas, at the union of the three churches in Feb. Pastor Crawford gave a pledge that in case of Mr. Richard's return to Chefoo should his members so desire they should be returned to his pastoral supervision, & whereas Mr. R. has returned & has resumed control of them, be it

Resolved, That the former members of the Chefoo church be & are hereby dismissed for the purpose of reconstituting the former church.

Thus we wash our hands of the whole disagreeable business. Mr. Jones wrote Mrs. Crawford of all the arrangements they had made saying they were constituted on a permanent basis—"subject always to the better plan of a union with Tungchow whenever desired." (!!) With regard to this last, our mission will say emphatically, "No more church unions, if you please. They bring nothing but jealousies, heart burnings, discontents. If your members wish to come to us, they must come one by one, each to be voted on according to his merits." Some came in under the union whom we would reject emphatically on individual merit. So the affair stands. But *our* course is clear. We keep the name "Tungchow Baptist Church": we shall work faithfully to build it up. The best elements of the North St. church will be absorbed into the future into our church: the worst will cease to claim to be Christians. They will not hold together as a church & they know it. The money is all the leaders care about. The humble, good Christians among them will, I believe, eventually come to us one by one.

We are all in usual health. With kindest regards & Christian affection, I am

Yrs. sincerely,

L. Moon.

Tungchow, China
Nov. 14, 1878
My dear Dr. Tupper,

In the account rendered of my travelling expenses, I stated that there remained in my hands one hundred & forty two dollars, nineteen cents ($142.19). I said that I would pay house rent for the current year out of that sum. I have now paid a year's rent, & send you the statement. The first payment I made was in Feb. last, & was for the quarter beginning in November, two months before I re-occupied the house. The year for which I have paid rent then ends to-day.

Statement

Left over from travelling expenses	$142.19
Interest on house money 5 months at 4 pr. ct.	_30.96_
	$173.15
Sums expended as	
pr. next page	_105.00_
Balance now in my hands	$ 68.15
Paid out in effort to purchase a house	
To writer of deed	$ 1.00
" middle man	2.00
" " " for getting rent reduced	_2.00_
on North St. house	
	$ 5.00
Rent on North St. House 1 year	_100.00_
	$105.00

The house money as I wrote you before is in the Shanghai Bank. It is put in for one year at 5 pr. cent interest. The interest is payable next October, but I have still the sixty eight dollars fifteen cents mentioned in the preceding page to meet the rent as it falls due next year.

    With kindest regards,
    Yours truly,
    L. Moon.

Tungchow, China
Dec. 9, 1878
My dear Dr. Tupper,

    I see from the Oct. number of the *Journal* that a lady will probably be sent to Canton to join Miss Whilden. I am induced by this circumstance to say something that has been on my mind sometime. I happened to cross the ocean in company with two friends, one sent out by the Woman's Union Missy. Soc. & one by the American Episcopal Board. One day at table the officer who was presiding said to the former of these ladies, "For how long do you go out?" She answered, "Five years." Turning to the other he asked, "And you?" She said, "Seven." Then he said to me, "And you?" "For life," I answered. "And what dreadful thing have you done at home," asked this man of the world in his jesting way, "that they should banish you for life?"

Now this conversation set me to thinking. The present plan on which our missionaries are sent out is that they are to stay for life, or until health breaks down. It is as if you said to a soldier whom you were sending to the front to do battle with the enemy, "Mind! no furloughs. We expect you to fall on the field." Yet, during the war, I never heard of a soldier who did not long for his furlough that he might look once more upon the dear home faces before he passed forever into the "eternal dark." Now for the practical application of what may seem rumbling talk. It seems to me that when you send out a new missionary it would be the right & kindly thing to say: "Go out & work to the best of your ability, & at the end of ten years come back to your native land for rest & recreation. Be assured of a cordial welcome back." My word for it the new missionary will work all the better if you give some such hope to stimulate in hours of weariness or depression.

We are in usual health. The country work being over for this year, we are devoting ourselves with renewed energy to the schools.

With kindest regards, I remain

Sincerely yours,

L. Moon.

Tungchow, China,

March 8, 1879

Reverend Dr. H. A. Tupper: —

My dear Brother,

Your letter Dec. 3rd came duly to hand as also the brief note of Jan. 8th accompanying the letter of Rev. Mr. Bennett & your reply to him.

I heartily acquiesce in the proposed investment of the house fund: it seems to me the wisest & is especially acceptable as relieving me of personal responsibility. The money is in the Shanghai Bank at the present at five pr. cent. It was deposited in Oct. for one year. Before next Oct. please direct me how to make the proper transfer of the funds to America.

One of the North St. brethren who was most disagreeable last summer has made friends. He first called on Mrs. Crawford & took her a pupil. Then he made me two calls & promised to put two sisters in school if it can be managed. (His father's family are all heathen). Last night he came to me to study the first chap. in Revelations, having previously requested me to help him. He is to come again next Tuesday night & I suppose on again one night every week until we go through the book. I am rather amused at the sudden intimacy that has thus sprung up. I said some extremely severe things to the young man last summer & offended him deeply. He did not come near me for months. *He deserved every word I said.* When Mr. Jones of the English Bapt. Mission was here he talked very seriously to this brother on the condition of his own heart. Mr. J. had heard only the young man's own account & drew his conclusions from that. Then came the Board's letter exhorting to harmony & love. So, as I have said, the young man has made friends. He wants Mrs. Crawford & myself to go out to his village in the spring & says he will go with us. He represents people out there as anxious to hear, villages are thick, & no foreigners have ever been to that neighborhood. Another of the North St. brother called this morning & asked if I wanted another pupil. He has a young relative he hopes to put into my school. I am confident the Board's letter has done good. I trust all will come right in time & those who throw away their religion will only show that they "went out from us because they were not of us."

I trust you will have a good meeting at the Convention. Our schools are doing well, church members manifest zeal & activity, & there are a number of inquirers. We have reason to "thank God & take courage."

Yrs. in the bonds of the gospel,

L. Moon.

Tungchow, China,
May 10, 1879
My dear Dr. Tupper,

Your letter of Jan. 15th addressed to the mission was rec'd some time since. It is pleasant to have the Sec. say "Well done" when he is fully informed of the circumstances that have rendered our position peculiarly trying and responsible.

The late cool spring weather has been unusually favorable for country work and we have been prosecuting it to the extent of our ability. In a former letter I gave you the dark side of this pioneer work, its trials and hardships: in this letter I should like to reverse the picture and show you the sunny side. Leaving behind you the city pent in its gray massive walls, with its thousands living in squalor and abject wretchedness, come abroad with me into the open country. Over there to your left is the blue sea, its waters flashing gloriously in the morning sunlight. Stretching in front of you & on all sides, far as the eye can reach, see boundless fields of grain rippling like waves of the sea in the soft spring breeze. As you go farther on, the scenery changes. Instead of this one broad plateau, there lie countless thousands of tablelands, giving endless variety to the scene. Perhaps you will think at first that the absence of trees is a grave defect in the landscape, but in time you will come to feel that the boundlessness of the prospect is in itself an added charm. No fences, no hedges, nothing to vex the eyes with a sense of limitation. Unconsciously your mind takes on a glad realization of freedom. "The heavy and the weary weight of all this unintelligible world" drops away, and you breath "an ample ether, a diviner air." There are scenes of beauty that stamp themselves ineffaceably upon the memory. A village nestles cosily in a green valley at the base of gradually ascending hills and tablelands; beyond it the sea with its every varying charms. As you ascend the view broadens. Farther and farther stretches out the sea as you turn backward to cast many a lingering gaze; before you, as you advance, an ever widening expanse of hill & dale and cultivated tableland. The pure air, the brilliant sunshine, the beauties of sea and shore and sky, these all combine to produce a feeling of exaltation in the soul. Nature wears a radiant smile for one who is accustomed to look upon her face with a loving eye.

So much for the effect of mere external objects. Recall for a moment the thoughts that crowd upon the mind. This ancient continent of Asia whose soil you are treading was the chosen theatre for the advent of the Son of God. In a rush of grateful emotion there came to your mind the lines of that grand old hymn the "Dies Irae," "Seeking me Thy worn feet hasted, On the cross Thy soul death tasted," and your heart is all aglow with longing to bear to others the priceless gift that you have received, that thus you may manifest your thankfulness & love to the giver. He "went about doing good"; in a humble manner you are trying to walk in his footsteps. As you wend your way from village to village, you feel it is no idle fancy that the Master walks beside you and you hear his voice saying gently, "Lo! I am with you always even unto the end." And the soul makes answer in the words of St. Bernard, that holy man of God, "Lord Jesus, thou art home and friends and father-land to me." Is it any wonder that as you draw near to the villages a feeling of exultation comes over you? That your heart goes up to God in glad thanksgiving that he has so trusted you as to commit to your hands this glorious gospel that you may convey its blessings to those who still sit in darkness? When the heart is full of such joy, it is no effort to speak to the people: you could not keep silent if you would. Mere physical hardships sink into merited insignificance. What does one care for comfortless inns, hard beds, hard fare, when all around is a world of joy and glory and beauty?

I returned yesterday from a short tour of four days made partly in company with Mrs. Holmes and partly alone. On the first day, being overtaken by rain, we had to hurry on to the inn, and therefore only visited four villages. The next day was one of cloudless sunshine, the villages were close together, and long ere night fall we had visited twelve. We were joined by an excellent native brother towards the close of this second day and he gave us effective assistance. The landlord of the inn where we were staying is a young teacher. He made no objection to the proposal to hold a night service in his school room for the benefit of the villagers and himself attended as did also his mother. As we came stumbling back in the darkness to our quarters at the inn, Mrs. H. said enthusiastically, "I like this sort of thing; it seems romantic." For myself, I was too prosaically tired to see any romance.

Rain fell in the night, but the next day was all that could be wished. Keeping together we visited nine villages, then parted, Mrs. H. and the deacon going eastward to keep an appointment with Mrs. Crawford who had that day left the city, and I returning to the inn. On the way back, I halted at two villages and had an enjoyable time talking to the women. That the men chose to listen too was no fault of mine! Arriving at the inn, I had scarcely got established on the "kong" before a party of men came in to make me a call. They had heard us at the first village we had visited in the morning. Being a large village, the native brother had made two long addresses on different streets. My visitors were extremely respectful in their manner and evidently anxious to hear more. I handed one of them a catechism which he read aloud with a running commentary of his own; naturally there were many connections to make in the course of his remarks, for the wisest of these heathen is "lower than a Christian child" in all that pertains to spiritual things. "The more I hear, the more I want to hear," he remarked to one of the others who assented warmly. Seeing he wished the book very much, I presented it to him & he took his leave with thanks. As the others still lingered, I opened a hymnbook & took for my text "Jesus Loves Me." They listened with such evident desire to hear more of Jesus that I felt sorry when the announcement of supper compelled them to retire. After supper the family all gathered in my apartment, a number of men & boys came in, and I was busy teaching the latter until about nine o'ck. When the male part of the visitors had gone, the young women of the family who has previously kept modestly in the background now came forward to be taught a hymn. Another half hour of hard work & they withdrew. Next day I returned home taking ten villages on the way.

I trust the Board will heed our modest request for two more missionaries. I say "modest" because we *ought* to have a dozen right away. If the statement which I observed in a recent religious newspaper, that "women do not make good pioneers" be true, then there is all the more need that you obviate the necessity of their engaging in such work. While it might not be in good taste to take issue on the opinion quoted above, it may be permitted to refer with just pride to the work done by Miss Rankin in Mexico. Entering alone and single-handed that priest-ridden land, she founded six churches before ill health compelled her to retire from her labors. Any better or more successful "pioneer" work than that would be hard to find.

I should be glad to call the attention of ladies who feel an interest in mission work, to the organ of the woman-workers of China. It is called "Woman's Work," is printed twice a year at Shanghai, and the cost including postage, is sixty-two cents pr. annum. Mrs. Yates is president of the Soc. under whose patronage the work is issued. The money should be sent to Mrs. J. W. Lambuth, Shanghai.

I trust you are having a pleasant and profitable meeting of the S. B. Convention and that the three interests in which as Baptists we are most concerned, the Seminary endowment, & the Home & Foreign mission work will receive an impetus which shall tell upon their future prosperity.

Yours sincerely,

L. Moon.

Tungchow,

Sept. 8, 1879

My dear Dr. Tupper,

Your kind letter of June 30th reached me in due season. I am glad you dissent from the view of Woman's work with which I took issue. I think it had error in it, with possibly a grain of truth, yet was so worded as to convey an erroneous impression against which I felt called to protest.

We hav begun country work again, Mrs. H. & I going out two successive days last week & visiting fourteen villages. We were delighted at the eagerness of the women to hear. Words flow naturally when one finds interested listeners. We hear from Dr. Graves the good news that he has already baptized seventy this year.

I am glad that prospects at home are so hopeful. The work out here never wore a more promising aspect.

Mary Hartwell is here preparing to be married. She is engaged to Mrs. Crawford's teacher, an excellent young man. She seems amiable, industrious, & economical, &, since the young folks made the match themselves contrary to Chinese custom, it is to be hoped they will demonstrate the superiority of the western ideas on that subject.

We are looking forward to Mr. Eager's coming with pleasure, & are no less pleased to kno that he expects to bring a fair lady with him.

We are in usual health except Mrs. Crawford who has not been well for some time.

Hav you eny rules for speling in the *For. Journal*? I asked bekaus I hav adopted the fonetic style of speling, but I shal not dare to spel that way if your compositor snubs me by putting my letters in type in the old way. Plese let me kno.

With kindest regards,
Yours sincerely,
L. Moon.
Published in the December 1879 *Foreign Mission Journal.*

Tungchow,
Sept. 21, 1879
Mi dir Dr. Tupper,

I encloz Dr. Crawford's receipt for the hous muney. Yu wil notice that he distinguishes between interest & principal. Part of the former, I hav already advanced in payment of hous-rent & more wil be needed before the close of the year. When I last rendered yu mi akkount of hous muney I had in mi hands

$$\$68.15 = 68150 \text{ cash}$$

I have paid out this year in hous-rent cash 75000, the mission being now my debtor to the amt 6850 cash, for hous-rent advanced. Twenty-five thousand more wil bi du in Dec. for which I wil kal on Dr. Crawford as wel as for the abuv 6850 cash. This wil leve, I think, about sixty dollars on hand to meet next year's rent. But of kours as it is all in Dr. Crawford's hands, I wil not need hereafter to send yu eny akount.

Wi ar all in usual helth & antisipating kuntry work with plezur as sun as musketos abate. With kindest regards,
Yurz sincerely,
L. Moon.
N.B. Don't yu admir the nü speling?
L. M.

Tungchow, China,
March 22, 1880
Rev. Dr. H. A. Tupper:—
My dear Brother,

Your kind letter of Jan. 26th reacht me last week.

I think the disposition you propose of the house-money is eminently wise & good. It meets my most hearty concurrence. I will write the ladies on the subject enclosing to you. If on perusal you approve, please communicate to them, otherwise suppress & write me what you would like said & I will copy.

What you say of our mutual friend is very pleasing to me. You are right in supposing that I "think very highly of him." (This is *not* to go into the *Journal!*) Thank you for the nice kind things you say to me personally. Would I merited them!

I have not time to-day to write you a long letter. Mrs. H. & I were out some days last week & met a most kindly reception. We had planned to start on another short tour tomorrow, but it is not certain the weather will permit.

We are looking eagerly for reinforcements, I especially as I am bored to death living alone. I don't find my own society either agreeable or edifying. I asked Mrs. Yates to stir you—i.e. the Board—up to send Mr. & Mrs. E. out as soon as possible. I really think a few more winters like the one just past would put an end to me. This is no joke, but dead earnest. *Verbum eat.* So send on our good brother & sister.

Dr. Crawford has not been well of late; the rest of us are in tolerably good health.

With kindest regards,
Sincerely yours,
L. Moon.
N. B.
This is not meant for the public.
L.M.

Tungchow, China,
May 22, 1880
Rev. Dr. H. A. Tupper: —
My dear Brother,

Your letter of March 30th containing enclosures from Charlottesville reached me on yesterday & I need not say gave me sincere pleasure. I am conscious that I have not written for the *Journal* as much as is proper or as I would wish to have done, but I have been exceedingly busy with country work & in the intervals between tours home work of various sorts would demand attention. I have also had many letters of inquiry to answer and as you know this takes up a great deal of time. Each girl in school is supported in whole or in part by some Socy. & this fact entails a good deal of writing to these various societies & besides there are many other letters of inquiry. I have hoped that these private letters might be accepted instead of something longer & more elaborate for the *Journal*. One more fact & my apology is ended: I once had strength enough to work all day in the villages & at night sit down on a "kong" & write off the day's experiences. But, somehow, mission life takes the strength & energy out of us before we know it, & we have to learn to be watchful & not overwork lest the time come too soon when we can work no more.

I fear that my letter in answer to yours about the final disposition of the house—money did not reach you in time for the finishing up the matter before the meeting of the Convention. I stated my cordial acquiescence in your proposed disposition of the money & also enclosed letters to the ladies of the Societies in Atlanta & Richmond about the matter.

Our mission are all in usual health. We are looking forward with very pleasant anticipations to the promised reinforcement. You must not fail to meet our expectations. Our need of new missionaries was never more urgent than at this time.

With kindest regards,
Yours truly,
L. Moon.
Published in the August 1880 *Foreign Mission Journal.*

Tungchow, China,
June 14, 1880
Rev. Dr. H. A. Tupper:—
My dear Brother,

I venture to write to you upon a matter which you may perhaps think is outside of my province, but if so I beg you to charitably overlook any mistake I may be making.

I happen to know through a mutual friend (Dr. Toy in fact) that Mr. Eager remained in America this year because he wished to discharg a debt contracted in his education. I am of the impression that for the last six years, at any rate, the last four years, he has been supporting himself & at the same time prosecuting his studies with a view to the missionary work. He has had to live in the most economical way & hence his opportunities for laying by anything in advance have not been great. Now a young man about to be married & about to leave America for many years, naturally needs money for various expenses that wil readili occur to your mind. I have heard from the older missionaries that our Board formerly allowed a married man a certain sum—three hundred dollars—for an outfit, this over & above his traveling expenses & his salary. It is supposed that this rule fell into desuetude in the hard times that followed the war, or the Board may have formally abolished it. I know that the Southern Pres. Board & the Woman's Board & the Congregational Board all allow for outfit & some for furniture. It seems to me that this last is unnecessary as any missy. by economy can gradually furnish a house out of his salary. I think our Board has been perfectly right if it has abolisht the rule allowing an outfit because the times were too hard for them to afford it, & I am sure that no missy. wisht it. But now, it seems to me, as times are so much better, it might be worth while to ask if the Board can not afford to return to the old rule. It seems to me that Mr. Eager's case is one that justifies such return, if any should. For instance, workers at home need books if they are not to fall hopelessly behind the times. How much more does a man coming out here need books to keep his mind awake & active when there is so much to depress him in all his surroundings. For a man to attempt to keep his mind strong & growing without books is like a workman's using his fingers instead of tools.

Please forgive me if I hav meddled in what does not concern me & set it down to a wish to do right, even if the wish has been ill-directed.

We are in tolerable health. Dr. Crawford is feeble. It is useless to say he should have help as soon as possible. We are looking forward with very pleasant anticipations to Mr. E's coming. To escape typhoons on the one hand, & on the other not to lose the coast steamers which stop running in cold weather, they shd. leave San Fran. by Oct. 1st. Earlier or later wd. be undesirable.

Yrs. truly,
L. Moon.

Tungchow,
Aug. 16, 1880
My dear Dr. Tupper,

I am afraid you will think I am veri fond of making suggestions, but I am going to venture once more & then quit—until next time. It occurs to me that Mrs. Holmes would be a good deal better for a change. She has been out in China now nearly eleven years, which is a longer time than most missionaries stay. As you know, at least one Board requires its missionaries to go home once in seven years. Nearly all permit the privilege once in ten years. When Mrs. H. came out, the understanding with Dr. Taylor was that it was for eight years. She has now stayed three beyond the time agreed upon. I don't know certainly that she would go home if invited, but I wish very much that the Board would give her an invitation. If Mr. & Mrs. Eager get out here this fall, they would be able in the course of six or eight months to take charge of Mrs. Holmes' school after a fashion, giving it at least a general superintendence, & thus they could work gradualli into it.

Allow me to congratulate you on the appearance of yor book & its favorable reception by the critics. I should send for it, but for the fact that you hav promist to send it. My friend Miss Safford, whom doutles yu remember, is spending several weeks with me & I am greatly enjoying her visit.

I am looking forward with great pleasure to the coming of Mr. & Mrs. Eager. I hear golden opinions of him from those who ought to know, & *he* writes in veri laudatori strain of the young lady. May I ask to be kindli remembered to your family? I retain the most delightful recollections of my visit to yr. hous.

Yours sincerely,
L. Moon.

Tungchow,
Sept. 11, 1880
Rev. Dr. H. A. Tupper:—
My dear Brother,

Yr. letter, ment to break the news of Mr. Eager's not kuming, reacht me yesterda. We had previousli heard thru Dr. Yates of the chang of purpose. My judgment goes fulli with the Board in the decision. A Bishop for Italy (for he wil be that in fact tho not in name) iz a matter of much more consequence than a man for Tungchow. At least so I think, looking at the question wideli & not az connected with mere local interests & wishes. I think I can heartily congratulate yu on the decision. In saying this, I speak only for myself. The rest of the mission think differentli & so does Dr. Yates who haz written yu on the subject. Of course the ladi had a right to her preferences & I think they should hav been considered. I am heartily glad that inclination & duty now go together in her case.

I hope yu wil send us a man & wife soon. I hav been thinking of asking you to send a lady to be associated with me. I think I kno just the lady, but I don't kno that she wd. come. I hav never written or spoken with her on the subject. Could the Board send a lady if the right one could be found? If I were askt what kind of woman, I shd. say, "Not young, of sincere piety & with a genuine love for children." I should not advise any young lady to try life out here; it is too hard & trying.

Yu say sum veri nice things about "our mutual frend" in which I agree, but I fancy he wd. be both amused and amazed at the amount of "humility" yu ascribe to him. I trust he haz a bright future before him at Harvard.

My frend Miss Safford haz left me for her home in Suchow. Mrs. Crawford & Minnie ar in Chefoo for a little holiday.

The kuntri iz ful of wild rumors, but negotiations with Russia ar resumed.

My school iz prospering in numbers being larger than ever before. This iz "unofficial," please.

With kindest regards & X^n affection,
Yrs. truly,
L. Moon.

Monday, Sept. 13
P.S.
I add a line or two that the promise of another man quite reconciles the mission to the loss of Mr. Eager. I had a little chat with Dr. Crawford

yesterday & he says he fully approves the action of the Board. We had heard thru Dr. Yates that Mr. E. was to go to Italy & had not heard that anyone was to be sent here in his place & naturally some of the mission felt a good deal troubled & I think somewhat hurt. But the new man will make it all right.

L. M.

Tungchow, China
Nov. 22, 1880
Rev. Dr. H. A. Tupper:
My dear Brother,

Your postal reacht me sometime after the book. On the reception of the latter, I wrote thanking you for it & expressing the pleasure I shd. take in reading it.

I shall be very glad to comply with the wish expressed in your postal. I have asked Mr. & Mrs. Kiwa (Mary Hartwell) to make out a map such as you desire. He will draw the map better & more accurately than I could & she will put down the names in English.

We have no stations in the ordinary acceptation of the word, that is, a place where a paid assistant holds service. Our Christians are scattered in various places & we visit them as we can. They are expected to meet on the Sabbath & hold religious services; some of them do & some do not. I have askt the makers of the map to note every place in which any of our members or the North St. members live. In some places there are only one or two, in others more. I am sorry to say they have a tendency to gravitate towards the city which is bad in some respects. Moving away from their old friends & neighbors, they have less reproach to endure as being Christians; I think it wd. be better for them to live it down at home & try to influence their own region. They are poor & hope to better themselves by moving to the city. Sometimes they do & very often they lose what little they bring with them.

The war rumors seem to have almost died out & things move on quietly as before, only there is constant drilling of troops. It is to be hoped that China will not attempt to cope with the power of Russia; right or wrong, she will be worsted in the war & would probably have to pay a larger indemnity than is now demanded.

The people grow more accessible. Dr. & Mrs. Crawford were out last week spending several days in a village where there are no Christians & they found great readiness to hear. Mrs. Holmes & I have been making some very pleasant day trips among the neighboring villages. Even these are growing friendly and manifest a willingness to be instructed. The good work grows & there are many causes of hopefulness.

I do not know whether you take the *Chinese Recorder*. I send you the latest number which contains an interesting article from Dr. Nevins on "Mission Work in Central Shantung." I thought you might like to reprint the article in whole or in part in your *Foreign Journal.*

With kindness regards,

Yrs sincerely,

L. Moon.

Tengchow
Dec. 14, 1880
Rev. Dr. H. A. Tupper
My dear Brother,

Herewith the map for wh. I am indebted to Mr. & Mrs. Kiwa who were so kind as to make it for me. I askt that every place should be put down where we have members, also all places where any of the North St. members live. You see our members liv mostli in villages not very distant from the city. I notice one place, Mer je ks, put down where we hav no members, I think. At Ning hai also, tho we once had members they are now excluded. Our mission force is too small to allow us to work in distant places. The Presbyterians are branching out in many directions & have stations scattered far & wide. They have rec'd in one field, some eighty accessions lately, but of these I don't know how many are children & infants.

Our thoughts are largely taken up with the impending war. It is said that forty Russian war vessels are expected in Yokahama, that the Admiral is to have a grand reception from the Emperor in Tokio & the probabilities seem to be that Japan will unite with Russia against China. We naturally feel somewhat unsettled, as it is not certain whether we shall be able to remain here with safety. There are a good many troops here now & more are coming. They are under good discipline & give us no real trouble, only some annoyance from their curiosity to see into our houses. A good many were at church yesterday both in the morning & afternoon & behaved very well.

Our missions are in usual health. With kindest regards,

Yrs. sincerely,

L. Moon.

Tengchow,
China.
May 21, 1883
Rev. H. A. Tupper. D. D.,
My dear Brother-

Yesterday was one of gladness for our church in this place. Seven were added to our number by baptism, among whom was Mrs. Pruitt. The latter came to China under the Presbyterian Board of Missions. She comes to us from conscientious convictions of duty. She has for several months, and has lately, returned from a long country tour. We have reason to congratulate ourselves on the accession to the mission & the church of one so active & energetic, and so thoroughly imbued with the missionary spirit.

The general outlook of the mission work is encouraging. Our congregations, especially at Sunday-School, have increased. The boy's school is prospering under Mr. Halcomb's judicious management. The school for girls is larger than ever before, & unless I can enlarge my accommodations I shall probably be compelled to decline applications. The mission has unanimously voted that such an enlargement is necessary for the proper prosecution of the school work. I believe the school would readily run up to fifty pupils if there were room. It used to be that we had to go out & seek pupils. Now parents seem anxious to have their daughters come.

In addition to school work, I carry on city visiting, as time and strength permit. I generally meet a cordial reception, & sometimes the message I bear is received with earnest attention. There seems to be a general breaking down of prejudice, which makes working in the city very different from what it was a few years ago.

That noble veteran, Dr. Crawford, is giving himself very earnestly to the work of preaching the gospel. He seems to me to be doing some of the best work of his life. His long residence here has not only given him a profound knowledge of the character of the people, & the proper way to approach them, but it has also given them a profound respect for him. He finds attentive audiences of well-dressed men in his street preaching.

With my kind regards, I am
Yours sincerely,
L. Moon.

July 23rd, 1883
Rev. Dr. H. A. Tupper:
My Dear Brother—

Your postal of May 23rd was received last week. All money contributed for pupils in my school is covered by the regular annual estimate. I have no extra expenses. Money is occasionally sent direct to me for some particular girl, but I turn it over to the treasurer of the mission. My school was full the last half session almost to its capacity of accommodation. If applications increase as they have done within the last year, I shall have to ask the Board to make an appropriation to enable me to enlarge my quarters. As a mere matter of business, it does not pay for a missionary to give her whole time and energy to the care of forty girls, when she could superintend a school of eighty or a hundred with about the same expenditure of time, and with far more pleasure and satisfaction to herself. I believe a school of a hundred girls could be built up in a few years, but to do this more room is imperatively needed. Please think the matter over. The mission voted unanimously some months ago that my school quarters ought to be enlarged. If you think the Board would favor such a plan, it is probable that it ought to be carried out about the close of this year. We must have the quarters first, and then the pupils will come.

At a meeting of the Tung Chow Baptist mission last week it was resolved unanimously that Miss Mattie Roberts, of Louisville, Ky., be invited to join the mission at Tung Chow with her future field undecided. This action looks to her being connected with the Hwang Hien mission, when that is opened. It is with great joy that I look forward to the establishment of this new interest. It is what we have earnestly desired for many years. I trust Laichowfu will be the next station in a chain of missions to reach finally the capital of the province, Chenanfu. I long to see Southern Baptists rise up to the measure of duty and privilege in giving the gospel to this people.

We are all in usual health. The missionaries for Whong Hien are full of enthusiasm and hope. I trust the Board will sanction their plans. Our brethren seem to be progressive and cautious in their views, ready to be guided by the opinions of older missionaries, and yet prepared to strike out new paths where their own judgement shows it to be desirable. Our mission is in hearty sympathy with the "new departure" in teaching English in the schools. Thirty years ago, doubtless, it was a great mistake. Times are now changed; "young China" is coming to the front, and the Christian church should keep abreast, should lead, in higher education of those who will help to direct the future of this great empire.

We had the great joy of welcoming Mrs. Crawford home about two weeks ago. She was looking worn on her arrival, but seems to be rallying in health and strength.

With very kind regards, yours sincerely,

L. Moon.

Unofficial

Tungchow, China,
Sept. 24, 1883
Rev. Dr. H. A. Tupper: —
My dear Brother,

Your letter of June 23rd & postal of July 20th have been duly rec'd. I will write to Mr. Stackhouse. He has been very kind & is very self-denying. I appreciate what he has done because I know he feels what he gives—& so do many others. But it is not of this I meant to write. I wish to have a chat with you, unofficially, face to face, about the school here, present and prospective. It seems to me that the time has come when we must arrive at a definite decision about the school for girls. The quarters are too small for more than forty. With forty, they are much crowded. Last session there were thirty-eight present. All have not returned & we have now thirty-two. Others will probably return. The question to be decided is, how far we shall expand our school work. It is my profound conviction that it does *not pay* a woman to give her life to teaching forty girls. I would not do it myself, nor advise any other woman to do it. A school of eighty or a hundred might repay the outlay & the sacrifice a woman makes of time & strength. Now shall we go on & have a large school? Or, has the time come & are we strong enough to make a decided stand on the question of foot-binding? Heretofore we have only used moral suasion. We have taken *all* who applied, if suitable, & only tried to induce parents to consent to unbind their feet. Shall we now say that we will in future take *no* girl with small feet? This would probably reduce the school to ten or fifteen girls in the course of time. Those now in school would be allowed to continue on the old terms. Perhaps about half have large feet now. Shall we make it a rule that *all* who come in shall unbind their feet? I would rather, as a matter of principle, have fifteen girls with large feet than fifty with small. *Under no circumstances do I wish to continue in school work.* I confess it would please my ambition to build up a big school, but I long to go out & talk to the thousands of women around me. I *hate* sham. If I pretend to have a school I want the best one that would repay the time spent on it, but I don't want a poor little affair that will drag on in the hands of the Chinese while I am half the time away on country work. If I am to devote myself to evangelistic work in the city & country, I *must* be free from the school. No woman, had she the strength of Hercules, could do justice to either, if she had to carry on both. Now please think it all over, tell me as a friend—not as secretary—what your judgment in the matter is—& then, as secy. turn over in your mind some plan to relieve me of the school. If Mrs. Holmes is coming back, I am willing to hold on a little longer for her sake—her heart is bound up in the school, but, if not, then I want to *give up school work permanently,* & go back to North St. to live, when the new mission is establisht at *Whonghien.* The North St. house will then be vacant.

We are all very busy & are all well.

With kindest regards,

Yrs.,

L. Moon.

Note:

Please don't think I am not heartily in sympathy with educational plans. I am, most thoroughly, but my own taste does not lie in that direction. I want my friend Mr. Halcomb to build up a self-supporting school of high grade & hope he will have the hearty support of the Board in his plans, & I want the *best* school for girls, if another lady will teach it & leave me free.

Tungchow, China

Feb. 11, 1884

Rev. Dr. H. A. Tupper:

My Dear Brother:

I am sorry to have to report that owing to fever among my pupils, I was compelled in December to disband the school. The first case occurred in Oct., the sufferer lingering on until the latter part of Dec. when she died. She was an extremely interesting and lovable child, the brightest and sweetest of the younger members of my flock. There were some ten other cases of fever, and fearing the further spread of the disease I thought it best to send away those that were well. One case still lingers on, having been ill now for about three months. This fever is regarded as very contagious. It does not seem best that the school should be resumed for sometime. Owing to the large increase in the numbers last year, the appropriation for expenses only lasted up to the first of November. I therefore began a new financial year at that date and shall draw from the treasurer only the amount needed for expenses up to the final closing of the school. Some expenses were incurred in sending the girls home, and a number who were sick had to be kept on some weeks longer. Two who lived far away have been compelled to remain up to the present time. I desire to express very hearty thanks to the friends whose contributions have helped to sustain the school. They will understand that the funds contributed for this year will not be drawn, but remain for disposal in the hands of the Board.

Not having the school to fill up my time and thoughts, I have decided to devote myself to country work and city visiting. It must be confessed that the latter is one of the most difficult departments of missionary work and one that produces few immediate results. The great difficulty is to get admission to the homes of the people. Though there is now no active hostility to foreigners in the city, there still continues the old, deep-rooted aversion to anything like social intercourse with us. However, there are families to which we are cordially welcomed and to such it is a pleasure to go. Let me describe a few visits I have recently made and these will give an idea of the work to be done. Today, being the fifteenth of the Chinese month, is one of the seasons set apart for worship at the temples. The worship is of the barest, most meager kind imaginable. Before the idols a few sticks of incense are burning & bowls of food are set out. In front of the fane is spread a straw mat. The worshippers come in, bow to the idols, kneel & knock their heads three times and take their departure. The whole time scarcely occupies two minutes. Sometimes paper is brought to be burned and this is cast into a small room outside especially prepared for the purpose. This paper represents money. This morning I wandered into a temple and was received by an aged priest. This temple is falling to decay and the priest said as my object was to do good it would be but carrying out my purpose if I would contribute to rebuilding & restoring this temple. As he is quite deaf, I found it difficult to convey to his mind the idea that missionaries had no sympathy with idolatry. A bright little grand-daughter of his, carrying in her arms a child almost half as big as herself, readily volunteered the opinion that the idols were nothing but mud, without spirit and not good for anything. On inquiring, I found she had heard this from a Christian neighbor. On leaving this temple, I went to see a family with whom I have some acquaintance. In a shrine built in the wall is a small image about half a foot high, called the "Heavenly Officer." In front of this was a table on which incense & offerings are placed. In the house was a table upon which was the family tablet and upon this table were many bowls of food. Incense was also burning. Here was a family evidently "wholly given to idolatry." They kindly invited me to a seat on the kong and I spent some time trying to tell them of Him who is the only Way.

One day last week, starting out alone, not knowing whither I should go, but praying that I might be guided to some work for the Master, I found myself after a considerable walk in a small village near the city. I accosted two men and asked if the women would not come out to talk. They said the Mandarins had ordered the women to stay indoors on account of the soldiers. One of the men, however, finally invited me to go in and very soon the room was full of people of all ages, men, women and children. The master of the house was a shop-keeper in the city and seemed to be a man of intelligence. He and his wife listened with great attention, the latter saying that what I was telling them was true. After a long talk, I took leave with cordial invitations from them to return. The same afternoon I went to visit one of my old friends and former neighbors. She is a woman who has heard the gospel probably for twenty years. I found her confined to the kong by a fall. She seemed glad to see me and I thought there was genuine interest in the way she listened to the "old, old story." Hers has been a sad life. Her children have all been taken from her, and finally her husband died, leaving her alone in the world.

I was much interested in some visits I made on another day last week. In the large yard was a swing about which was gathered a merry party of girls. Some of them followed me into the house and set themselves to learn part of a hymn. A good many boys also came in and I had a busy time teaching. On leaving, I was invited into another house where I found a very pleasant old gentleman, a retired merchant. We had a talk in which he brought out the usual notions about worshipping "Heaven & Earth" and one's parents. He had never found time, he said, to go to any church to hear preaching. I presented him a copy of Matthew's Gospel which he seemed glad to get.

There is one encouraging feature in this work which I desire to mention and that is the difference in the way many people listen from what they used to do some years ago. Formerly, it was with the greatest difficulty the women could be induced to listen at all. You would scarcely have begun before they would interrupt with frivolous questions, or would drown your voice in general conversation. Now, they often listen in silence and it is easy to read in their faces the conviction that these words are true. They often say they believe and some speak contemptuously of the idols. The great difficulty in their way is the fear as to what others would say. Our work continues to be among the respectable poor and the middle classes. The aristocracy still regard us with lofty disdain.

We have had the great pleasure lately of welcoming Miss Roberts to our mission and I esteem myself particularly blessed in having her with me. Her bright, cheery spirit makes sunshine in the house. If you have any more like her, please send them on forthwith! She is getting on well with the language and bids fair to be a very good speaker.

Dr. Crawford has not been well of late. Others of the mission are in usual health.

With kindest regards,
Yours truly,
L. Moon.

Tungchow, China
Nov. 3, 1884
My dear Dr. Tupper:

Our mission has suffered a very sad & painful loss. Our dear friend & sister, Mrs. Pruitt, was taken from us on the 19th of October. She had been ill about six weeks from a fever peculiar to this country. Her illness was not considered alarming at first & she was hopeful of recovery up to the end. On the day of her death she was brighter than she had been for a week. She took her food with relish & talked cheerfully. About an hour after supper, suddenly, without any warning, she passed away. Her death was painless. Thus has departed to her reward one who fell as truly a martyr as the saints of old who laid down their lives for the Lord Jesus. For her we can only rejoice that the Master has bidden her "come up higher." She has entered upon the nobler work & the unending bliss of Heaven. For ourselves, we mourn the sundering of tender ties; the loss of her sweet & helpful companionship; we grieve that we shall hear no more on earth her cheerful, kindly voice & see no more her bright, sunny face.

Mrs. Pruitt came to China not quite three years ago in connection with the Northern Presbyterian Board & was stationed in Chefoo. From the time of her arrival, she set herself diligently & faithfully to the acquisition of the language & she made rapid progress. She continued to be a persevering student & even in her last illness would try to learn orally.

She was united to Mr. Pruitt in Sept. 1882 & was thenceforth connected with our mission in Tungchow. From the time of her coming among us, she identified herself heartily with the work of the mission. She took charge of a class in Sunday school & all can testify to the faithfulness with which she taught it. One of the members of this class was unusually dull & Mrs. Pruitt would go to her home during the week & teach her the lesson for the coming Sabbath. Whatever Mrs. Pruitt undertook, she could always be depended upon to perform. Having kindly consented to teach a class in my school last year, every day found her promptly & punctually at her post although she had to come across the city to do less than an hour's work.

In the spring of 1883 she made a long tour in the company with her husband & Mr. Halcomb. The Chinese admired her personal appearance & her gentle, winning manners drew the women in crowds around her. In the autumn of the same year she made a tour with Mr. Pruitt, & on their return planned a number of short tours which she was providentially hindered from making. Last spring, again in company with Mr. Pruitt & Mr. Halcomb, she made a very long & fatiguing tour. Her ardent enthusiasm, earnest zeal, & the incessant demands of the work no doubt carried her far beyond her strength. She said, after her return, that often during the trip, she would get in from the day's work too tired even to talk English. She said she would throw herself on the "kong" in utter exhaustion. She also suffered during this trip from sore throat, brought on by constant talking to the women. She had many invitations to visit them in their homes & she felt that she could not refuse even when too tired to go. She was looking badly on her return to the city, but that seemed only natural after the weariness of her long & exhausting labors. The protracted absence from home had caused many arrears in household affairs & with her characteristic energy & cheerful self-forgetfulness she set to work. Ever thoughtful & considerate of others, she never spared herself. She was not well during the summer, but still there was nothing to awaken alarm. The treacherous fever took hold of her so gradually that her friends were not aware that she was sick. After she was too unwell to work, she accused herself of being only "idle." Her last act before giving up & yielding to the disease was to help a friend who was very busy preparing to go to America.

Her patience & gentleness throughout her long illness was wonderful. She said that although she could not understand why God had sent the illness yet that it was all right & she submitted implicitly to His will. She was most touchingly thoughtful of those who had the care of her, expressing constant solicitude lest they should be worried. She made attendance upon her sick bed a delight to those who were privileged to minister to her. As she lay ill there, she seemed to take more thought for their comfort than they did for hers.

The Chinese unite in speaking warmly in her praise. They talk especially of her great kindness, unselfishness & interest in them & their children. She won their love & respect as few are able to do.

To the projected Whong hien mission, the loss is most heavy; Mrs. Pruitt was the only lady in that mission ready for work.

Of her beautiful home life, of her loving devotion to her husband, of his unspeakable loss, it would not be fitting to tell in a paper intended for publication.

Though she was with us but a little more than two years, we have cause to thank God that He sent her to us. For that brief time, she gave us a shining example of earnest devotion to God's work, & her beautiful self-sacrificing life will not have been in vain if it shall stir us to imitation. The memory of such a life will be an abiding inspiration.

L. Moon.

Tungchow,
March 4, 1885
My dear Dr. Tupper,

Your letter of Dec. 6th only reacht me last night. I reply immediately & allow my letter to take its chance of getting through before the threatened blockage begins.

I prefer to speak only for myself as regards the question of a school. I am decidedly the friend of schools & should cheerfully help in building one up. I do not wish to engage in that work myself.

I feel it due to any lady who may be planning to come out here to open a day school to say *most emphatically* that it would be worse than any wild goose chase. Day schools for boys *have been utter failures*. A day school for girls would not stand *even the* ghost of a chance. For a woman to come out here with a noble ideal of a good work to be done & to find her cherisht hope *an absolute impossibility* would be a crushing disappointment. Of course, if she were elastic in her nature, she could turn to other work. But she ought not to be allowed to come out under a misapprehension. In Canton, day schools are a success because of a demand for the education of girls. Here there is absolutely no such demand. We have labored for years to create it but thus far without success. Of course boarding schools are perfectly feasible for the reason that they offer outside inducements. If the lady's purpose is to open a boarding school, after two or three years' study of the language, she would be ready to enter upon such work. To undertake it earlier would scarcely be wise. During this time of waiting, I would cheerfully invite her to remain with me if it suited her. I am, in fact, the only happy possessor of a spare room in the mission, at present. Owing to the failure of the Whong Hien mission to secure a house, we are considerably crowded at present. Mr. Halcomb is intending to fix up the school quarters here for a temporary residence & keep house. I am keeping house in Mrs. Holmes' former residence. Mr. & Mrs. Halcomb will be on the same premises—we will share one yard in common. When the Whong Hien mission gets started, I wish to move back to North St. & work my old parish from that centre. I have still worked it since removing to this place, but it involves a somewhat long walk to get over there. I am not *anxious* to move, but the understanding with Mr. Pruitt is that when he gives up that house I expect to return to it. It may be two or three years before he will be able to get quarters in Whong Hien, if the war lasts—or he may get a house sooner if the consul bestirs himself rigorously. I have been keeping house now about eight years & could not be content or happy under any other circumstances. In fact, the *sine qua non* of my remaining in China would always be a home of my own. Of course I should not object to another lady's sharing it with me if we liked each other on trial. I shouldn't like to pledge myself beforehand to live with a lady I had never seen. Would you? Nor should I like a lady to come out here pledged to live with me, for she might think me "cranky" & disagreeable. On the whole, I would rather invite her as I did Miss Roberts, to make her home with me as long as it suited her convenience. This would prevent embarrassment on both sides. I *should* like very much to have a lady divide the country work with me, but I should like to know her before asking her to live with me permanently.

I have said a good deal I did not think of writing when I began this letter. But perfect frankness is always best & may prevent serious mistakes. If a lady comes to reopen the school, personally I can pledge cooperation. The rest of the mission can speak for themselves.

If our latest rumors of the war are correct, we are likely to have the French here soon. We propose to stay at our post though it may be one of danger. We do not wish to lose the opportunity of showing to the people that we are their true friends, even though our stay may involve some risk. Of course all work will be suspended & we shall have to remember the lines of Milton, "They also serve who only stand and wait." Waiting is the hardest kind of work, but God knows best & we may joyfully leave all in His hands.

With best regards,

Yours sincerely,

L. Moon

Tungchow,
Apr. 4, 1885
My dear Dr. Tupper,

I feel compelled to write you in a way which is not agreeable to myself & which may seem to you ungracious. But there is no help for it. There has been great conflict of opinion in what was formerly the Tungchow mission. As you know, we have now two missions, the Tungchow & Whanghein. Nearly two years ago Dr. Crawford formed a plan of getting the Board to make changes in the rules under which we came out & have been going on these many years. The majority of the mission made so determined & resolute a stand against the proposed changes that he did not send his suggestions to the Board. Now he goes to Richmond to press in person his peculiar views. While we are perfectly willing that he should freely carry out his view so far as himself & his wife are concerned, & also so far as he can induce others to accept them freely & without official pressures, we *are not willing* that those views should be forced upon those of us who do not see our way to accepting or even approving them. Dr. Crawford insists that his plan will give perfect freedom to all parties. As the rest of us see it—it would make him, through the Board, dictator not only for life, but after he has passed from earthly existence. His plan included every cash we should spend for mission work & extended even to the regulation of salaries! If that be freedom—give me slavery!

As to the proposed plan of having one mission—the Shantung mission—as I see it, it would but perpetuate disagreements. Now, if a man shows himself disposed to be tyrannical, there is some escape by forming a new mission in which he has no power to annoy. If there were a Shantung mission what way of escape would be left from perpetual and ever reoccurring disagreements? I believe that the only hope of peace is in having independent missions—as we now have—responsible to the Board alone.

I have not written this in any spirit of unkindness to Dr. Crawford. I told him I should write to the Board about the matters upon which we disagree. This is in no sense an accusation of him. As he will see the Board in person, it is right that they should know that he represents *absolutely nobody* but himself & wife. While we are willing that he should have perfect freedom, we are not disposed to submit ourselves to dictatorship. All we ask is the same freedom that we concede.

I regret the necessity of writing this letter, but I think it right that the Board should be informed of the state of affairs as seen from a different stand-point from Dr. Crawford's.

With the best regards,

Yours truly

L. Moon.

Tungchow, China,

June 27, 1885

Rev. Dr. H. A. Tupper:—

My dear Brother,

The May no. of the *Foreign Journal* has just reached me. I find in it a quotation from my article in *Woman's Work* of last November. Mention is made of three classes of unmarried women among missionaries. I wrote the article from deep, intense sympathy with my suffering sisters. I have belonged heretofore in the third class who were free. It seems to be the purpose of the committee to relegate me henceforth to the first class. I distinctively declined to be so relegated.

Will you be so kind as to request the Board to appropriate the proper sum—say $550.00 (five hundred fifty dollars) to pay my return passage to Va.? On arrival I will send in my resignation in due form. I regret the necessity of taking this step, but any other course is impossible. I wish to leave here in the later part of Dec. & should be glad therefore of an immediate response.

Yours, with kindest feelings,

L. Moon.

Tungchow,

July 17, 1885

Rev. Dr. H. A. Tupper:-

My dear Brother,

Your letter of June 5th reacht me this morning. I echo most heartily your wish that you could talk with us face to face. In an hour's talk you could be put in possession of facts that might be useful in forming an opinion of mission matters in Tungchow. In default of such personal talk, I will tell you briefly of how matters have gone here. I will not go back farther than the early part of 1884, about the time Miss Roberts joined the Mission. Previous to her arrival Dr. Crawford informed me privately that he intended to call a mission meeting, lay down the office of pastor & call upon the young brethren to take matters in charge. He gave to me as his reason that he was not only unable to get on with his fellow missionaries but that he had alienated the Chinese from him & that his withdrawal was absolutely essential. Shortly after Miss Roberts' arrival, he called the mission meeting, stated his purpose & requested the young brethren to consider the matter as to who should succeed him in the pastorate. This was anything but welcome to Mr. Pruitt & Mr. Halcomb. Their hearts were set on going to Whong Hien & the Board had already sanctioned this purpose. Nevertheless, laying aside their own wishes, they consented to give up their cherisht plans & Mr. Pruitt gave Dr. Crawford to understand that he would accept the pastorate. Before the final steps were taken, however, it became manifest to Mr. Pruitt that he was to be a mere figure-head to do the preaching while Dr. Crawford & his Chinese deacon would continue to rule the church. As a self-respecting man, Mr. Pruitt could not consent to occupy such a position & he withdrew his formerly yielded consent. Mr. Halcomb never felt called to accept a permanent position here & declined to take the question into consideration. Dr. Crawford therefore retained the pastorate & matters went on as before. He continued as he had done almost from the time Mr. Halcomb & Mr. Pruitt arrived to *demand* in the most imperious manner that they should definitely pledge themselves to his views—views on the school question, I beg you to observe that had never been heard of until the winter of 1882, while Mrs. Crawford was in America & after Mrs. Holmes had left China. Previous to that period, our every energy had been given to building up schools. Now, on Dr. Crawford's mere demand, & without gaining the assent of our judgment, the brethren were required to subscribe to these new views. The same imperious demand was made with regard to the employment of native assistants. The brethren replied that while their judgment thus far was against the employment of native assistants at the same time they could not give any pledge on the subject. It would be too tedious to tell of the incessant recurring to the same ever-tedious theme, the ever repeated annoying demands that the brethren should stultify themselves by absolute submission & of their mild, but firm refusal to bind themselves to a fixt policy in so early a stage of their missionary career. (Note: It took Dr. Crawford twenty years to find out the folly of schools. He wisht others to reach that point in as many months. Naturally they declined when they saw, as the result of schools, the best & most efficient members of our church.)

I will now relate the latest phase of the question about the pastorate here. We had a mission meeting to consider a proposition from our

Presbyterian friends. When that had been disposed of, Dr. Crawford stated that he had told the native church that he would resign his pastorate on the following Sabbath. He stated to us his plan. A young man named *Wong*, not yet even a licentiate, was to do the preaching during Dr. Crawford's absence. Mr. Davault, who had been here about two months & who could probably understand a few dozen Chinese words & who was not even a member of our church, was to decide when Mr. Wong had preacht all we could endure of his sermons & was thereupon to invite Mr. Pruitt or Mr. Halcomb, both of them members of our church & both speaking Chinese wel, to take Mr. Wong's place for a Sunday. This most absurd & ridiculous plan met with prompt & decided opposition on the part of the majority of the mission. So decidedly did some of us express our opinion of the matter in private that Dr. Crawford felt constrained to abandon it without calling a mission meeting for discussion. He withdrew the resignation he had offered the church & still holds the position of pastor, all things being left during his absence in Mrs. Crawford's hands. This arrangement is perfectly satisfactory to all parties. Mrs. Crawford is a woman, I need not say, of excellent judgment & great tack. Dr. Crawford once gone, she cordially invited the young brethren to take charge of the church and Sunday school in his absence. They were only too glad to throw themselves heartily into the work of building up the church. They preach, preside at church meetings, lecture on Thursday evenings, & Mr. Halcomb has charge of the Sunday school.

Every thing goes on in the most perfect and beautiful harmony. Since the lamented death of our dear Mrs. Halcomb, the brethren have thought it best to relinquish the design of going to Whong hien. They have therefore connected themselves again with the Tungchow mission. Our mission meetings, the retrospect of which used to be a constant matter of humiliation & self-reproach for unseemly wrangling, are now perfectly serene & untroubled. We meet, elect a moderator, the business is stated promptly & at once disposed of, & then one of the gentlemen closes with prayer. Formally, Dr. Crawford always assumed that he was moderator & he used his position to drag in, on all occasions, his peculiar views on mission policy. A business meeting which should have taken twenty minutes, would be dragged on for two hours in worse than profitless discussion of the same ever recurring themes.

As Dr. Crawford has utterly failed to carry with him the judgment of his associates, we do not think it right that he should try to *force* his views upon us practically without our consent, by going home to influence the Board in person. He promist us positively that nothing should be attempted without full & free discussion & consultation between the three missions in China. A time was set when the whole matter should come up. That time passed & nothing was said. Months passed & the whole matter seemed to have fallen into oblivion. Suddenly we are informed that Dr. Crawford is going to America & he declines to tell us what he means to do there. We feel that he has not kept faith with us. The only hint he gives us of his purpose is in the announcement at the Union prayer meeting a day or two before his departure that he is going to America to try to unite the Richmond & Boston Boards on his policy.

With regard to Dr. Crawford's proposition to divide fields, I think there is no especial dislike felt to that by the gentlemen of the mission whom alone it concerns. Only I must tell you an amusing little item of the proposed division. The Tungchow line was to run within 15 *li* (5 Eng. miles) of Whong hien city. Thus the native brethren living in five miles of Whong hien would be required to come twenty miles (sixty *li*) to Tungchow for communion instead of being allowed to cast in their lot with the church that was to have been established at Whong Hien city. Yet Dr. Crawford could not see the impolicy of this as regards the natives, its injustice as regards the Whong hien foreign pastor, & its general absurdity as regards practicability!

My letter thus far has been taken up with general mission matters. If you will kindly permit, I should like to ask a question on a subject which concerns me personally. Can you tell me—or rather will you tell me—if the China committee proposes to make any changes in the status of unmarried women in the missions? Here in Tungchow the ladies have always been admitted to mission meetings on equal terms with the gentlemen of the mission. For a long time, you know, the mission consisted of only Dr. & Mrs. Crawford & Mrs. Holmes. Then my sister came & these four made up the mission. Later, I joined it & the mission consisted of one man & four women. We met & consulted always on equal terms. At one time, as you know, the mission was left entirely in the hands of women—Mrs. Holmes, Mrs. Crawford & myself. It was at a very trying time, owing to difficulties with the North St. faction, but we weathered the storm. When Miss Roberts came, no one ever dreamed of questioning her right to enter the mission on equal terms. Our mission meetings are held in a private parlor. They are simply a company of men & women met together to consult about matters in which all are equally concerned. To exclude the married ladies from these meetings might be unwise, but it could hardly be deemed unjust as they would be represented by their husbands. To exclude the unmarried ladies, would be a most glaring piece of injustice, in my opinion. To such exclusion

I could never submit & retain my self respect. I have heretofore rejoiced in the fact that I belonged to a mission in which all my rights were secured. I have felt great sympathy with ladies in the Southern Presbyterian mission & the English Episcopal mission for the way in which their rights were ignored. It was the deep feeling of the injustice & the unwisdom of this course that led me in "Woman's Work" to advocate a broader & juster view. Having my own rights secured, I felt it a duty to raise my voice in behalf of my friends who were less happily situated. I presume the China committee is laboring under a misapprehension of facts. I suppose they are unaware that the ladies here, whether married or single, have always occupied precisely the same position as the gentlemen. Otherwise I cannot see why they felt called upon to say that they "do not endorse" my position. If it indeed be their real purpose to deny to the ladies of this mission rights that have never heretofore been questioned, then, sorrowfully, but as a matter of self respect & duty there can be no course open to me but to sever my connection with the Board.

With very cordial greetings,
Yours sincerely,
L. Moon.

Tungchow,
Oct. 19, 1885
Rev. Dr. H. A. Tupper:
My dear Brother,

I promist Mr. Halcomb sometime ago that I would make a statement to you with regard to the condition of the roofs on this place. You are aware that he repaired the school premises expecting to live there for a time. Afterwards, on Mrs. Halcomb's death, the premises were handed over to Mr. Joiner, who lived there until his removal to Whong hien. As you know, we were greatly pressed for room after the new missionaries came. As the Whong hien house seemed unattainable, Mr. Halcomb was compelled to make the temporary arrangements here. He found that the roofs needed repairing—or, rather, entire renewing, in order to render the houses habitable. Roofing is expensive. In the part of the premises I occupy, I was also compelled to attend to the roofing. Some of it had to be entirely renewed. The Chinese say that a good thatched roof will last twenty years. I hope, therefore, that the present expense, though regrettable, is a good investment. If the roofs had not been renewed, some of them would have tumbled in. Chinese houses are built in rows, one story high. Hence the necessity for so much roofing.

Mr. Halcomb is away on a three months' tour. He writes cheerfully of his work. Mr. Pruitt is also away on a long tour. Mrs. Crawford's health is much better and she is able to renew her country work. She finds encouraging indications of interest. I have made several short trips this fall. The people are increasingly friendly. The result of the French War seems to have been good in opening the eyes of the people to the fact that we are their friends & that we are under the protection of the Chinese government. The conduct of the government towards foreigners during the war was that of a civilized power. China has made a vast stride during the last few years in her attitude towards foreigners. Our position here is far different from what it was ever before. In my own experience, I am met with smiling faces & cordial greetings where there use to be only coldness. We can readily get lodgings now in private families in the country. It used to be difficult often to secure our nights at an inn.

I expect to start in a day or two for *Pingtu*, a city three hundred & forty *li* from here. This will be the most distant trip I have ever taken. I shall go by way of Whong hien to see our missionaries in their new quarters. I presume someone has written you of the satisfactory conclusion of the long negotiation for the Whong hien house, & also of the fact that the station has been opened there. We feel very much encouraged and now our thoughts turn naturally to pushing farther westward & opening a new station as soon as the Board sees its way to the men & the means. Whong hien ought to be only the first in a long chain of stations reaching to the capital, Che man fu.

With kindest regards,

Yours sincerely,

L. Moon.

Tungchow, Nov. 17, 1885

Rev. Dr. H. A. Tupper: —

My dear Brother,

At a recent meeting of our Mission, I was directed to write you on two points.

Brethren Davault & Joiner have recently removed to Whonghien. The question was brought up whether the expenses of their removal fell properly on them personally or whether those expenses should be paid by the Mission. We had no precedent to guide us, & it was decided to refer the matter directly to the Board for decision. By "removal" is meant not only themselves but also their household & kitchen furniture. The Board will know what is customary in such cases, and we ask that they let us know what is the rule. If you decide that it is right for the Mission to pay expenses of removal, the brethren will send you their account.

The second matter about which I was directed to communicate with the Board was with regard to opening at the very earliest practicable date, a new station, to be located at the city of *Pingtu*. This city is about 115 Eng. miles from Tungchow, being three days' journey beyond Whonghien. The Mission directed me to ask that two married men be sent out for work at Pingtu. Considerable work has already been done there by our brethren Pruitt & Halcomb. Mrs. Pruitt also did valuable work there during her too-brief missionary career. We have already a hold there in the fact that several of our church members here are from Pingtu. Some of them have borne there fruitful testimony to the gospel among their own relatives, and it is among these that I believe we shall receive some of the first fruits of our future work.

Without wishing to raise hopes too high, I should like to emphasize very strongly the fact that the location of the proposed new station seems to our judgment most admirable. It is in a rich & fertile country. Our work would be mainly among a well-to-do middle class, whether in the city or the country. There is none of that grinding poverty which is such a drawback to mission work in this region. As the strongest reason for wishing to start a station in the Pingtu region, the fact should be mentioned that the most glorious triumphs of the gospel in this Province have been in the interior. There the Eng. Baptists & the Northern Presbyterians have in a few years gathered in many hundreds of converts, while in the coast stations the work advances very, very slowly.

Some time ago, Mr. Halcomb & Mr. Pruitt sketched out & sent to the Board a plan of future operations in our Province. Their idea was that Whonghien should be the first in a long chain of new stations to stretch on to the Capital as our goal. The Mission now asks the Board to enable us to take the next step in the occupancy of the Province. The two brethren above mentioned propose to continue to work in Pingtu & the neighboring region as they have done in the past without formally opening a station there at present. But as soon as the Board can send us two married men for Pingtu we wish the station to be opened & Mr. Pruitt & Mr. Halcomb will settle there permanently. Meanwhile I propose to spend a large portion of the next year or two in Pingtu trying to push on woman's work in that region. Not long ago I made a short stay there & I was much delighted with the wide-open door for woman's work. I have seen nothing comparable to it in my whole missionary experience. Such eager drinking-in of the truth, such teachableness, I have never seen before. There are many hundreds of women in that region who belong to religious sects. These women are mostly devout worshipers of Buddha & abstain from animal food. Such women leaven a community wherever they are & I regard them as the most hopeful material upon which to work. They are deeply & earnestly religious. They have thought much about the soul & concerning the future life. They are groping ignorantly after God, if "haply they may feel after & find Him," & I doubt not that many of them will eagerly embrace the truth if presented to them lovingly & earnestly. In working in a region where there are already native religious sects there is the very great advantage that the minds of the people are familiar with the idea of joining a religious sect, & that it carries no odium with it. Here, it is considered very disgraceful to join a Christian church. I believe there would be comparatively little of that feeling where the community is already leavened by religious ideas. Here we have to meet, not Buddhism, but blank atheism.

We have found the people of Pingtu friendly. I think there would be no difficulty in getting as many houses as may be needed without appeal to the secular arm to enforce our Treaty rights. When I was there a short time ago I was offered a house. I declined because I did not like the locality as being too public & because I was not free to pledge the rent. I ventured, however, to take four rooms in a nice Chinese family in exactly the locality I wished. The rent is only Tls. 18 *per annum* & I felt sure both the Mission & the Board would sanction the outlay. I was told I could have the rooms three years or five years if I wished.

Our station at *Shangtswang* of which Mr. Halcomb is pastor is less than fifty Eng. miles from Pingtu & can therefore be much more advantageously worked from that city than from Tungchow.

In behalf of the Mission, the above is respectfully submitted.

L. Moon, Secy. of Tungchow Bapt. Mission

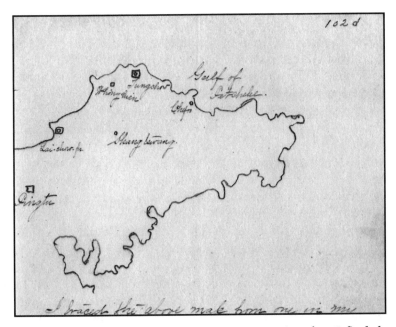

I traced the above map from one in my possession, but I find that the relative location of *Shangtswang* is entirely wrong. On the above map it is put 30 Eng. miles from Tungchow, whereas it is more nearly 70 Eng. miles. It should be placed about 20 Eng. miles nearer Pingtu, while Pingtu itself should be placed some twenty-five miles farther from Tungchow. Roughly speaking, from Tungchow to Whonghien = 20 miles. Chinese say 60 *li*. From Tungchow to Shangtswang = 66 2/3 Eng. miles = 200 *li*. From Tungchow to Pingtu = 113 1/3 Eng. miles = 340 *li*. From Pingtu to Shangtswang = 46 2/3 Eng. miles =140 *li*.

Pingtu, March 12, 1886
Rev. Dr. H. A. Tupper:
My dear Brother,

I have recently returned from a visit to *Shangtswang*. A few items concerning the little body of Christians nestled among the hills there may not be without interest. The church, as you are aware, is what was formerly known as the North St. church of Tungchow. For some years they were without a pastor. In the spring of 1884, Mr. Halcomb assumed that office. The church at that time was threatened with dangers from two sources. Many who had seemed formerly to "run well" and who had held positions of influence in the church had practically renounced the faith; some had even gone back to idolatry. Among the faithful little band living at *Shangtswang*, two of the best brethren were alienated from each other and it was difficult to secure their harmonious co-operation in the affairs of the church. Here then were two problems to be solved, two difficulties to be overcome: to cast out the worthless and unprofitable members, and to reconcile the good and worthy, that they might heartily unite in building up the church. In less than two years, our brother Halcomb has the satisfaction of seeing one of these difficulties entirely removed and the other in a fair way to be fully accomplished. The brethren who were alienated are now reconciled and are working harmoniously together. Some of the worst offenders have been excluded and others will follow.

On my recent visit, it was delightful to see how thoroughly the pastor had gained the confidence and support of his people. An exceedingly difficult and complicated case had arisen. A member who had seemed unusually earnest and faithful had attempted to commit a crime. In this he was foiled and had been put in prison. While in prison another church member had made use of a foreigner's name to get him cruelly beaten. This later outrage had aroused much sympathy for the original offender and there was some danger lest his crime should be forgotten on account of the cruel injustice of which he had been the victim. He was now out of prison and came to the meeting. His manifest purpose was to compel the church to espouse his private quarrel. His demand was that they should immediately expel the other man or himself. He proposed to ignore the pastor and insist the church should back him or exclude him. Up to this time he had been a trusted leader, but now that he arrayed himself against the pastor and tried to force his case upon the church, it was simply delightful that the brethren stood firm and declined to allow the case to be brought up. Both offenders richly deserve exclusion, but, in the present heated state of opinion, the pastor deemed it wise to defer the case until the church could not only be fully informed as to the facts, but could look at them dispassionately.

The *Shangtswang* church provides its own house of worship. They also support a school. Thus the problem of self-support is in the process of being satisfactorily solved. As a body of earnest, faithful, warm-hearted Christians, the brethren and sisters at *Shangtswang* compare favorably with Christians in America. The Chinaman is accused of being unemotional. Yet, last Sunday, as the good deacon handed around the bread of communion, I noticed that his tears were flowing fast. I have heard the pastor say that he has seen the whole body of communicants melted to tears. Occasionally one or another declines to commune; something is on his conscience and he dares not partake. During church meeting, if the discussion grows a little sharp and bids fair to become personal, one or another of the older brethren quietly gets up and leaves, a gentle hint to warmer spirits to cool off.

L. Moon

Tungchow, July 10, 1886
Rev. Dr. H. A. Tupper:-
My dear Brother,

I sent you at close of last year a report of work done. Shortly after this, I went to P'ingtu visiting Shangtswang on the way. Just before my departure for P'ingtu, I rec'd a letter from the man whom I had rented rooms saying that I could not have them. On my arrival at P'ingtu, a good many houses were offered me, mostly inferior. I finally rented one which, with some improvements, was reasonably comfortable. The rent is twenty-five thousand cash a year, say, about twenty-four dollars. It is high rent from a Chinese point of view, but foreigners always have to pay more than natives. It is not a house that would do for permanent residence, but I don't mind "roughing it" for a year or two. The locality is a good one for work, the neighbors being friendly. I had a great many visitors & numerous invitations to visit. From Dec. 16 to June 5, I made 122 visits. Besides this, I made 33 visits to villages. In visiting a village, my custom was to spend the day. There was usually a crowd & I met frequently with earnest, serious women. The more I saw of that region, the more convinced I was that it is an admirable location for a new mission. I think a mission could be established & conducted there without heavy expense. Our idea is to rent good native houses & fit them up in comfortable foreign style. A good house could be rented at about one hundred & fifty dollars a year. It would take, say, two hundred taels to fit it up. We are opposed to building foreign chapels, thinking them a great mistake in our part of China. A small humble room, with a few very plain benches in Chinese style, would be proper, & if in time we have converts, they should themselves provide the place of worship. For our part of China, we see evil & only evil in the employment of paid native assistants. I do not know decidedly what will be the view of the mission finally on the school question. At present, the trend of opinion is that the natives are able & should support their own schools. As regards girls' schools, it is different. There are no schools for girls. Yet we incline to think it better to teach them as we can in their home rather than gather them into schools. Day schools for girls might be useful, would be inexpensive, &

would not be subject to objections as holding out pecuniary advantages to pupils.

I speak of three matters simply to show our wish to go forward on the least expensive plan. Of course we would not favor it if we did not think it also the best; I am speaking now *only for our part of China.* What we need sorely is more men & women. Immense fields lie untoucht for want of laborers to occupy them. For myself, my idea is not to settle in P'ingtu but, when once a mission is established there, to push on to some new field & break the ground for others to come later. This, of course, with due deference to the wishes of the Board & also with due regard to my own health. I don't know how long I could stand the rough life in new places. What I want now is to beg you to send us six new missionaries for P'ingtu. You know the Mission has askt for two married couples. In addition to this, I think two single ladies could find abundance of work in that region. The ladies should, of course, have their own establishment. The rent for three houses would not probably exceed five hundred dollars. No doubt the S. Schools of S. C. could send out & sustain two ladies if properly stirred up. I should take great pleasure in looking after the comfort of the ladies until they should be able to look after themselves. They could come at first to my house here in Tungchow, though I think it would be wise for them to go as soon as possible to their final destination. The dialect differs somewhat from that spoken here & would be best learned on the spot.

I expect to return to P'ingtu in Sept. I shall probably go by Shangtswang & purpose remaining there about two weeks. The school there was flourishing at latest reports, but we have some fear that the teacher may be allured away by the offer of better pay elsewhere. The school is supported by the church. Chinese cannot pay high salaries. While they pay from twenty to thirty dollars a year, possibly forty if the teacher is a first class graduate, the foreigner comes along & spoils everything by giving between fifty and sixty dollars to the merest tyros. So we run up prices & then wonder why the natives don't support their pastors & teachers!

Hoping that the Board will in time, see its way to sending us the new workers we ask. I remain

Yours sincerely,

L. Moon.

Private & Confidential

Tungchow, July 27, 1886
Rev. Dr. H. A. Tupper: —
My dear Brother,

In a letter of last year you say, with regard to a communication of mine, "I wish our Board had such a correspondent in each of our Missions." It has occurred to me that much good & no harm might be done if I should write you with regard to a subject brought to your notice in a recent letter by my friend & brother Rev. N. W. Halcomb.

The step he has taken of offering his resignation is deeply regretted by both Mrs. Crawford & myself. We thought such haste unwise & urged delay. Whilst admitting that, if he definitely settles down into the views given in his letter, he cannot remain a missionary, we felt very strongly indeed that he should take ample time for deliberate consideration of these questions & that any haste was to be deprecated for his own sake, as well as for the sake of the mission. On the other hand, a delicate sense of honor led him to feel that he was not free to investigate the questions at issue without undue bias toward a certain conclusion so long as he was the representative of the Board. Feeling himself free now, he has entered upon the question of the Divinity of our Lord in a spirit of candor & reverence from which I augur the happiest results. Let me say here that while he has endured mental tortures from these doubts, he manifests the Christian grace of gentleness, meekness & humility in an unusual degree. His character seems to me a singular blending of strength & sweetness, such as one rarely meets.

Can you wonder that we grieve to lose him as a co-worker here? Mrs. Crawford remarkt not long ago that she had expected more of him than of any of our young men, that he is more aggressive than any of the others, & that having had larger experience of life at home, he was better fitted to grapple with problems out here. Dr. Yates thinks so highly of him, that he has repeatedly attempted to get him to go to Ching Kiang. I mention all this to show how very valuable a worker we all regard him. That the Whonghien mission was set on foot finally was due to his energetic presentation of the case to our counsel at Chefoo. If he should never do another thing for our Mission, in my judgment he has *more than repaid* by services rendered any expenses to which the Board has been put on his account.

It is proper to mention the fact that Mr. Davault's health has suddenly given way. It is understood that his lungs are affected. We do not *know* that this will issue in his final loss to the work. Supposing he should be compelled to leave Whonghien, as now seems probable, what should be done? It would seem hard to ask Mr. Pruitt to go alone to occupy a position which Mr. Davault has found unendurable with even a wife by his side. Could Mr. Halcomb be induced to reconsider his determination, *in case Mr. Davault really breaks down at Whonghien,* he and Mr. Pruitt could go back to their old plan of going to Whonghien. I only learned a few days ago *why* they did not go there, an intimation that they would not be welcome to one to whom they had generously resigned their claim on the house there!!

I am writing this without consulting anyone. It seems right to mention these facts to you. I fear Mr. Halcomb might be annoyed & would disapprove if he knew of my writing. But I don't feel like keeping still when the strongest man we have seems about to leave us. I have an abiding faith that he will come out into a clearer light than ever before. I believe his feet will get upon a foundation that nothing can shake. Meanwhile I deprecate haste. We sorely need here his good judgment, energy & common sense. It has occurred to me that a telegram to wait followed by a kind brotherly letter from you might yet save him to the work here by giving him time to settle into firm faith. I say this not unmindful of the fact which he insists upon that he has been growing more unsettled for years. It looks to me like a crisis after which, old foundations being unsettled, he will come back to a faith never to be shaken. I give this, of course, only as my personal opinion. I know that his mind is made up that he ought to go & I know that Dr. Yates fully agrees with him. That his heart is still fully in the missionary work is proved conclusively by the fact that he was negotiating for a house in Pingtu & was making his arrangements to go out this fall & spend the winter there. He was full of plans of work & usefulness, but Dr. Yates' advice, coinciding with his own judgment, decided him to offer his resignation. Mrs. Crawford & I did all we could in protest to keep the letter back.

Please regard this letter as *strictly* confidential. Mr. Davault is here for his health—the second time in the last two months. He has clearly assumed responsibilities in Whonghien beyond & above his strengths & his preparation. He has not been here two years & has assumed heavy responsibilities. No wonder he has sunk under them. He gets better as soon as he throws them off & comes away, but Mrs. Davault insists that *Whonghien* is to blame, that lack of society is the trouble & C. & C. We think, poor fellow, that it is consumption & of course the disease is aggravated by his depressing surroundings and heavy responsibilities.

Begging you will regard my communication as meant for your eyes alone, I am, with Christian love,

Your coworker for the Chinese,
L. Moon.

Private & Confidential

Tungchow, Aug. 7, 1886
Rev. Dr. H. A. Tupper:—
My dear Brother,

At a recent meeting of the Tungchow mission, we laid some plans for pushing our work into the interior, a thing upon which our hearts are much set. What we want first is that you send us two married couples & two single ladies for P'ingtu. Meantime, we who are on the field will try to prepare that region for a settled station. For preparatory work, I take P'ingtu as my special province. Mr. Pruitt also works out there & Mr. Halcomb has done not a little work there for some years past. Mrs. Crawford chose as her field for pioneer work, Laichowfu. This city is 100 *li* or one day's journey, this side of P'ingtu. It is on the great road leading out west & is two days' journey beyond Whonghien. After we get missionaries settled at P'ingtu we want a station opened at Laichowfu. We still plan for a third station, the place not yet selected. Our idea is for the older missionaries who are acclimated & can "rough it" to help start the new stations by doing the preliminary work. Messrs. Halcomb & Pruitt have worked in the Laichowfu region for some years on their spring & fall tours. My idea is that for interior work we should develop what is called "woman's work for woman." That is, I favor the appointment of two unmarried ladies to each interior station as it is opened. The field for woman's work is simply boundless. If the Board should decide to go largely into the plan of sending ladies out, my long experience & observation suggests that we plan to make them comfortable & happy. They should have a comfortable home provided for them, two living together. This would be no more expensive than a home for a married couple. I think it should be understood that they be not only allowed, but urged, to come to the coast every summer for recuperation. My plan would be that they come, at their own expense, to Tungchow where they would have sea bathing & where their rasped nerves would have some "surcease" of the trial of being reviled every time they set foot out of doors. People at home don't understand what a dreadful trial that grows to be & how good it is to get away from that burden awhile. My house here, with the rooms Mr. Halcomb put in order & alas! never occupied, owing to Mrs. Halcomb's death, would accommodate, say three ladies besides myself for the summer. At other times, we would go to the interior. I wish to keep my home here as a refuge & place of rest for myself & others in case of sickness & in summer. I am willing to "rough it" nine or ten months if I can come to a comfortable home for recuperation in summer. Now, if you send us young ladies, I propose to take them into my heart & hold to them the place of a mother. If older, more mature ladies, I wish to do for them a sister's part. I have opposed ladies coming out because I know some people regarded it as a burden to be asked to take ladies into their family or to help them get started. My idea would be that my long experience & the fact that I know just how a woman feels coming out here alone, would enable me to give effectual help & in the beginning to make a happy home for those who come. Miss Roberts said she had a "happy home" with me & I should like to do the same for others.

If you keep up with the Southern Meth. mission, you will see that they are pushing woman's work. Dr. Allen askt for ten ladies at one time. He wants young ladies for indoor work & mature women for outside work. I don't care about the age, but I see a vast field for the steady development of woman's work. Among missionaries for the interior, it seems to me exceedingly desirable that there should be a doctor. One doctor, settled at some central point, could attend to the health of at least three stations, I should think. By the new rules, I see that doctors' bills are no longer allowed. If the Board would send out a doctor, of course the missionaries could still pay him just as they would have to pay the doctor in any other mission. A doctor in a new place conciliates prejudice enormously. If he would sell his medicine to the natives & even charge rich patients for services, no possible harm could come.

We want to be very economical in carrying out all plans for expansion. Our notion would be to rent & fit up good native houses & build *no foreign chapels*. These only create prejudice & opposition in our part of the country. The early plan of the "church in the house" until the natives can build their own churches, seems best for this region.

I wrote you confidentially how deeply Mrs. Crawford & I regretted what seemed undue haste in our brother Halcomb in offering his resignation. I have never wavered in my belief that he would come out into a bright faith & that he would get his feet upon a rock that would be immovable. I am more convinced of that than ever after a month's daily study with him. He is our strongest man, energetic, active, aggressive. His departure would be a heavy loss. I believe his heart is deeply interested in the mission work & that a grand field is ready for him among the educated & official class. It was a member of that class that *offered* him a house in P'ingtu. Mr. Halcomb's scientific attainments give him a position in Chinese eyes which would be simply invaluable in new stations. I should intensely regret it if his letter of resignation should be acted upon & accepted. It seems to me it would be a heavy loss to the mission. Of course, if the views he exprest in that letter were settled, none of us would wish him to stay. He could do no good. But, with time he will work clear of most of these doubts & difficulties & we would keep a most valuable man on the field.

Mr. Pruitt is a growing man, a very fine preacher, a man of good judgment & of a very gentle & winning spirit. Mr. Davault is better, but his health will be cause of anxiety. He is still here & will be for some time.

Please consider all this as strictly confidential. I would not even *hint* to folks here some of the things I have written.

Yrs. with X^n affection,

L. Moon.

Whonghien, Jan. 1, 1887
Rev. Dr. H. A. Tupper:—
My dear Brother,

I found your letter of Oct. 28 awaiting me on my return from P'ingtu last week. We deplore with you the loss of our brother Halcomb from the mission work. He is a man of high & noble purposes & of a deeply religious nature. It is the very depth & intensity of his religious earnestness that has led him into doubts. I have never wavered in my conviction that he would settle down into a firm faith that nothing can shake.

I write now to request you to make application to the Board in my name for leave to return to America. I do not think it right or wise, in general, for a missionary to remain abroad more than ten years. It will be ten years next Oct. since I left Albemarle *en route* for China, ten years next Dec. since I arrived in Tungchow. During that time, I have lived alone, & since Mrs. Holmes' departure have worked alone. I begin to feel the effect of the long continued strain, upon my energy & upon my spirits. The next step might be to fall into ill-health & that I decidedly wish to avoid, with two examples before me as Miss Whilden & Mrs. Holmes. I write about the matter thus early because I would like to receive an answer before we make up our estimates in July.

I am spending part of the winter in Whonghien. The doctor forbade Mr. Davault's staying here this winter & I offered to exchange houses with him. After Mr. Joiner's attacks of something like paralysis, it seemed better for Mrs. Joiner not to be without a neighbor to call on in case of need. In the spring I want to make some trips in the neighborhood of Tungchow & then go to P'ingtu. The latter seems to me a fine region for work & I hope some day the Board can occupy it as a permanent station.

With kindest regards,

Yours sincerely

L. Moon.

P.S.

I have not signed the rules owing to a scruple about something in the Preamble. It will be necessary for me to have a full & free talk with you on important matters when I see you, &, with your permission, I will defer the question of the rules until that time.

L. M.

P.S. 2nd

Mr. Joiner has just been over to talk about the horse business. If he can continue working as he has been doing this fall, I think it will pay the Board to make some arrangement with him. The case is different from what it is about Tungchow. Here, the work is close at hand & to be had pretty much all the year around. Those of us who lived in Tungchow & kept our own animals, did not wish the Board to pay for them when we could do at most only two or three months' of country work in the spring & fall each. But Mr. Joiner lives in the country, with accessible villages all around, & the case seems to me, upon consideration, to be different.

L. M.

Tungchow,

July 19, 1887

Rev. Dr. H. A. Tupper:—

My dear Brother,

Please thank the Board in my name for the "cordial invitation" to return to America, contained in your letter of June 7th. I realize the inexpediency of any missionary's going home under existing circumstances, if it can be avoided. I have decided to try to hold on until next June (1888) if I find that my health justifies it. I have an intense horror of going home "broken down" to be of no use to myself or anybody else. Keeping such possibility in view & trying to avoid it, I shall try to do the best work I can in the coming year. My throat has troubled me, at intervals, for some years & for a short time last month I lost my voice. If this should again be the case for any length of time, it seems to me it would be better to return to America earlier than the time above indicated, as, once there, I should be no expense to the Board.

I have felt very sorry for all your trouble & anxiety about the late debt upon the Board & rejoiced heartily that you were able to make so gratifying a report to the Convention. We do so long for some new missionaries, but realize the fact that the Board can only act as the churches provide the means. I am very especially anxious that the work at P'ingtu (*Pingdoo*) should be pushed. Brethren Halcomb, Pruitt & Mrs. Pruitt in her short missionary life, did no little work there. I have sacrificed more in health & in comfort for that region than for any other. I believe that a good foundation has been laid for a permanent station. I do hope the Board will keep the request of our mission to open a station there as one of the possibilities of a not very remote future. I always leave P'ingtu with regret & go back to it with joy. The affectionate kindness of the people awakens a grateful affection for them in my own heart. The opportunities for work are simply boundless. The children would beg me to go to their homes as if it were a great favor. Going out to make a visit by invitation, I have had to refuse invitation after invitation as I would pass along the street. I made about eighty visits in two months & might have made many more but for lack of time & strength. When not visiting, girls were constantly at my house learning. I suppose I taught some fifty or sixty. These, in turn, frequently teach others, their older sisters at home, or their younger brothers & sisters. I could have spent my time pleasantly & profitably in simply teaching those bright, affectionate girls, but I had to remember that the work among the women was of chief importance.

Perhaps you will accuse me of having P'ingtu "on the brain." I certainly have it on my heart. Please do not put this personal letter in the *Journal*.

With very cordial regards,
Yours sincerely,
L. Moon.

Private

Chinkiang
Aug. 23, 1888
Rev. Dr. H. A. Tupper:—
My dear Brother,

I came here in July expecting to remain a few days, at most a week, & I have allowed myself to remain until this time, with a purpose to stay a month longer. I think the Board will not object when I have stated the reason for my stay. As you know, Mr. Bryan has been alone here, with a heavy burden of work & responsibility. All this he has borne with strength, courage & success. So far as the work among the men is concerned, it has gone on satisfactorily. But the work for women has not even made a beginning, or a beginning so feeble as to amount to nothing. The trouble has been just this: missionary ladies of all denominations (married) have held aloof from the work, devoting themselves to the care of their families & to housekeeping. Mr. Bryan naturally & rightly desires better things for his wife. Unfortunately, Mrs. Hunnex fell into the ways of the place & Mr. Hunnex felt bound to uphold her. He therefore discouraged Mrs. Bryan from attempting to learn the Chinese characters. Spite of all this & other drawbacks, Mrs. Bryan wishes to work so far as her health & strength permit, but she is timid & inexperienced. She needs to be shown how to get hold of work, as well as how to do it. I should have felt very helpless, at first, without the assistance of experienced missionaries, & I know from experience the difficulties in the way of a beginner. Mr. Bryan says that Mrs. Hunnex is of this disposition that she will do whatever she sees Mrs. Bryan do. He thought that if I could aid in getting work started here among the women that I would accomplish more for the general cause of Baptist missions than by going back sooner to my own field, P'ingtu. I think there is a fine field here for woman's work & wish that there were ladies here who could give their whole time to it. I have made some visits with Mrs. Bryan & some alone, have gone into the native city once with Mr. Bryan & we plan to go repeatedly. I have also been visiting the villages near here & I shall continue to do so. I find the people polite & friendly. I have gone a good deal to the chapel, but the woman do not come there, as yet, in numbers though Mr. Bryan thinks that there is an increase in the attendance of woman on Sunday.

I hope the Board will not disapprove of my stay here. In addition to the reasons given above, I had the personal one of need of mental change. I have worked so hard at P'ingtu & have been so much alone there, that I was mentally jaded. I thought it would not be wrong to remain in bright & pleasant society, if I could, at the same, do a good work as a missionary. I believe that my stay here has been blessed of God. I am exceedingly anxious to hear of reinforcements for Shantung. The people of *Säling* (P'ingtu village) are urgent to have me live among them. They say that they must *have* a teacher that many of them are determined to be Christians, & that no amount of obloquy can keep them back. I am willing to remain a reasonable time in P'ingtu, but I need the change home very seriously, & I think I ought to be relieved. I am trying now to get strength of body & soul to plunge again into that burial alive, but I ought to have permanent relief. We have to fight heathenism on one hand & the tremendous prestige of Presbyterian overwhelming numbers. We ought to have men & women in something like the numbers of the Presbyterians & the Eng. Baptists, & I confidently believe that we would have hundreds, yea thousands, of inquirers & converts. I think I know whereof I speak for I have lived right down among the people & I *know* they can be won by loving self-sacrifice on the part of missionaries—but we must have the missionaries.

I write now partly on a matter of business. I have in the Hong Kong & Shanghai Banking Corporation, a deposit that will amount to about Tls. 1,000 (one thousand) next March. It has occurred to me that the Board might be willing to borrow it of me at 6 pr. cent. I should probably leave it in their hands for many years, using only the interest annually. My present Deposit Receipt expires March 12th, 1889. I should wish to hear from you with regard to the matter before the close of this year. Being at P'ingtu, I shall require time to make necessary arrangements. I sometimes get "snowed up" & cut-off from postal communication.

Hoping to hear of reinforcements for Shantung & especially for P'ingtu, I am, with cordial regards,

Yours sincerely,

L. Moon.

Chinkiang,
Aug. 27, 1888
Rev. Dr. H. A. Tupper:—
My dear Brother,

Thanks for your prompt reply to my letter of May 24th & also for the hope you hold out of a "woman-reinforcement." How I wish you could send out two women this fall for P'ingtu! Is that one of the possibilities? I am anxious that they should come & make a beginning before I leave for America. I should like to go with them to P'ingtu & introduce them to my numerous friends there. This would be a great help to them after I should be gone. The Chinese would accept them readily as my successors even though they could do no work at first.

I am very glad of your suggestion to the Executive Committee & take this as permission to write directly to them & urge the work. I should be most heartily glad of ten women for the P'ingtu region. Nobody who has not seen can imagine the wide field opened there for woman's work. I would I had a thousand lives that I might give them to the women of China! As it is, I can only beg that other women & many of them be sent. Above all, we need mature women. The Chinese have a high respect for such, but, for many reasons, I think young women had best not be sent. It would not be proper, in Chinese eyes, for young women to go out in the independent way necessary in doing rough country work in the interior. Besides, it seems to me too hard on the young ladies themselves. Of course, there may be exceptional cases.

I am very desirous to go home next year; I think my health requires it. Still, I am not willing to go until P'ingtu is provided for. When once that is done, I can go home happy & with a clear conscience. But I *cannot* leave those eager people without the certainty that others will carry on the work. Of course, if we don't carry on the work, another mission will step in & reap the fruits of work already done. That is one strong reason for holding my post until new workers come. We ought to have a very strong force at P'ingtu & then push on to other places. If only our people would wake up! I am here trying to give a little push to woman's work, at Mr. Bryan's very urgent request. He has made me many tempting offers to work here permanently & Dr. Yates also wished me to come, but I do not see my way to do more than give a little temporary help. I have visited some villages & also been into the native city. Mr. Bryan thinks the attendance of women has increased at chapel on Sundays. There were about twenty yesterday at Sunday School & preaching in the morning & a few in the afternoon. The service in the afternoon consisted of singing & addresses by two of the brethren. Mr. Bryan knows how to put his members to work. The prospect here seems to me very bright & encouraging & Mr. Bryan is most emphatically "the right man in the right place."

I wrote you fully, a few days ago, my reasons for remaining here longer than I had intended. I hope the Board will approve. In addition to the fact that I can work here as readily as in Shantung, I felt the need of change. I am very happy here & the sunshine will go with me, in memory, when I plunge again into the hard life of the interior. Thanks for your cheering words.

Sincerely yours,

L. Moon.

Tungchow,
Oct. 5, 1888
My dear Dr. Tupper,

I wrote you from Chinkiang offering to lend the Board about one thousand dollars. The amount exactly, at present, in Tls. is 953.93. This is on fixed deposit in Shanghai & will amount to something over one thousand dollars when payable March 23, 1889. I write now to make a slight change in my offer. I propose to lend the money one year to the Board, free of interest, provided it is used to send two woman for work in Pingtu, the said missionaries to be sent just as soon as possible. I wish to leave the money in the Board's hands for several years,—after the first year drawing interest annually at six *per cent*. In case of my death, I should wish the money, principal & interest, paid to my natural heirs.

Please let me know immediately the decision of the Board, as owing to my being in Pingtu, there will be delay at this end of the line in my receiving your reply. If my proposition is accepted, I will turn over the money to the Mission Treasurer, Rev. C. W. Pruitt, on March 23rd 1889.

There is sore need of help in Pingtu. Two men reached here on Sunday from Sahling, (in Pingtu) the village of which I have previously written. The women & girls interested in the gospel got impatient of my long delay & these men set out to seek me, hoping to meet me on the way & return with me. As they did not meet me, they came on here. They are to go back with me next week to Pingtu, by way of Shangtswang. The little flock at *Shangtswang* has been sorely afflicted. Several of them have had cholera, & two women & one child succumbed to the disease. I am going out with the double purpose of trying to comfort them in their afflictions & of consulting with them as to what can best be done for the prosperity of the church. My membership is there. Now that Mr. Pruitt has given up the pastorate there, the direction of affairs falls to me. I shall be virtually the pastor. In any case the responsibility would be great, but now it is doubly so owing to the discouragement of the members & to the difficulty which led to Mr. Pruitt's withdrawal. I am hopeful, however, with God's blessing, of rallying the members to work for our Lord. There are some good & faithful ones there. I have several plans in mind for them, the details of which it is not necessary to state. In addition to the interests of *Shangtswang*, there is the responsibility of pushing the growing and very hopeful work in Pingtu city. Several women there are under regular instruction. Besides this, there is the village *Sahling*, where thirty persons meet on the Sabbath for worship. Mrs. Crawford & I will visit them soon & hope Mr. Pruitt will go out later. I shall spend a month or longer at the village as soon as possible. I think it would be a capital centre from which to work the neighboring villages. I hear that persons in several villages are interested. To push this work we *must* have *many* women as soon as possible. Please send two immediately & two more as soon as possible. I believe we should have large results in the near future if we only had the workers. The responsibility of the Pingtu region falls chiefly on me as I am the only one who can stay there for any length of time. Others go for a month or six weeks & must come back to duties at Tungchow & Whanghien. You see that I need co-workers as soon as they can be sent. I ought to be relieved so as to go home next year. I should wish to go to America in October of next year at the latest, if four women could be sent out in the spring. My house here would be their home till they get into work, but please appoint them for *Pingtu*, not *Tungchow*.

I have much at heart the interests of the work in Chinkiang. Two women are needed there immediately. Two should be sent also for Yangchow. Our well-beloved brother Bryan has done grandly, but he should be heavily reinforced. The odds of heathenism & pedobaptism make a hard fight for Baptists everywhere. We ought to have a line of stations from Shanghai, Soochow, Chinkiang &c. running up and connecting with us here. Then we could help each other & present an imposing front to Pedobaptists, as well as gain *prestige* among the heathen by numbers. As it is, we are swamped—ground between two millstones. These things ought not so to be.

On last Sunday, Mr. Pruitt had the happiness to baptize his wife. A young girl of seventeen, one of my former pupils, was also baptized. Mr. Pruitt has gone South for a change. He was run down in health & greatly needed a change. He will visit Shanghai, Soochow & Chinkiang. He will be of untold help to our comparatively new missionaries in those places (Shanghai & Chinkiang.) They will help him by companionship & talk about the home land. Mr. Pruitt feels keenly his loneliness here as the only young man in the Mission. He took his Chinese clothes along & proposes to spend part of his outing in helping Mr. Bryan open Yangchow, that grand old city, with its half a million inhabitants. Only the Inland Mission is working there now. They are mostly Baptist. We ought to occupy Yangchow immediately. Presbyterians are rushing to occupy cities on the Grand Canal going North from Chinkiang. When once they have occupied a city, they profess to think it discourteous for us to go in!! On the South, towards Soochow, the Methodists are occupying, or preparing to occupy, the chief cities. Yangchow is famous for old associations & bids fair, in the near future, to be of greatly enhanced importance. It is a very famous city in Chinese history. There is much wealth there & there are many handsome shops.

I shall wait longingly the promise of reinforcements in the near future. The Chinese are delighted at the promise I have held out that two women will be sent for Pingtu. They will be lovingly welcomed as religious teachers by many who are just emerging from heathenism. It is not as of old. The heathen are seeking us—begging, almost imploring to be taught. And we are so weak—weak in numbers—none of us strong in health—& the work presses. We overdo our strength. If we are not reinforced heavily—disaster will follow. Some of us may break down or die. Others will go in & reap the fruit of our labors in the past. But I hope better things though I thus speak.

With xn love,

Yrs.,

L. Moon.

Tungchow,

Nov. 6, 1888

My dear Dr. Tupper,

I write to urge you most earnestly that *four* woman be sent out next year to join me in work. As you know, many more than that are needed in the Pingtu region. I should be content with two to begin with out there, & the promise of eight more. Just now, I urge that two be sent immediately for Pingtu & two to work in the Tungchow region. The work is opening up admirably, but I can not do it alone. The hard pioneer work is done. What is needed now is women to do patient teaching, living out in the villages most of the time. This involves physical hardships & privations. Therefore, *strong* women are needed—vigorous, healthy women. And they must not be young. The Chinese profoundly respect women of middle age or elderly women, but young women would meet with unpleasant things & they ought not to do country work. If we had schools, it would be all right to send young women to work in them.

I think you know I would not ask ladies to come here if I did not think the time & occasion ripe for their work. Years ago I disapproved of women coming to Tungchow to work because the conditions of life here were too hard & the work accessible too little & too difficult, it seemed to me, to justify the sacrifice. Now, the way is open & I urge that many women be sent & sent as promptly as possible.

I trust also that Mr. Bryan's plea for lady workers will meet a prompt response. There is a grand field for woman's work in Chinkiang.

I have been spending three weeks in a region about thirteen miles from here. I could spend three months there profitably, but cannot spare the time. A vast field Mrs. Holmes & I used to work together has been untouched for years. Alas! alas! I could wish myself *five* women instead of but one.

Mrs. Crawford & I go out to Pingtu this week. Mr. Pruitt will probably go next week.

With Christian love,

Yrs.,

L. Moon.

Pingtu, Jan. 8, 1889

Rev. Dr. H. A. Tupper:

My dear Brother,

Please accept my hearty thanks for your kind letter of Oct. 24. My annual report which was already on its way to Tungchow before your letter came & which I asked Mr. Pruitt to forward you, will serve in part as a reply to your suggestion that I return immediately to America. At the present juncture of affairs, it seems to me absolutely necessary that I remain at my post. The work here needs me. I look eagerly for the coming of others to whom I may hand over the responsibility of the work. When that shall have been done with a clear conscience & a joyful spirit, I can turn my face homewards, but not till then unless my health should really break down. That a change is imperatively needed, I am fully aware, but the circumstances are such that I must run even a serious risk rather than leave. We *must* have two women & at least one family for Pingtu as soon as possible. We ought, in the course of time, to have not less than three families here & all the single women you can send. I consent to leave, however, as soon as two women are here with sufficient knowledge of the language to take over the work among the women & children. While I do not a little for the men & boys, I don't feel bound to stay on their account. Still, I must add that the work is suffering & will continue to suffer in that department for want of a man living on the spot.

I fear you over-rate my ability to arouse S.B. women. Nevertheless, I will gladly do what I can to that end. What I hope to see is a band of ardent, enthusiastic, experienced Christian women occupying a line of stations extending from Pingtu on the north, & from Chinkiang on the south, making a succession of stations uniting the two. That seems to me a purpose worthy of the energies of Southern Baptist women. It is the goal to which I would wish to point their aspirations, if the Board approve. To succeed in this, a mighty wave of enthusiasm for Woman's Work for Woman must be stirred. How shall we do it?

With regard to the women who should come, I would emphasize the word "experienced." The responsibilities are so heavy & the physical hardships are so many that they should not be undertaken by young women. There is so much work to be done, too, that ought to be done by men. A young woman could not do such work & retain the respect of Chinese men.

Allow me to say that the speediest way of affording me rest in accordance with the kind purport of your letter is at once to hurry forward reinforcements to the front. Two women for Pingtu immediately!

I returned yesterday from a visit to *Saling*. During the ten days I was there, I taught women & girls in a small inner room, while the men & boys learned as best they could in the outer room which is used as a chapel. None of these people have been admitted to church privileges, yet they had worship every night but one while I was there, with three services on Sunday. It was enough to make one's heart ache to see these sheep without a shepherd. It was touching to hear their prayers that God would move the hearts of pastors in American Baptist churches that they might be willing to come & teach them, or to send men to teach them. The movement in that region is growing, but a man is needed to push it. Several letters have been placed in my hands to be forwarded the Board asking for a pastor. My decided opinion (pardon me for volunteering it) is that if ministers cannot be found to come, earnest hearted laymen would do invaluable work. Such a man could do everything except administer the ordinances. The China Inland Mission is full of laymen some of whom give their wealth as well as themselves.

I shall send the letters to Mr. Pruitt asking him to endorse the request and forward the letter to you. After this move was on foot among the Chinese—indeed just in the midst of it—I had a letter from Mr. Pruitt in which he said it was absolutely necessary that we should have men here at Pingtu. He saw the difficulties of the situation just as the Chinese were feeling the pressing need.

Hoping to hear soon of two women for Pingtu,

Yours sincerely,

L. Moon.

Tungchow, March 23, 1889
Rev. Dr. H. A. Tupper:
My dear Brother,

As I have much at heart the prosperity of our mission work in China, I trust you will pardon the expression of the opinion on two points. I. The need of physicians. There should be one (married) for Pingtu immediately. The nearest doctor is at *Wei hien,* a distance of sixty miles. He is a Presbyterian. *We lose immensely in prestige* in Chinese eyes by being so very dependent on another denomination. For years our mission has helped to sustain a Presbyterian doctor here in Tungchow. This, of course, is to help build up their mission at our expense. Not only that. In case of protracted sickness, much time is lost. In case of married couples, I have known several instances in which one was drawn off for months & the station closed while the other was seeking medical attendance here or elsewhere. With a doctor at the station, many, many months of work might be saved.

With regard to Pingtu, I plead for a physician as a matter of humanity. Suppose, for instance, a man with a family should go to Pingtu to live. His wife & little ones ought not to be allowed to run the risk of no medical help nearer than 60 miles.

II. There should be more than one man at Soochow. A mission force of less than four men at one station seems a great mistake. In Soochow, the Methodists have a *very exceptionally strong mission.* They have Dr. Park, with a splendid hospital for men. They have native graduates in medicine mission employ. They have Dr. Mildred Phillip, with hospital recently opened, for women. They have boarding schools for boys & for girls. There are two Presbyterian missions in Soochow, Northern & Southern. Practically, these three missions are one as against Baptists. They have also single women for work in hospital, schools & visiting. Now, send one Baptist man & wife there & he is practically crushed beforehand. All the *prestige* of years & of numbers is on the Pedobaptist side. It is because I know & have known for years by hard experience what it is to fight against heaviest odds, not only of heathenism but of Pedobaptism, that I raise my earnest protest against a similar state of things in Soochow. Our brother Tatum ought to have three men to go with him to Soochow to open the station & as many single women as the mission then formed should desire.

It is impossible to express too strongly the absolute certainty of failure if one man goes alone with such heavy odds against him. Remember how pathetically our well-beloved brother Bryan pleaded for helpers. Yet he began in Chinkiang on tolerably even terms as to time & he had the *prestige* of locality, a handsome church building & c. Yet he felt that the odds were against him in having there so many Pedobaptists.

Trusting you will excuse this expression of opinion for the sake of the motive which prompts it,

Yrs. sincerely,

L. Moon.

From Miss Lottie Moon
Reaping

PINGTU, October 17, 1889

Rev. Dr. H. A. Tupper:

My dear Brother—You will be pleased to know that a church has been organized at Saling, a village about ten miles from Pingtu city. I was disappointed that more were not ready for baptism. A number of women are interested; some of them, I hope, are converted. What is very remarkable, is the way the truth has seized hold of the young women. Not only in families where the men are interested, but in families where there is bitter opposition and even persecution, young women are eagerly studying Christian books. One very fine young woman is steadfast, though every member of her family opposes except a younger sister, who was once interested, but has fallen away. In another family the young daughter holds out against the bitter opposition of both her mother and grand-mother. In connection with the baptism of one young woman there was a wonderful manifestation of God's over-ruling providence. She had lately been married into a heathen family and her mother-in-law was full of suspicions. She came, however, to see for herself. On the day of the baptism, perhaps an hour and a half before it was to take place, this heathen mother-in-law came to me and said, "Have you examined my daughter-in-law?" I said that I did not know that she wished to be examined. "Yes," she said, "she is so eager and anxious about it that I have had to do her work for her." Here the young woman appeared and confirmed her mother-in-law's statement of her wish to be baptized. After her baptism, her mother-in-law was all kindness, remaining at home to receive her when she should return from the baptismal waters. The young woman's father spoke of it as a case in which faith had removed a mountain. It had been simply inconceivable that this woman should consent to her daughter-in-law's baptism, yet, of her own accord, she preferred the request for her. Another providential circumstance was the absence of the young husband who would have opposed. Another young woman who was baptized had evidently gone through much mental suffering. She is to be married in a short time into a heathen family, the time of marriage having been hurried up expressly to prevent her receiving Christian instruction. She feels she may be going to great persecution and oppression on account of her faith. She resolved to follow her Lord in baptism, cost what it might. It was a joy to see her radiant face after the ordinance. While the little church was being organized she sat beside me. Impulsively she threw her arms around me and said, in whispered words, how could she ever thank me aright for having come to tell her the good news of salvation. Her whole soul overflowed with joy. In the evening, at prayers, I asked her to lead, and I never heard such a prayer from Chinese lips—rarely from any lips. She seemed in the very presence of God, talking with him face to face, with filial reverence pouring forth her deep thankfulness, pleading to be kept from sin, imploring with intense anxiety the conversion of her heathen neighbors and friends, and asking God's blessing upon the missionaries. I expect her to be a great power in the large village to which she goes. Already one village is opened by the marriage of the young woman whose mother-in-law asked baptism for her. We made a call there on the day of our return to the city and were received with most eager cordiality. The mother-in-law is herself interested now, and I am to go back and spend several days. I look for her conversion and that she will become a Christian leader in her village. She is a fine, frank woman, strong, decided and energetic. Once converted, she would be a power for good. One of the beautiful things about this movement, is the eagerness with which those who are interested tell the good news far and wide. It is like a protracted meeting where Christians are deeply stirred for the conversion of their friends and relatives. One very interesting case is that of an old man of eighty, a learned teacher, for whom his daughter and son are anxious. He had not spoken to this daughter for twenty years, but now he asks her earnest questions about the way of salvation. As yet he has seen no missionary, but I am to make a visit to his village, and expect to talk with him. It is a somewhat difficult case. Some forty years or more ago the old man was guilty of the fearful sin of putting away his wife for no cause and bringing in another woman whom he had enticed away from her husband. The wronged wife lived on to old age in the same court-yard with her supplanter, and because her daughter refused to recognize the interloper as her mother, the father refused all communications with her. Now, in their old age, these two guilty people feel that they have sinned. The woman is afflicted with a loathsome disease, which she says is God's judgment on her. The old man is eagerly asking what he must do to be saved.

The movement is spreading in all directions. New inquirers are constantly being brought in. It was feared that the baptism would shock Chinese prejudice and that there would be a falling off of interest. Instead, four new inquirers of excellent character presented themselves that very day. One of the men baptized told me that he had sat up half the night after his baptism instructing two of these new inquirers. As to the men already baptized, and the women, too, they have had a basis of moral training for years in the "Venerable Heaven Sect." The former leader of that sect at Saling preached at his own charges for twenty years and built up a following of about forty men and women. They propagated their doctrine secretly, being afraid of persecution, and a common saying among them is, the more one is persecuted the stronger he becomes. One young woman of whom I had great hopes has proved an exception, however, to this rule. Married into a heathen family, at first she was firm, but, on the death of her father-in-law, wearying of the struggle, she fell into idolatry. When the two young women, her close friends and companions, were baptized, she was deeply stirred. As we returned from the water, she walked with me, and I spoke some solemn words about the great sin into which she had fallen. Later, she shut herself in a room alone, threw herself on a "kong," and wept bitterly.

The leader of whom I spoke above is a most admirable character, humble, godly, sincere. Wherever he goes in the prosecution of his business, he never fails to speak a word in season. He gives whole days to instructing inquirers, entertaining them often at his own expense. His open, free-handed hospitality has often put me to shame. It seems to me that all these years God has been leading him. Now, from a most joyful Christian experience, he speaks to his neighbors and friends of this great salvation. I have never seen brighter evidences of sound conversion than in the case of this man and of the young woman to whose prayer I alluded above.

On the morning after the baptisms, the second brother of this man was asked to lead in prayer. I was touched by one part of his prayer. He said, "The Chinese are as sheep without a shepherd," and he prayed the Holy Spirit to move upon the hearts of pastors in America to come and take the oversight of this flock.

If there were men on the spot to push the movement, I believe we should have such wide-spread ingatherings as the English Baptists have had and are constantly having. They baptized one hundred and twenty this fall, and have besides four hundred learners.

Yours sincerely,
L. Moon.
Published in the January 1890 *Foreign Mission Journal.*

From Miss Lottie Moon

Tungchow, July 1, 1890
Rev. Dr. H. A. Tupper:

My Dear Brother—Miss Barton and I returned last week from Pingtu, where we had been spending two months with Miss Knight. We left the latter well and happy in her cozy Chinese home, fitted up at her own expense. Miss Knight thinks she will be ready this autumn to take over the work among the women in the Pingtu region. This will leave me free to introduce Miss Barton in my field near Tungchow, which she has kindly consented to take. Her gifts of mind and heart will make her a valuable worker. In the two months recently spent in Pingtu, she greatly endeared herself both to Christians and heathen. Her knowledge of medicine opened a wide door for her in heathen homes.

On arrival at Whanghien, we found the other members of the mission awaiting us, according to previous appointment. Several committees were instructed to write to the Board with regard to a speedy increase of our force. You will hear from us on the subject in due time. *Apropos* of a request from the mission for two single women to work the region east and southeast of Tungchow, I may be permitted to quote some remarks of Rev. J. Hudson Taylor on "Woman's Work," at the recent Missionary Conference in Shanghai. He said: "This Conference should make clear the need of women. The results of their work are indeed a surprise. Are not the parts of China which are closed to us open to women? There is less fear of women as political agents. They are allowed to go where male missionaries cannot enter. Women often have invitations to go and stay as guests. The influence of these visits prepares the way for the male missionaries who may follow. In some place where male missionaries are coldly received, women can get a footing. This occurred in Lanchoufu, the capital of Kansuh, where an unmarried women got a house inside the city, when the male missionary had to stay outside the walls. This gradually opened the way for a married missionary. We have not yet learned how God can use single ladies in opening China."

I am happy to say that persecution at Säling has measurably subsided. The brethren have been allowed to return to their homes and to follow their usual avocations unmolested. Young women belonging to heathen families, who have accepted Christ, are still sorely ill-treated in their own homes. They bear it nobly, bravely, uncomplainingly. The brethren are enthusiastic and hopeful. The new interest reported last year at *Li tz Yuen* is growing healthfully. This work was begun, and has been pushed almost exclusively by the native brethren. Miss Knight, Miss Barton and I were asked recently to visit the village and teach the women how to keep the "Rest Day." I regard the work there as very promising.

Yours sincerely,

L. Moon

Published in the October 1890 *Foreign Mission Journal.*

Scottsville,

Oct. 10, 1891

Rev. Dr. H. A. Tupper:

My dear Brother,

Thanks for your note of welcome. It is indeed good to be "home again." I am thoroughly enjoying my rest. Its calm was slightly disturbed by a request from Baltimore to attend the Md. Association. I was disposed to go, but only thinking about it made my head hurt. I therefore wrote Mrs. Rowland that I had been so unmerciful to myself in China that I thought it time to call a halt now & take needed rest. I have been often warned by missionaries not to begin work until thoroughly rested lest the home-coming should do more harm than good. My present purpose is to keep quiet all this winter. I don't think my head will ever get well without perfect rest.

I should be glad to give you any information as to Chinese affairs. Mrs. Crawford begged me to urge on the Board the need of additional reinforcements for North China. We sorely need now six more families—two for each station—& two single women for Tungchow. You remember the Mission formally asked for the latter more than a year ago. It might as well be frankly said that only single women can be depended on to do evangelistic work. Except Mrs. League, we have had no married woman to undertake work of that sort since the death of the first Mrs. Pruitt. Mrs. Crawford, of course, is also an exception. Ladies with families cannot, & indeed ought not to do country work. Their work lies immediately around their homes. In North China, the very large majority of the people are in villages. To reach them, one must be away from home a good part of the year. It is manifest, then, that we must have single women to do this work. As I have often said, they should not be young. The nearer forty the better, I think. It is a pleasant fact that the older a single woman grows the more the Chinese reverence her. I have often had them tell me that when I die I shall become a god! So much by way of enforcing our plea for two more ladies for Tungchow.

Also, at Mr. Britton's request, I put in a plea for Soochow. That point ought to have not less than three more families. The Pedobaptist influence there is simply overwhelming. Without a strong mission there, I honestly believe it a waste of a man's life to live there. I was with the Brittons about two weeks in Shanghai & was very much pleased with their quiet good sense & goodness.

Could you give me Mrs. Holmes' address?

My sister joins me in kind regards. She & I are living alone, my brother having moved from Albemarle. I am planning to carry her off with me when I return to China & she approves the plan.

Yrs. sincerely,
L. Moon.

Scottsville,
Feb. 19, 1892
Rev. Dr. H. A. Tupper:
My dear Brother,

As the warm friend of the Board & also of my beloved brother Pruitt, I am deeply troubled at the probability of his not being sent back to China. Without consulting her, I venture to enclose for your & Dr. Bell's perusal a letter rec'd yesterday from Mrs. Pruitt. If Mr. Pruitt should not return to China & to his old post at Hwanghien, it will be the severest blow our much afflicted North China mission has had since Mrs. Bostick's lamented death. Mr. Pruitt has done & can do for the Hwanghien station what no other man has done or can do. He went there when the name of the foreigner was utterly odious to the Chinese. Fearful blunders had been made in the beginning of the station which we feared that twenty years of holy living would not & could not retrieve. Mr. & Mrs. Pruitt went there, however, & set quietly to work. In *five* years, the change made was amazing. I know whereof I speak. I spent a winter in Hwanghien (1885-86) & the place was absolutely closed to all mission effort. I had scarcely a visitor & there was not a house, except among the few Christians, open to me in all that region. Last spring, at Mrs. Pruitt's request, I spent about two weeks helping her in the work around her home. I was never more surprised & delighted in my life. I found that, instead of being hated & despised, we were welcomed heartily into many families & in some there was an eager desire to hear the gospel. Unlike Tungchow, Hwanghien is a rich & prosperous region. I found that Mr. Pruitt was visited by men belonging to leading families. Mr. Pruitt is a scholar by nature & by training. He is the *only* scholar in the North China mission. He is the only man we have whose tastes & habits fit him to do literary work of high value. Some years ago, there was a proposition from the Northern Baptists to our mission & to the Eng. Baptist mission for a joint translation of the New Testament. It was a source of mortification to me that there was not a man in the mission at that time with sufficient scholarship for such a work. Most missionaries content themselves with a sufficient knowledge of the spoken & written language to preach & converse with the immense masses of uncultivated people. Mr. Pruitt, while not neglecting the masses, has fitted himself for work among the rich & highly cultured classes. He is the only man in the mission thus far who has shown ability to win the higher social class. Miss Fields once said, & said truly, that the second decade of a missionary's life is the best. In the first, he only learns how to work. Mr. Pruitt, should he return to China, would have before him the best work of his life. The Chinese think a great deal of manners. I regret to say that some missionaries, from a Chinese standpoint, are simply boors. Mr. Pruitt's Chinese manners are perfect. Cordial, graceful & elegant, they are very winning. Among the gentlemen of our mission, Mr. Pruitt is prime favorite with the native Christians.

Some years ago, I was anxious for Mr. Pruitt to move to P'ingtu. After seeing the work in Hwanghien last spring, I urged upon him & especially upon the Mission that he ought not to leave Hwanghien. No other man could gain in ten years the hold he now has on the Hwanghien community. It was the judgment of the whole mission that Mr. Pruitt should remain at Hwanghien & Mr. League should go to P'ingtu.

It has seemed to me right to state these facts for the information of the Board. I have been intimately acquainted for years with Mr. & Mrs. Pruitt and I *know* that they have always been warm friends of the Board. I know, too, that they are not extremists in anything, but are cautious & moderate in their views.

Now, I know that the easy answer to all this will be to say "let Mr. Pruitt sign the amended Rules & all will be well." I shall write him today & as a friend & sister suggest this course. It is by no means certain that my suggestion will have weight. Then, are we to lose the most promising male missionary that we have in North China? The man who can do for the grand Hwanghien work what no other can, the *only* man who knows how to reach the higher classes & the only one whose scholarship puts him on a level with cultured Chinese. That is to me a very painful thought. To fail to send such a man back to such a work seems to me a very grave responsibility.

The thought has occurred to me that some medium course might be found. The Board regards itself as badly treated. On the other hand, Mr. Pruitt feels aggrieved. He thinks that the penalty inflicted in declining to send him back to China out of all proportion to the offense. Cannot Christian love come in here & triumph over every obstacle? If in politics, arbitration saves from disastrous wars, would it be out of place to avert grievous disaster from our Lord's work in China by privately submitting this matter to the arbitration of three men, one to be chosen by the Board, one by Mr. Pruitt & a third by the two selected? All could be pledged to strict secrecy & the Board & Mr. Pruitt could pledge themselves in advance to abide by the decision of the three arbitrators.

May I ask that this letter be read to the Board, as it is written from a profound sense of duty?

With kind regards,
Yours sincerely,
L. Moon.

Scottsville,
March 21, 1892
Reverend Dr. H. A. Tupper:-
My dear Brother,

A letter from Mr. Pruitt written the day after you saw him gave me the joyful news that all was right between the Board & himself. You have well characterized him as "a noble & lovely man, gentlemen & Christian."

The news from Mr. Bostick is what I have been expecting. As to the question of an "independent missionary," I think his acceptability to the Mission as a body would depend upon what "policy" he should pursue. As Mr. Bostick is the originator of the famous "Articles of Agreement," I don't think he would be likely soon to go into anything unacceptable to others in the Mission. To speak frankly, we missionaries "bore the compass" in our methods so constantly that I shouldn't be astonished, should I live ten years longer—to see bro. Bostick an ardent advocate of schools, native preachers & Bible women!!! This is not saying anything to his disadvantage. It is only saying that we all try all plans & as none of them are perfect, we throw them overboard & try something else. It is like Chinese modes of conveyance. The last used always seems the worst. The *tia chiao* is intolerable until we try the *shentz*, that being unpleasant, we try the *cant*; the later being atrocious we take the sedan chair and then we go back to the *tia chiao* as being after all not so bad.

To return to the question of an independent missionary. We Baptists are so very weak in Shantung & the Presbyterians are so very strong & unscrupulous & aggressive in their dealing with us as a Mission that the loss of *one* Baptist from our force is a very serious matter. The Chinese wouldn't at all understand *why* Mr. Bostick should leave on account of differences with the Board of which they never heard. Mr. Bostick's departure would be only one of many heavy blows the Mission & work have sustained. I think if he stays he would work harmoniously with the Mission. He is active & earnest & feels himself called of God to the work. I should be very sorry indeed to see him lost to the work & I am sure that every member of the Mission would feel in the same way & would rejoice to have him stay as an "independent missionary." This is not to say that we agree with him in all his views. Some of us differ with him radically on important points.

Yrs. sincerely,

L. Moon.

Scottsville,
June 20, 1892
Reverend Dr. H. A. Tupper:
My dear Brother,

Mrs. Memmler of Cartersville, Ga., writes that she has made application to be sent to China & adds that you think her age an insufferable objection. You have always received my suggestions so kindly, even when not adopting them, that I am emboldened, in this present instance, to express my dissent from your view. Mrs. Memmler is a woman of high culture who has always kept habits of study. She has an unusually quick mind. At fifty years of age, she would hold her own in acquiring a foreign language, if pitted against ordinary women of thirty. She will be a power wherever she is & I believe would be a power for good in North China. She has a rare gift for winning children & that is just what we need. I have seen her recently in her own home and therefore speak from personal observations.

Some years ago, the S. Presbyterian Committee allowed a lady to go out whose age was forty-seven. She is acknowledged to be one of the best & most useful missionaries they have. Dr. Nathan Brown of Yokahama (now deceased) spent twenty years in Burmah or Siam before going to his life work in Japan. In the early days in China, the language was much more difficult to acquire than it now is because there were so few helps. Now, with excellent lesson books and lexicons, the language is not much more difficult than any European tongue. In North China especially, the language is easy because the spoken & printed language are the same. While Dr. Yates may have advised that no one be sent over thirty—I think that advice would not hold good with regard to North China where the language has only four tones & where it could be learned both by the eye & ear at the same time. Trusting you will excuse this statement, I remain

Yrs truly,
L. Moon.

Scottsville, Va.,
Feb. 4, 1893
Rev. Dr. H. A. Tupper:
My dear Brother,

I know Dr. Hartwell & have a high regard for him as a X^{ian} brother, but his return means *"war to the knife"* between the Mission of the Board & that of the "Gospel" brethren. The very thought of it makes me heart-sick. It would be a simple waste of one's life to work in China under the painful & sad experiences which I know so well soon after first going to China. For him to go, is to make several people throw away their lives in the effort to build up work on a different line. The man that uses money has it always in his power to draw off the converts & to neutralize the influence of those who don't use money. The use or non-use is a matter of principle. It seems to me that we ought not to throw obstacles in the way of brethren who are conscientious in their method of work. For Dr. Hartwell to go, would mean the re-introduction of the system of paid preachers, schools &c., out of which we have painfully worked.

I enclose the first letter I have ever had from Mr. King which will throw some light on the subject. It was meant only for my eye, but may do good under the circumstances.

My objections are not personal to Dr. Hartwell. I should rejoice to see him go to Central China (say Chinkiang) or to Canton. For him to go to Shantung, would be nothing short of utter ruin to some of the interests already there. Don't you notice what Dr. Taylor says in his last letter about the difficulty of getting Italian churches on a self-supporting basis because of plethora of funds in Pedobaptist hands? He didn't dare to leave a church he mentioned without a pastor because some Pedobaptists would "take them up." Well, alas! alas! our best Chinese X^{ians} could be "taken up" & made helpless when we are only getting them now to walk. I write hastily because I want to send this off immediately. Be assured of my hearty sympathy in all these difficulties & my hearty loyalty to the Board. At the same time, I can't help standing firmly for what I believe to be right principles of mission work & *must* deeply deprecate the utter confusion that a change of mission policy would mean. It would be against the feelings of the majority of our Shantung mission, I think. If Mr. Pruitt has changed, it is since I saw him.

Yrs. sincerely,

L. Moon.

P.S.

I should think well of "recommending that the Board retain position in Shantung province.....re-inforce the work," but *not* ask Dr. Hartwell to return to Shantung. May the Lord direct us out of all this muddle, for only He can!

Yrs. sincerely,

L.M.

Scottsville,

Feb. 6, 1893

Rev. Dr. H. A. Tupper:

My dear Brother,

You have done me the honor to say that in conferences on Shantung, my letters are useful. It is therefore imperative that I should speak with absolute frankness. Had I known that the Board had it in mind to reverse the mission policy that has prevailed in our mission for several years passed, I should not have urged a continuance in Shantung on those lines. I should had said at once: Give up Shantung. In the interest of peace, depart in peace.

Had I known that Mr. Pruitt had changed his views of mission policy, I should never have urged his return to Shantung. Far better that he should go to Chinkiang.

For the Board to re-open the Chefoo station with Dr. Hartwell there, seems to me a violation of the law of Christian love. To do this, would absolutely ruin the work of the Gospel brethren at Tungchow. The only condition on which a new mission policy ought to be inaugurated in Shantung is that of putting a wide distance between the Board's work & that of the other mission. The Board might withdraw to P'ingtu, returning *Shangtswang*, & let Laichowfu be a boundary beyond which we would not go. That is to say, throw them in Laichowfu for good measure & let us keep ourselves rigidly with our faces pointing southward toward the Chinkiang mission coming up to meet us. This, it seems to me, would be a generous division of territory. The latest account of the Swedish brethren is that they were not pleased with *Laiyang* & would not go there. They were negotiating for a house at *Kiao chow*. This precludes our going there, by the Shantung unwritten law of mission comity. *Echowfu*, which we had wished to occupy, has been pre-empted by a heavy Presbyterian force, so we are shut out there. But there are a plenty of places, no fear about that.

I am compelled to say that unless some rigid division of territory be adopted, so as to minimize the harm done to the work of our brethren, it is impossible for me to work in Shantung. I can not waste my life in pulling down God's work that other brethren & sisters whom I know & love, are building up. I cannot be a party to inflicting on Southern Baptist brethren & sisters what I have had to endure for years at the hands of Presbyterians. I will have no share in neutralizing the influence & undermining the work of men & women who, I believe, have been called of God to do His work. Better ten thousand times to hand over the whole work to the Gospel brethren as fast as they are able to take our places. I don't believe in giving up until they *are* able because this would be to hand over the work to the Presbyterians. Pardon me for repeating to you what I said in a letter to Mrs. Crawford last week that, for Southern Baptists, instead of fighting the common foe, to turn their guns on each other, would be madness. Since such is my deliberate opinion, I shall have to ask the Board to transfer me elsewhere, if the fight is resolved upon. I have been in one terrible fight & I know that it would be renewed, probably with added bitterness, for there would be more contestants. Such mission quarrels embitter life, make work unfruitful, extend to the Chinese, & prevent the growth of the missionary in spirituality. How can one love God & commune with Him while he is in a hand-to-hand conflict with Christian brethren? Then there are social alienations that are simply disgraceful. Life, wouldn't be worth living if that old feud is to be revived. The Board has never known, can never know, all the harm it did, all the pain & shame to those who have to be dragged into it. May God avert such a curse from the Shantung work as its renewal! Ten thousand times rather withdraw us all!

You will perhaps have noticed Mr. King's proposition that the Board keep up its present force. That about tallies with what you proposed last summer.

Personally, I find a difficulty in deciding to what point to ask to be transferred. There are Presbyterians & Methodists at Chinkiang & I am *sick to death* of fighting. I don't want to go where there are any but Baptists. I have thought of Quinsan. If my health would stand it, I should not mind living there alone. I have thought of Japan. Would the Board consider a proposition to transfer me to that country? Other denominations have transferred veteran Chinese workers to that country & with good effect. The S. Methodist mission was opened very satisfactorially by Dr. Lambuth who had probably worked in Shanghai twenty-five or thirty years. Mrs. Randolph of the S. Pres. mission was transferred to Japan after ten or more years in China. Dr. Brown, Northern Baptist, was transferred after twenty years of work in Burmah or Siam, I forget which. The fact is, I suspect I should get horribly homesick for Shantung, if exiled to Central China. If I could plunge into a new life in Japan, I should not feel the change half so much. I believe Shantung to be a far better field for mission work than Central China. Those who know the people of both sections say so. Naturally, having my roots already deep in Shantung & especially in P'ingtu, it will be a trial to be plucked up & re-planted. But—a wounded conscience who can bear?

Better the pain of leaving Shantung than to sin against God by injuring my neighbor's work. –

I failed to explain in a former letter how our business matters are transacted independently of having a mission station in Chefoo. In P'ingtu, a merchant buys our personal cheques on Shanghai bank, drawn in favor of Messrs. Sing Tai & Co. of Chefoo. The latter advances the silver on site to the P'ingtu merchant. The P'ingtu merchant lets us have cash or silver as we may need when he buys the cheque. It is a convenience to him, to Sing Tai & Co. & to ourselves. The Mission Treasurer either sends us cheques on Shanghai, or, at the beginning of each quarter, notifies the Bank to place to each missionary's private account what is due.—Our business agent, Mr. Smith, attends to letters, parcels, meeting new missionaries &c., & for this we pay him not out of mission funds, but on private account.

Hoping you will take kindly my frankness,

Yrs. sincerely,

L. Moon.

Scottsville,

Feb. 10, 1893

Rev. Dr. H. A. Tupper:

My dear Brother,

Many thanks for your prompt reply to my letters, relieving my mind of self-conjured spectres.

I have tried throughout to take a broad view of the whole situation. My judgment & my sympathy have been & are with the Board. In a less degree, my sympathy goes out to the Gospel brethren & very especially to Mrs. Crawford. I feel assured that Shantung is one of the best fields for work in China. If, without organic connection, the three missions, our own, the Gospel mission & the Swedish, can work harmoniously, I believe we shall make a forward movement that will rejoice us all. Mrs. Crawford writes of revived interest in the long dormant field east of Tungchow. The native brethren are arousing themselves to work & some converts are desiring baptism. The reports from *P'ingtu* & *Shangtswang* are encouraging. We believe that the work is now in better shape than it has been for years & we confidently expect progress.

My health has so much improved that it seems right to ask the Board to send me back to China next fall. I should like to leave here about the middle of Sept., spend ten days in Chicago, (of course at my own expense,) & sail early in Oct. Would this meet the approbation of the Board? When last the subject of my remaining at Tungchow was mentioned, I suggested that the question be left in abeyance. I should like to lay the two sides of the question before you & to be guided in the matter by the wishes of the Board. In desiring to remain at Tungchow, I have been moved not only by certain personal considerations, one of which was health, but by the fact that I thought I was needed there. In my later years at P'ingtu, I promised myself to atone for neglect of the Tungchow work by going back there. You know we asked for *two* single women for that work besides Miss Barton & myself. Miss Barton's health has been so poor that she can do no work except teach her Sunday school class & study some. She *will* study, though forbidden by the doctor. Mrs. Bostick's health precludes work except the little she can do in S. school & in her own home. Thus a heavy burden falls on Mrs. Crawford. She alone is left for that hard country work & she is no longer young,—she is past sixty. She works westward while my work has been east & southeast of the city,—a field Mrs. Holmes & I worked together for years. I have felt that I ought not to leave that field unless other women could be found to take up the work there. The strong probability is that Miss Barton will be compelled to return to America. That being the case, I should be left as the only representative of the Board at Tungchow. Under such circumstances, it does not seem right for me to stand in the way of the Board's positive wish to withdraw entirely from Tungchow. It has occurred to me that one cause of the difference in my health at Tungchow & P'ingtu may be the different style of living. Miss Knight has perfect health at P'ingtu. She lives in Chinese style by day, but retires at night to a comfortable, well-furnished room in foreign style. I have "roughed it" throughout on Chinese kongs or beds because I did not expect to remain in Pingtu. If I should fit up, say four rooms, in foreign style as I had at Tungchow, live by day with the Chinese on kongs, but retire at sunset to comfortable quarters, I think it very probable I should retain my health. At any rate, in case of sickness, I could be comfortable. If it be the Board's preference that I go to P'ingtu permanently, I am entirely willing. I could not fail to be happy there because I love the people more than any other Chinese. Then Miss Knight is there to whom I am devoted. I should earnestly hope that the Board would reinforce the P'ingtu station, giving us four families & two single women besides Miss Knight & myself. As between Tungchow & P'ingtu, I leave the matter absolutely with the Board & shall be perfectly content whatever may be the decision. I should say that the people of the P'ingtu region seem to me to be more religious naturally than those on the coast & that it is therefore a *better* field, in my opinion, than the other.

I will cheerfully do the "kindly office" you ask.

No one can defend Brother Bostick's course in some matters, though we may try to make excuses. His wife was ill & the Board's letter of limitation reached him two weeks after the time expired. Mrs. Crawford says that for Mrs. B. to travel now means *death*.

With warm thanks for your unvarying kindness,

Yrs. sincerely,

L. Moon.

Scottsville, Va.
Feb. 13, 1893
Rev. Dr. H. A. Tupper:
My dear Brother,

Thanks for your letter including the resolutions. I am interested in whatever concerns Shantung. I am sorry we have lost Mr. League. He was one of our best missionaries. I can not but hope that some way will be found for him to remain on the field. He is too valuable a worker for us to afford to lose & his little wife has made one of the most energetic missionaries we have had. I do not forget that it was due to their unselfish giving up of their sweet home at Hwanghien & removal to P'ingtu that I was enabled to return to America.

Mr. League's resignation is doubtless the last that will be offered. Now we may plan definitely for the future. If it is decided that we retain Hwanghien, two more families should be sent there, one of the men being a physician. The strong, well managed missions all go now on the plan of massing rather than scattering their forces. At one time, the Eng. Baptists had about twenty missionaries at *Tsingchowfu*. This, however, was not a permanent force. They have since settled at *Cheoping* & have tried to effect a lodgment at *Tsinanfu*, the capital of the province. The minimum force of the Presbyterians is at Chefoo where they have three families. At Tungchow, they aim to keep four families & usually there are one or more single women. At *Weihsien*, westward beyond *Laichowfu*, they have a heavy force,—several families, several single women & two or three doctors, male or female, among them.

At P'ingtu, as I mentioned in my last letter, we ought to have three more families & one of the men ought to be a physician. In addition, we should keep four single women at work in that region. Having equipped Hwanghien & P'ingtu properly, we ought to plan to occupy some other city, either *Laichowfu*, to connect us properly with Hwanghien, or some city south of P'ingtu. I met a young man last summer in Reidsville, N. C., who said he wished to do pioneer work & supposing that he would go out under the Board, I suggested to him the opening of *Laichowfu*. He has written recently asking questions about that city & also inquiring as to the advantages of going out under the Board. He said that the matter was not yet settled & that he would "consider well" before going out independently. He is a very fine young man & is taking a partial course at the Seminary, at the same time studying medicine. His knowledge of medicine would make him doubly valuable for opening a new station. He expects to be ready to go in Dec., after the meeting of the N. C. Convention.

Mrs. Crawford & I have been very desirous that the two missions should work practically as one & that the needs of either should be supplemented by the other. If the Board thinks this unadvisable, we could divide the field & keep out of each other's territory, but retain a general co-operation. For instance, it would not do to rend the infant association because the missionaries belong to different organizations. N^n & S^n Baptists co-operate in associations in China. How much more should Southern Baptists! Earnestly hoping that the B^d will grant us the men & women needed, I remain

    Yrs. sincerely,
    L. Moon.

Scottsville,
Apr. 8, 1893
Dear Dr. Tupper,

I have just returned from Baltimore & wish to speak of two young ladies who wish to be missionaries. Both are members of Dr. Wharton's church. One of them, Miss Clara Woolford, is a leading church worker. She has made her record during eleven years of faithful service, seven, I believe, in the Brantly Church. When Dr. Wharton was told that she was thinking of going to a foreign field, he said it "would break him up," but added that, "if the Lord wanted her, he would give her up." There is not a dissenting voice as to her fitness. Her mind was not quite fully made up. She has an aged father, but he tells her to follow her sense of duty. I think she will go. We talked freely about the North China work & she wishes to be with me; at first, in my own home, &, later, with me or in her own separate work, as may seem best. For the first two years, anyhow, with me, & I have promised to watch over & help her in every way. She is, I think, about twenty-eight years of age, a lovely, refined, noble Christian woman. Now, I beg, do let us have her in Shantung. She is exactly the woman with whom I should like to work & be associated.

The other candidate is a Miss Graves, who has impressed me very favorably indeed. I think she would make an admirable worker. But she has only lately come into the church & is still an untried worker. The ladies think that she had better prove herself a year or two, at home, first, & I think so too. She works in a factory, but her failure in culture does not seem to me against her. She is a woman evidently of much force of character. She has a strong, good face & I believe would be a first class worker, in time. I think, with some preliminary home training in her own church, that she could become, in the interior of Shantung, a most trusty worker, the centre of her own work with women & children. I think her strong, brave & trustworthy. In manner, she is quiet & very earnest. She is a woman who will grow, I believe, in every way. Her pastor is very enthusiastic about her & wants her to go out with me this fall. By the way, you have never answered my request about starting this coming Sept. I think Miss Graves would do better to wait & Mrs. Pollard seems now to think so. That was the general sentiment of the ladies, so far as I know. I did not see Dr. Wharton after hearing from the ladies, Miss Armstrong, Mrs. White, & Mrs. Cross. The latter two ladies want to try Miss Graves first in her own church work & I think they are right. Miss Woolford is one of a trio, consisting of Mrs. Cross & Mrs. White & herself, upon whom Dr. Wharton relies.

Hoping that you will consider favorably my petition for Miss Woolford to work with me, I am

Yrs. sincerely,

L. Moon

Scottsville, Va.,

May 23, 1893

Dear Dr. Tupper,

In your letter of Feb. 8th you say, (4.) "so far from 'making war,' the Board would much rather quit the field of Shantung." In a letter rec'd from Mrs. Crawford today, she said, "The movement means 'war' & war to the death." She also speaks of it as a "design to inaugurate a warfare & stamp out the work of thirty years, to swamp Shantung with money."

In (5.) you say "I presume the Committee would not even mention the name of Dr. H. to the Board, knowing the opposition of missionaries, or of even one missionary" –

Mrs. Crawford says, "There seems to be a real desire to destroy, to stamp out every vestige of the work which has been done, or may be done by those who do not see as they do. We were prepared to go along working in harmony as Baptist brethren, & supposed they would do the same as you,

King, Sears, Misses Fannie & Laura desire. But no—they not only mean to ignore our right of existence, but to declare an exterminating war upon us."

I write the above that you may see that I correctly represented matters when I said that Dr. Hartwell's appointment meant "war to the knife" with our "Gospel" brethren.

I write now to inquire if it is too late for the Board to reconsider its action in the matter. Would it be possible, at this late hour, to allow the missionaries who adhere to the Board to withdraw from Shantung? This was proposed last fall. I hear that there will be other resignations sent in when news reaches Shantung of Dr. Hartwell's appointment, resignations of extremely valuable workers who have heretofore adhered to the Board. Much as I love Shantung, I should rather leave there than have any share in strife.

May I ask you, as a kindness to me, to consider this letter official & as meant to be read to the F. M. Board?

Yrs. sincerely,

L. Moon.

Scottsville, Va.

June 10, 1893

Dear Dr. Tupper,

Thanks for your kind letter. I do not feel worthy of the nice things you so good naturedly say, yet I appreciate the kindness.

Only the future can show whether the sending of Dr. Hartwell is wise or not. I am not sanguine of good results, but no one will rejoice more than I if they come. As you know, my strong objection was not personal. I feared & still fear, social alienation & bitterness. I presume the Board does not know half that I know. Neither, I suppose, does Mr. Pruitt. The alienations—the fact that Mrs. Crawford was kept in months of torturing suspense because her husband's life was threatened by a violent & desperate man—a man in good standing in Dr. Hartwell's church,—the fact that other church members endeavored to extort money from Dr. C. unlawfully,—these and many other painful things we were absolutely dumb about to new missionaries. They were too painful to be talked about. Yet the Crawfords can't forget them or cease to feel that Dr. Hartwell gave a certain moral support to the bad & wicked men in his church who were persecuting Dr. Crawford. Thus much by way of explanation of my lack of faith in any good to come out of the present movement.

I have been in correspondence with Mrs. Yates about getting a transfer to Central China & she has been very kind & cordial about it. Mr. Bryan has long wanted me to work with him; he urged it when at Chinkiang. Again, at Yangchow, he & Mrs. Bryan wanted me, & only last winter I had a letter expressing an earnest wish that I should join them at Shanghai. I thought my mind was fully made up to ask such transfer. Still, I do not wish to act hastily. After reading your letter yesterday, it occurred to me that I might wait the turn of events. I prefer Shantung always. If the hopes of the Board & of my good friend & brother, Mr. Pruitt are realized & we can have a cordial, peaceful separation, without social bitternesses—brother refusing to speak to brother,—&c. &c.,—I am quite ready to go on cheerfully with my work in Shantung. But if old sores are to be re-opened & old quarrels begun again, for the sake of my own soul, I must get out of Shantung. If I go back there, it would have to be with the distinct reserve of my right to ask the Board to transfer me to Central China, if, for any cause, I find life in Shantung intolerable.

I am warmly a friend of some of the Gospel brethren, as you know. I should not make one particle of difference, here or in China, in my treatment of them & of the brethren in our own mission. I should invite them & their families just as cordially to my hospitality & render them every kindness in my power. Also, if I am asked, as I have been, to let a young lady go with me who is to belong to the "Gospel Mission," I should think myself something less than a Christian should I fail to do cordially a sister's part to that young lady. In a word, if, as you suggest, the noble office of peace maker is in any measure to be mine, it can only be by the frankest kindness on my part to brethren & sisters, in both missions, who differ from me in opinion. We are all equally honest & sincere & we all need kindness in the trials that are before us. God help us if we forget that we are brothers & sisters—Christians alike, with allegiances to one Master! The "Gospel Mission" is now an accomplished fact & its members are entitled to the same social courtesies that Baptist missionaries extend to Presbyterians & Methodists & others.

My sister joins me in kind regards.

Yours sincerely,

L. Moon.

Excerpts of Moon's Letters, 1872-1893

Enclosed please find a postal order for $5.00. It is meant for Dr. Cote's church in Rome. Were my ability commensurate with my will, the contribution would be much larger. Should you acknowledge the reception of this sum in the *Herald*, please put it as from "Virginian."
Lottie Moon to H. A. Tupper
May 25, 1872

Your kind letter of Aug. 20th was rec'd yesterday, & also one from Miss Clayton of Atlanta which I suppose you forwarded. I have just been writing a long letter to the Ladies of the W.M.S. of Atlanta & there is a paragraph in that letter I wish to submit to your consideration. It is as follows: "The assurance that the house will be built fills me with satisfaction, I sincerely believe that our usefulness will be enhanced by having a separate dwelling. I should like to consult with the Ladies of your society as to what had better be done with the money as it is collected. As the contributions are mostly small, we could hardly expect the Board at Richmond to keep a separate account of them, & so it seems there might be a probability of their being swallowed up in the general fund. After mature consideration, it seems to me that it would be best for your society to appoint a Treasurer for these funds and to request other societies to send all money for the house directly to that lady. The latter could place the money on deposit at a bank, making it payable to the society on-demand. When the whole amount has been raised, it would be advisable then to send it to Dr. Tupper."
Lottie Moon to H. A. Tupper
October 24, 1874

You are right in your conclusion that heathen nations are not necessarily devoid of civilization. Speaking of artists, there are men in the South of China who really deserve the name. Mr. Crawford has a portrait hanging in his parlor, which was painted by a Chinaman, from a photograph & I am sure that a foreign painter would have done no better. It is a picture of President Davis, and, as a gentleman from an American man-of-war remarked to me a day or two since, "I could recognize that picture across the street." He said the likeness was perfect.
Lottie Moon to H. A. Tupper
October 24, 1874

I see that you are calling for a missionary for Tung Chow. Supposing that before very long you will be sending out re-inforcements, I think I had better inform you as to the value of the American Trade dollar in this section, so that you can advise any one coming here not to purchase it in San Francisco. Our party were informed when in that city that the Trade dollar was made expressly for use in China. We purchased, more or less largely, at a premium of three per cent over gold. When we reached Shanghai, we found that neither foreign merchants nor Chinese would take our luckless dollars. The most of mine are lying still in my desk. Even those who have American postage stamps for sale object to receiving the American Trade dollar in exchange. I am told that the shrewd Chinese in San Francisco purchase the Trade dollar in large quantities, export it to China, & melt it up. I learn, however, that it is current in Hong Kong.

Lottie Moon to H.A.Tupper
December 28, 1874

As I write, the old woman who goes out visiting with me comes in. I thought surely, with the ground covered with snow, she would hardly make her appearance to-day, but she is really indefatigable. The branch of work to which I am especially devoting myself, is regular, systematic visiting. I feel a good deal encouraged by the kind reception that I meet. Not of course that personal kindness means spiritual interest, but it is more pleasant to visit those who receive you cordially & address you respectfully, than it is to go among those who greet your appearance with the words, "The devil old woman has come!"

Lottie Moon to H.A.Tupper
December 28, 1874

The members of our mission are in usual health. With the opening of spring, we are resuming country work with great delight. The people receive us most kindly. In the city, too, there seems to be a wave of kindly feeling of which we seek to take advantage while it lasts. Until some absurd rumor gets afloat, we will have pretty ready access to the homes of the city people. Then, perhaps for months, only a very few will dare to let us enter their houses. But the work is God's & we do not fear the final result. "The heathen *shall* be given to His son for his inheritance," & we must be content to await His Own time.

Lottie Moon to J. C. Williams
February 25, 1876

Turning to more pleasant topics, I am glad to say that our mission work continues encouraging. The schools are progressing most satisfactorily. Mrs. Holmes' girls' school now numbers 17. One of her pupils, who has been in school several years & is about sixteen, went to the country last week to be married. According to Chinese custom, a bride spends most of the first year after her marriage with her mother. The mother of the pupil above mentioned has arranged with the family into which she marries that she is to return to school shortly after her marriage. If she returns to school, & another pupil of last session comes back according to promise, the total number will be nineteen, & Mrs. Holmes' maximum is twenty. She has not room for more. It is a subject of constant admiration & surprise to me, how Mrs. Holmes manages to build up her girls' school in the face of so many obstacles.

Lottie Moon to H. A. Tupper
March 20, 1876

You will rejoice to learn that Corea is at last opened to the world. To think, too, that Japan has done it! It is reported in the Shanghai papers that three Corean ports are to be opened. Thus wonderfully is God using one heathen nation to open another heathen country for the gospel. A young king of Corea is said to be now in power & to be a man of liberal policy. It is said that China has advised this action on the part of Corea. The immediate cause of the opening was a demand on the part of Japan for satisfaction from the Corean government, a Japanese vessel having been fired on from a Corean fort.

Lottie Moon to H. A. Tupper
March 20, 1876

About remaining at North Street permanently, I am indifferent. Any decision the Board makes will be agreeable to me. I only wish it to be distinctly understood that I will neither go nor stay on the decision of any Chinaman or body of Chinamen. My private residence is no concern of the North Street church, any more than Dr. Warren's private residence is the concern of the African church in Richmond. I earnestly seek the good of the North Street church & have tried to be friends with them. At the same time, my self-respect compels me to say that they have by right no voice in this matter, nor will I allow them to usurp it. To do them justice, they have never attempted it.

Lottie Moon to H. A. Tupper
September 18, 1876

If a new missionary should come out, a married man, the place is eminently fitted for such occupancy. Any friend of Mr. Hartwell's, approved by the Board, would receive the most cordial welcome & every possible assistance from every member of our mission. We are prepared to love & co-operate with any one whom the Board will send us. There is only one matter which we should wish to deprecate in advance, & that is the employment of *paid assistants.* For another missionary in Tung Chow to employ them would greatly hamper us in our efforts to induce the natives to work simply for the love of Christ & because they esteem it an honor so to work. Heretofore we have had a fight to keep down the element in our church which wished to demand that we should employ men to preach. If it is understood that the Board has adopted this policy for Tung Chow of not employing paid assistants, it would greatly strengthen our hands. With us it is a vital principle, though we would never dream of wishing to impose it upon other missions. All we ask is free play here for what we regard as the right mission policy.

Lottie Moon to H. A. Tupper
September 18, 1876

I have had to write with so many interruptions that my letter seems hardly an answer to yours. Like yourself I am "anxious that every root of bitterness should be removed." Thank you for your trust in us that we will do all in our power "to conciliate the regards of the North Street church & to preserve the bonds of peace." I could mention many instances in which my sister & I have tried to help them, but I should feel ashamed to seem to make much of trifles. From Pastor & school down to the humblest member living in the city, we have sought to aid them as we could. We seem to have gained Pastor *Woo's* confidence & regard. As to any influence with the church, I must own to signal failure. The anti-foreign spirit is there, & only the grace of God can eradicate it. I should be glad to attend their service frequently, but I do not think they would like it. My sister said once to the pastor: "I would attend your church often, but your members are not partial to foreigners." He smiled, & made no reply. I have only attended there once & that was on a rainy Sunday. It seemed a little bit curious to be put off with the women & children into the little side room adjoining the chapel. This innovation has been introduced since Mr. Hartwell left, I am told. The men & boys have the chapel all to themselves. When we have union prayer meetings, however, the women muster in force from the other two churches & we are allowed the honor of sitting with the men. It is but just to say that this idea of separating men & women in worship is not confined to the Chinese. Dr. Williamson, Scotch Pres. at Chefoo, goes even farther. He has services for the men at one hour, & for the women at another.

Lottie Moon to H. A. Tupper
September 19, 1876

Every Sunday, private members of all the churches go out to preach. Sometimes they meet a good reception, often the reverse. When I say preach, I include in it talking by the wayside to one or more. The men go out in the morning. In the evening such women as are of suitable age go out visiting especially to carry the gospel message to others. They nearly always report a kind reception. Once in two week's our prayer meeting is in especial reference to this work & the brethren are expected to tell what they have done. *Woo shen sung* has been particularly active in setting the plan to work among his members. I was very much pleased one Sunday as I stepped out of my street door to see & hear one of the North Street brethren talking of Jesus to a man who seemed to be listening very attentively. It made my heart glow as I passed on my way through scenes of traffic. It is pleasant to know that there are many such witnesses for God on the streets of this heathen city every Sunday.

Lottie Moon to H. A. Tupper
September 19, 1876

Poor Mrs. Holmes! it nearly breaks my heart for her to give up her boy. I almost fear she cannot bear it. Even the anticipation has produced a restlessness that I have not seen before in her manner. She meant to have written Dr. Dickenson by this mail, but she told me last night she was not equal to the effort. For my own part, I feel like urging her to go home with him. I do not believe God requires such sacrifice of natural affection. As to her school, my sister is willing to take it in her absence if she will go, & I would take my sister's. At present, however, Mrs. Holmes is firm in her resolve to send Landrum.

Lottie Moon to H. A. Tupper
September 19, 1876

Mrs. Crawford says, "The North St. boys have ceased to come to sing. They missed two days—Thursday & Saturday. Saturday evening I met one of them & asked him what was the matter. He said he did not know, 'Woo shen sung pu kyer ky'u.'" (Mr. Woo does not allow us to go.) "Two other weeks have passed & neither boys nor a word of explanation has come. Perhaps they had instructions from America. I don't know."

Lottie Moon to H. A. Tupper
February 22, 1877

A letter rec'd from Miss Pitman last night informs me that her party leaves New York Oct. 20th or 22nd. I prefer you should decide whether I go with them or not. As I wrote you, there would be no advantage in my getting to Tung Chow earlier than the Chinese New Year. There would be next to nothing to do. Soon after that time, our Spring work begins. Schools open & we resume our city visiting & country trips. This being the case, I am not *anxious* to leave here earlier than the middle of Dec., so as to be in time for the 1st Jan. steamer. If it is certain that Mr. and Mrs. Simmons can go then, I would prefer to wait for them. Of course *to them,* it is important to go as soon as possible, for they have the language to learn. If they can not go until next Spring, however, I should very deeply regret to lose the opportunity now offered of agreeable company as far as Japan. I can look out for myself, once there.

Lottie Moon to H. A. Tupper
September 27, 1877

Resolutions of
Woman's Miss. Soc. Richmond

1. Resolved that, the balance of the Moon house fund now in the hands of the Treasurer of the Foreign Mission Board, and contributed by this society, be used to send Miss Lottie Moon to China.
2. Resolved that, while this society do not think it advisable to bind themselves to refund the money should it be needed for the house. They will, if that necessity shall arise, take the matter into consideration.
3. Resolved that, in the event of the Ladies of Georgia not continuing the support of Miss Moon, this Society will adopt her as their missionary.
4. Resolved that, this Society invite Miss Moon to visit them before she leaves for China, at such time as will best suit her convenience.

Adopted by W. Miss. Soc. Oct. 9, 1877

I hope that the reasons given in the enclosed letter for declining the position of "Mary Harley Missionary" will seem to you sufficient. The suggestion I make to the Committee is made with all deference to the Board as the deciding power. I have heretofore deprecated the sending of unmarried women to Shantung. In the Tungchow region, work is done under such discouraging auspices in the city, and under such physical hardships in the country, that it has not seemed to me right to encourage ladies to go there. Here things are different. City & country are alike accessible. Ladies could, from a comfortable home in the city, work not only the city but a country region full of villages. To go out for a day to a village, returning at night, while it is very wearisome to mind & body, is not physically wearing. It is the long tours, the "knocking about" in inns, the publicity that wear one out. Still, there are draw-backs to life in the interior & ladies should not come without being made fully aware of just what they are undertaking. It is literally true that there is absolutely nothing to attract one but abundance of hard work. If a woman can be content to bound her life within very narrow limits for the sake of the good she may do, the work would reward the self-denial.

Lottie Moon to H. A. Tupper
March 20, 1886

The native brethren are doing admirably, but there should be foreign brethren resident in Pingtu to lead them. The work is very encouraging and I think we should have large ingatherings had we the proper working force. Last year some of the brethren were discouraged because no pastor could be found to go and live among them. I said, "No matter! We *natives* will push the work!" Well "we natives" mean to push it still, but we wish you would send us some foreign brethren to help! Besides brethren, I put in a plea for two more women for Pingtu. I have already written, by order of the mission, asking for two more for Tungchow. With three here and four in Pingtu, we would have a tolerably good beginning of woman's work in Shantung.

Lottie Moon to H. A. Tupper
July 29, 1890

How I wish the coming Centennial might be utilized to stir up an interest in Missions in all our S. B. churches! I am getting very covetous, but it is for money to be poured into the Lord's treasury, that so the gospel may be given to "every creature."

Lottie Moon to H. A. Tupper
July 29, 1890

Thanks for your kind invitation which I highly appreciate, but I think it best, at present, to tarry quietly at home. Yet I should be glad to talk over North China matters with you, according to your wish. If you could come up to Scottsville some day reaching there at twelve o'c'k, my sister would meet you at the train & bring you out to our little home. We dwell in a "wel, modest" house about a mile out of town. You could return by the 3.25 P.M. train, but I think that would hardly give time for a full conference on our North China mission matters. There are two hotels in town & you might pass the night at one of them, leaving by five o'c'k train in the morning. My sister & I would be pleased to have you take dinner & supper with us. This arrangement would give ample time to confer about the needs of the mission & for any information you may desire. If it meets your approval, please send me a note a day or two in advance. I am sometimes away from home, & we do not always send to the P. O. everyday.

Lottie Moon to H. A. Tupper
November 3, 1891

We are pleased to learn that you will be with us on Tuesday next. I write to suggest that in Scottsville you go to the Powers house. I don't know that one hotel is any better than the other, but we think you would prefer the one where there is no bar-room. Besides, Mr. Powers is an active worker in the Scottsville church & his eldest daughter, Miss Annie, is President of the Woman's Miss. Society. The society has been entirely overshadowed by another, the Ladies' Aid Society which is absorbed in local interests. Nearly the same members compose both societies, the officers being different. Miss Annie is anxious to have an efficient society, but she has been hampered in the way I mentioned. I should be glad if you would make her acquaintance & encourage her & suggest to her methods of making the meetings more interesting. The pastor, Mr. Daniel, told them last Wednesday that there was no reason why this should not be made the best society in the state.

Lottie Moon to H. A. Tupper
November 6, 1891

Further reflection convinces me of the impossibility of my working in Shantung under a change of mission policy. If that has been decided upon, please request the Board to transfer me to Japan. Knowing as I do the circumstances of that past awful time, it would take the optimism of a Gladstone or the malice of a fiend, if I could have any part in Dr. Hartwell's return to Shantung.

Lottie Moon to H. A. Tupper
February 7, 1893

Living quietly alone, it has sufficed heretofore, but spring is approaching, my health is better & I wish to go about more. I desire to attend the Convention in May, to visit Miss Knight's family & to make some other trips. To accomplish these things, I must ask the Board to increase my allowance to fifty dollars a month. In connection with this subject, I may say that I took a number of trips last year to speak to various societies about mission work. In most cases, they offered to defray my expenses, & with two partial exceptions, I declined, telling them to send the money to Richmond instead. I did this because I wished to do some work for the Centennial at my own charges.

Lottie Moon to H. A. Tupper
February 20, 1893

At our mission meeting in 1890, held at Hwanghien, it was voted unanimously that we ask for *two* ladies to work with me east of Tungchow. Mrs. Crawford & I were appointed a committee to inform the Board of the wish of the mission. I wrote the letter & Mrs. Crawford & I signed it, but we have never had a reply. Perhaps the letter failed to reach you. I recall the matter now by way of answer to your query as to whether my application for a lady would equal that of the mission. I feel sure that a cordial welcome would be given to all who may be sent. As to a home, there is no trouble about that. I can always look after newcomers for a year or two, until they have time to look around & decide what they wish to do. There is a very wide open door for woman's work, in the interior especially. Miss Barton & Miss Knight would always join me cordially in caring for newcomers, so I think there need be no hesitation on that score.

Lottie Moon to H. A. Tupper
April 13, 1893

I observe in a recent copy of the *Religious Herald* (recent to me, but old to you) that Mr. Matheny has begun to write up the Gospel Mission in that paper. He has wished to edit a paper in the interests of that movement, but I suppose the time is not yet ripe for such an enterprise. I think that the friends of the Board ought to know what the leaders of this movement mean. I do not wish to appear publicly in the papers as opposing their plans, but I should like to give you some facts to be used at your discretion, in conversation or in print. There has been a great outcry against "Centralization." "Local churches to the front," says Dr. Crawford. "No need of paid agents," says Mr. Herring. "This movement is not antagonistic to the Board," it is declared. "It is meant to supplement the Board." Now for *facts.* It is no secret here that Mr. Bostick has declared it his purpose to "smash the Board" and "wipe out the Convention." A Central Committee was suggested to Mr. Herring from China. He replied, "That will grow up naturally. If we should speak of it now, it would ruin us." Miss Barton is my authority for these facts. She says that there is to be a Central Committee and a salaried agent. Thus it is designed to have a new board under the name of Central Committee and also a *de facto* Secretary,—a field-secretary, he might be styled . . .

I write to you, because I want you to know the facts and because I believe that a word from you now and then in the *Herald* or *Biblical Recorder* might do a world of good. I am too far off to take a share in any discussion until it might be too late. There ought to be some thoroughly informed person on the spot, not officially connected with the Board. It occurred to me that you would not object to knowing how things have worked here and in this letter, I have given you a slight insight into matters. The whole story would go back about thirty years. I have been connected with the mission about twenty.

Lottie Moon to Mr. Saunders
January 12, 1894

THE LOTTIE MOON

CORRESPONDENCE

II. FOREIGN MISSION

JOURNAL ENTRIES

"Let us pray that grace may everywhere abound ..."

Foreign Mission Journal Entries

Lottie Moon wrote numerous articles for the *Foreign Mission Journal,* a periodical published by the Foreign Mission Board of the Southern Baptist Convention. These articles were designed both to inform her American readers about Chinese culture and folkways, as well as explain how missionaries conducted their work.

Moon's careful eye for detail, coupled with her engaging writing style, still make for informative and entertaining reading. Readers may notice that she wrote fewer articles for the *Foreign Mission Journal* under R. J. Willingham's tenure as Corresponding Secretary of the Foreign Mission Board than she did for his predecessor, H. A. Tupper. This is due largely to the fact that Southern Baptists were expanding their international missionary ventures at the turn of the century and space in the *Foreign Mission Journal* was becoming scarce. Her earlier works, especially, "Good Points and Bad Points in Chinese Christians," "Houses-The Kitchen God-Buddhist Ideas About Animal Food," "Chinese Superstitions-Transmigration," and "Polygamy," remain especially instructive.

Of course, Lottie Moon's name is most often associated with an annual "Christmas Offering" collected within Southern Baptist Churches under the aegis of The Woman's Missionary Union. Named in honor of Moon, this offering is earmarked for supporting international missionaries. The articles titled "An Earnest Plea for Helpers," and "From Miss Lottie Moon," published in the August 1887 and December 1887 editions of the *Foreign Mission Journal* respectively, provide background information regarding this offering's beginnings.

A TRIP TO THE COUNTRY

It was a bright sunny day in the middle of November. For some days previous, bleak cold blasts had caused us to draw our wrappings closer about us as we went hither and thither on mission work intent. Now, there was scarce a breath to stir the foliage yet lingering on the trees. "We are all going for a pic-nic" was the announcement this bright sunny morning as the writer sat wearily following the teacher's pronunciation of a Chinese lesson. A pic-nic! Truly it had a pleasant sound, but would it be right to lose a day from the study of the language? A little explanation served to clear up matters. The ladies of the mission proposed to visit some of the country villages for the purpose of imparting religious instructions, and as they would take their dinners and spend the day, they styled the expedition a pic-nic. There would be no harm in accepting such an invitation as this, since mingling with the people is one of the best methods of acquiring the language.

As we left the mission premises, we met a native Christian woman accompanied by a forlorn looking specimen of humanity. The only clothing to his waist was a piece of matting on skin drawn around his shoulders and held by each hand. His head was destitute of the customary pig-tail as he had been destined for the priesthood. A few days before, one of the native women had come to Mrs. Crawford and Mrs. Holmes to ask if they would take the boy. She said he was an orphan and had run away from the temple at which he had been placed to be trained as priest. He came to the temple here, but the priests refused to receive him, saying they already had more than they wanted. Each of the ladies expressed a readiness to take him, but his fear of the foreigners led him to decline coming. Finally, however, necessity proved stronger than fear and he presented himself before us. Clothes were provided for him and the day after his coming he was placed at school.

To proceed, however, with the account of our day in the country. Our party consisted of four ladies and a native brother, one of the deacons of our church. One of the ladies led the advance gallantly, mounted on her donkey, and a wonderful little donkey it was, for actually during the whole day, we did not observe it bite or kick or indeed commit any act unworthy a most gentlemanly animal. To be sure, our ears were now and then regaled with his melodious notes but what of that? A donkey may surely express his feelings as well as other folks.

The other ladies followed in chairs borne by coolies while the deacon walked. On turning into Main street we found it thronged with people and animals. The shops displayed their wares in tempting profusion; provision and fruit vendors had spread these articles on the streets, on the bridges; while immense baskets of various vegetables were visible on either side. Peddlers of every description were bearing their baskets on poles suspended over the shoulder. Our course was constantly impeded, in the narrow street, by pack-mules or human burden-bearers. The musical tinkling of bells warned us to stand aside for the passage of that peculiar Chinese conveyance, the *shentz.* Just outside the city gate we had to halt for the passage of a train of mules loaded with immense bundles of faggots. The unusual crowd in the street had not caused us any especial surprise, but as we advanced into the suburbs we knew not what to make of the throng of men and animals. The women too had crowded to the doors and were looking on with intensity. Their gaze was at once turned on the foreigners and they exclaimed, "They are going to the theatre." The mystery of the crowd was thus explained. John Chinaman was bent on taking a holiday and really it was astonishing to see him look so gay. For the nonce, his usual stolidity seemed laid aside, and he laughed and cracked his jokes like anybody else.

Here, in the suburbs, seemed a good place to begin our mission work for the day. Mrs. H. dismounted from the donkey, and the chair-bearers put down their burdens. The aim of the ladies was to approach the Chinese women, but the latter were very timid and fled into their homes if any effort was made to go near them. The men and boys gathered around curious to see the foreigners. One object was thus gained; an audience was secured for our native brother. Though a lay member, he preaches frequently, especially during these expeditions to the country. Some listened curiously, while one face at least expressed real interest. Finding it impossible to reach the women, we moved on and soon came in view of the theatre. The crowd were standing in a dense mass in the open air. The theatre was a small rude structure of matting, designed probably to serve as a stage for actors and musicians. We passed to the rear of the crowd, and halted on the other side. Now the foreigners constituted to many of them a more wonderful sight than even the theatre and they gathered in knots about us eager to hear us talk.

One of the chair-bearers is a Christian and he seized the occasion to say some words to the men and boys around. They would possibly have heard him attentively but for the presence of one young man whose mocking witticisms set them all to laughing. With an audience in such a mood, a chair-bearer stands but a poor chance. His very occupation precludes, to the Chinese mind, the idea of his making a public address. They listened with respect to the deacon who went professedly as a preacher.

After a short halt, we proceeded towards one of the neighboring villages. All along our road were Chinese walking or riding. On our arrival at the village, we sat down in the street and waited to see what could be done for the women. Here, too, they were afraid of foreign people. The men and boys did not seem to share this feeling. The ladies talked to some of these and again our good deacon found a small audience. As may be imagined, it is exceedingly difficult to enchain the attention of such hearers for any length of time. Some will hear perhaps half a dozen sentences, others will tarry a little longer, while a few will stay up to the close of the remarks. Now and then a running fire of questions is poured in and the sermon becomes for the time only an answer to these. When they cease, the speaker goes on with his discourse. We tarried at this village some time and then moved on to another. So far as we know, the gospel had never been proclaimed here, and yet the simple villagers received us most cordially. Women, children, and a few men gathered around us immediately. We had halted intending to take our dinner, but the work seemed too pressing and first must the bread of life be presented to these needy souls.

At length we sat down to our meal and the scene was doubtless as novel to the Chinese as to ourselves. They crowded so close as almost to touch us and were interested in all we did. The knives and forks seemed to awaken especial attention. It is a habit of the Chinese to comment freely on all they see, and their unsophisticated remarks are often amusing though personal.

When the dinner was ended, the ladies again taught the women and children. One of the latter earned a copy of the "Happy Land" in Chinese as a reward for learning a small portion of the hymns. The bright red paper on which it was written doubtless formed the incentive to the effort. We gave away several copies of this hymn, won on the same condition. It was hard to leave so interesting a people, but there are hundreds of other villages all around that have never heard the gospel and to one of these we _____ this village, it was enough to break one's heart to pass so many houses with women standing at the doors and reflect that so few had heard us, that it had been simply impossible to reach more than a very small number.

As we approached the next village, the quick ear of an experienced missionary caught the word "devil." This sound used to be far more common than now. In the city, Tung Chow, the Mandarin has forbidden the offensive epithet. Probably we were the first foreigners to visit the village we were nearing. We went bravely on, though aware of almost certain opposition. Mrs. H's donkey was hitched to a wall and our chairs were put down in the street. Some women looked curiously at us from their street doors. A man came up evidently angry and excited and talked with our deacon who vainly endeavored to impart to him some religious instruction. He was full of bitter contempt and wanted to hear nothing of this new doctrine. He ordered the women indoors and they obeyed in a frightened manner, closing the door after them. He then walked off, doubtless deeming himself the master of the situation. The street was almost empty. A few children were visible, but they now held off from us and it seemed that we would have to beat an ignominious retreat. Luckily, rather let us say providentially, Mrs. Crawford had taken her position lower down the street, out of reach of our opponent's voice. The women gathered about her gradually and this gave courage to others who now collected in sufficient numbers to give work to each of the ladies who could speak the language. As Mrs. H walked triumphantly to her donkey, she exclaimed, "This village is conquered."

Our day's work was now ended. Wearied in body, but cheered in soul by the thought of the good done, we turned our faces homeward. The scene was indeed lovely as we neared the city. There lay the blue sea, sleeping in tranquil beauty as if no storm had ever ruffled its surface; from its bosom rose islands bathed in purple light; off in the distance a single sail dotted the picture. The sun was approaching its decline and cast mingled light and shadow on the grassy mounds of the Chinese cemeteries on either side. The laborers were still at their toil, for not yet had that darkness descended which entitles the ploughman to 'homeward plod his weary way.'

Our road lay again near the theatre and the crowd was slowly dispersing. They looked curiously at us, but it was too late to make any efforts for their good. John was doubtless tired by his unwanted holiday as we were ourselves by our day of travel and of labor. In comparative quiet they wended their way home.

The country people are more ready to receive the gospel than those in the city. Hence, the need of earnest effort in the battle to bring down the suspicion almost universal towards foreigners. Hence, too, the Lord's call for men to labor as evangelists among these villages. It is said that in three years' time one could hardly visit them all, so numerous are they. Mr. Crawford is over-tasked in the many demands upon him. He has three Chinese services every Sabbath, besides attending and conducting in his turn the English service. In addition to this, the conduct of the Thursday night prayer-meeting and the teachers' meeting devolves upon him. Then there are theological students who look to him for training. Along with this work of pastor and professor, he preaches in the streets of this city and acts as an evangelist in the country. It is not right for the brethren at home to leave him to toil on year after year unaided, and, when this noble soldier of the cross has "fallen asleep," who will fill his place?

Women, too, may find more than will fill their _____ many such! In city and in village, thousands of women will never hear the gospel until women bear it to them. They will admit women, but men can not gain acceptance to their homes, nor will they come to church. The only way for them to hear the good news of salvation is from the lips of foreign women. Are there not some, yea many, who find it in their hearts to say, "Here am I; send me?"

Foreign Mission Journal.
Published in the March 1874

NOTES FROM NORTH CHINA

In the mission field, sectarian differences seem so unimportant that what affects one denomination, whether for good or ill, is keenly felt by all. This has been evinced recently in events which have stirred our hearts first with joy and gladness and subsequently with indignation and sorrow.

During last year, a wonderful work of grace was manifest under the ministry of Rev. Mr. Corbett of the Northern Pres. Mission, at one of his out-stations. Large numbers of people were interested in the gospel, and almost a whole village became Christian. Mr. Corbett deemed it wise, in this state of things, to remain in that region at least during the winter. He therefore sent for a few household conveniences, and had his children to join him. For a while everything went on well. But the history of the church is the same in all ages. Where God's ministers are most successful, there the powers of darkness marshal their forces for the conflict. "The blood of martyrs is the seed of the church." As it has been elsewhere, so must it be in China. A violent persecution arose. An appeal was made to the local magistrate for protection, and he declared himself powerless to render any assistance, saying that he himself feared the violence of the mob. He advised Mr. Corbett to leave. The latter, however, stood his ground until a personal attack was made on him by stoning. Some of the native Christians were beaten and one of them was seriously injured. Mr. Corbett began to think it was time to remove his children to a place of safety. The result proved that this decision did not come a moment too soon. About two o'c'k in the night, he set out, and the next day about nine an enraged multitude came to the inn he had left with the design of killing him. In the mean time, tidings of Mr. Corbett's difficulties had reached the missionaries at Chefoo, and Rev. Mr. Eckard determined to go to his assistance, and at least bring away the children. Taking a different road from that Mr. Corbett was travelling, they failed to meet. On Mr. Eckard's arrival in the disaffected region, there was great excitement. He took refuge in an inn, securing the doors, and the mob stoned the building two hours. Finding Mr. Corbett had left, Mr. Eckard also returned home.

Much uneasiness was felt on account of the native Christians. It was known that a strong persecution was going on, and that they were standing firm under these trials. The news comes very recently that certainly one man has been killed and rumor swells the number to seven. Any appeal to justice seems worse than useless. The facts are probably that the officials are the instigators of these outrages. Mr. Corbett, through the American consul, represented the matter to the proper Chinese authority. The latter replied, after some delay, that he had investigated the matter and that it was thus: Some of the church members had attempted to kidnap a boy in order to force him to join the church, and that the crowd interfered and rescued him on hearing his loud cries. The Christians then tried to kidnap a man, and the crowd, justly indignant, interposed and saved the intended victim. As to Mr. Corbett himself, he said that no offence had been offered him further than this, that he had taken his children to the theatre to amuse them, and that the crowd, not being used to foreign children, pressed around to see them, and that Mr. Corbett then used very improper and unbecoming language. The magistrate stated further that when the people went to Mr. Corbett's house, it was because they had heard tales of his kidnapping children; they had therefore gone peaceably to investigate the matter for themselves.

As regards the property Mr. Corbett has lost, there seems at present no hope of restitution. It is easy to denounce these outrages in no measured terms, but we blush to think they have their counterparts in the justice meted out to the Chinese in San Francisco.

Here in Tungchow, affairs are moving on pretty much as usual. We notice with pleasure an increased attendance on preaching. Another man has been received for baptism. He dates his first convictions to hearing the Christians talk about keeping the Sabbath. He says he never before heard of a

Sabbath except at the New Year, & his attention was at once arrested. He has endured firmly a cruel persecution at the hands of his wife.

This city offers a very wide field of usefulness for an active, energetic man, while the surrounding country is full of villages where the gospel has never been preached. Another minister is sadly needed to take some of the burden from Mr. Crawford. What with a regular pastorate, street preaching, itinerating, and instructing a Theological class, making books, and writing hymns,—he is doing the work that ought to be shared. It is too much for one man.

The ladies of the mission are doing what they can to bear the word of life to the people, but the force *is wholly inadequate to the work*. We are already sadly foreboding the departure of one of our most efficient missionaries. In three or four years at most Mrs. Holmes must go home for the education of her son. In the meantime, however, it would seem the part of wisdom that two ladies should be sent out that they may learn the language & thus be prepared to take charge of the girls' boarding school. We say two simply because it would not be desirable or pleasant for a lady to live alone. One of the Presbyterian ladies here is trying this, and she finds it very lonely.

We believe that there are men and women in our Southern Baptist churches who but require to be assured of the pressing demand for more laborers in some specific field, in order to respond, "Send us." We believe, too, that the money needed is in the denomination and that it will be forthcoming. We are convinced that the brethren and sisters at home will not allow these missions which God has blessed so abundantly to languish for want of more laborers or of material support. In this faith we wait, believing we shall hear from home that the needed re-inforcements will be sent.

L. Moon.
Tung Chow, March 9, 1874
Published in the June 1874
Foreign Mission Journal

INTERESTING EXTRACTS FROM LETTER OF MISS LOTTIE MOON, TUNG CHOW,

To Woman's Missionary Society of Atlanta, Georgia:

Not Devils

I am sure your hearts will be greatly rejoiced to know that the work here has never been more encouraging. Last Sabbath we had the largest congregation I have ever seen in our church, and many of them listened most attentively. The city has been crowded for more than a week with students who have come up to the examination. They exhibit a more teachable spirit than heretofore, and Mr. Crawford's study has been daily thronged with interested auditors. The contempt for foreigners seems to be giving way to a feeling of respect. Trifles often show the drift of popular sentiment. Instead of hearing the offensive words "foreign devils" applied to us in the city, we hear now "foreign people," "foreign lady-teachers," sometimes spoken as we pass along the streets.

Persecution

Our hearts were made glad last Sabbath by the baptism of an individual who has interested us by his firm stand under the persecutions of his heathen family. They fastened him in a room without food or water, and endeavored to starve him into submission. Providentially, they did not take away his Christian books. He studied these more closely than ever. The pangs of hunger he satisfied by eating some raw beans he found in the room, and when he wanted water he commenced to dig a well in the room in which he was confined. Chinese houses are built on the ground and do not have plank floors as with us. When the family discovered the well-digging they yielded. They had no wish to ruin their dwelling. The man has shown that he is made of stern stuff, and we hope he will be very useful as a Christian.

Mrs. Holmes' Proposed Return

Mrs. Holmes has a girls' boarding school. The Chinese do not believe in educating women. Hence it is a very slow and difficult work to gather even a few girls for instruction. Very few of the women read at all. Mrs. Holmes' success has been gratifying. Unfortunately she must return to America, in about four years, to educate her son. We are very desirous that two ladies should be sent out, in the mean time, to learn the language, that they may take her place. One lady would find it lonely; indeed, it would not be at all desirable for one to live alone. Ladies out here are trying it, but, I am afraid, at the expense of health and happiness. Should two ladies come to take Mrs. Holmes' house, one might take charge of the school, and the other could devote her time to visiting among the women. The matter in which I am most concerned now, is the building of a house for my sister and myself.

House For The Misses Moon

A lot adjoining the church has already been purchased. We confidently trust that our Christian sisters will furnish the funds for the building. Our desire is to have this house as a new centre of influence. Experience shows that more work can be done, and more good accomplished by scattering the mission forces. Of course, we would find it more pleasant in many respects to continue members of the Mr. Crawford's family, but for the interest of the mission it would be better to have a separate establishment. My sister wishes to have a boarding-school for girls.

Discount And Premium Matrimony

A frequent question of Chinese women is if I have a mother-in-law? Mr. Crawford suggested an easy way to dispose of their astonishment when they hear of my destitution. It is to tell them that mothers-in-law are too hard to get along with—that I fear they will beat me. This joke amuses them invariably, because they all know how hard a time a Chinese daughter-in-law must have. The women who asked today seemed shocked that a person of my age was unmarried. She inquired about my family; seemed to pity my forlorn state, and said she would get me some relations of my name.

Disposing Of Rude Boys

We then went to a house where a number of boys, a dozen or more, came swarming into the court. They evidently came to have their fun out of me; they were very disorderly. Finally I raised up very straight, looked full at them, and gave them a little talk about manners; this quieted them awhile; when they began to be obstreperous again I told one of them, individually, that he had no manners. They all took this hint, and I had a very pleasant time teaching them; they learned rapidly, both the Catechism and "Happy Land."

"Revealed Unto Babes"

At another house two women learned very fast; I say women, but one was a girl about twelve or thirteen, already married, however. There was a little child about three years old. They said it knew some of "Happy Land." My sister asked, "Who is the True God's Son?" The little thing replied, in a very sweet voice, "Jesus."
Published in the July 1874 *Foreign Mission Journal.*

FOR THE *HOME & FOREIGN JOURNAL*

In a former letter, some mention was made of the work in Chemi under the labors of Rev. Mr. Corbett of the Presbyterian mission, of the determined opposition that arose, culminating in an assault upon him and a subsequent attempt to take his life, & followed by a violent persecution of the native Christians. At one time, there was a report that at least one of the latter had been murdered. Fortunately, however, they did not proceed to such extremities.

Every friend of missions as well as every missionary, owes a debt of gratitude to Mr. Shepherd, American consul at Tientsin, that he has not allowed the perpetration of these outrages against Mr. Corbett to go unpunished. The Chinese officials were in full sympathy with the rioters and used every expedient to shield them from justice. With a patience that never flagged, with a determined resolution that nothing could turn aside, Mr. Shepherd literally fought his way day by day demolishing every stronghold of lies, until finally the *Taotai* was compelled to concede his just demands. The guilty parties were punished by beating or imprisonment, & the restoration of the stolen property or its equivalent in money was guaranteed. The men were likewise compelled to sign a bond not to molest Mr. Corbett any more.

After the trial was concluded, those who had been beaten went home & reported that the affair had gone in their favor, and that Mr. Corbett had received punishment. While they were busily circulating such falsehoods, who should make his appearance at Chemi, but the very man whom they were boasting they should kill next time, and whom they were now representing as having lost the suit. They all fled in utter consternation. Mr. Corbett says he was never so well treated before as on this visit, that the very dogs did not bark at him. He reports that the persecution last fall against the native Christians was very violent, but that they have stood firm. At one time they could not go on the street without being reviled in a matter shocking even to Chinese ears, accustomed as they are to hear foul language. When a Christian would take his produce to market, the heathen women would band together & take it from him by force. These Christians have at present no pastor, but they meet every Sabbath for prayer & praise, & to catechise each other. Mr. C. says that the women learn to read faster than the men, & the children most rapidly of all. In this city the good effect of the trial was at once apparent. People are no longer so afraid to receive us into their houses & in visiting among the women there is a decidedly increased cordiality on their part.

During the trial above mentioned there occurred a new & rather ludicrous application of the title "D.D.," usually read Doctor of Divinity. The acting clerk of the court was a missionary who had a right to append those letters to his name. The consul, not understanding Chinese, found it difficult to keep in his mind the names of the various witnesses, so, in order to distinguish them, in jotting down his notes, he would give each witness some name by which to keep him distinct from the rest. Among others was a man whom the consul found it convenient to designate as the donkey driver. "I will put him down as D.D.," he said. Just then a gentlemen who was acting as an interpreter gave a comical glance at the clerk. The consul, at once divining the joke, said gravely, "I mean no disrespect to Dr.——." Of course the court was convulsed with laughter, & the term "D.D.," in this section, at least, will often bring up visions of a certain long eared animal and his driver.

We are earnestly hoping that the Board will ere long send us re-enforcements. A man is sadly needed, while there is work for as many women as will come.

L. Moon.

Tung Chow,

June 29, 1874
Published in the September 1874 *Foreign Mission Journal*

FROM MISS LOTTIE MOON

Good And Bad Points In Chinese Christians

During the three years I was in China, I never knew a church member refuse to pray in public. I heard poor prayers and embarrassed prayers—but no refusal to pray when called on.

All try to sing. Even the little children six or seven years old bring their hymn-books and use them.

The three churches in Tung Chow, two Baptist and one Presbyterian, have agreed that the members, male and female, shall give one hour of every Sabbath to making known the gospel among their heathen neighbors, friends, acquaintances, or, in short, wherever they can find a listener. This plan was commenced last summer and has been enthusiastically prosecuted.

The worst feature in the character of a converted Chinaman is that he does not feel the guilt of sin. In general, any Chinaman will admit that all are sinners, but it is a sad fact that even the most advanced christians among them do not feel the enormity of sin as an offence against God.

Akin to this is the lack of the emotional in Chinese christianity. How often have I heard the lament among old missionaries: "If they could only feel! If there were only some way to arouse them from their stolidity!"

Shall we not pray that God will bless and sanctify to his glory the good points in these our dear brethren, and that the Holy Spirit will guide them into all truth, thus correcting and subduing their faults?

Published in the May 1877 *Foreign Mission Journal.*

SUNDAY IN CHINA

If there is anything calculated to make one *feel* the fact of being in a heathen land, it is to pass through the streets on the Sabbath. Stepping out of your street door, on your way to church, you find yourself at once in the middle of a busy throng. Perhaps it is market day, & the streets are lined on either side with bags of grain, donkeys, mules, & men. A busy traffic is going on. Everywhere, as you proceed on your way, are evidence of a land without a Sabbath. Hawkers vend their wares, pedlars call attention to their goods, children play about the streets, men gossip or discuss business—the busy tide of life rolls on. Probably not one in all that vast throng is aware that it is the Lord's holy day. How you long to see this thoughtless, careless, busy multitude, wending its way to the house of God!

But there is a brighter side to the picture. Arrived at church, you behold a quiet, orderly, well-dressed congregation assembled to worship the True God. Among them, too, are heathen, some of whom are hearing, for the first time, the story of God's love. The thought of being in God's house is peculiarly sweet in a heathen land. Outside, Satan reigns; "gross darkness covers the people." Within, God shows Himself gracious to His own chosen ones.

L. Moon.
Published in the August 1877 *Foreign Mission Journal.*

FACTS FOR SOUTHERN BAPTISTS TO PONDER

In the vast continent of Africa, we have one white missionary & one colored. In Japan we have—not one. In Burmah, Siam, India, the isles of the ocean,—not one. In China we have at present eight missionaries. Putting the population of China at four hundred million, this gives one missionary for fifty million people. Yet, we call ourselves Missionary Baptists.

Our Lord says, "Go ye into all the world & preach the gospel to every creature." Are we obeying this command?

L. Moon
Published in the September 1877 *Foreign Mission Journal.*

Miss Moon's Journal

Tung Chow, China, March 29, 1880
Mrs. V. L. McWilliams, Cor. Sec. W. M. Soc.,
Blue Mountain, Miss.:
My dear Sister,

Your letter of January 26th was received by the last American mail. You kindly left it to my choice to reply to you directly or through the columns of the *Foreign Journal*. Scarcely a mail arrives from America without bringing several letters of inquiry. Some of them require a direct personal answer, but a letter of the nature of yours may be answered in such general terms as might perhaps interest a larger circle than your own society. With this end in view, I kept the following journal during a short tour last week, and hope you will accept it instead of a formal letter.

Journal

March 24, 1880

About nine o'clock A. M., had you been near the east gate of Tung Chow you might have seen emerging from its portals two individuals different in appearance and dress from the blue-robed crowd passing in and out. These two were walking rapidly and talking as they went, giving no manner of heed to the people about them. The people on their part scarce noticed the two, being accustomed so many years to the sight of foreigners. In the rear followed two sedan-chairs, borne each on the shoulders of two men. A little behind was a donkey laden with bedding, a box and some baskets of provisions. The morning was bright and beautiful, the air and the sunlight exhilarating. Our travelers walked on still in busy talk, taking in almost unconsciously the delightful influences around until, after some miles, a sense of fatigue suggested the propriety of using the chairs. Meantime village after village had been past, but all so near the city that we did not care to halt, and as we went on there were villages "to right of" us, villages "to left of" us, villages "in front of" us. Our road lay right through some of them, but still we kept our onward way. Like that eccentric youth with his remarkable banner, we heeded not the alluring voices that bade us "stay and rest;" if, unlike him, our motto was not "excelsior," it was at least "forward." We had markĕd out a certain plan of campaign and we did not intend to be turned aside from its prosecution. After going about eight miles we reached the intended scene of operations, the cluster of villages known as *Wandzeko*.

These villages heretofore had had the reputation with us of being hard and unmanageable, especially the first one of them. Our chairs were set down and soon the people began to gather. We taught and talked awhile, and as we left we agreed that "this was the best audience in every respect that we had ever had in this village." As we went on, "still the wonder grew." There were large crowds, but they were so quiet and attentive and some of them so anxious to hear, that it was easy and pleasant to speak. Leaving the third village we stopped by the wayside to take our lunch. Some boys and men found us out and came to see the wild beasts eat. Mrs. H. in *her* turn found them out, for no sooner was she done eating than she commenced a vigorous attack on the catechism. I was not so good. I stole a few moments to dip into a story in "Littell," in which I was interested. The next village was not many yards away. The people had seen us and were waiting on the street for us. The four villages in this cluster, like the three visited in the morning are so close together as to be separated only by a stream or a crossing. You have to inquire where another village begins, or you would be in danger of thinking them all one. In each village we gave them a talk. It was only a little after three o'clock when we had finished the whole group of seven.

Further on was a large village known to us of old as unfriendly to foreigners; still we had no wish to avoid it. Reaching this village we divided forces and had a not unpleasant time. True, nobody cared to hear the word of life, but they were willing enough to chat about indifferent matters. One's age is always a subject of profound interest. If you once tell them, they will never forget the interesting item; should you return ten years hence they would say, "She was here ten years ago and was such an age, and now she is so and so." There is no chance to escape this dreadful question in China. Just "screw your courage to the sticking place," and say it out boldly; it will become easier every time. In fact one tells it just about as in America we answer an inquiry as to health, "Pretty well, I thank you." I should like to tell in an episodical way of the first time this question met me in all its bold atrocity. I have often thought it very amusing, but I did not find it at all funny at the time. I had just landed in Chefoo a day or two previous. My kind hostess proposed one afternoon that I should take a ride out to the Scotch Presbyterian mission, some two miles away. The members of the mission were supposed to be absent, but the buildings were worth seeing. So, mounted on a donkey and in charge of a Chinaman, I set out, arrived on the grounds and looking leisurely around, what was my surprise and chagrin to see a gentleman emerge from a building and advance towards me. I wished to beat a hasty retreat, but knew not a word of Chinese and could not give the order. The gentleman advanced courteously. I introduced myself, and he gave me a cordial invitation to go in and make a visit. He led the way into a cozy library where we had a pleasant chat. The lady of the house came in, and they proposed to take me around and show me the church, the hospital, and something of their work. It was the evening of the women's meeting, and they would like me to look in. My kind hosts told them I was just from America, and that I had come to teach the women the gospel. Then arose a clamor I did not at all comprehend. "They are asking your age," my hostess said with a quiet smile, "but you need not tell them if you do not like." Do you think I could stand such a challenge?

But to return to my story. Leaving the large village with a feeling of satisfaction that at least friendly relations had been maintained, we passed on to a small village not far distant. Here one woman especially interested us by her friendliness and readiness to hear. Her liking seemed to grow the longer we stayed, and her grateful feeling overflowed when Mrs. H. gave her son a book. She followed us beyond the village as we were leaving, saying, "Be sure to come here next time you visit the country; if you want food, you can have it; if you want water it is here." Nearly the whole village followed, while there was an overflow from the large village we had previously visited, to meet us on our return. We felt quite grand receiving such a popular ovation. As we passed on through the large village, the crowd continually increased. Finally they said, "Stop awhile and enjoy yourselves." Elated by such distinguished attention, we paused with gracious smiles to look upon our admirers. "Come see the devils," called out one of them to a friend. Fancy the sudden downfall of vanity!

Our course lay now across green fields of young wheat. Over to the left was the sea dotted with white sails, and behind us the sun, sinking towards its decline, was casting long mellow rays of light. The country people, busy here and there at their work, enlivened the landscape with their garments of bright blue.

After some travel, we drew near another group of villages, the scenery meanwhile growing constantly more charming. Three villages nestled cozily in the valley into which we were descending, while a fourth touched the sea. The fields grew ever greener, the sun sank lower and lower, while under the soft rays of the moon, now trembling into view in the eastern sky, the sea was no longer blue, but a shining white. The picturesque village, the fishing boats, the steep cliffs—rising abruptly on one side, but sinking away to a smooth beach on the other—all these formed a picture which will long abide in memory. Reaching the first of this group of villages, we were soon surrounded by an eager crowd. The usual teaching and talk followed; and now, the sun having sunk behind the hills, and only its reflection being visible, we hurried on to the village where we were to spend the night. Our way lay still adown the sloping valley, and having reached the village, we wound through various narrow streets until, a hundred or two yards from the sea, we entered our quarters for the night. Passing through the court-yard, which served at once for stable, pig-pen, barn, and yard for the inn, we entered the kitchen, which opened into the apartment where we were to spend the night. The glories of sky and sun and sea and shore were now all gone. Black walls, a ceiling with smoke seemingly some inches thick, a brick bed on which was a torn mat, various vessels of grain, beans, flour, a sort of bureau, a window that cannot be opened—such the scene. The men are about to crowd in, but I motion them back: "We are women," I say, "you must not come in." The man who has entered retreats, the bedding and provisions are brought in, and we proceed to make ourselves comfortable as circumstances permit. But outside, the yard is filled with an eager crowd wishing to catch sight of us, and it is all our chair-bearers can do to get them out with the promise that tomorrow after breakfast they shall both see and hear us. Mrs. H., meanwhile, has discovered that the "kong" is not a bed of roses. "How can any civilized people live this way?" she asks, with a touch of impatience. Wonderingly, I answer, "Do you think the Chinese civilized?" "I don't mean the Chinese," she responds, "I mean ourselves." But supper comes after awhile, and laughing and chatting over it, we forget our surroundings. We are too tired to have the people come in, so Mrs. Holmes settles down to "Littell," and I sit down to write this diary.

Published in the June 1880 *Foreign Mission Journal.*

MISS L. MOON'S JOURNAL

In the June number of our paper the experience of Miss Moon in a trip to the country on March 24, 1880, was given from her diary addressed to Mrs. V. L. McWilliams, Corresponding Secretary Woman's Missionary Society, Blue Mountain, Miss. What occurred in the next three days on the same excursion is given below, also taken from her journal.

March 25

The woes of last night, who could picture? If we hung up a curtain before the window, thus closing the narrow aperture which admitted the air, we should suffocate; if we did not hang it up, the moonlight streaming through the translucent paper, would keep us awake. Not having the resolution to suffocate outright, and not wishing to lie awake all night, we adopted half measures; the curtain was hung up enough to suffocate, but not enough to exclude the light. In the opposite room snored "mine host;" outside the donkey brayed at intervals long and loud, and on toward the "small, wee hours," the cock lifted up his melodious voice. Two or three hours of troubled slumber, the day dawns, and the woman of the inn is already demanding admittance on some household errand. After breakfast we hurry out to escape the smoke with which our room is beginning to be filled from the kitchen. The yard is full of people, and Mrs. H[olmes], takes them in charge. I stroll up the street where there are a few women in view. Taking my seat on a large rock I call out: "Come over and get acquainted." A man standing near says, "Begin to explain (books) and they will come." In a few minutes I am surrounded by a large crowd all eager to see and too excited to listen. Today we have visited in all twelve villages. At some of them the demand for books was greater than we could meet; the school boys were especially eager to get them. Passing from one village to another, I felt some plucking at my sleeve and holding on as I was walking. Turning to see who it was, a boy said confidently, "Won't you give *me* a book?" Pretty soon he was holding on to my other arm as if afraid I would get away from him, a number of other boys keeping close and wanting books, too. The chair being reached, all the books I had were given away. Mrs. H. had a large crowd around her, and I took my seat off at some distance. Pretty soon my boyish friend took his seat beside me, with the same confidential air, pulled the catechism out of his sleeve (the sleeve is the Chinaman's pocket), and began to read, while I looked on to help him out, and other boys gathered around to listen. After we left this village Mrs. H., remembering suddenly that she had lent a man her last book returned to claim it. She found the man reading aloud to two others, and all so intensely interested that she had not the heart to take it away. We had a somewhat amusing time when we stopped for lunch. We try if possible to elude the crowd at such times, but rarely succeed. There was a temple standing some distance from a village at which we had talked, and we decided to enter the yard, close the doors and keep the crowd out if they should follow. This was easier to plan than to accomplish. Our chairs were set down on the raised place in front of the temple door. All was so clean and bright and quiet that we began to congratulate ourselves upon our good fortune. But you can't balk a Chinaman in that way. They knocked so fiercely at the doors that the priest was afraid that they would be broken in, and therefore, opened them. The crowd and we ourselves were amused, and we made a compromise. Not a foot was to be set on the platform where we were sitting, but they might stand below and see us to their hearts' content. "Why don't you go home and get your dinner?" said Mrs. H. to one of them. "If I should go home to get my dinner, when I came back you would be gone," he answered. When our meal was over, the restriction was removed and the crowd pressed around us. A very lively conversation here followed with the men, mainly about the customs of our country.

Tonight we are at *San-she-pu,* ten miles from the city, in very comfortable quarters. We have stopped here so often that we feel quite at home.

March 26

We seem to have become one of the "institutions" of this region. The people now look for our coming from year to year. At the first village at which we stopped this morning, a young woman came up laughing with pleasure. "You've come again," she said, "the same who were here before." "Yes, the same, and we have come to tell you the same things we told you before. You can't have forgotten them all?" No, she remembered some.

At the next village there was a woman from the city who claimed Mrs. H. as an old acquaintance. After a talk on the street, Mrs. H. accepted an invitation to visit the family to which she belonged, and it turned out to be one of the most aristocratic of the village. Meantime I was surrounded by a crowd who listened very well. I took occasion to advert to one of the crying sins of this part of the world—cursing. I asked if the children of that village cursed. "No," said an old woman, "they don't know how to curse." Of course this was false, but I seemed to accept her word for the time. When through with my talk, I said pleasantly, "When I came into this village, some children cursed me." They expressed much surprise, and wanted to know how it was. "Why," I said, raising my voice to imitate the children, they said, "The devil old women have come." The crowd laughed and the women became apologetic. "Next time I come tell them to say a foreign woman has come, or a teacher has come to explain books." If we had felt any wounded pride at the unflattering designation, it would have been soothed at the next village at being addressed as "Venerable teacher." We had but one unpleasant experience today. This was at a village where they used to manifest their hatred by not coming near us. Today they crowded about us, but there was not a little rudeness.

At the last village we visited today the inhabitants were exceedingly friendly. We were each invited to make a visit and accepted. My hostess said I must not laugh at her humble quarters, and I assured her there was no danger of that. I was somewhat agreeably surprised on entering the yard to note the neatness and cleanliness; the farm produce was well stacked, and the yard was nicely swept. Inside was also attractive. The "kong" was covered with pretty, new and clean matting, and the bedding, of which there was abundance, was neatly folded on one side. I was invited to mount the "kong" an invitation I rarely decline. The hostess and another old woman sat on each side of me; pipes were produced, and I was invited to smoke. I explained that women do not smoke in my country. They lighted their pipes and smoked away during the rest of my visit.

The room was filled with women and children, who stood in front of the "kong." My glove was past around for examination, and as usual elicited the remark that foreigners are "skillful." "We are skillful, you say, but there is one thing we can't do; we can't make gods." The woman looked greatly surprised. "We can make steamboats and sewing machines, but not gods." Her face expressed still a puzzled surprise. "What, not if you could see one of our gods, couldn't you make them?" "No," I replied, "we can't make gods." I think she was beginning to feel a little contempt, when the woman standing by who saw the point, said with a laugh, "They don't *want* gods; they don't allow the worship of mud images." At this moment, being called to go, the conversation could not be pursued.

The keeper of the inn at which we are staying is a young teacher. He seems to be entirely free from the arrogance and hatred of foreigners that usually characterize his class. He has a very nice school of twenty pupils. As soon as they were dismissed for the day, which was a little before sunset, they came quietly and stood outside our door, modestly doubting if they would be admitted. Mrs. H. invited them in, and in a few moments they were eagerly committing to memory and singing "Jesus Loves Me." Here I cannot but pause to pay a very high tribute to the good manners, the docility, and the wonderful application of Chinese boys. Take them as a class, in power of steady application they far surpass Western students.

March 27

Today there is a high wind blowing from the North, last night there was rain; our wisest course would have been to come straight home. Instead we halted at five villages. Our road lay through a region where the people are not friendly; nobody cared to hear, and I had the feeling that we were spending our strength for naught. We had meant to visit nine or ten villages, but yielding to the force of circumstances, we gladly set out for home. But "home" after an absence of several days does not always mean quiet or rest. There are the accumulated matters of the past days to be attended to; people come in to call, or somebody wants medicine. Happily, however, when the night descends, you may shut out the Chinese faces and voices, of which you are inexpressibly weary, and sink at last into quiet repose.

L. M.

Published in the August 1880 *Foreign Mission Journal.*

FROM MISS LOTTIE MOON

Three Days Among The Villages

It had grown so hot a few weeks since that it seemed there must be an end of country work for this season; but a heavy rain, fortunately for us, if not for the husbandman, having cooled the atmosphere, we took advantage of this favoring circumstance and started out for a short tour. Leaving the city about eight o'clock, we were soon in the open country. Having passed through various villages, all of which we had previously visited, we began to descend a rugged plateau by one of the worst roads imaginable. But the badness of the road is more than compensated by the wildness of the scenery. Terrace rises above terrace, all reclaimed from rude Nature's hand by ages of incessant toil. Hillsides, which in our favored land would never know a touch of the plough, are here crowned with the result of patient labor. The longer one lives in China the more respect is felt for the patient industry of its people. Early and late they toil, often for a bare subsistence, and making a support where a white man would give up in despair.

Descending the plateau on which we had been traveling for some miles, we emerged into a narrow but pretty valley, at the head of which was a village called *Shang-ko-fing-gia.* Scarcely had we entered the village when a woman greeted me very cordially and insisted that I should go at once to her house. I had known her a long time, but had not seen her for several years. After some general conversation she spoke of her son's death. I told her that as soon as I entered her gate I had thought of him. This seemed to touch her, and her eyes filled with tears. She said that when I had visited the village before her heart had been too full of grief to come near me. I told her I had understood that. The Heavenly Father, she said, had treated her hardly in taking this child from her. It was, indeed, pleasant to be able to assure her that this "child of her affection" was safe in the heavenly fold, and that it was in tenderest love that God had taken him. It was a joy to speak to her of the hope of reunion beyond the grave. Taking leave of our friendly hostess, we found an audience on the street, some of whom listened with an attention truly gratifying. The next village might be said almost to touch the one we just left. Here were a larger number of hearers, but none especially attentive. Passing on to the next village, which was less than a quarter of a mile distant, we halted for our lunch in a picturesque spot, beside a clear and beautiful stream. The immense rocks obstructing its course gave an air of wildness to the scene; the grass was green to the water's edge; while the trees, bending their long branches from above, mingled "shadows dark" with "sunlight sheen." Opposite was a small shrine to some heathen god. Taking the meal leisurely, the people had time to gather. Then, under the shade of a fruit tree, Mrs. H. told them the story of the creation and of the fall of man as narrated in the opening chapters of Genesis. When she had ended, a pleasant-faced old lady, who had listened attentively, asked promptly, "How old are you?" I then took my turn, but had scarcely begun before the same question was put. Answering this and some other personal questions, I talked on a while, after which followed a sort of general conversation with the men, who sat or stood around our chairs, smoking their pipes, and for the most part, well disposed to be instructed. Leaving them, we took our course up the stream, following its winding way, enjoying the bright sunshine, the shadows flecking the grass, the cool breeze gently swaying the tree tops, the fields of waving green.

Such hours as these repay the self-denial of country work. Crossing the stream, our way lay along a deep gorge, then gradually up a plateau, and before very long we entered the beautiful and fertile Whong-hien valley. Our road lay through several villages, but as we had recently visited them, we did not care to stop. However, in the last of the group, receiving repeated invitations to halt, and the chair-bearers wishing to rest, we had our chairs set down on a quiet street. Immediately the people came crowding around. A woman begged assistance for some disease from which she was suffering. After directing her where to find medical advice in the city, her request served as an opening for a talk: "We have not come to cure diseases, nor to see the country, nor to ask anything from you, but we have come to bring you a message." "What message?" someone in the crowd naturally asks, and thus the way is fairly opened. They listen well and intelligently, especially the men, but towards the last there was rather more of excited arguing on the part of some of them than I find agreeable. We parted in a very friendly way, however, one old man receiving a book for which he had previously made request. As we were leaving I noticed a group listening as one read aloud from this book.

Our course lay still through the *Whong-hien* valley. The road was wretched enough in many places, but far as the eye could reach on either side was one scene of beauty—vast fields of green wheat, rolling lands, with low hills, and the horizon bounded with ranges of mountains, to which the distance lent a soft, purplish tinge. The corn and the *gowliang* (for which I know no English name) were about two inches above the ground, while the millet was just beginning fairly to show itself. After witnessing a famine, one comes to take a deep interest in the annual crops. One learns to watch the clouds if too much rain has fallen, or to look with intense longing for the clouds if there has been too little. One notes with anxious interest the growth of the standing crops, and forecasts the probabilities of a plentiful or scanty harvest. Just now the prospect for wheat is very fine if we can only have twenty days of clear weather.

We met people coming from market with bags of grain over their shoulders, and we saw scholars returning to their homes from the examinations now being held in the city. We overtook one nice looking young man, who, according to Chinese custom, inquired "Where are you going?" and "where do you come from?" Then he asked the chair-bearer at what "preaching-hall" I lived. One of them replied, "North Street." "Why is it," he asked, "that when we go there they shut the door?" Thinking this a somewhat personal question, I told him "there was no gentleman living there, but only a woman, that is, myself." Then, "thinks I to myself," how pleasant it will be when our promised reinforcements come, and there will be no need to shut the door on these scholars!

We were at our journey's end much earlier than usual, but the quarters were by no means inviting. They were far too public—the inn being on the Main street, where a market is frequently held, and there were other reasons that made us unwilling to remain there.

As we started out the second morning one of the first objects that attracted our attention was a group of women beside a stream washing clothes. Their method certainly has the merit of convenience—the only utensils needed being a flat rock placed in the edge of the stream and a round stick, very much like a rolling pin, to beat the clothes, which are alternately placed on the rock and dipped into the water. When the garment is washed, they spread it out on the ground to dry. The ironing (?) is done at home, after the clothes have been starched. A thick, flat stone is brought into requisition, the garment is placed thereon, and now two round sticks are used. A skillful woman brings these down upon the clothes with a wonderful rapidity and with quite a musical rhythm in her successive blows. It is astonishing that clothes come out of this process looking as nice as if they had been carefully ironed.

There being no bridge over the stream to which allusion was made above, our chair-bearers took off their shoes and waded across. The road was now smooth and level, on each side well-worn ruts indicating the use of wheeled vehicles. We are sometimes amused in reading the home papers, at the blunders made in statements about China. For instance, not long ago there was a statement to the effect that while the Chinese have wheel-barrows, they have no carriages. Now, the real truth of the case is, that the Chinese classics, books perhaps four thousand years old, speak constantly of carriages. Doubtless they were rude and clumsy vehicles without springs, probably pretty much such as they use at the present day, but still such as may, with propriety, be denominated carriages. Speaking of blunders, we were somewhat surprised to see a statement that "beginning in Shantung a year ago, the church now numbers two hundred." One would infer from this that Shantung is some city, and that until a year ago no missionaries had lived there. In point of fact, Shantung is a large province, with probably thirty millions of inhabitants; missionaries of various denominations have been working in Chefoo and Tungchow, which are both in Shantung, for nearly twenty years, and there are little churches and mission stations scattered in various parts of the province. In Tungchow alone the Baptist and Presbyterian churches number together more than two hundred members. In the region of *Ching-chow-fu*, a large city in this province, the English Baptists have a large and prosperous work, while the Northern Presbyterians have been established several years in *Che-nan-fu*, the provincial capital.

But to return to my story: Our course lay through the most charming country. There were seemingly endless fields of grain. Scattered about at no remote distance from each other were cozy looking villages embowered in green trees; and in the distance, bounding at once the view before us and the horizon beyond, were the same low ranges of mountains, giving definiteness to the view and forming a soft and lovely background to the bright scene before us. I wished while in the first village we visited that day that I had pencil and paper to put down, on the spot, the remarks made as Mrs. H. was trying to gain the attention of the women who came around. Failing that, I will throw together some incidents of the day's experience. Imagine the missionary with a book in her hand, sitting or standing, as may be most convenient, and trying to fix the attention of the women on the most important subjects. "I have come to tell you something very important," says the lady. "You must listen well. I ask these children not to make a noise." "How old are you?" inquires some one. Answer and go on: "If it were not very important, we would not take all this trouble to come here to tell you." Audible approval. "Good people," they say, "come here to tell us a good doctrine. Listen to what they say." "Sad it is," goes on the lady, "that you all here, almost without exception, worship mud images, and you do not know that it is a sin. We have come to tell you that it is a sin against the Heavenly Father." "How many children have you?" "One," says Mrs. H., if she happens to be the speaker. "Boy or girl?" "How old is he?" "Is he married?" The missionary goes on with her talk. ("How white her hand is!" "She doesn't look more than seventeen or eighteen." "How pretty she is?" "The fact is, their water and earth (climate) is better than ours.") "Pray don't talk," says the lady, "when I am through you may talk as much as you like." "Be quiet; don't talk," they say to each other. Silence two minutes, while the lady resumes her talk: "People cannot transmigrate, neither are they like lamps that go out, nor are they annihilated, nor does the wind blow them away, nor do they go to the temple after death to drink the soup of forgetfulness." "What! don't transmigrate?" exclaims some astonished listener. "No; after death there are but two places, a heaven of boundless happiness, a hell of endless suffering." "Can we women go to heaven?" they ask in accents of utter doubt. And so the talk goes on. The women are mere children in mind. Now and then there is one of intelligence, eager to learn and evidently having thought earnestly over the questions of human destiny, but the majority have minds utterly vacant.

The scene I have endeavored to describe above is mainly confined to a first visit to a village. The excitement and the eager curiosity to see and to ask personal questions almost prevents the possibility of any fixed attention. Still, they get not a little truth in this irregular way; and a year hence, if permitted to re-visit these villages, they will probably welcome us as old acquaintances—tell us things we have told them today, and listen with eagerness to what we shall say. It is really hard work to keep one's wits to answer promptly every question, and then to go on with one's talk just where it was left off; or if the question be something connected with the subject, to interweave the answer so as to make no serious break in your connected discourse.

We visited nine villages during the second day of our tour. After our return to the inn, we were fortunate in procuring quarters in a private family. A woman who lives in a very retired way consented to take us in, not only at this time, but whenever we may have occasion to visit this region. Scarcely had we gotten into our new apartments before they were filled with women and children, who congratulated themselves that we were now where they could visit us. The woman of the house has an only son, living somewhere among the Russians. To our surprise, we found here very handsome fashion-plates, gotten up in Paris for the Russian market. They also showed us a Russian coin, some foreign photographs, a lead pencil, &c. It seemed rather odd in that out-of-the-way village to find people ahead of ourselves in Paris fashions, and to be shown a Russian kopek—a coin we never saw in our lives before! Who will say after this that China does not move? The family insisted that the absent son is in our country, and it is useless to deny the "soft impeachment." All foreigners are alike to them, and there is but one "outside country." They have caught up some Russian words from the traveled member of the family, and as they air their knowledge, and Mrs. H. replies she doesn't know the words, they remark sagely to each other, "Ah! she does not understand because she lives in a different country." No wonder they make this explanation, for two Chinamen living five hundred miles apart are wholly unable to understand each other's spoken language.

On the third and last day of our tour we visited eight villages, and among them one of the three largest in this province. It is said to have one thousand families. In one village where we had acquaintances, we made a ceremonious call, and were treated with great politeness, a courtly gentleman escorting us as we took our leave, and asking us to call again. In their ancestral hall hangs a genealogical chart which goes back eight generations. Each name is accompanied with a picture, supposed to be a portrait.

Our course this last day lay mostly near the sea shore, and a part of it through scenery both wild and grand. Hills, valleys and endless plateaus seemed tossed together in the wildest confusion. The road, now winding around some rocky ledge, now suddenly descending to a great depth, and again as suddenly ascending, it was impossible to keep one's chair. The grandeur of the scene was a feast to the eye, but the enjoyment was marred by excessive fatigue. At last, after many weary miles, the city burst upon our view, and we gladly entered its walls just as the sun, looking like a ball of fire, was sinking below the horizon.

L. Moon.

Tungchow, June 4, 1880

Published in the September 1880 *Foreign Mission Journal.*

FROM MISS MOON, OF TUNG CHOW

HOUSES—THE KITCHEN GOD—BUDDHIST IDEAS
ABOUT ANIMAL FOOD

In this part of China, especially in the cities, the houses are well built. They are constructed mostly of stone, and some of them, from the outside, present an imposing aspect. No house can be said properly to front the street as in western lands. On the contrary, except the street door, only dead walls meet the eye of the passing gazer. This remark applies only to dwelling houses, however; the shops all open on the street. The street door of the better houses is massive, painted a shining black, set off sometimes with gay red panels above, or, if the owner be a literary man, with large gilt Chinese characters, indicating the grade to which he has attained in the government examinations. Usually, also, even on the doors of the very poor, are pasted long, broad strips of red paper, on which has been written some ethical sentence from the works of the ancient worthies of China. The effect is ornamental and pleasing to the eye. The street door is furnished with wooden bolts within, and even in the day-time, such is the cautious temper of the people, the door is often shut fast, and one has to knock a weary time before getting admission. A heavy iron ring on each door serves as a knocker. Before gaining admission the usual question "Who?" or "Who knocks the gate?" must be answered; and the answer always is, "I,"—it probably being supposed that the voice will convey all the needed information as to who the special "I" may be. Having gained entrance, one passes through a covered way which leads into a court-yard, and upon this court-yard front two or three buildings.

Chinese houses in this section are usually built in rows. A wealthy family will have five or six such rows of houses, one built back of the other, with a little intervening yard. The main room in the first row will probably be the ancestral hall, which is usually a large and handsome room, hung with scrolls, and occasionally with pictures, and having ancestral tablets, with vases in front of them, for burning incense. This room also serves as a sort of study for the gentleman of the house, and here he receives his literary friends. The other rows of houses are used by the various branches of the family. The Chinese mode of living is patriarchal—many generations dwelling under one roof, or rather series of roofs. To divide the property and dwell apart is exceedingly disgraceful in Chinese eyes. One street door serves for all. Say there are six rows of houses, the persons dwelling in the sixth will have to pass through all the other five in order to get access to the street. Each row contains 3 main apartments, a middle room with doors opening into the court-yard in front and the court-yard in the rear, and two doors opening into interior rooms. The middle room serves as a kitchen—and usually has two brick ovens. These are connected by flues with the brick beds in the adjoining rooms, and keep them comfortably warm in winter, but unendurably hot in summer. A foreigner, after tossing restlessly all night on one of those hot "kongs," is ready to declare that life is not worth living under such conditions but evidently the native enjoys being roasted alive. Above one of the brick ovens in the kitchen is pasted the god, *Dzord-wong*, with a shelf below him, on which stands the incense vase. This god is burned at the new year, a clean new god being bought for half a cent to supply his place, the old one being supposed to ascend to heaven and give account of the deeds of the family. Here are some of the things forbidden in the presence of the kitchen god: "Do not strike the oven, do not burn paper in it, do not sing foolish songs, do not curse people, do not cut up vegetables on the oven, do not burn unclean fuel there, do not burn there old clothes or shoes. Do not use your feet to stir the fire. Knife or axe do not put on the oven. The broom put aside out of sight. Beef or dog meat you must not eat. If a family be thus clean, it is well. It is not allowed to speak bad words in the god's presence. On the day when *Dzord-wong* rules you should not scrape the oven, lest the god be frightened away." There are certain days on which these things are forbidden, as, in the first month on the second, eighth, ninth, twelfth and twenty-seventh days. Scarcely any two months are alike as to the days, except that the twenty-seventh day of each month is sacred to this god.

The reader will have noted above that beef is put in the same class with dog's meat. Indeed the Chinaman looks upon the eating of beef pretty much with the same kind of horror we would feel in eating the flesh of the horse. The cow grows up along with a man's children. They pet it and love it as a calf. When it is older it draws the plow alongside the patient donkey. To a Chinaman it seems the height of ingratitude and cruelty to use its milk or slay it for food. The strict Buddhist will not touch animal food. Perhaps the following extract from a Buddhist book may interest the reader as giving the Buddhist feeling upon this subject: "All men love life. All creatures have the same instinct. How can one kill them for the gratification of one's appetite? To use a sharp knife, plunging it into their hearts, to flay them, to cut off the scales of a fish, to tear the shells from turtles and terrapins, to plunge living things into hot water, to salt them—great is the torture of these dumb creatures, though they have no power to express their anguish, and men who do these deeds have deadly enemies in the victims of their cruelty. Such men, dying, descend to hell. After enduring great torments, they are changed into animals. Those animals they have slain now wreak their vengeance upon them. For every life he has taken, the culprit shall himself once die, (transmigrating for this purpose into some living creature.) When the retribution is complete, then again will he become a human being; he shall have many sicknesses, and not many years shall he live, losing his life, whether by the sting of venomous reptiles, by the tiger's violence, by the soldier's sword, by the magistrate's sentence, or by poison—some of these shall be his lot because he took away life.

"I entreat men with tears. I dare not say you should altogether refrain from animal food; I only exhort you not to slay. Let a family forbid slaughter: its members will receive divine protection. Their troubles will be removed far away. Their lives will be very long. Their descendants will be filial. Their blessings will be multiplied, and words cannot express them. Should they constantly set free living things, and constantly chant prayers, not only will their happiness be increased, but, in the matter of transmigration, everything will be in accordance with their wishes. If they wish again to become men, this is allowed; if they desire not to transmigrate, their wish is gratified. They do not descend into hell.

"Ye good men, you have a method of attaining to this, I invite you to turn your hearts, make a firm resolve and use this means. Then you need not repent. If you cannot carry out this, go and exhort other men and your merits will not be few."

It was mentioned above that a Chinese house usually contains three principal apartments, the middle room which is the kitchen, and two inner rooms. In these latter the family life goes on. Running the whole length of the room, say about ten feet in length, and five in breadth, is the "kong" or brick bed. This is spread with matting, and here the women sit during the day, and here the family sleep at night. Here also the lady of the house receives and entertains her guests, the visitor being invited to get up on the "kong" and the inevitable pipes being hospitably brought forth with urgent invitations to smoke. This invitation is rarely declined, for smoking is universal with women as well as men.

The floors are of brick in the better houses; among the middle class and poor people, there are only dirt floors. Windows are of wood, bars, say an inch apart, over which is pasted translucent paper. Occasionally, just in the centre of the window is a bit of glass two or three inches long, permitting one to see out. The rooms of Chinese houses are very small, and one often wonders how the inhabitants find breathing space, especially as the windows are often so constructed that they cannot be opened.

The furniture in the houses of the rich, though not abundant, is often handsome, being set off by exquisite varnishing, and kept bright and polished by daily rubbing. It usually consists of a large wardrobe and a sort of bureau, with a chair or two. The middle class will probably have a bureau and a chair, and the poor no furniture at all. The bedding which consists of wadded coverlets, is neatly rolled up during the day and placed on one end of the "kong." The richer people live in considerable comfort; but an ordinary Chinese house of the middle and poorer classes, the dirt, confusion, and disorder are simply appalling. The smoke-blackened walls, the dust-covered furniture, the impure air, the disgusting odors—all these combine to render a Chinese home anything but attractive in the eyes of the "foreigner in far Cathay." The best specimens of comfortable living are to be found mainly in the cities, and occasionally in a large town. The homes of the country people are dirtier, more smoke-blackened, the furniture less or more dust-covered, and the yards are usually filled with farm produce. Add to this the pig-pen under the window, and the stable a few feet from the door, and the charms of such rural life are more readily imagined than described.

Chinese houses having been depictured above, albeit imperfectly, the next article will tell of the people who inhabit them.

L. Moon.

Tung Chow, March 3, 1881

Published in the June 1881 *Foreign Mission Journal.*

CHINESE SUPERSTITIONS—TRANSMIGRATION

Tung Chow, March 19, 1884

It is popularly believed that each person has three souls. At death, one soul is interred with the body. A hole is left at the side of the grave for the exit of the spirit. Offerings of food are made on set occasions, and the spirit is supposed to consume them in some ethereal way. Another soul is supposed to take up its abode in the ancestral tablet, and this is also worshipped with incense, offerings of food, and prostrations. A third soul is supposed to go to the temple and there to drink the "soup of forgetfulness." It is the last soul that is believed to transmigrate. The belief in transmigration is as universal among the Chinese as it seems to have been among the Jews in the time of our Lord. A Chinese woman, arguing with a missionary with regard to the doctrine of transmigration, related a story which she regarded as furnishing irresistible proof of the facts of which she was personally cognizant. A woman gave birth to a daughter, and in her disappointment that it was not a son, strangled her. A second and third daughter met the same fate. On occasion of the murder of the third child, the father remonstrated with the mother on her cruelty, but finally allowed her to have her way. One night, in a dream, a being appeared to him and said: "I have been to your house three times, and you would not allow me to live. When it is day, I shall go again, and this time I shall injure you." He awoke in great terror; fell asleep, and the dream was twice repeated. He related this to his wife. On the morrow she died in giving birth to a fourth child. The explanation on psychological grounds is simple. In drinking the "soup of forgetfulness," the soul is supposed to lose all memory of its past. There are rare cases, however, in which such is not the case. A singular story is told, the main facts of which are known to a great many persons, and are avouched by two Christians, who could have no motives for falsehood. Ninety years ago there lived in the village of San Jeow, thirty-five *li* from Tung Chow, a fisherman who traded in a certain kind of black fish, and from this circumstance was popularly known as "Black fish Jeow." The fisherman was accustomed to hawk his fish about the country, and even extended his travels as far as Wei Hein, some hundreds of miles distant. An intimate friend of the fisherman died. Ten years after his death the fisherman was in the neighborhood of Wei Hein selling his fish, when he fell in with a party of school-boys. One of these addressed him as "Black fish Jeow," and he stated that in a former existence he had lived in the village of San Jeow under such a name, and proceeded to relate a number of incidents connected with his former life there, and mentioned circumstances known only to the fisherman and his deceased friend. The fisherman was amazed to recognize in this school-boy of ten the aged friend who had died ten years previous. When the boy had grown to be a young man of twenty, he went to visit the former scene of his existence. There he had been poor; now he was the heir of wealth. He found the former companion of his life an aged woman of eighty. He was exceedingly gratified that his daughter-in-law recognized him, and in reward he presented her with fifty taels of silver. He ever retained an affection for his old village, and all who visited him from that region were cordially received and hospitably entertained. Persons connected with the officials from his old country were accustomed to call at his house for hospitality, as he always asserted that he still belonged to his old district. The main facts of this story are said to be well attested. How are they to be explained? Making due allowances for exaggerations and additions to the story, we may suppose that the school-boy's imagination had been fired by stories of transmigration, and that he had some general knowledge of the fisherman by hearsay. His name and place of abode would be generally known in the region through which he travelled, and nothing would be more natural than for a boy to prefix his nickname, "Black fish," on seeing in what he dealt. The fisherman's surprise would probably arrest the boy's attention, and the thought would be suggested to his imagination that he was the hero of an actual transmigration. The rest of the story would follow as a matter of course. A Chinese Christian asserts Satanic agency, declaring that the boy was possessed of the devil, who revealed to him the facts.

The Chinese fully believe in demoniacal possession. They also speak of persons as "possessed of the fox," or "possessed of the weazel." Witches worship the spirit of the fox, and are supposed to have its help in injuring others. These witches also have the reputation of being able to cure diseases.

L. Moon.

Published in the June 1884 *Foreign Mission Journal.*

STRANGE CUSTOMS AND IDEAS

In visiting among the Chinese one meets with customs that seem odd and even very abhorrent to the Western mind. As I was passing along the street on yesterday, I was accosted by an acquaintance and cordially invited to enter. On going into the house the first sight that met my astonished gaze was a large black coffin. It was placed in the centre of a room through which the family and all visitors must constantly pass, a room in which the family cooking is also done. Here this ghastly object has stood for more than three months awaiting burial. The woman I was visiting, who is a daughter-in-law of the deceased, rattled on, laughing and talking in the liveliest way. She said the venerable lady had died and that they did not have the money necessary to bury her. Sometimes a family will expend more than a thousand dollars on a funeral. A fortune-teller must be paid to select a lucky place for burial. Priests are engaged to celebrate the funeral rites. A band of musicians is hired who make right[?] hideous with their din. Open house is kept for days and there is much feasting and jollity. In the funeral procession there is not a little barbaric pomp and show.

When the sick are found to be dying the friends hasten to put on them their best clothing in order that they may make a good appearance in the other world. The dying must be removed from the "kong" (brick bed) lest the spirit should enter it and remain. If, unfortunately, death should take place before removal, the kong must be pulled down. After death, paper money is burned that so the deceased may be able to pay his way in the under world. Paper horses and carriages and servants are also burned. It is desired that the dead shall keep up the same state to which he has been accustomed in this world.

The Chinese believe that each person has three souls. One is supposed to enter the tablet which is kept at home to be worshipped; another is said to go into the tomb, and to this offerings of food and money are also made on set occasions; a third is supposed to go to a temple and drink a beverage of forgetfulness, after which it transmigrates according to the deeds done in the body. A wicked man will become an animal; the very good man may hope to be a god. A good woman is allowed to believe that she may become a man when her period of existence in this world again rolls around.

Lottie Moon.

Tungchow, 1884

Published in the August 1884 *Foreign Mission Journal.*

LUNG SAN TIEN

June 4, 1884

If only a machine could be invented to grind out answers! It must be admitted that patience less than angelic would grow weary of the seemingly endless round of questions. "Where do you live?" "How old are you?" "What is your name?" "How many are there in your family?" "Are your mother and father still living?" "Have you children?" "Did you make this dress or hire somebody to do it?" "Did a tailor make it?" "Did you make your hat?" "What did it cost?" "Did you make your gloves?" "What did they cost?" "Did you make your shoes?" "Have you holes in your ears?" "Why don't you wear earrings?" "What do you eat?" "Do you eat pork? beef? mutton? eggs? rice? chicken?" "Aren't you cold?" "Has your brother any children?" "Has your sister any children?" "How old were you when your parents died?" "Do you sleep on a kong or on a bed?" "Don't you get cold sleeping on a bed?" "From what country are you?" "Do you make the whole journey by water?" "How long does it take?" "What is the distance?" "Do they till the ground in your country?" "Have you mountains?" "Do you go on a steamer?" "What does it cost?" "Don't you get seasick?" "How long have you been in China?" "Which country is best, yours or ours?" "Don't the women rule in your country?" "Do you go home every year?" "How often do you go?" "Is your country east or west from here?" The monotony of answering precisely the same questions put by some dozens of people in the course of an hour, and this not once, but some thousands of time, would be endurable were monotony the only drawback. The utterance of Chinese demands an expulsive energy which so strains the muscles of the throat as to render even ordinary conversation physically wearisome. When more than one's strength is needed to talk on matters of the highest moment, when one's articulation begins to fail, and the speaker longs to relapse into utter silence, that so wearied muscles may rest,—how delightful would it be to turn a crank and have the machine say, "I am an American." "I have been in China ten years." "I'm not cold." "People are alike everywhere in thinking their own country the best," and so on, till, as on the hand-organ, it is all ground out and the instrument goes back to the first tune.

The Chinese are a kind-hearted, friendly race when once you know them and come to live among them in a familiar way. They are disposed to be neighborly, and are kind in sickness. I have been troubled with a sprain, and two different neighbors have sent me a plant, the decoction of which, they say, will reduce the swelling. The women are much more friendly than the men. It sometimes happens that I am sent for to visit a family, and the remark slips out that the men are away, and therefore they ask me. The other day I was urged to visit a certain family. The little daughter and a young relative came to conduct me. We had quite a walk through the village, and at last came in view of the house. To the chagrin of my young conductors, a man of the family was loading a donkey near the door. As soon as he caught sight of the hated foreigner he began to utter some very uncomplimentary remarks about the "devil-woman," and my young friends slunk back in alarm. The daughter said in an undertone to the cousin: "Don't tell that I brought her here." The man sternly demanded what I had come for, and the young cousin said that I had only come on the street to enjoy myself. As the remarks were not addressed to me, I passed on in silence and was soon invited into another house. In a few minutes the room was jammed with a chattering crowd of women, the window was down tight, and the kong on which I sat was very hot. I did what was possible to get their attention, and talked to such as would listen; then as soon as politeness allowed, took my leave. I was asked into another house where the kong was cold, and I got the window put up. The room was filled at once, and I talked to them a good while. Then some men came in and the women scattered. The men were evidently hostile, though maintaining a show of outward politeness, and I immediately withdrew. Then one of my young friends dragged me to a third visit, much against my will, for I was wearied in body, and for the time, disheartened by so much unkindness. The woman for whom the visit was intended received me kindly and learned some in the catechism. In a few minutes a man appeared, looking like a small thunder cloud. As the woman is a widow and free to do as she likes, I gave myself no concern about the young man's looks.

I listened to an odd conversation this morning. Two old women had been moaning to each other their sad lot. One of them remarked that she was only sixty-four years old and that she ought to have more strength. The other said, in the most natural way in the world, "Have you a coffin?" "Oh, yes." In turn she inquired her companion's age. "Sixty-nine." "You only lack one year of seventy; have you a coffin?" She replied that she had thought of providing herself with that very necessary article, but somebody had said that she was not likely to die within six months, and so the matter had been postponed. This reminds me of a visit I paid in the city a month or two ago. The old lady was a stranger to me, but welcomed me cordially. In her small room was a large unpainted coffin, which she graciously explained, she had provided for herself. She seemed to regard it affectionately as the place of her future repose. The top was not dry, and one end of it rested on the coffin while the other was supported on the kong. This "kong" be it understood, is a brick bed spread with matting, on which the Chinese sit by day and sleep at night. The old woman cheerfully remarked that the top would be dry in a few days and then it would be placed on the coffin. It is childless people, or people whose children are undutiful, who think it necessary to provide themselves coffins. The Chinese have a great desire for what they regard as a respectable burial, and for that reason they provide themselves good coffins if they have reason to believe that this will not be done by surviving relatives.

June 5. I heard this morning of a strange custom that tradition reports to have prevailed in China in former times. When people arrived at sixty years of age, it was the custom to prepare for them a place of sepulture, in which they were placed. Food was put in sufficient for a few days, the tomb was closed, and the aged parent was left to die. I have not been able to ascertain how long ago this barbarous custom existed. Some years ago I noticed, near Tung Chow, what seemed to have been a subterranean passage, which had caved in. Upon inquiry I was told that in the olden time a man had here buried alive his aged parents.

As I was teaching the catechism this morning to the widow above referred to, she remarked to a neighbor who was admiring the readiness with which she learned: "I have no other thought but this." The neighbor replied, "You are like my eldest son. He is all the time reading these books; even at his meals he reads the New Testament." This same woman told me the other day that her son had been better since he had been reading my books. A catechism given to his daughter first attracted his attention, then a little hymn book, and afterward he seemed literally to devour the "Peep of Day." He spoke of one of the miracles and said emphatically that this proved that Jesus is the True God. His daughter and niece are bright girls and have both learned some in the catechism and hymn book. I spent a good part of last Sunday morning teaching these girls in their own home, the women of the family listening with great interest.

Tung Chow, June 6th. Yesterday I visited a village, and as I was talking to the women one of them interrupted with the question: "If we don't worship the idols, what must we worship?" Not caring to break the thread of my talk, I made no reply. She repeated the question, and to my delighted surprise, a girl answered, with an earnest look: "Worship the True God. Worship Jesus."

As I came home to-day we halted for the chair-bearers to rest at a village, where I recently spent a few days. A pleasant looking boy hung about my chair, and I inquired if he had learned any in the catechism when I was staying in the village. On his answering in the affirmative, I questioned him and found he could answer four pages. Pretty soon he disappeared and presently returned bringing a handful of beautiful, fragrant roses, which he presented with a beaming smile. A simple gift of flowers is a small thing from our point of view; it seems only an amiable, boyish kindness. To one who has lived long in China, trifles like this mean a good deal more. They mean that old prejudices are passing away, and that the people are learning to regard missionaries as friends who have come here to do them good, no longer as "devils" to be feared, hated, and despised. As one of the signs of the times, the gift of a handful of flowers is not devoid of significance.

L. Moon.

Published in the September 1884 *Foreign Mission Journal.*

WHEAT HARVEST

Wheat harvest in the region around Tungchow begins usually about the 20th of June. It is a season that is anticipated with much joy. True, there is hard work, but at the same time there is feasting and jollity. The whole village becomes a scene of happy activity. In general, women do not share the outdoor labors of the men; times of harvest furnish an exception to this rule. The men go out to the fields, while the women, girls and smaller children, down to the least babies, take their places on the threshing floor. The floor is on a level spot and is rolled until it is perfectly firm and smooth. The wheat is pulled up by the roots and tied into bundles. Mules and donkeys are then heavily laden and led away to the threshing floor. The women unload the animals and then, with a chopper, cut the bundles in two, the roots being piled in one place and the heads in another. These roots are afterwards used as fuel. The wheat is stacked at night and in the day is spread out on the threshing floor for sunning until it is perfectly dry. A good deal of the wheat drops out as the drying process goes on and is carefully swept up. The main mass, however, has yet to be disengaged from the straw and chaff. The wheat is spread out on the threshing floor and is threshed by means of a stone roller. This roller is dragged around by a blind-folded donkey, urged on by the whip of a driver. The mode of cleaning is like that of the Bible times. The wheat and chaff are tossed up; the wheat falls into a pile and the chaff flies before the wind. This process is repeated until the wheat is perfectly clean.

During the wheat harvest the price of labor advances. The usual pay for a man's work a day is about twelve or fifteen cents, without food. During the wheat harvest food is provided of the best quality, with Chinese wine at dinner, and the pay ranges from about fourteen cents a day as high as fifty cents. In the neighboring county, Whanghien, high prices prevail, and from forty to fifty cents seems to be the rule.

L. Moon.

Tung Chow, July 7, 1884

Published in the November 1884 *Foreign Mission Journal.*

FROM MISS LOTTIE MOON

A late Shanghai paper contains the following interesting item: "There has been over $1,000 contributed, without solicitation, by the Chinese gentlemen of Shanghai for the sufferers by the recent earthquake in Charleston, S. C."

For Gen. Grant's monument the great Chinese Viceroy, *Li,* sent a liberal subscription. These kindly acts of heathen people are in pleasing contrast to the treatment Chinese receive in some parts of America.

The same paper contains an extract from an English paper giving some interesting facts concerning the China Inland Mission. This mission was begun twenty-one years ago, and has sent out two hundred missionaries. These missionaries go out with the understanding that they have no claim upon any person or society for a salary. They receive funds in proportion to the funds of the mission. "There is now a missionary stationed in nearly every province; but several of the provinces are each as large as the whole of England, with a population equal to Great Britain. There are still one thousand walled cities, besides smaller towns and villages, without a single Christian missionary in them. England, with the population of one province in China, has 35,000 ordained ministers."

It is stated that negotiations are nearly completed for ceding Macao to Portugal. China has four European nations as near neighbors: Russia on the North, England at Hong Kong, and in Burmah, France in Anam, and

Portugal at Macao. On the score of influence the latter may be counted out. Russia, as unscrupulous, aggressive and constantly encroaching, is to be feared and watched. England is China's natural ally, and statesmen of both nations seem conscious of the fact, as witness the late treaty negotiated between the two countries on the conquest of Burmah by the English. China concedes substantial advantages, and England permits the highest spiritual (Buddhist) authority in Burmah to continue the accustomed tribute, formerly paid by the civil power, to the Dragon throne. France, after the experiences of the late war, will find it to her interest to keep on good terms with China.

Besides these European nations, China has a near neighbor Japan, which is being rapidly westernized and Christianized. In time these influences must tell in favor of the spread of Christianity in China. The influence of Europeans in government employ in many departments must also tell in the way of breaking down prejudices and thus of indirectly aiding the work of the missionary. For instance, we now and then find Chinese soldiers who "keep worship day," that is to say, who refrain from drill on Sundays. To this they were habituated under their European drill-master, and even when no longer under his control some of them keep up the custom, at least for a time. The high character of men in the Customs' Service has also, no doubt, exerted a good influence on the Chinese mind. It is said but that one defalcation has ever occurred in this service, though more than twenty years have elapsed since its establishment. The sum was at once made good by the Head of the Service out of his own private resources.

Looking at China's relations with foreign powers, and at changes going on in her own borders, everything seems propitious for the earnest prosecution of the mission work. But, oh! the fewness of the workers. In Shantung, for instance, with its twenty-nine million inhabitants, we have eight missionaries, that is, one missionary to three million six hundred thousand people. Well may Dr. Ellis, quoting "that grand old Scotch apostolic missionary," say we are "playing at missions."

L. Moon.

Whanghien, Jan. 12, 1887

Published in the April 1887 *Foreign Mission Journal.*

POLYGAMY

Pingtu, China, Jan. 12, 1886

I was invited last Sunday to visit a mandarin's family, but declined on the plea that I do not go out on the Sabbath. I was asked to appoint a time for the visit, and I named this morning. Accordingly about half past eleven o'clock, a woman came to conduct me to the official residence. I was led through the large public gateway across a yard, then into another yard somewhat smaller, whence we turned to the left through an arched way leading to the private residence. A young fellow went ahead and announced my arrival. I followed immediately, and my presence seemed to produce some confusion; evidently I was not expected so early. A scene met my astonished and pitying gaze, such as I have never witnessed in the lowest hovels of beggary. An elderly woman was in the act of rising. Her hair was unkempt, her face unwashed, and seemingly smeared with soot, while her dress was disgustingly filthy. On a table beside her implements for opium smoking told a sad tale. A servant was engaged in combing a little girl's hair. She hastily swept off the dust from the torn matting which covered a wooden bedstead, and invited me to sit, saying, apologetically, that they had not expected me so soon. I entered into conversation with her, and in a few moments two blind men came in. One of them inquired what was meant by the Sabbath. Ascertaining that the elderly woman who had awakened my pity was the mandarin's legal wife, I made an effort to form her acquaintance. Hearing she was not well, I went back to her bed insisting that she should not rise. I had opportunity now to observe that, in this bitter January weather, her wooden bed was just opposite the open door, in the very coldest part of a very cold room, that the bed was barely covered with one poor rug, and must have been hard and cold beyond description, and that she had but one single covering. I attempted to sit down on the edge of the bed, but the servant interfered, and hurried me away to my original seat. After some further delay, a man wearing a wadded satin garment emerged from an inner apartment and passed rapidly out. This was the mandarin. I was now invited to enter the inner room, the comfort of which was in painful contrast to the squalor and wretchedness of the outer apartment. A couch extending the whole length of one side of the room was spread with felt rugs, and on one side was neatly folded an abundance of bedding. On the other side of the room was a wooden bedstead, likewise well provided with an abundance of cover, folded up for the day, as is the Chinese custom. A fire was burning in a Chinese stove, on which was a tea-kettle with hot tea. As I entered a woman with a pleasant face, but evidently in poor health, greeted me in Chinese fashion, clasping her hands in front and bowing. On inquiring I was told that this was the lady of the house. Here, then, for the first time, I beheld the practical working of polygamy. The wife of the man's youth, whose crime was that her male children had all died, was cast off and reduced to a state of abject squalor and wretchedness, while another woman was brought in to take her place, and here, right before her eyes, was living in luxury, with servants to anticipate her every want.

Apologists for the polygamist tell us of the cruelty of requiring a man who wishes to become a member of the church to give up the mother of his children. In the case before me it is the mother of living children, two grown and married daughters, who has been put away. The woman who supplanted her is childless, except that she has two adopted children, a boy and a girl. Now the question arises, if an adopted son can fulfil all the requirements of ancestral worship, why was not a son adopted in the first place? Why should not the lawful wife have been allowed to adopt a son to take the place of those she had lost, and why should she not thus have been spared the bitter trial of seeing a stranger brought in to supplant her? O, the cruelty of this horrible system of polygamy! Yet your Christian missionary apologists will tell us that if the man will only promise to take no additional wives we should condone his past and receive him for baptism! Fancy a Mormon asking for baptism and receiving a gracious permission from the Baptist pastor to retain his half dozen wives!

But to my story. After some little talk with the lady, the two blind men entered. They were said to be fine musicians, and I asked them to play and sing. Two instruments hanging on the wall were taken down and the musicians prepared to comply with my request. One instrument was similar to a guitar and the other seemed to be a castanet. The musician with the guitar played a rapid and lively prelude, and then the other one burst out singing, bringing in the castanet at intervals as additional accompaniment. Then the first musician, all the time playing rapidly, seemed to answer him, and so they sang, alternately, till finally, towards the close, they sang together. It was not by any means bad music, though the accompaniment was monotonous. Meantime the lady has settled herself to her accustomed morning smoke. With her head resting on a pillow, she reclined on one side of the couch while I sat on the other. Beside her had been placed a waiter holding the usual paraphernalia of opium smoking. She would take a bit of prepared opium on something that looked very much like a knitting-needle, and hold it over the flame of a lamp. When it grew soft in the flame, she would put it into the opium pipe, apply the pipe to the flame and draw deep whiffs. The faint, sweet odor of the burning opium is unlike anything else, and can never be mistaken; one often notices it in passing opium dens. The musicians kept up their apparently endless duet, the opium began to affect my head, and seeing no prospect of doing any good I was wishing I could make my escape. After awhile the smoking ceased, though the music did not, and the lady left the room to get her breakfast. She returned at last, the duet meantime having come to a close, and I talked with her and taught her adopted son. She inquired what people were permitted to join the church, and asked if we had separate churches for men and women. I warned her of the sin of opium smoking, but felt that all such warning was in vain. I could not but feel sorry for the adopted son, a bright, polite, rosy-cheeked boy, the very picture of health. Yet what hope, humanly speaking, can there be for him with such examples hourly before his eyes? I was disgusted with the whole scene, and gladly availed myself of the fact that it was my dinner time, in order to effect my escape. As I went out I paused to speak to the unfortunate woman who sat in squalid misery on the side of her wretched wooden bed. Years ago this miserable creature was probably a happy wife and mother, living in comfort, with servants to wait on her. Now she is an outcast, ill-clad, in abject poverty, her daughters far away, her sons in the grave, and, in the adjoining room, separated only by a curtain over the doorway, lives in luxury the woman who has supplanted her and the man who was the husband of her youth. Should this man apply for membership in our church, could the decision be left to me, I should say to him: "Put away the woman who has supplanted your lawful wife and restore the latter to her rightful place in your house, and so give proof of the sincerity of your repentance. After that we will talk about admitting you as a candidate for baptism."

L. Moon.

Published in the May 1886 *Foreign Mission Journal.*

FROM MISS LOTTIE MOON

Tungchow

In working recently in the country near Tungchow, I have been much encouraged by the manifest changes in the attitude of the people towards foreigners. Everywhere I have been met with pleasant words and smiling faces. At only one village this spring have I witnessed any manifestation of the old hostility. I was talking with some women when an elderly man of respectable appearance came on the scene and spoke in an undertone. He passed on and immediately they began to make excuse that it was cold, and to go into their houses. I comprehended at once what had taken place, and looking at the cause of the interruption as he disappeared, I thought, "Poor, old man, you have not many years in which to do this bad work. When you are gone there will be none here to oppose." We met him as we were leaving the village. I suppose he had gone on that street to see that I should get no audience there.

I was much gratified to find the two villages where I am accustomed to stay evidence of real progress. There seemed to me to be a beginning of genuine interest. One should not be discouraged by the extremely slow progress of the gospel in the heathen lands. To be impatient of early results is as if pioneers, in an unbroken wilderness, with forests to be cut down, houses to be built, lands to be cleared, the soil to be plowed and sown, should be dissatisfied that houses do not grow up by magic, nor broad acres, in a moment, wave with golden harvests. The hearty pioneer plods on patiently, year after year, and in time he reaps the reward of his labor. So in heathen lands we must wait patiently during the time of seed-sowing. The harvest will come in time, and in China what a harvest it will be! We should remember that the Chinese are not a small community of savages who gape in astonishment at Western civilization. On the contrary, China had a respectable civilization when our own ancestors had not emerged from barbarism. Proud of her government, proud of her ancient civilization, proud of her literature, it is no wonder that China has striven to keep out influences from the West. She has striven in vain, and is being more and more drawn into the current. China and the West have misunderstood each other. China has judged the West from having opium forced upon her by a Western power. The West has judged China by its emigrants, forgetting the fact that, as a rule, the best representatives of a nation do not emigrate. It is time that this mutual misunderstanding should cease. In China we see many multiplied proofs of a deep and abiding change. Much of the former hostility to foreigners was due to ignorance, which is rapidly passing away. In the West a similar ignorance exists with regard to China. Many intelligent people still look on the Chinese as barbarian. It is to be deplored that they do not read and inform themselves as to the real facts. With such a work as

Williams' *Middle Kingdom* accessible to all, ignorance about China is inexcusable.

L. Moon.

Published in the July 1887 *Foreign Mission Journal.*

FROM MISS LOTTIE MOON

AN EARNEST PLEA FOR HELPERS

Perhaps one of the blessings to be extracted from the denominational differences is that they may be legitimately used to stir up a rightful emulation. For several years, some kind, unknown friend has sent me the "Woman's Missionary Advocate," which is the organ of the Southern Methodist women. In reading this monthly I have been deeply impressed with the intense earnestness of the women who direct the work at home, and with the prompt response made by the Methodist sisterhood to every demand, whether for money to sustain the work, or for consecrated women to carry it on. Last December a noble young missionary fell at her post. Immediately the cry went through the women of the church that her place must be promptly filled. From China went the plea that the workers on the field were overburdened, and that overwork meant death to some of them; that they must be reinforced or disaster would result. Already the news comes that two new missionaries would be on their way to China in March, and that two more would leave in the following autumn. The Southern Methodist women manifest an intense enthusiasm for foreign missions. They give freely and cheerfully. Now the painful question arises: What is the matter, that we Baptists give so little? Whose the fault? Is it a fact that our women are lacking in the enthusiasm, the organizing power, and the executive ability that so conspicuously distinguishes our Methodist sisters? It is certain that women can be found willing and glad to come and work for God in China. The lack is not of women who would come, but of money to send and sustain them. Here, in Pingtu, there is a wide-open door for woman's work. It could be indefinitely enlarged if there were women to do the work. Already, as I am doing it, the work naturally divides itself into city and country work and into work for the girls and for the women. Though I have been here nearly two weeks, I have not been able to spare even a day for the country. Three unmarried women could find abundance of work to do here. There should be some one to give herself up wholly to teaching the girls. The latter are allowed great freedom; more than I ever saw anywhere else in China. They marry much later than in the Tungchow region, where, owing to poverty, on the one hand, and the wish of the intending mother-in-law for a servant, on the other hand, shockingly early marriages are the rule rather than the exception. The girls here remind me of the American girls in their freedom, sweetness, modesty, and docility. I could imagine no nobler life than one spent in teaching such girls to follow in the footsteps of our blessed Lord.

There should be a woman here to visit from house to house, a most hopeful and promising sphere for activity. Lastly, there should be some one, strong in body, cheerful and indomitable in spirit, to do the country work.

The more I see of the field, the more deeply I am impressed that it is one we should occupy. The affectionateness and docility of the women, their freedom, the general politeness and kindness of the people; all these are a new revelation to me of fine possibilities in the Chinese character. I feel that I would gladly give my life to working among such a people and regard it as a joy and privilege. Yet, to women who may think of coming, I would say, count well the cost. You must give up all that you hold dear, and live a life that is, outside of your work, narrow and contracted to the last degree. If you really love the work, it will atone for all you give up, and when your work is ended and you go Home, to see the Master's smile and hear his voice of welcome will more than repay your toils amid the heathen.

L. Moon.
Pingtu, May 4, 1887
Published in the August 1887 *Foreign Mission Journal.*

SHANTUNG AS A MISSION FIELD

There are some special reasons why Shantung should be regarded as one of the best fields for mission work.

1. The climate is good. After being acclimated, with reasonable prudence, missionaries enjoy as good health as most people in America. It has been proved by actual experience that missionaries may occupy native houses, properly fitted up, & not suffer in health. In Southern & Central China, foreign houses must be erected or the result would probably be disastrous.

2. The spoken & the book language are the same. Thus the missionary is spared an immense expenditure of time, strength & toil in the acquisition of the language. While the spoken & written language are different, the missionary finds himself confronted with the task of learning two difficult languages before he can feel himself fully equipped for work. When he has mastered the written language, he realizes that it is an instrument which will avail him only in communicating the gospel to the educated. The illiterate masses, & especially the women & girls, will always be debarred the use of books if they must acquire a language in order to learn to read. Where the spoken & written are the same, the poorest peasant, with perseverance & industry may learn to read the Word of God.

3. There is comparatively little prejudice against foreigners. There is none of that hatred which has broken out elsewhere in riots & houseburning & serious endangering of the lives of foreigners. There is also none of the bitterness felt in some parts of China on account of outrages committed on Chinese in America. The influence of the great *Viceroy Li* is powerful in this province. Among other instances, his well-known friendliness to foreigners was manifested by the interposition which secured our mission a foot-hold in Whonghien. It is not probable that there will ever again be serious difficulty in procuring houses wherever desired in the province.

4. The people are a fine race & well worth the devotion of one's life for their evangelization. A province that produced such sages as Confucius & Mencius is not to be lightly or contemptuously regarded. The men are manly & independent in their bearing. In some parts of the province, the women have great freedom of action. Societies for religious worship flourish among the women & one may see them going up to the temples in companies for worship. Members of these societies also meet twice a month for worship in private houses.

5. In the interior of the province, missions have been very successful. The English Baptists have a flourishing mission at Chingchowfu, begun about eleven years ago. They have not far from a thousand converts. The work is largely self-propagating. The Northern Presbyterians who have a number of missionaries working in the interior have also gathered in numerous converts. The Congregationalists are working successfully in the northwest corner of the province.

The time seems ripe for our mission to emulate the example of others & push on into the interior. We were the first to enter Shantung & yet for years we have lagged behind others in the prosecution of the work. The more I see of the people in the interior the more intensively desirous I become that they shall have the gospel preached to them. Here, at P'ingtu, there is ready access to the homes of the people. Not only am I constantly sent for to go to their homes, but I rarely go out for a walk without being invited into one or more houses. The children beg me to visit their homes as if I would be conferring a great favor. The men, if they are at home during my visits, talk pleasantly & invite me to return. The girls & women have great freedom. I have been told that the women go to the large market gatherings & I see girls on the street selling their straw braid to the itinerant buyers. The girls are sweet, affectionate & modest. With proper instruction & training, they would develop into fine, intelligent women.

The dark side of the picture is the prevalence of opium smoking. It is painful to see families going down that were once prosperous. Of my immediate near neighbors, last year, four were opium smokers. One has since died & another moved. For opium smoking, there is no remedy but the gospel. It has saved some & might save many more. A mission here in P'ingtu, consisting of three families & two unmarried women, once started, would not be a very expensive luxury for Southern Baptists. With no paid assistants, with no foreign houses or churches, & no boarding schools, such a mission, once set going, could be carried on annually at a cost of six thousand dollars. Wouldn't such an investment pay better, say, than twenty-five thousand dollars contributed by one man for a memorial church in a city already supplied with churches? Why can't we have a "Memorial" mission? When will some rich Baptist come forward & start a mission which would give the gospel to some hundreds of thousands of people? When will some church say, "We will sustain one missionary in P'ingtu," & not only say it, but raise the money and send the missionary?

L. Moon.

P'ingtu, May 17th 1887

Published in the September 1887 *Foreign Mission Journal.*

THE BREAKING DOWN OF MISSIONARIES

When an army is in the field & a fight is coming on, it is wise to send the sick to the rear. Many a noble life has been uselessly wasted by the determination to be in the battle at all hazards. Men, scarcely able to rise from their beds, have dragged themselves to certain death, impelled by patriotism or driven by the fear of their comrades' sneers. In the army of the Lord, it is no mere idle boast to say that foreign missionaries constitute the van. Theirs is the post of honor; it is they who are obeying in person the last command of their risen Lord. Theirs is the post of danger. The time may have passed in China at least, when a missionary has cause to fear personal violence. Yet there remains the climate with its subtle influence, sapping a man's vitality almost without his consciousness, until he awakes to find himself a physical wreck. There is the fierce, pitiless Eastern sun blazing down fifteen hours a day for many months in succession till the very sunlight is heart-sickening. There are the physical hardships necessitated by his work of which one is ashamed to talk, less he should seem to be complaining. There is the crowd, often hostile, always curious, pressing upon & around him until his nerves are worn beyond endurance. There is exposure to loathsome diseases in unavoidable contact with all conditions of people. There is, wearing upon the mind, the ever present depressing consciousness of being hated by the people, one he (is?) giving his life to save. In the missionary's surroundings, there is everything to drag him down spiritually & mentally & nothing to lift him up. Then, as regards the work to be done, there grows upon him the feeling of overwhelming odds in the contest. He looks forth & sees villages on all sides as far as the eye can reach & knows that beyond these they go, on & on, until the imagination wearies in the effort to grasp their numbers. Then there are the great cities in few of which is there any resident missionary. The sense of responsibility presses upon him & with it the feeling of powerlessness to effect anything. Fancy one man set to meet the spiritual wants, say of the whole state of Georgia & you will have some conception of the case in heathen lands. Last year, a Methodist missionary wrote to the Woman's Board urging that reinforcements be immediately sent. He described how those already here were overworked & added that failure to send reinforcements meant death to some of those already on the field. Ten years ago the Missionary Conference which met in Shanghai, sent forth a stirring appeal for more laborers. "Many among us," says this paper, "are tempted too undertake many duties. Hence, the broken health & early death of not a few of our best men." Those words are as true now as when they were penned. A missionary who has passed safely through the trying time of acclimation & who has been enabled by the blessing of God to continue in the field, watches with painful interest & sympathy the breaking down of new missionaries. I knew a party of five young Presbyterians missionaries who came out to Shantung in the fall of 1881. They were followed a little later by three others. A brighter, livelier, more hopeful set of young people, it would have been hard to find. Among them were characters of rare worth & beautiful consecration. Of these eight, within four years & half, three were filling graves in Tungchow or Weihien, three had returned to America to remain, & two were left.

A good many years ago three Presbyterian missionaries opened a station in the capitol of this province. Of these three, one lost his reason & with his wife was sent home & one died. The mission has been repeatedly reinforced & now numbers six on the field & two on furlough.

The Weihien mission, began by the Presbyterians in 1883, has suffered heavy losses. Two of its members returned to America in that same year, one died in the following year & another in 1886. A physician who was sent out to the mission in 1884 broke down & went home in about two & half years. By repeated reinforcements of experienced missionaries from other stations, the mission now numbers six.

Facts such as these seem to teach some serious lessons. First, a lesson of sympathy. Give the returned missionary a cheerful welcome, even if he breaks down in two or three years, remembering that in his place you might not have done so well as he did. Second, a lesson of caution. It seems exceedingly unwise to put upon new missionaries the heavy responsibilities connected with opening a new station. New missionaries break down or die under overwhelming burdens, the weight of which is largely due to their inexperience & ignorance of the language & the ways of the people. It would be well if young missionaries could be held back from all work except that of learning the language until they are acclimated. Third, a lesson of prudent provision. The minimum force of a new station should be at least six missionaries, & more if possible to provide against the certainty of illness, departure or death. Lastly, *when the sick and wounded are borne to the rear there is all the more pressing need for reinforcements to be sent speedily to the front.*

L. Moon.
Tungchow, July 27, 1887
Published in the October 1887 *Foreign Mission Journal.*

FOR THE *FOREIGN JOURNAL*

I copy from a Shanghi paper as follows: "Some very important memorials from censors have lately been presented to the Throne bearing on the subject of education, in which foreign & scientific studies are recognized & recommended as qualifying for honors. This is the beginning of the greatest revolution which China has ever witnessed, compared to which the mere change of a dynasty is but a passing accident. A censor, *Chan Sui-yung*, recognizing the importance of foreign affairs, recommends that of the smaller officials within Peking, who are recommended for merit, the foreign-educated & those who understand international affairs should be placed at the head of the list. Further, that mathematicians should enjoy equal privileges in literary examinations with those who understand the Monogolian dialects. *Ch'un* is highly pleased with the proposals, & has submitted them for favorable consideration to the Boards of Civil Office & of Rites."

Ch'un is the father of the young Emperor. Contrary to all expectation, the Prince has shown himself liberal & enlightened. When he came into office a few years ago, as leader of the war party, grave fears were entertained of a reactionary policy on the part of China towards all foreigners. The Prince was supposed to be a foreign-hater, yet never before have foreigners been more sure of protection to life & property & of kindly treatment by the common people.

France has again lost ground in China, a fact which no one but the French will regret. Heretofore that country has been the acknowledged protector of Roman Catholics in China, of whatever nationality. The German & Italian Governments have given orders to their respective representatives to extend the usual civil protection to Roman Catholic missionaries of their respective nationalities. The Roman Catholic Bishop at Peking has received from the Chinese Government the dignity of a red button & thus holds rank, in some sense, as a Chinese official. He will be able now effectively to protect his co-religionists throughout China & will no longer be liable to the suspicions of being an emissary of France.

Great changes are going on in China; wonderful progress is being made. The question comes up, What are Southern Baptists doing to utilize the opportunities now offered? Here in Shantung where we ought to have a hundred missionaries, we have just *eight*? How long is this state of things to continue? How long is the "King's business" to go undone? How many million more of souls are to pass into eternity without having heard the name of Jesus?

During my recent visit to P'ingtu, I was more than ever impressed with the desirability of opening a mission station there. I cannot speak too warmly & gratefully of the kindness of the people. The opportunities for work are limited simply by the strength of the workers. I was there about two months. During that time, I made eighty visits to heathen homes, besides teaching daily in my own "hired house." From after breakfast till sun-set with a rest at noon, I was constantly busy. It was almost like having a school. Sometimes as many as a dozen girls would be learning at once. Towards the last, my throat became so sore & cough so bad that I had to give up teaching. The girls would say, "No matter. Bring out the book & we will study ourselves." I had also to decline visiting. In all my experience in China, I had never seen anywhere such readiness to learn & such freedom from prejudice against foreigners. Again I plead for a mission station to be opened at P'ingtu. In this connection, however, let me say that no one should go there to live who has the slightest predisposition to lung disease. Consumption is very prevalent, especially, I was told among young people. In the spring, the dust proves to be fearful. It rises, almost like a cloud, obscuring the air. I noticed that it affected the lungs of the children & I presume it causes consumption. Otherwise, the people seem very healthy.

L. Moon.
Tungchow,
June 29, 1887
Published in the October 1887 *Foreign Mission Journal*

FROM MISS LOTTIE MOON

In a former letter I called attention to the work of Southern Methodists women, endeavoring to use it as an incentive to stir up the women of our Southern Baptist churches to a greater zeal in the cause of missions. I have lately been reading the minutes of the ninth annual meeting of the Woman's Board of Missions, M. E., South and find that in the year ending in June, they raised over sixty-six thousand dollars. Their work in China alone involved the expenditure of more than thirty-four thousand dollars, besides which they have missions in Mexico, Brazil, and the Indian Territory. They have nine workers in China, with four more under appointment and two others recommended by the committee for appointment. I notice that when a candidate is appointed, straightway some conference society pledges her support in whole or in part. One lady is to be sent out by means of the liberal offer of a Nashville gentleman, to contribute six hundred dollars for travelling expenses. A gentleman in Kansas gave five thousand dollars to build a church in Shanghai in connection with woman's work there.

The efficient officers of this Methodist Woman's organization do their work without pay. Travelling and office expenses are allowed the President of the Board of Missions. This money is to be used at her discretion in visiting conference societies that are not able to pay her expenses. Office expenses alone are allowed the Corresponding Secretary and her assistant, and also to the Treasurer. A sum is appropriated for publications, postage, and mite boxes. The expenses for all purposes are less than seventeen hundred dollars. In a word, Southern Methodist women, in one year, have contributed to missions, clear of all expenses, nearly sixty-five thousand dollars! Doesn't this put us Baptist women to shame? For one, I confess I am heartily ashamed.

In the matter of appointments to mission work, extreme care is taken in the selection of candidates, and, judging by the high character and efficient work of Southern Methodist women in China, this care is not exercised in vain. Candidates are sent up by the societies of their respective conferences. There is a standing committee on examination of candidates. Above this is a committee on missionary candidates appointed at the annual meeting. There is also an educational committee, whose duty it is to ascertain if the applicant comes up to the required standard in education. When the candidate has satisfactorily passed these various examining committees the case comes before the Board, and the applicant, if accepted, is recommended to the Bishop for appointment.

I am convinced that one of the chief reasons our Southern Baptist women do so little is the lack of organization. Why should we not learn from these noble Methodist women, and instead of the paltry offerings we make, do something that will prove that we are really in earnest in claiming to be followers of him who, "though he was rich, for our sake became poor?" How do these Methodist women raise so much money? By prayer and self-denial. Note the resolution "unanimously approved" by the meeting above:

"*Resolved*, That this Board recommend to the Woman's Missionary Society to observe the week preceding Christmas as a week of prayer and self-denial." In preparation for this,

"*Resolved,* That we agree to pray every evening for six months, dating from June 25, 1887, for the outpouring of the Holy Spirit on the Woman's Missionary Society and its work at home and in the foreign fields."

Its "work at home," be it noted, is to arouse an interest and collect money for the foreign field, as also the Indian Territory.

Need it be said, why the week before Christmas is chosen? Is not "the festive season when families and friends exchange gifts in memory of The Gift laid on the altar of the world for the redemption of the human race, the most appropriate time to consecrate a portion from abounding riches and scant poverty to send forth the good tidings of great joy into all the earth?"

In seeking organization we do not need to adopt plans or methods unsuitable to the views, or repugnant to the tastes of our brethren. What we want is not power, but simply combination in order to elicit the largest possible giving. Power of appointment and of disbursing fund should be left, as heretofore, in the hands of the Foreign Mission Board. Separate organization is undesirable, and would do harm; but organization in subordination to the Board is the imperative need of the hour.

Some years ago the Southern Methodist mission in China had run down to the lowest water-mark; the rising of the tide seems to have begun with the enlisting of the women of the church in the cause of missions. The previously unexampled increase in missionary zeal and activity in the Northern Presbyterian church is attributed to the same reason—the thorough awakening of the women of the church upon the subject of missions. In like manner, until the women of the Southern Baptist churches are thoroughly aroused, we shall continue to go on in our present "hand to mouth" system. We shall continue to see mission stations so poorly manned that missionaries break down from overwork, loneliness, and isolation; we shall continue to see promising mission fields unentered and old stations languishing; and we shall continue to see other denominations no richer and no better educated than ours, outstripping us in the race. I wonder how many of us really believe that "it is more blessed to give than to receive." A woman who accepts that statement of our Lord Jesus Christ as a fact, and not as "impractical idealism," will make giving a principle of her life. She will lay aside sacredly not less than one-tenth of her income or her earnings as the Lord's money, which she would no more dare to touch for personal use than she would steal. How many there are among our women, alas! alas! who imagine that because "Jesus paid it all," they need pay nothing, forgetting that the prime object of their salvation was that they should follow in the footsteps of Jesus Christ in bringing back a lost world to God, and so aid in bringing the answer to the petition our Lord taught his disciples: "Thy kingdom come."

L. Moon.

Tungchow, Sept. 15, 1887

Published in the December 1887 *Foreign Mission Journal.*

FROM MISS LOTTIE MOON

A Hard Question—An Earnest Appeal

With that omniscience which awakens the wondering admiration of the uninitiated, a Baptist editor declared last year that it would be impossible for those who embrace the "new theology" to take a strong interest in foreign missions, that belief in a "second probation" is incompatible with earnest effort for the conversion of the heathen. Pondering the question of the indifference of Southern Baptists to missions, in the new light cast upon my ignorance by this wise editor, I conclude that the large majority of Southern Baptists have adopted the "new theology." Else, why this strange indifference to missions? Why these scant contributions? Why does money fail to be forthcoming when approved men and women are asking to be sent to proclaim the "unsearchable riches of Christ" to the heathen?

The needs of these people press upon my soul, and I cannot be silent. It is grievous to think of these human souls going down to death without even one opportunity of hearing the name of Jesus. People talk vaguely about the heathen, picturing them as scarcely human, or at best, as ignorant barbarians. If they could live among them as I do, they would find in the men much to respect and admire; in the women and girls they would see many sweet and loving traits of character. They would feel, pressing upon their heart and conscience, the duty of giving the gospel to them. It does seem strange that when men and women can be found willing to risk life—or, at least, health and strength—in order that these people may hear the gospel, that Christians withhold the means to send them. Once more I urge upon the consciences of my Christian brethren and sisters the claims of these people among whom I dwell. Here I am working alone in a city of many thousand inhabitants, with numberless villages clustered around or stretching away in the illuminate distance: how many can I reach?

It fills one with sorrow to see these people so earnest in their worship of false gods, seeking to work out their salvation by supposed works of merit, with no one to tell them of a better way. Then, to remember the wealth hoarded in Christian coffers! the money lavished on fine dresses and costly living! Is it not time for Christian men and women to return to the simplicity of earlier times? Should we not press it home upon our consciences that the sole object of our conversion was not the salvation of our own souls, but that we might become co-workers with our Lord and Master in the conversion of the world?

I left Tungchow nearly two weeks ago, spending a Sabbath at Shangtswang on my way to this place. There were three services during the day, conducted by the younger brethren. A Presbyterian missionary, Dr. Nevins, who has just passed through here, told me that he stopped on his journey hither at a village about five miles from Shangtswang, and that he found that the Christians sustained a good reputation among the heathen.

I have been in Pingtu nearly a week, and find the people as kind and friendly as ever. A few days ago, visiting a family, I was talking with two men, and they volunteered the assurance that all like to have me there, that there are none who are unwilling. I rarely go on the street without invitations to visit, which I cannot accept for lack of time. At present I spend mornings at home, chiefly in teaching the girls, and go in the afternoon to some village. The weather is now beautiful for the latter work. It is delightful to go out into this fertile country, smiling with rich harvests, which the people are not busy gathering—a charming contrast to the Tungchow region, where a severe drought has prevailed, and scarcely half crops have been made.

I am told that a telegraph line is being put up just outside the city limits. Though there will probably not be a station here, it will make me feel in the civilized world once more just to see the wire.

L. Moon
Pingtu, Oct. 3, 1887
Published in the January 1888 *Foreign Mission Journal.*

From Miss Lottie Moon

We are told that Jesus went about among the cities and villages "preaching the gospel of the kingdom" and it is added that when he saw the multitude as sheep without a shepherd, he was moved with compassion. No heart that has truly caught the Master's spirit can look out on the vast multitudes of heathen and fail to be moved with a like pity. Not merely tens—nor hundreds—nor thousands, but millions are moving resistlessly on in the downward path. Who lifts a helping hand to stay their course? How are these people to be saved without the gospel? "How shall they hear without a preacher? And how shall they preach except they be sent?" "Narrow is the gate and straight the way, that leadeth unto life, and few be they that find it." Neither these heathen nor their forefathers ever heard of the narrow gate. Once more I desire to plead the cause of the people among whom I am living. Pingtu is a walled city with suburbs on all sides. The suburbs contain a population probably not less than the city itself. In all directions are encircling villages. Stretching northward and eastward as far as Tungchow and Chefoo, a distance of more than one hundred miles, there is not one resident missionary. Westward, there is a mission-station of Presbyterians, distant from here sixty miles. To the south, stretching on for hundreds of miles, I know of no mission-station. Members of our mission have worked in this region now for several years, coming all the way from Tungchow. What can two or three accomplish in the way of reaching these hundreds of thousands? The itinerant missionary comes, spends a few days at an inn and is gone. This is all his time allows, for he feels that there are many other places with pressing claims upon him. The majority of the natives look upon him as a "devil" to be hated; even the best disposed regard him as an enthusiast who is trying to lay up merit for his own sake. Here and there, however, is a man who becomes interested in the gospel; he listens to instruction and has vague desires after a better life. He has before him a fearful conflict. There are family influences, there are superstitions of ages, there is obloquy and hatred. The newly awakened man needs the moral support of the missionary's presence. Is it a wonder that many give up in despair, thinking it is no use to try, and that they can't walk this hard path alone? Suppose there are converts; they need to be taught how to live the Christian life. They need before them actual examples of holy Christian living.

It is absolutely certain that our mission force in Shantung is utterly inadequate. In this large province, with probably thirty million inhabitants, we have at present but one station, and that not strongly manned. We were the first to enter this field, and to-day we are the weakest mission, with perhaps one exception. These things ought not to be so. There should be steadfast resolve to push the work on into the interior; to establish new stations as rapidly as possible and to man them thoroughly, that there shall be no more disastrous failures. All this means an immense increase in contributions to the mission cause and consecrated men and women ready to lay all upon God's altar, that these precious souls may be saved.

"Then saith he unto his disciples, the harvest truly is plenteous, but the laborers are few. Pray ye, therefore, the Lord of the harvest, that He send forth laborers into His harvest."

L. Moon.

PINGTU, Feb. 29, 1888

Published in the June 1888 *Foreign Mission Journal.*

FROM MISS LOTTIE MOON

The Heathen's Blindness—Our Duty

I wish it were possible to get people who are interested in Foreign Missions to understand something of the immensity of the work to be done. I do not refer now to the enormous numbers of the heathen or the vast extent of the countries yet unevangelized. I am thinking only of what has to be done in even one small community, merely to make a beginning. The Chinaman, as regards foreigners, stands somewhat as our customs did one hundred years ago; the alien is a natural enemy, to be hated and despised. He is a being of inferior civilization, to be regarded and treated as a "devil." Go into one of their temples and see the grotesque and hideous images that represent to them the "devils" of their Buddhist hell and you will understand how the Chinaman regards the foreigner upon whom he bestows this complimentary epithet. The missionary comes in and settles down among the natives. His first object is to convince them that he is human and that he is their sincere friend. By patience and gentleness and unwearied love, he wins upon them until there begins to be a diversion in sentiment. There are those who will hate him to the end, but others come to recognize that he is both wiser and better than themselves. Now begins the work of teaching with some hope of making a real impression. These heathen are not only without a knowledge of the gospel, but their minds are full of superstitions and false notions. At every step, the missionary must remove error as he tries to teach the truth. He tells them of a soul to be saved or lost, and they answer that there are three souls, one of which will go through endless transmigration. He tells them of the state of the soul after death and they answer that according to their accepted opinion, the soul goes to a temple where it remains two days, after which the son of the deceased burns a paper horse on which the soul is sent away to the destined place in the spirit world. Tell them of the different states of the righteous and the wicked as being the just sequel of life on earth, and they answer, "Yes, those who are poor and suffer here will suffer in the other world; those who are prosperous here will be prosperous there." Tell them of the falseness of idols, and they quote the proverb, "Worship them and they are gods; don't worship, and they are mud images." We will suppose, however, that some faint glimmerings dawn upon them of a desire for better things. They confess that the idols are false, that there is but one True God, and that He alone is the lawful object of worship. They say that they do not know how to pray, and the missionary endeavors to teach them. Their spiritual darkness is absolutely inconceivable to one who has not seen it. A sample form of prayer is presented (I) pray (the) Heavenly Father (to) pity me (and) forgive my sins. "Ah! Yes," says one, "pray to heaven and to father and mother." Another who always associates heaven and earth as two gods, says, "Just so. That's what we do, pray to heaven and earth." Still a third caught by the similarity between the Chinese words for father and happiness, says, "Yes, pray to heaven for happiness." The missionary, undiscouraged, patiently teaches them the glorious truth of the Fatherhood of God until he is satisfied that the learner has at least caught a glimpse of the meaning and then he passes on to talk of sin and the need of its forgiveness. The hearer readily admits the fact of sin and the necessity of forgiveness, but thinks it must be obtained by outward work of merit, such as burning incense, knocking heads and chanting prayers. A simple, brief form of prayer has to be explained over and over, sentence by sentence, and sometimes word by word. Even a person who reads and who goes glibly over the words, has but slight conception of the spiritual meaning. The prayer being learned, the learner consents to begin to pray for himself. It is easy to see that such a one has taken only a first faint, feeble step in the divine life. How many never go beyond that! What watch care is needed, what prayer for God's Spirit, what constant instruction of this poor soul, how does it need guidance and instruction that it may walk worthy of the calling wherewith it has been called! Now let it be borne in mind that the case above presented is not a solitary one, but that it is fairly representative of every man, woman and child in a heathen community.

In view of such facts, it is plain that even to make a beginning in the conversion of China to the religion of our Lord Jesus Christ, there must be an immense increase in our mission force. The Presbyterians, who are already enormously ahead of us in numbers, have asked this year for fourteen clerical and medical missionaries and as many young ladies as are wishing to come. Assuming that the majority of the fourteen will be married men, the number asked for this year is over thirty. In contrast with our two feebly manned stations, the Presbyterians have already four stations, each with three or four times as many men as we have at a station. They have, in other words, twice as many men for any given station as we have for all Shantung.

"They that sow bountifully shall reap also bountifully," is as true in spiritual things as in material. Until our people at home are thoroughly aroused on the subject of Foreign Missions and contribute largely of their means to the cause, we have no right to expect that God will bless us with extended success. Has not the time come for a change that shall amount to a reformation on our part?

L. MOON.
Pingtu, March 30th, 1888.
Published in the August 1888 *Foreign Mission Journal.*

FROM MISS LOTTIE MOON

A Growing Work
Pingtu, May 25, 1888

I mentioned in a former letter that there seemed to be an advance in the work here. It takes heathen people a good while to learn the real object of a missionary's coming among them. There is a great rush in the first stage, from mere idle curiosity to see the foreigner. I trust we have passed that stage here to a large extent, and that the time has come when we may expect fruit from the labor expended. Mrs. Crawford came out in April, and we have been engaged in incessant teaching, either at home or in the houses of the people. We are beset with invitations, and sometimes have to make engagements days in advance. We are invited into scores of places, each of which becomes for the time a centre of teaching; the neighbors flock in, and many of them set to work earnestly to learn.

In a letter recently published in the *Foreign Mission Journal,* Mr. Pruitt mentions a village where some were "fully persuaded," and only needed further instruction. We returned a few days ago from a visit to this village. Of fifty families in the village, I was told that about twenty were interested in the gospel. We worked at the rate of twelve hours a day. I never saw such hungering and thirsting to be taught the way of life. Mrs. Crawford, who is not strong in health, instructed the men, besides taking a share, as she could command the time, with the women and children. It was simply impossible to meet the urgent necessities of the case. Four workers would have found their hands full, and we were only two. Old women and their little grand-children would be learning from the same page. Mothers of families were there eager to be taught. Bright, lovely young girls would pore all day and half the night over the hymns and prayers we were teaching them. Before we were through with breakfast, numbers of girls and women would be awaiting permission to enter, and would work steadily at their books until time for dinner; after a noon-day rest, we would again admit them, and only cease work in time for a walk before dark. Then, after supper, came another spell of teaching which lasted till midnight. Many of the girls laid aside their straw-plaiting, or sewing or spinning, that they might devote themselves entirely to learning. There were crowds of visitors from neighboring villages for whom we could do almost nothing, although many of them were eager to be taught.

On Sunday, I was filled with wonder, as I saw an orderly assembly of at least twenty-five persons sitting quietly through a Christian service, and themselves taking an intelligent part in the worship. The singing was spirited and good. During the prayer, there was perfect quiet, and as Mrs. Crawford read and commented on the third chapter of John's gospel, there was earnest, thoughtful attention. These people belong to a sect known as the "Venerable Heaven Sect." Their leader is a man of great force of character and fine natural ability. Their doctrines are propagated orally. Any one who has learned them is permitted to write them down for his own use, but the book is not allowed to be copied, and when worn out is to be burned. From all that we can learn, we have come to believe that this religion has been handed down orally and secretly, with many corruptions in the transmission, from early Nestorian teachings. The difference between members of this sect and ordinary Chinese is most marked. They have deep spiritual desires, and earnest aspirations for salvation from sin and its penalty. There is a gentleness and a sweetness in the women and girls, and a kindness and sincerity in the men that I have seen nowhere else. Seeing the eagerness with which they accepted our teaching, we could only compare them in our minds to Jewish proselytes of apostolic times. It seemed as if they could not give us up. Whenever we spoke of leaving they would entreat us to stay longer. When finally we felt ourselves breaking down, we tore ourselves away, amid the regrets and the tears of those we had been teaching. They urged us to return as soon as possible and arrange for a longer stay.

None but a heart of stone could turn away from such urgent pleadings. I had previously planned to leave immediately for a return to America, after an absence of more than ten years. Instead, I have promised these people to return here in August and teach them. One of the men, after hearing of this decision, spoke very feelingly of the sacrifice involved, and especially of the disappointment to those who were expecting me "at home," and then he buried his face in his hands and wept. His brother, the leader, came up to the city to visit us on the day of our return, and wept at the thought of parting with us for even a few months. We leave in a few days for the coast, Mrs. Crawford to work in the country near Tungchow, and I for a season of rest and change. Mrs. Crawford has given time and labor here in Pingtu which she could ill afford to spare from her own large field west of Tungchow, stretching half way to Whanghein. As I saw her last week instructing patiently for hours the men who eagerly gathered around her, my memory was haunted by the words of Scripture: "That no man take thy crown." It seemed to me that here was a woman doing the work of some young man among Southern Baptists in America who *ought* to be here, and that when the harvest should be garnered in Heaven and the laborers receive their reward, the Master would place on her head the crown that should have been his! As was remarked in an editorial in the *Journal*, women are doing their own work and much of that which properly belongs to men. It was also stated elsewhere that no trained young men are offering for China. More and more some of us on the field are beginning to think that there is great need here of earnest lay workers. Consecrated, godly laymen, of sound practical sense and good education, would find here a magnificent field for all their energies. The China Inland Mission is largely made up of the lay element. The head of the English Baptist Mission at Chingchowfu, one of the most successful in China, objects to having the title "Rev." prefixed to his name. The field here in Pingtu seems to be ripening for a great harvest. The question is, shall we reap it? Or shall others come in and reap the benefit of labors already expended? The calls upon us are more than we have time or strength to meet and the field is constantly widening. Some have taken down their kitchen gods; others have ceased to worship at the temples. Books and leaflets are begged and many learn in their own homes. In the village mentioned above, the more advanced teach those who have made less progress. It is simply wonderful that Christian hymns are sung in so many heathen homes. There are, in the city and the country, perhaps twenty who might be classed as inquirers. It would be utterly impossible to state the number who are learning or have been taught hymns and prayers. While I would be exceedingly cautious of raising unfounded expectations, it is impossible to exaggerate the readiness of the people to receive us. This does not mean an immediate ingathering of converts, but it is a very loud demand for more workers.

There was One, who for "us sinners and our salvation," left the glories of heaven and sojourned upon this earth in weariness and woe, amid those who hated him and finally took his life. There was another, his chosen missionary, who preached the gospel "in much patience, in afflictions, in necessities, in distresses, in stripes, in imprisonments, in tumults, in labors, in watchings, in fastings; as sorrowful, yet always rejoicing; as poor, yet making many rich; as having nothing, and yet possessing all things." The Son of God and his humble disciple, the apostle to the Gentiles! "Who follows in their train?" Will not *you* who read these lines say, "Here am I, send me."

L. Moon.

Published in the September 1888 *Foreign Mission Journal.*

CHINKIANG

Chinkiang is situated on the Yangtse river, one hundred and fifty-seven miles from Shanghai, from which place it is easily accessible by steamer. Besides Roman Catholics, there are three Protestant denominations working here. Our mission has a most eligible location for work. One is surprised at the unwisdom displayed in building a number of foreign houses off on the hill in entire isolation from the natives. It would seem to be inconvenient for the men of the missions to reach any work, but it becomes almost an impossibility for their wives to get access to the people. A woman with young children may put in some moments of work daily if she is near the natives and close to the chapel, but if she must spend an hour or two on the road in order to reach any work it is almost certain she will do none. In this respect, we have decidedly the advantage over the Methodist and Presbyterian missions here. While their houses are off on the hills, far away from their chapels and from the natives, our chapel is at the head of the principal business street, and both mission houses are in a stone's throw of the chapel. The latter is a very pretty and convenient building. With windows thrown wide open and the breeze coming in, with the organ and lively hymns, it is a bright, attractive spot. On the ringing of the bell, the natives drop in rapidly. After a good deal of singing, Mr. Bryan talks in an easy conversational style and readily holds the attention of the audience. He is usually assisted by some of the church members. An elderly man, recently baptized is already making himself useful in talking to the heathen. Last Sunday afternoon we had a service somewhat unique for China. Five natives were appointed to speak and each was limited to ten minutes. The subject was sin, and the first four speakers were to discuss it, each in one special aspect, while the fifth summed up and connected the whole. The first four speakers were all members of the Baptist church here, while the fifth is connected with another denomination. It is very pleasant to observe that Mr. Bryan understands the art of setting his members to work. Of the native assistants last Sunday all were unpaid volunteers, and to all it was a coveted honor to be put up to speak. The audience was remarkably quiet and well behaved, and there was very little going out during the addresses. Mr. Bryan has great tact in managing a Chinese audience. "We have a custom here," he will say, "that the good people sit down and the bad people stand up." In a few moments, each Chinaman has asserted his goodness by seating himself. I was much amused last Sunday by the coolness with which Mr. Bryan stood up in his foreign dress before his Chinese audience and claimed to be a native of this place. "You judge a man," he said, "not by his outward appearance but by his dialect. Of the men who have just spoken to you, one came from such a place as you can tell by his dialect, another from some other place and so on for all the five speakers, but you can see," he added, "that I am a native because I speak the dialect." A ripple of subdued amusement passed over the audience, and then they listened attentively to this "native" as he gave them a talk about sin and urged them to accept the Saviour. On yesterday afternoon the church members assembled to study a portion of the Scripture, and one of them brought a number of his friends. About fifteen took part in the lesson, while an interested audience looked on and listened. Mr. Bryan seems to me to be emphatically the "right man in the right place." He is closely confined now to chapel preaching, but plans, when Mr. Hunnex shall have come, to do some general evangelistic work. His heart is set on opening a mission at Yangchow, a large city of half a million inhabitants, some twenty miles distant from Chinkiang by water. As yet the China Inland Mission is the only Protestant mission working there, but the Presbyterians are planning to begin a mission there. I earnestly add my entreaties to those of Mr. Bryan that the Board will send a man and wife immediately to prepare for work in Yangchow. Mr. Bryan is also very desirous of having a single woman to work here among the women. There seems to me to be a very fine opening here for such work. The women are friendly and accessible. I believe that in two or three years an experienced worker would have her hands full. A beginner, with the language to learn, would have to go more slowly and feel her way cautiously until she learned how to work. But for either, whether experienced or otherwise, there is a grand field here absolutely untouched thus far. Of the single ladies connected with the Methodists, one is a doctor, who works chiefly at her dispensary, and the other has a small boarding school. In this great city, with its outlying villages, there is no one whose sole work it is to go out and carry the glad news of salvation to the homes of the people. For such work single women are especially fitted as being free from domestic cares and duties. There is, no doubt, a work among the families of church members which can best be done by the pastor's wife, but if she has little children demanding her constant care, she cannot do any very extensive work among outsiders and especially among the villages. Of all the missions of our Board in China that I have seen, there seems to me none more important than this. With wisdom and prudence on the part of those in charge, I doubt not that a strong, aggressive church can be built up here. The members have a mind to work and the pernicious system of paid assistants has not been introduced. Thus far, the work among the women has not kept pace with that among the men. Mrs. Bryan, with delicate health and the care of two little children, has been much hampered in her efforts to acquire the language. She attends chapel services, to which a few women and children come, and she has done some visiting. With improved health and more experience, she is capable of doing very valuable work.

The new mission house is nearly completed, and will be ready for occupancy about the first of October, when Mr. Bryan will move in, vacating his present quarters in time for Mr. Hunnex, who is expected in October.

L. Moon
Chinkiang, August 1, 1888
Published in the November 1888 *Foreign Mission Journal.*

WORKERS FOR SHANTUNG

The Presbyterian mission in this province has "seventeen ordained missionaries, fourteen wives of missionaries, five unmarried female missionaries;" and yet "in view of the great need of more missionaries in the province of Shantung," the mission "has made an earnest appeal to the Presbyterian Board of Foreign Missions for an addition to the working force

of ten ordained ministers, two physicians and three unmarried ladies."
Assuming that most of the men who come out will be married, this means
an addition of nearly thirty to their present force of thirty-six.

We have six missionaries in Shantung, and we ask for thirty new ones.
Suppose we get them, our force will run up to thirty-six, just the number the
Presbyterians now have. Supposing they get the reinforcement asked for, as
they surely will, they would still nearly double us in numbers.

When Southern Baptists get sufficiently in earnest to properly man old
stations and open new ones, they may expect the Lord to smile upon the
work of their representatives in Shantung. To expect two men and four
women, one of whom does not yet know the language, to have a very large
measure of success is to go against the usual precedents. It is true that God
does sometimes bless with great success a small force, as in the case of the
workers among the Telugus, but this was under the exceptional
circumstances of a famine, which opened the hearts of the people. Those
who have the most men and women in the field will, other things being
equal, have the most converts. According to the sowing, so the reaping. In
the physical world, one hundred men can plough and sow more land that
five men, and when the harvest time comes, the reaping will be in
proportion to the sowing. So in missions. "They that sow sparingly, shall
reap also sparingly." It makes one heartsick to see how denominational
papers blow the trumpets over "four men, possibly five, for China." We
ought to have four men properly to man one station! Yet we are bidden to
exult over four men as if they were four hundred!! "O, Lord, how long?"
When will our people wake up to the needs of China's perishing millions.
When will Southern Baptist laymen come out at their own charges to do
mission work, as is done by many in the China Inland Mission and by some
in the English Baptist Mission? When will the time come when dozens, yea,
hundreds of churches, shall send out and support each its own foreign
missionary? Where is there a strong city church that could not, as part of its
regular church work, send out, as did the church at Antioch, its own foreign
missionaries? Why should not the First Church in Richmond choose its man
and say to the Board, "We will support this man (and wife) in China." Why
should not the Second Church say, "There is a crying need of woman
workers in Pingtu; we will sustain with our prayers, our sympathies, and our
money, some godly, consecrated women to be appointed by the Board as our
missionary." Souls are perishing for lack of knowledge; missionaries who
need rest are wearing themselves out with overwork, and are heartsick at the
apathy of the home churches, and over the waters is wafted to their ears,

with a loud sound of rejoicing "four, possibly five, men for China!!!" May God open our hearts and our purses, and may the good news soon come, "Thirty seed sowers for Shantung, one family and two single ladies for Chinkiang, four families and two unmarried ladies for Yangchow." Then shall our hearts be glad, and the work of the Lord shall prosper in our hands.

L. MOON.
Chinkiang, Sept. 11, 1888
Published in the December 1888 *Foreign Mission Journal.*

FROM MISS LOTTIE MOON

Kiangsu
The name of this province is taken from the first syllable of the provincial capital and *Su* of Suchow, the chief city. It is bounded on the north by Shantung, on the east by the Yellow Sea, on the west by Ngankin and on the south by Chehkiang. Its area equals that of Pennsylvania in square miles, or England without Scotland and Wales. According to Williams' *Middle Kingdom,* "the staple productions are grain, cotton, tea, silk and rice, and most kinds of manufactures are here carried to the greatest perfection. The people have an exceptional reputation for intelligence and wit, and ____ its cities present a gayer aspect and are adorned with better structures than any other in the empire."

"Probably no other country of equal extent is better watered than Kiangsu. The Great River, the Grand Canal, many smaller streams and canals, and a succession of lakes along the line of the canal, afford easy communication through every part. There are three large lakes in the province, while a third lies partly in Kiangsu and partly in Chehkiang. Nanking is the capital of the province. The largest seaport in Kiangsu is Shanghai, now become one of the leading emporia in Asia."

Chinkiang, our most recently established mission in Kiangsu, is situated at the junction of the Grand Canal with the Yangtsz river. "Its position renders it the key of the country, in respect to the transport of produce, taxes and provisions for Peking. _____ The country in the vicinity is well cultivated, moderately hilly, and presents a characteristic view of Chinese life and action."

In a province of this size, Southern Baptists, having entered more than forty years ago, have two mission stations, neither one of which is properly manned. In Shanghai, we have one family and Mrs. Yates; in Chinkiang, two families. The Southern Methodists, besides their very strong force in Soochow, their flourishing work in Hanziang and the newly opened station at Kading, have in Shanghai alone three families and six single women. They are about to build a large training home for unmarried women in Shanghai. At the four stations just mentioned, they have fourteen single women, one of whom is a doctor in charge of a hospital for women. In a recent "Woman's Missionary Advocate," I note the appointment of another young lady for China. And still the call goes forth for more workers and Southern Methodist women respond nobly to every demand from China.

In Chinkiang, the Northern Methodists have two families and two single women, while another unmarried woman is expected to join them this fall. The Presbyterians have one family and one unmarried man in Chinkiang. Practically, as opposed to Baptist principles, Methodists and Presbyterians are one. We may say then that while we have in Chinkiang two families, the Pedobaptists have four men and five women. This disparity in numbers ought not to be allowed to continue. After nearly fifteen years experience in China, I am convinced that the minimum force at any station should never be allowed to fall below three families. It is absolutely certain that there will be sickness, breaking down of health, it may be death, in the course of even a few years. At least three men are needed in any given station, to accomplish anything bordering on aggressive work. To expect one man, or even two, to build up a strong local church, to itinerate in the neighboring country, to push out and start new stations, to plant scores of infant churches in the villages around the mission station, is simply to demand impossibilities. In Chinkiang to-day we should have not less than three families and two single women.

Our brother Bryan's heart turns eagerly to Yangchow, that great city, famous in ancient annals of China, and now one of the wealthiest and most populous cities of Central China. It is situated on the Grand Canal, about twenty miles from Chinkiang. From a Chinese standpoint, Yangchow is a place of great importance on account of its wealth, its trade, its literary men, and its being the residence of so many officials. It is supposed that the first great railroad in China will run from Peking to Chinkiang by way of Yangchow. Should this be the case, the importance of the latter city would be greatly enhanced and its commerce largely increased.

At present, China Inland Mission is the only one working there. The Inland Mission, while undenominational, is largely Baptist in principles and practice. The Methodists have bought land in Yangchow, but have not yet settled there. The Southern Presbyterians are planning to begin a mission there at an early day.

It would be wise should our Board grant at once our brother Bryan's request for four families and two single women for Yangchow. The sooner we get a settled work there the better. The mission in Central China should work north to meet the Shantung mission working south, on the same line. The two missions are united in policy and could work harmoniously together.

L. Moon
Tungchow, October 10, 1888
Published in the January 1889 *Foreign Mission Journal.*

FROM MISS LOTTIE MOON

Recently, on a Sunday which I was spending in a village near Pingtu city, two men came to me with the request that I would conduct the general services. They wished me to read and explain, to a mixed audience of men and women, the parable of the prodigal son. I replied that no one should undertake to speak without preparation, and that I had made none. (I had been busy all the morning teaching the women and girls.) After awhile they came again to know my decision. I said, "It is not the custom of the Ancient church that women preach to men." I could not, however, hinder their calling upon me to lead in prayer. Need I say that, as I tried to lead their devotions, it was hard to keep back the tears of pity for those sheep without a shepherd? Men asking to be taught and no one to teach them. We read of one who "came forth and saw a great multitude, and he had compassion on them because they were as sheep not having a shepherd." And how did he show his compassion? "He began to teach them many things." Brethren, ministers and students for the ministry, who may read these lines, does there dwell in your hearts none of that divine compassion which stirred the heart of Jesus Christ, and which led him to "teach" the multitude "many things?"

Thirty miles from Pingtu city is a gold mine. Nestled close among low-lying hills are two foreign houses and the buildings over the mine. Several American miners are there in the employ of the Chinese government. These men are living a hard, dull, isolated life, in a remote region, far from home and friends, with the sole purpose of worldly gain. So much for the devotees of Mammon. One cannot help asking sadly, why is love of gold more potent than love of souls? The number of men mining and prospecting for gold in Shantung is more than double the number of men representing Southern Baptists! What a lesson for Southern Baptists to ponder!

L. Moon.

PINGTU, Feb. 9, 1889

Published in the May 1889 *Foreign Mission Journal.*

WHY MANY MISSIONARIES ARE NEEDED

"The harvest is plenteous, the laborers are few." Those now on the field cannot possibly reach the millions of perishing souls.

The religion of Jesus Christ has an ethical as well as a doctrinal side. Plato said in substance, if you would teach a child, be yourself what you wish to teach. We know the power of example even in Christian lands. We know how one holy man leavens a whole community, and leaves behind him, when he has ascended, the fragrance of a stainless life. Think what a power for good such a life would be in a heathen community. The missionary comes into such a community, and accompanying the faithful preaching of the word, the Holy Spirit convicts men "of sin and of righteousness, and of judgment." Many hearts are stirred, but these newly awakened souls are bound in the chains of old habits. How even to be truthful is a hard problem confronting them. How when reviled, not to revile again; how when hated and persecuted, not to hate in return, but to love instead—what a trial of flesh and blood! Most of the converts, especially the women, cannot read. Now what these people need—next to the grace of God in their hearts—is to see the life of Jesus Christ set before them in the concrete, in the holy life of the missionary. They must see him meek under reviling, if they are to learn to be meek. They must see him gentle and mild and kind, under rude provocations. They must see him brave and firm, and strong, where to yield would be to betray the truth. From him—comparing his life with the law laid down in the New Testament—they must learn to mould their lives. How shall they fashion themselves after the example of one whom they see but once in six months, or even once a year, or sometimes once in two or three years? In order profoundly to influence people, one must live among them. One's daily life must be open to inspection. How shall people know whether or not a man is Christ-like, if they rarely see him? For example, what influence would a man living in Richmond be likely to exercise upon people on the borders of the Ohio river by going out there once or twice a year and spending two days in one town, a week in another, a few days in a third, and so on for a month, supposing those people on the Ohio river to be wholly unacquainted with Christian truth, or just beginning to come out from idolatry? Yet this is practically what much mission work amounts to, so long as the mission force is so small.

The population of Shantung, estimated some time ago at twenty-nine million, is largely rural. It may be truthfully said, that in moral worth, the country people are the hope of Shantung. Among them there is comparatively little opium smoking. There is much more freedom for the women. In villages, even young women are allowed to go out freely. In cities, girls over fourteen are strictly secluded, are not permitted to go out unattended, or to go out at all, except at holiday times.

The village population, while the best and most accessible, is widely scattered over a vast area. To reach them, a large force of missionaries is absolutely needed. The work is exceedingly hard and trying. Accommodations are poor, and proper food difficult or impossible to be obtained. There should be a sufficient number of missionaries to divide this hard work, relieving each other by turns, that so the probabilities of breaking down may be reduced. Work in the cities, carried on from one's settled home—even though that home be a plain Chinese house—is, with regard to physical comfort, comparatively easy. There should be a sufficient force to alternate, so that while some were out doing the very hard work, others might be (comparatively) resting, in order to take their turn. It is as an army. If one man must mount guard day and night without relief, he will finally drop down at his post. So, in missions, there is an immense amount of overwork that ought to be obviated by having more workers.

The call of the Shantung mission for "thirty seed-sowers," is moderate in the extreme. Thirty new men and women would only put us on a temporary equality with a mission which enlarges its numbers every year. The Presbyterians have now four stations all well manned, and are planning to open two new ones. When our new men come, we shall have in all Shantung three men—one less that the Presbyterians have in Tungchow alone!

Thirty men and women to labor among nearly thirty million heathen! In the sight of Jesus Christ who commanded to "make disciples of all the nations," in view of one million unredeemed souls swept into eternity this year by famine and flood, is not the call for "thirty seed-sowers for Shantung" sadly below what we should ask?

L. Moon.
Published in the December 1889 *Foreign Mission Journal.*

FROM MISS LOTTIE MOON

A Visit To Saling

Our visit was timed so that we might be present on the occasion of the departure of one of our young Christians, recently baptized for the home of her heathen mother-in-law. Some of her friends had urged my going on the ground that my presence would give her necessary encouragement. I replied that I had no doubts as to her firmness, that I felt assured she would be faithful, even unto death if need should be, but that I would go simply because I loved her. The day for the wedding had been set for Sunday. We arose early on that day and held a service of prayer with the bride and her friends before the bridegroom came to claim her. Her face was radiant with a holy joy that now the time had come for her to suffer for her Lord. None of us knew to what she was going, and many tears were falling as the prayer went up for a blessing on our young sister. After her departure, the usual Sunday service was held in the chapel. The brother who led in prayer broke down into uncontrollable sobbing as he prayed for her who had just left us. She is greatly beloved, and many fears were felt that she would be persecuted on account of her faith. We knew that, on the third day, according to custom, there would arise the question of worship at the ancestral graves. What would be the result of her refusal none could say. That evening I received a message from the bride to be "at peace" concerning her. She was reported as cheerful and confident. Next day, how glad we were when she came back and told the story of the triumph of her lovely Christian spirit! The young husband, in his first conversation with her, inquired why she would not worship at the graves. In her beautiful, modest way, she told him her reasons, and he said it would displease his elders, but that she must speak to his mother on the subject. Finally he said, "It shall be as you wish." "Not as I wish," she gently answered, "but as the Heavenly Father wills;" and she told him her pity for him, and her earnest wish that he, too, should not worship at the graves. In her first talk with the new—the always dreaded mother-in-law—she showed the same gentle tact and unwavering firmness. The result was that everything was yielded to her wishes, and no sinful conformity was demanded of her. On the third morning, as she was to take her final departure from the home of her childhood, she came to ask for Christian books, that she might teach her new relatives. Her whole soul was flooded with joy. She had given herself up to suffer for her Lord, and lo! his mighty hand had made all things smooth before her.

Before her departure we had a few delightful moments of prayer and praise in her old home, which was crowded with relatives and friends. I have since heard that wherever she went that day, to the various feasts spread for her according to Chinese custom, she spoke out fearlessly, urging upon the heathen women the holy doctrine in which she believed. She felt herself inspired by the Holy Spirit; and looking upon the almost angelic loveliness of her sweet face, one could not doubt that she was right in this belief.

As I have mentioned before, one of the most pleasing features of the movement at Saling is the zeal with which the converts and inquirers make known the gospel to others. At home, abroad, wherever they may be, the chief thought of many of them seems to be to tell the glad tidings. Men seek out their friends and urge them to accept this doctrine that has come down from Heaven; women carry it to their relatives on their visits to them; little children learn Christian prayers and hymns, and become missionaries to their parents. So, from Saling a power is radiating that shall, in God's good time, bring light, and peace and joy, into many a home now dark in the blackness of heathenism. The quondam leader of the "Venerable Heaven Sect" goes actively among his former adherents, telling them of the "better way" he has found. To one village, about two miles from the city, he has gone repeatedly. Recently he called there, and the inquirers constrained him to tarry and tell them more fully of the great salvation. A more joyful, happy Christian than this man I have never seen. Humble, godly, sincere, he is indeed a "bright and shining light." One day, as he was preaching here on the street, a man called out, "How much money do you get for preaching?" "I get no money," was the answer. "Why, then, do you preach?" "For the sake of the Heavenly Father," he replied. Recently he was at a wedding feast, and observing that the guests at the same table with himself all kept silent, he said: "Don't let me keep you from talking, I am only a plain country man just like yourselves." They answered that they feared their talking would keep him from speaking. He replied, that if they were willing to hear, he would gladly preach to them, and they assured him of their willingness.

Two days ago a young man sent in his name and asked permission to call. He was from the village above mentioned, about two miles out from the city. He has belonged to the "Venerable Heaven Sect" about nine years, and has the moral culture which the sincere adherents of that sect all have. I was much pleased by his manner and appearance. He can not read, but is eager to learn. He is about thirty years of age. It was pleasant to listen while a member of the Saling church who came in that morning, instructed him from the fullness of his own joyful experience. As he told him of the sacrifice on the cross for our redemption, the inquirer's face was radiant with joy. Unconsciously he laughed aloud, and said, "I can't help believing—I can't help acting out (my belief)."

The Christians at Saling seem to have increased greatly in spiritual strength since their baptism. The influence on the inquirers has also been excellent. One woman went off to herself and wept that "these children" (the two young women who were baptized) should precede her into the kingdom of heaven. Another woman told me that the sight of the baptism had made her very anxious. Her husband bitterly opposes, and he persecutes their son who is interested. He threatens to turn him out of doors—an appalling threat to a man with wife and little children to support. Another case of persecution, is a young woman—a strong, brave, noble girl—whom they have threatened to sell off into Manchuria. She says she is not afraid; that if we meet no more on earth, we shall meet in heaven.

Another young woman, who, after her marriage last winter, fell into sinful conformity with idolatry, seems now to be repentant. They have threatened to beat her, and, if finally she doesn't yield, to divorce her.

The gratitude of these women brought out from heathenism, is often touchingly expressed. They say, "If you had not come to tell us, we should never have known this great salvation; but for you, we should go to hell." Surely there can be no deeper joy than that of saving souls!

Miss Knight in her two visits to Saling, has greatly endeared herself to the Christians and inquirers by her kind and affectionate manner. I hope that in a few months I shall be able to resign the work there entirely into her hands.

L. Moon.
PINGTU, Nov. 1, 1889
Published in the February 1890 *Foreign Mission Journal.*

FROM MISS LOTTIE MOON

Healthy Growth In Pingtu Neighborhood
PINGTU, Aug. 25, 1890

I had the satisfaction on yesterday, of hearing from a Pingtu city woman that she purposes asking for baptism at the next communion season at *Saling*. The city work, though first begun, has never been as hopeful as that in the country, and this is the first applicant for baptism in connection with my work here. Several men, relatives of this woman's husband, whose business led them to Tungchow, have been connected for years with the church there or with the one at Shangtswang. A young lady, the daughter of one of our near neighbors, seems also greatly stirred on the subject of baptism, but has not made formal application. Her sister suggested that her future mother-in-law would be offended by her taking such a step, but she replied that she was not afraid. These things do not always turn out in accordance with our fears, if only the daughter-in-law is brave and firm. A very noble young woman at Saling has suffered much for the faith from her own father and other members of her family. They threatened to sell her off into Manchuria, and finally to punish her for her resolute persistence, betrothed her, contrary to Chinese custom, to a man much older than herself, whose family was socially inferior to her own. Whatever her inward rebellion against this hard lot, she had no alternative, under Chinese law, but to fulfil the engagement contracted for her. Being a handsome, attractive and very clever young woman, she had no difficulty in gaining the good will of her husband, who permitted her to do as she pleased. Soon after her marriage, while on a visit to her father's house at Saling she was baptized. This greatly incensed her father and her aunt, the parties who had been responsible for her betrothal, and they succeeded in arousing the anger of her mother-in-law against her. The latter was intending to treat her harshly when an elderly teacher, a relative of the family, came in and inquired of what offence the new daughter-in-law had been accused. He also asked to see her books. The young lady brought them out and having a gift of natural eloquence, expounded to the teacher the truths of Christianity. He pronounced her books and her doctrine good and charged her mother-in-law to treat her kindly and not to interfere with her keeping the Rest Day. When Sunday came the young lady told her mother-in-law that she would do no work on that day. The mother-in-law said: "The north room is vacant; go in there and have your worship." At noon she brought in her dinner which she had cooked for her.

The teacher above mentioned has sent a request to our brother Tan to visit him, as he is interested in the gospel. The village where he lives is about seven miles from Saling.

Brother Tan is a very happy Christian. He says he thanks God for the persecution last winter, that he sees now the great blessing it has proved to be in the progress of the work. Two fine men living in Li-tz-yuen ascribe their interest in the gospel to his firm endurance of suffering. He had often urged on them the claims of the gospel without arousing their active interest. Their families are also interested. Brother Tan says that he is constantly meeting the men who carried him off and beat him last winter. They are all his relatives. He says that he takes pains to be kind to them and that they look very much ashamed. His hope and prayer is to win them to God.

I trust that the work in Li-tz-yuen is growing healthfully and that, in time, a church there will be the result of our brother Tan's faithful labors. He has not been alone in labor there, however. Two of the other brethren, Mr. Yuen and Mr. Li, have repeatedly visited the village. The brethren keep up service in the city at Li-tz-yuen and at Saling. They are encouraged always to plan and control these services themselves, that so the whole movement may continue as spontaneous in its growth as it has been from its inception. Thank God! all have a mind to work, whether men or women. Two women, neither of whom is a church member, lately volunteered to lead in prayer in the Sunday service here (for women only) while I was in Tungchow.

My beloved colleague, Miss Knight, has remained bravely alone at her post during two months of this summer. Her health has been good and she has worked steadily at the language. I have not words to tell the joy and comfort she has been to me since her coming more than a year ago. Our neighbors love her and she dwells among them as one of themselves. It is a perpetual delight to me to see the bright, brave, sunny spirit in which she lives a life that to some natures would seem unendurable. "The love of Christ constraineth her."

L. M.

Published in the January 1891 *Foreign Mission Journal.*

LETTERS FROM THE MISSIONS

Miss Lottie Moon's Diary
Saling, Oct. 13, 1890
An old lady from *Hwao huoa t'un* wishes to be baptized. She has belonged to a native sect and had been for years seeking the forgiveness of sins. She repeated the required forms ten thousand two hundred times. This obtains

forgiveness of sins, as proof whereof, a paper is given (for sixty-four small cash) stating name, age and circumstances of the holder, and that she is entitled to go on board the boat and be received by the Venerable Mother to promised felicity. The old lady has also for years practiced abstinence from certain kinds of food on the first and the fifteenth of each month for the purpose of storing up merit. Now she abandons all this, accepts Christ as her Lord and asks for baptism. She is nearly seventy years old.

Oct. 14—Last night fire-crackers were exploded by some under pretence of passing the New Year! This as a preventive of cholera and other diseases, it being supposed that when the New Year comes in, all will be well. It is rumored that the Emperor, at the approaching New Year, will skip over a year in his reckoning, and instead of calling it the seventeenth of his reign, will designate it the eighteenth, because of *Tao Kuang's* seventeenth year was one of misfortune. In the present reign disasters have "followed fast and followed faster," and there is fear of worse.

Oct. 15—I was sorry when I had spoken joyfully of Heavenly recognition when the two women to whom I was talking spoke sadly of their mother whom they did not hope to meet in the "better land." A young woman, one of the church members here, told me recently that she had been thinking sorrowfully much of late of her mother—the beloved mother—who had died before the good news of salvation came.

Deaths and marriages are the order of the day now. Many have died of cholera and other diseases in the neighboring villages. The Christians in attending funerals give offence by not going to the temples or burning paper money and incense to the dead. If a man is at once pleasant and firm it is easier for him. The relatives say, "You stay and watch the door while we go to the temple." Here, as elsewhere, it is easier to be a decided Christian than a half-hearted one.

The ninth month is abundant in marriages because it is a time of leisure. The crops are mostly gathered in and people can spare time for enjoyment. When there is a wedding, connections of the family send gifts of food to aid in the entertainment of guests. The usual contribution here is forty loaves of bread. An odd custom of the Chinese is to return a part of the gift. Of the forty loaves, ten or twenty are sent back to the giver.

Oct. 16—The position of a Christian daughter-in-law in a heathen family is one of great difficulty. She is regarded as the property of the family to which she has been given by her own parents. Especially trying is her condition when a death occurs among her husband's relatives. She must then either give up Christianity or come to a direct issue with the family. She is required to worship the dead, and, as a part of the funeral ceremonies, to go in procession to the temple. At a set time she is expected to worship the tablet of the deceased. When first married, in this region, she must go to the ancestral burying place and worship the dead. There are young women who resolutely refuse to do these things. In some cases the demand has been waived. Where inheritance of property is involved, the difficulty is greatly increased. For instance, a man or a woman dies childless. Among the nearest kin an heir is sought, the condition of inheritance being that the heir and his family worship the deceased. A Christian girl married into a heathen family and refusing to worship in such a case, causes the forfeiture of the inheritance and excites intense anger and resentment in her husband and his family.

The Romanists, following counsels of Paul, meet the difficulty by encouraging Christian girls to remain unmarried at home. When one sees the trials and temptations to which beloved Christian girls are exposed by contracting such marriages, one wishes that Protestant missionaries would, "by reason of the present distress," say to Christian fathers in China as Paul said to the Corinthians, "He that giveth her not in marriage shall do better."

Oct. 18—One is surprised to learn that leprosy is a frequent disease in this region. The Chinese say that it is not contagious, but that it is hereditary, sometimes, like consumption, skipping a generation. They also say that smallpox is not contagious. Leprosy is represented as curable, if taken in time. The diseased part must be cut out, and thus, they say, a radical cure is effected.

Oct. 20—There is much that is interesting and a good deal that is amusing to a foreigner sojourning temporarily in a Chinese village. On Saturday we had two dramatic surprises enacted on the stage of Saling life. There is a well-to-do family here whose discordant elements do not combine harmoniously. The stepmother and sister-in-law are supposed to oppress the daughters of the family, all of whom are married now except the youngest. At a recent gathering of the sisters on occasion of a funeral, no doubt the matter was discussed and their uncle came over, on Saturday, from his village to Saling to remonstrate with the unkind stepmother and sister-in-law on their treatment of his nieces. The two women took umbrage, attacked the guest in their own house and pursued him to the street, where bystanders interfered. Conduct so outrageous demanded prompt reparation, and all that afternoon, curious eyes peering in at the street might have seen two discomfited women kneeling to implore pardon, and finally when the guest departed, these same women escorted him to the street door with every mark of polite respect. As one of the nieces is a Christian girl, it may be supposed that this discomfiture of the stepmother and sister-in-law did not create any sympathy in the Christians here. This Christian girl was given in marriage some months ago to a family below her own social position as a punishment for refusing to abandon her faith. Being a handsome, clever girl, she has won her husband's regard and he readily humors her wishes. The Chinese custom is for young women recently married to spend most of their time during the first year at their father's house. When one reflects that Chinese girls see their husbands for the first time when the wedding takes place and that they have no friends or acquaintances in their new home, one perceives the humanity of this custom. This Christian girl was married off purposely to a man living at a distance. The family declining recently to send for her as they should have done, she induced her husband to escort her to the house of a maternal relative. Thence, with his approval, she walked over on yesterday to Saling, asserting her right to remain in her father's house so long as she chooses. It was indeed a glad welcome that she received from the Christians here. It being Sunday, she went, on arrival, to the chapel, and learning there of my being here came immediately to see me. Her entrance made a sensation. We had supposed her twenty *li* away with no prospect of coming and yet here she was smiling and happy, overjoyed to greet us as we were to see her.

Published in the March 1891 *Foreign Mission Journal.*

LETTERS FROM THE MISSIONS

Miss Lottie Moon's Diary
[Continued.]

The other surprise on Saturday was more tragic. A young man belonging to a Christian family has for years lived unhappily with his wife. Recently he withdrew to his grandfather's, and sulked for a week. He was persuaded finally to go home. Having done some work in a way that was unsatisfactory to his wife, she reproached him in her accustomed harsh manner. Resenting it bitterly, he demanded of his stepmother that she should divorce her. His mother reasoned with him, saying that was not the Christian way of doing things, that his wife had been here for years, and that there was a child involved. He replied, "If you won't divorce her, you don't want me," and rushed away. He was followed, and also a man passing on the road saw him leap into a well, and at once gave the alarm. He was promptly rescued, in a speechless condition. Whether it was the shock of his cold plunge, or whether it was the consciousness of having asserted himself in this emphatic manner that restored his self-respect, "deponent saith not," but it is certain that, on the next day, his bearing was more manly than it had been in a long time. The family were much distressed by his attempted suicide, and were full of thankfulness to God that his purpose had been frustrated.

Oct. 22—It was touching to witness the meeting between the young man above mentioned and the good woman, his uncle's wife, who had watched over and cherished him in his helpless infancy and childhood. He threw himself on the ground, burying his face in his hands in an agony of grief, crying out how could he dare to see her. (She had been absent attending a funeral and had just returned.) She wept over him as a mother over her own child, pleading with him never to repeat the rash act, and telling him of God's great mercy in his having been rescued. For simple, unaffected, unconscious goodness, this woman seems to me to bear the palm among our dear Saling friends.

Pretty little *Kai*, brave, noble girl that she is, came in two days ago, sweet and sad, but smiling still, and told us how she had won the victory through God's mercy. None of the family went to the temple on occasion of the funeral of her husband's aunt. The purpose to make her husband the heir of his uncle was frustrated by her firm refusal to join in idolatrous worship at the funeral. The family are very angry with her, especially her husband. One of our Christian women asked, the other day, if she ought to attend funerals. Mistaking the purport of her inquiry, I replied that if her strength was not sufficient, she ought not to go. She said that women naturally preferred the retirement of their own homes, but that she felt she ought to go in order to bear witness for the Lord. She is now away attending a funeral, and I doubt not, will, on every fitting occasion, speak a word for the Master. Some time ago her daughter's husband told her that if her daughters were to be taught Christianity they would not be allowed to go to her house. "As to whether they come or not," she replied, "that I cannot control, but you may be sure that, as soon as they enter my gate, they will be taught Christianity."

Oct. 23—Having been pressingly invited to visit a family named *Tan*, I went on yesterday. They received me very cordially, and the conversation was at first on general topics. Soon it became manifest that they wanted to hear the gospel. The epidemic (cholera) has alarmed the woman of the family, making her anxious and uneasy. This family once seemed hopefully interested, but a question of inheritance coming up, the father yielded to temptation. With the help of his clan, he forcibly diverted the succession of property from the son of his cousin, who is the leader of the Christians here, and had it settled on his own son. It was the ever-recurring question of ancestral worship. The deed probably proved less profitable than it promised. The funeral expenses were heavy, involving repeated feasts to the members of the clan who aided him in the transaction. The man himself, who was previously hardworking and industrious, seems to have fallen into drinking habits.

Oct. 24—Tomorrow closes one of the most pleasant visits I have ever made here. There has been the kind of work I like best, quiet teaching of Christians and inquirers. They bring to the missionary many questions of conscience and of daily duty. To give wise direction in such cases, is not the least important part of the religious teacher's work. In the evenings, such Christians and inquirers as care to study, gather around the table, some learning hymns and others the New Testament. One bright young woman reads in Acts, or commits to memory in Matthew. Her mother toils painfully over the second chapter of Matthew. A dear young Christian boy learns from the same page of the Gospel as an elderly relative, past fifty. A promising young man who sometimes conducts the Sunday services, brings, now and then, a parable or other passage in the Gospels or Acts for explanation. Thus the time has slipped by in happy work, and tomorrow I leave these dear Saling Christians with a deeper love for them than before, with a clearer perception of their difficulties and a warmer sympathy with their efforts to lead true and holy lives.

During this visit I have been especially gratified to note their cheerful, patient industry. The persecution has ceased, and our brethren go about their farm work or other business unmolested, ready to speak a word for the Lord as occasion offers. Not long ago one of them went out for two days on an itinerating tour, casting himself on the hospitality of the heathen. He said that he lacked for nothing. Some kind man or good women to whom he had preached would be sure to offer him food when the time came.

The church at Saling seems to have in itself the elements of steady growth. Its members are active in propagating the truth. As there is no resident pastor, the services on Sunday are conducted, according to convenience, by four of the brethren. When the three accustomed leaders are absent, from sickness or any other cause, a young brother who is bright, earnest and faithful, steps forward and takes modestly the place of leader, as he did twice on last Sunday.

L. MOON
Published in the April 1891 *Foreign Mission Journal.*

A Chinese Heroine

Miss L. Moon

In the Province of Shantung, not far from Pingtu city, lies a little village, *Saling.* In this village, of three girls, constant associates and intimate friends, who manifested an interest in the gospel, the least interesting was perhaps *Yen.* The girls were betrothed into heathen families, and *Yen* was the first called upon to fulfill the engagement made for her by her elders. As the time drew near a change seemed to come over the girl. Her spiritual life was evidently deepening. Instead of being absorbed, as would be natural at such a time, in the preparation of her wedding outfit, her whole mind was given to thoughts on spiritual things. Her anxiety grew intense lest during the heathen ceremonies attendant on her marriage her courage should fail her, and she should be led into idolatry. She felt that the salvation of her soul was at stake. She expressed the feeling that death would be welcome as a release from the dreaded marriage. She grew pale and was deeply thoughtful. Her mind dwelt constantly on the fearful thought that she might succumb in the hour of trial. Her cousin, who is about two years older, did everything in her power to cheer and encourage her. She bade her not be anxious, assuring her that at the moment of trial the Holy Spirit would put into her mouth fitting words.

On the morning appointed for her wedding, *Yen* appeared to have recovered her spirits. Unlike most Chinese girls on such occasions, she was neither absorbed in her toilet, nor did she sit in stupid silence to be gazed upon. She was gravely collected in her manner, but her previous sadness seemed to have passed away. Not much help, except of a passive kind, did she get from her mother. Peremptorily she declined to take some little thing connected with an idolatrous rite and her mother assented.

The day after her marriage she returned home, according to the custom of the region where she dwells. There was a bright gayety about her which well became her, and she gave a very lively account to her young companions of the company at the wedding feast. That evening she was in her place at worship, though her young husband and his friends refused to attend. Before the service began she was busy learning these texts: "He that endureth to the end, the same shall be saved." "Be not afraid of them which kill the body, but are not able to kill the soul: but rather fear him which is able to destroy both soul and body in hell." "He that doth not take his cross and follow after me is not worthy of me." She knew that on the next day would be the hour of supreme trial, and she endeavored to fortify her soul with the words of him whom she acknowledged as her Lord. According to the prevalent custom, on the third day, the newly wedded pair go to the family burial place to worship the dead. They must also perform ancestral worship at home. With regard to the latter, *Yen* peremptorily cut short—by telling him that his suggestion came from the devil—her brother's Jesuitical advice that she conform outwardly, while in her heart her worship should be given to God.

On the eventful morning I called to see her, and found her extremely busy packing her belongings for final departure from her father's house. She seemed again greatly depressed. There was neither time nor opportunity for talk, and I could only whisper as I took my leave: "He that taketh not up his cross," &c., and I added, "Don't forget." "I know; I will not forget," she answered. I feared that her courage had failed, and I left the house with a heavy heart. I knew that her brothers, so far from aiding her, were rather throwing their influence in the opposite scale. In that frail girl's heart, sustained and strengthened by the Holy Spirit, there was but one fear; the fear lest she should deny her Lord. She was praying as she stepped into the conveyance that was to take her back to her husband's home.

That evening we were electrified at the close of our worship by learning that *Yen* had come off victorious in the hour of trial. She resolutely refused to worship at the graves, and with equal determination declined to worship ancestors at home.

Yen told us afterwards that this was her prayer as she drew near to the burial place: "Heavenly Father, I am willing to suffer. I am willing to take the cross for the Saviour's sake. Heavenly Father, help me!" Her prayer was heard.

Strange to say, beyond a little temporary vexation on the part of the husband and his family, no unpleasant consequences have followed.

Published in the May 1893 *Foreign Mission Journal.*

ERRORS ABOUT THE CHINESE

There are certain popular errors in thinking and speaking about the Chinese that ought to be corrected whenever an opportunity occurs. A returned missionary is often pained by flippant remarks which have their root in ignorance. We make the same mistakes in our estimate of the Chinese that they make about ourselves. Because they wear a style of dress different from our own, we look on them practically as "outside barbarians." They call us "devils" popularly, and Chinese officials formerly habitually designated the foreigner, in state papers, as "barbarians." "Heathen Chinese" is a popular epithet in America. A missionary in Japan, as quoted in the *Missionary Review of the World*, wisely insists that we cease to use the word heathen. He says, "The worst people in our so-called Christian civilization use this word most freely. Gamblers, hard drinkers, pharisaical moralists, low politicians cannot sing changes enough on it. 'The heathen Chinese,' 'the heathen Jap,' are the words of human beings who never had a noble thought toward the people of another nation, nor a spark of true patriotism. So that I would raise this question: Isn't it time that we missionaries part company with those who roll this word *heathen* under their tongues as a sweet morsel of contempt? Shall we Christians at home or in mission field be courteous in preaching the gladdest tidings on earth, or not?"

To this the answer may be made that the word "heathen," like the word "pagan," originally meant no discourtesy. In the early days Christianity had its first triumphs in the cities. The country people clung to their old forms of worship, and in the Latin tongue *pagani*, country folks, became synonymous with non-Christian. So, among our own ancestors, heathen meant originally dwellers on the heath, and as these people continued to reject Christianity long after people in the towns and cities had accepted it, the term came to mean non-Christian. Originally, then, the words "heathen" and "pagan" were not terms of reproach. In the course of the ages, a new meaning has been read into these words, especially the former, a meaning often distinctly contemptuous. It is, therefore, time that the followers of Jesus revise their language and learn to speak respectfully of non-Christian peoples. The missionary quoted above tells us that the Japanese are exceedingly sensitive as regards the application of the word to themselves. The apostle commands us to "be courteous." If the term "heathen Jap" gives pain to one human being, no Christian should ever again allow it to pass his lips.

An incident will show the animus of the men who delight to use the word "heathen" as a term of contempt, and also the feelings of answering scorn awakened in the minds of English-speaking Chinese.

During the rainy season, when the mud lay fifteen inches deep in the streets of San Francisco, a Chinaman, dressed in violet satin, was picking his steps over a plank at a crossing, when a citizen advanced from the opposite direction and jostled him in the mud. The sight of the Chinaman floundering in the mud greatly delighted the crowd. Having recovered his footing, and shaken the dirt from his satin robe, looking mildly around and bowing politely, he said: "You Christian, me heathen; good-bye."

Some writer has well remarked that when our own heathen ancestors were skulking in the forests of Northern Europe, the Chinese already had a respectable civilization. A thousand years ago, China was the most civilized country on the globe. The reports brought back by Marco Polo, the famous Venetian traveler, of the magnificence of the Chinese emperor and of the splendors of his court, were received with wondering astonishment in semi-barbarous Europe.

Chinese civilization seemed to come to a standstill, while that of Europe continues to advance. Nevertheless, much remains in the "Great Middle Kingdom" that deserves our profound respect.

I had intended to write on other points, but lack of space forbids.

L. MOON.

Published in the May 1893 *Foreign Mission Journal.*

EXCERPTS AND BRIEF ENTRIES

After the New Year, I began visiting every day. I am happy to say that I am most cordially received. A wonderful change has come over many of the people of Tung Chow since I used to know them some years ago. There is a readiness—in some cases an apparent eagerness—to hear the gospel, which has been a surprise and delight to me. I thoroughly enjoy the work, and am happy in it. I often think, while teaching the women and children, what a pity it is that Christian women, who want to make the most of their lives, don't come out here and plunge, heart and soul, into this blessed work. On all sides we hear words of cheer. The dark night of patient waiting is passing away. Never before were the prospects so bright.

I expect to begin country work in about two weeks. That has always heretofore been more hopeful than the city work. We long to see both prosper. We desire to see our church crowded with city people and country churches springing up all over the land. For this we labor and pray and wait.

May God help you and the Board to sustain the heavy burdens that fall upon you.

Yours sincerely,

L. MOON

Tung Chow, China

Published in the July 1894 *Foreign Mission Journal.*

GOOD CHEER

P.O. Chefoo

Tungchow, Oct. 1, 1894

During the month of July, I devoted myself to the study of Chinese and to such work as I could do at home or at church. In August, I resumed my country work and have steadily prosecuted it up to the present time. My aim is to visit the villages within reach going out daily from my own home. I have thus far visited fifty-three and shall continue this work some time.

The people were never more friendly. This is especially gratifying, as the villages near the city used to be hostile. A new generation has grown up with kindlier feelings toward the foreigner. I never found mission work more enjoyable. To go out daily among a kindly people, amid enchanting views of nature, everywhere one turns catching lovely glimpses of sea or distant hills or quiet valleys, all this is to me delightful. My work is done mostly out of doors. The country people, at this season, are on the streets or the harvest floors a good part of the time. I constantly thank God that he has given me work that I love so much amid scenes so beautiful. Returning about sunset or later, as we approach the grim old city walls, a home feeling comes over me, with a sense of thankfulness that, after the hard work and physical weariness of the day, I shall have the quiet rest that is found only in one's own home. I am very happy in the work and in my surroundings.

The war is a source of sorrow. Thus far China has been unsuccessful and naturally all my sympathies are with the land I love. The Chinese government is sincere in its desire to protect missionaries. Here, we have a good many soldiers, but under admirable control.

I trust the financial skies are brightening and that you will be able to send us more missionaries. We need them sorely. Our force is wholly inadequate at all stations and we ought to open another station in the near future.

Dr. and Mrs. Hartwell started to-day for Pingtu to attend mission meeting. They will be present at the dedication of the new chapel at Saling. This chapel has been built by the natives and the missionaries without expense to the Foreign Mission Board.

Please allow me to correct a mistake about the number of our churches. We have four, one at Tungchow, one at Shangtswang, one at Hwanghien and one at Saling in Pingtu. The Shangtswang church has very strangely dropped out in notices of our North China work.

With best wishes for the work committed to your hands and for yourself in that work.

Yours sincerely,

L. MOON

Published in the January 1895 *Foreign Mission Journal.*

EXCITEMENT AND SAFETY

Tungchow

Dr. Hartwell is able to sit up now a short while daily. He hopes to "crawl out" and resume work in the course of three weeks.

We have been in the midst of intense excitement on account of the nearness of the war. Rumors that China will ask for peace, fill all with delight. Our work has gone on as usual. I think the church here is doing admirably. The meetings have been kept up with spirit during Dr. Hartwell's illness. One good result of the war has been to draw the people and the missionaries closer together. The common danger has made a bond of sympathy. Strange to say, the danger dreaded was not from the Japanese, but from the Chinese soldiers. The people greatly feared that if the Japanese men-of-war should appear, their own soldiers would loot and fire the city.

The country people feared lest disorganized bands of soldiers would rob and commit outrages. As long as the missionaries are here, the sense of security to some extent continues. The people think we are well informed and that we would leave, if there was danger. The country people tell me that so long as I go to the country they feel safe. If I did not go they would feel sure that there was trouble here in the city, either from the coming of the Japanese or from their own soldiers. The city people say that their soldiers behave better on account of our being here. I have never been received so cordially in the country as at present. People come around to talk about the war, and when that has been discussed, they will listen to the gospel. With Christian regards,

Yours sincerely,

L. MOON

Published in the February 1895 *Foreign Mission Journal.*

Miss Lottie Moon writes interestingly from Tung Chow, China, of her work. After describing some work in general, she says:

"During the quarter I have visited forty-nine villages. I have gone out for half a day, or day. In a few cases, where the distance was greater, I have spent several nights at one village, making it a centre of work for the surrounding region. I am happy to report that, in general, I have been most cordially received. In one village the welcome was not only cordial, but warmly affectionate. I had not been able to go to them when the terror of invasion was upon us, and they heard that I had left Tung Chow. I assured them that I had remained quietly at home, trusting the good providence of the Heavenly Father. One old lady said I had been accused of being a Japanese spy, but that she had warmly defended me. I noticed that the kitchen god had disappeared from this old lady's wall, as also from that of her daughter-in-law. In another village, the neighbors assured me that a certain woman had given up all idolatry. This woman seems to me earnest and prayerful.

"There have been thirty baptisms thus far, this year in the Tung Chow and Hwang-Hien stations, and there are still others asking for baptisms, or for instruction. One very pleasant thing about it is that many of these come from Christian families, though there are some outsiders. One girl of about ten or eleven years of age is in the fourth generation of Christians on her mother's side, and in the third on her father's. Her mother, as a young bridge[?]in a heathen family, endured faithfully severe persecution, and lately has had the joy of seeing her husband and other members of the family put on Christ in baptism.

"During part of the quarter we have had the valuable aid of our Bro. and Sister Sears. He had preached frequently and she has visited in the city, as time and strength permitted."

Published in the November 1895 *Foreign Mission Journal.*

ONE OF MISS MOON'S MORNINGS

Tungchow, China
July 21, 1898

My Dear Children,

I will tell you how I spent this morning. After breakfast I called in a boy for a lesson in English. He is a little chap, without father or mother. He is bright and good, and trustworthy. I had thought that some day I would teach him English, but did not tell him my intention. He determined he would learn English, so every day when I would be busy in the dining-room he would ask me, "What is this called?" He quite persecuted me, haunting me wherever he could to get new English words. I was much pleased with his eagerness to learn, and struck by his clever way of getting taught. I told him to borrow the cook's primer until I could send to Chefoo and get one for him. Such a happy boy! It is a great pleasure to teach him.

This is my holiday time, and four of my school boys were cleaning up my yard for me. I promised them ten cash apiece for cleaning each yard. There are three yards. The boys are little fellows, and were very much pleased to earn some money to spend as they like. They had two rough knives with which they cut the grass, and they pulled up the weeds and swept the paved walks. As they finished this morning's task I found two boys waiting for me. They were from a village, and had called to see me. I asked if they had come to the city to "hear theatricals." They said, "No," they had come to "eat wine." By this they meant that they were invited to a feast. I asked them in and read and talked to them. I read them part of a hymn that begins "Come, ye sinners, poor and wretched," and inquired if they knew what it meant. Then, as they did not understand it, I explained the meaning. I let them read some in the "Peep of Day," and showed them pictures of Bethlehem and Jerusalem. When they were leaving I gave them each a picture. I asked them to come to Sunday school next Sunday. As they were about to go a young man came in who is to be married next week. He asked me to write and request Pastor Pruitt to perform the ceremony. I told him that Mr. Pruitt would be here for the wedding.

When he went away I told my cook that I had time then to teach him. He read to me the fifth chapter of Matthew, and afterwards I gave him a lesson in his English primer. One of my school boys hung around, and finally wanted to know if he might go to the sea. I consented, but said if he would wait a while I would pay the money due. So, I brought out a heavy string of five hundred Chinese brass cash, and counted out to each boy twenty cash. They went off happy to the sea. Tomorrow they must clean up a yard they did not finish today.

I went out to a village called Mung Chia last week, and while there I began to write an article for you, but was interrupted and did not have time to complete it.

Your friend,

L. MOON

Published in the October 1898 *Foreign Mission Journal.*

FROM MISS LOTTIE MOON

I am very glad indeed to learn of the valuable reinforcement in store for the Hwanghien station. Couldn't you send out with the party that promised additional woman for Tungchow? Miss Dutton and I cannot undertake the work that will need to be done. Four single women for Tungchow is the smallest number that could meet the exigencies of the work, even supposing it should only remain where it was before.

Missionaries all over China are expecting unprecedented growth in the work after an assured peace. It would be wise to prepare for such growth.

My stay in Japan has been very beneficial to my health. For six years and a half I had had neither rest nor change, and was feeling seriously the need of both. I hope to do better work when I go back.

It is my hope to leave here in February, and to reach Tungchow about March 12th. The Chinese New Year falls about February 20th, and the holidays are over twenty days later. The rowdy element is always in evidence during the New Year's holidays, and I do not think it would be safe to go to Tungchow until they are over.

Yours sincerely,

L. MOON.

Published in the March 1901 *Foreign Mission Journal*

MISS LOTTIE MOON, TENGCHOW, CHINA:

My work goes on as usual. The school numbers thirty-six names, but the attendance of some pupils is irregular. Some are always present. The discipline is satisfactory and the children do well in their studies. In the advanced department there are seventeen boys. About a dozen learn Arithmetic and Geography. All learn the New Testament, or some Christian book. The same is true of the primary children, of whom there are nineteen enrolled. Two children dropped out of school to attend a Government school just opened this year, and one young man left to go to work.

These Government schools offer inducements in cash and promises of employment to successful students in the civil service. Unfortunately, there is no religious freedom in Government schools. I regret the fact that some church members send their children to these schools. It is deeply to be regretted, as the children are compelled to worship Confucius.

Published in the August 1906 *Foreign Mission Journal.*

A BRIEF REPORT FROM MISS MOON

The Tengchow Station asked me to take charge of two additional day schools. These two, with the Memorial School in North St., occupy a part of five mornings in the week. I am glad to report them all as doing well. The number of girls in attendance is increasing. This gives me special pleasure. In one school, out of sixteen pupils, ten are girls. The schoolroom in that school is provided by Mrs. Lan, without charge to the Mission. She sends four girls to the school. In the Memorial School we have seven girls, with the prospect of perhaps two more. The three schools number nearly sixty pupils.

In addition to the oversight of those schools, I also prosecute city visiting. Mrs. Kiang, a Bible woman who is supported by the Tengchow Baptist Woman's Missionary Society, goes out with me on four afternoons in the week. On Sunday mornings, I am the responsible person for the Sunday school in the Memorial School building. Mr. Wu is the faithful superintendent of the school. He is supported by the B.Y.P.U. of the Charlottesville, Va., First church.

On Sunday afternoons I attend Sunday school in our church. The school is flourishing. We are greatly indebted to Dr. Frost for an ample supply of Sunday school cards.

With very cordial regards and earnest prayers for the work committed to your hands, I remain

Yours sincerely,

L. Moon

Tengchowfu, China, April 3, 1907

Published in the August 1907 *Foreign Mission Journal.*

THE LOTTIE MOON

CORRESPONDENCE

III. THE WILLINGHAM YEARS

1893-1912

"Let us gather jewels for a crown above..."

THE R. J. WILLINGHAM LETTERS
1893—1912

When H. A. Tupper retired in 1893, the Foreign Mission Board's trustees tapped Robert Josiah Willingham as his successor. Willingham was a well-known pastor with a keen interest in missionary work and a reputation for strong administrative skills. Under his leadership the Foreign Mission Board increased its missionary force from 94 to 294 in 7 different countries.

The correspondence between Moon and Willingham suggests that she did not have the same type of personal rapport with the new Corresponding Secretary of the Board that she enjoyed with his predecessor. Moon's letters to Willingham have an almost business-like tone and are much less personal than the ones she wrote to Tupper, perhaps because she and Willingham were not close personal acquaintances prior to his accepting the Corresponding Secretary's position. Likewise, Moon wrote few articles for the *Foreign Mission Journal* after Tupper's retirement. Yet, this is probably because Southern Baptists were expanding their missionary ventures and *Journal* space for individual missionary writings was becoming increasingly limited.

These minor details notwithstanding, Moon's letters to Willingham remain especially instructive. She wrote regarding regular missionary needs and reminded him of the need for more workers. One fascinating letter dated January 21, 1905 explains how difficult it is to learn Chinese. Many of her letters, particularly the one dated February 26, 1901, offer gripping first-hand accounts of life during the Boxer Rebellion and how military tensions spilled over into civilian life.

Scottsville,
Albemarle Co., Va.,
Sept. 5, 1893
Rev. Dr. R. J. Willingham:—
My dear Brother,

I have been waiting for you to get settled in harness, before writing with regard to my return to China.

In my latest communication from Dr. Tupper on that subject, it was agreed that I should go this fall, but the time was not appointed. It has been my wish to sail from San Francisco on the "China" on Nov. 21st. Please let me know what are the probabilities of my getting off at that time.

Yours sincerely,
L. Moon.
(Shantung, North China Mission)

Scottsville,
Albemarle Co.,
Va.,
Oct. 5, 1893
Rev. Dr. R. J. Willingham:
My dear Brother,

I expect to leave on next Monday, Oct. 9, for Chicago, to be gone about fifteen days. I read with satisfaction in the last *F. M. Journal* that I am to sail from San Francisco, Nov. 21. If nothing unforeseen occurs, I shall be ready to go at that time. I should not like to start with less than three hundred dollars ($300^{00}) for travelling expenses. If any should be left over, I should pay it into the hands of the Mission Treasurer.

I suppose I can make the trip to San Francisco in six days. My thought is to leave here Nov. 13th which would be Monday, & so reach San Fran. on Saturday. The time of sailing of vessels is not absolutely fixed, but is subject to change without announcement. So it is as well to be a day or two ahead of time. It might be well to inquire of Mr. John D. Potts, Passenger Agent C&O Road, Richmond, about getting a through ticket to San Fran. Possibly, reduced rates might be obtained. Steamer agents allow 20 pr. cent off to missionaries, naval officers & government officials.

Yrs. sincerely,
L. Moon.

P. O. Chefoo,
Feb. 28, 1894
Dear Dr. Willingham,

Mr. Pruitt writes me that you wish the views of each member of the mission on the salary question. I have never thought the salary excessive. On the contrary, it seems to me reasonable. Some missionaries have heavy doctors' bills—or dental—to pay. Some need change of air to recuperate health. If the salary is cut down to a mere living, such needed change would be impossible.

Some missionaries habitually use a part of their salary in mission work, as, for instance, paying salary of personal teacher, paying their own itinerating expenses, & sometimes house rent in the interior. Some missionaries use a part of their salaries to help build churches or to sustain schools. Just now, we have been called upon to help our Christians at Säling to put up a church. The Christians there are poor & have given, both in labor & money, according to their ability. They asked our help and it has been gladly given. I believe that the moral effect is much better if the natives know that we give out of our salaries. Otherwise, they would think that a rich F.M. Board ought to do it all. It is right for us to set them an example of giving. I am unalterably opposed to calling on the Board to help build churches in this part of China. When there is a push to Christianity,—as there certainly will be sooner or later,—we shall need *thousands* of churches. The wealthiest Board could not meet the demand. Now, every village has its temple or temples. Then, every village must have its church. We must lay the foundation right by teaching them to build their own churches from the first. It is a blessing to them & to us if out of our salaries we may help them. When the rush comes, of course, salaries could not go very far, but the principle of self help would have been established. They would know that we would not ask the Board to build churches that ought to be built out of funds collected on the field.

Missionaries ought to do at least as much in charity as people in their native land. "The poor we have with us always." I happen to know of a missionary who has for many years almost entirely supported an aged widow & who has recently been compelled by the necessities of the situation to promise to almost support another, so long as the said missionary lives. Who could endure to see an aged & worthy Christian sister begging her bread from door to door? Could one be a Christian & allow a fellow Christian to suffer for food or clothing?

Missionaries whose salaries are so low that necessity compels them to seem stingy, or whose theory of missions or whose natural disposition leads them to pecuniary meanness, lose the respect of the natives.

We must entertain our friends occasionally, both native & foreign. To do this, of course, requires more than a bare living.

I know that the F. M. Board is baring intolerable burdens & these ought to be lifted. I know also that a good deal has been said about excessive salaries.

I should not object in the least to having my salary put at five hundred dollars ($500.00). I should not be willing to have it put lower. Hoping that this will meet the approval of the Board, I am

Sincerely yours,

L. Moon.

Tungchow,
China,
(P. O. Chefoo,)
March 3, 1894
Dear Dr. Willingham:

We are feeling much encouraged by the large attendance at our annual meeting, which has just occurred. There were six applicants for baptism, of whom three were received & three deferred. Two of those baptized were from the *Shangtswang* region, & their membership properly belongs there. Brethren were present from *Säling* (P'ingtu), seeking aid in building a church. Until recently, they have worshipped in a private house. Last year, with commendable effort & self denial, they built a school house, & have been using it for a double purpose.

Now, they propose to enlarge this house sufficiently to meet comfortably the needs of public worship. They are poor, but earnest. Dr. Hartwell tells of their effort to extinguish a small debt on the school house during his visit to Säling in January. He says they took up three successive collections at one service, & the debt was met. I told him that these brethren deserved to be put along with Dr. Hatcher in making collections. The Tungchow church cheerfully voted twenty thousand cash to aid in building at Säling. The missionaries also gladly contributed to the same good purpose. Miss Knight had promised to give the foundation stones for the building. The Säling brethren went away delighted with the meeting & especially cheered by the help so cordially rendered.

We have a magnificent field extending over a hundred miles from the coast. There is imperative need of more workers for the three stations already occupied, besides the necessity already existing of pushing on to open new stations. Railroads are coming & then all China will be open as never before. A railway is now in actual operation from Tientsin to Shanhaikwan. By reference to a map, it will be seen that the latter is situated at the base of the Great Wall. Preparations are said to be well advanced for the extension of the railway from the foot of the Great Wall to the *Taling* river. One difficulty of the route is the blasting needed to carry it through some spurs of the "Long White Mountain." The *Taling* River is very wide & deep at the point where it has to be crossed & an excellent bridge will be required. The terminus of the road, for the present, is to be Moukden, in the province of Shingking, Manchuria. Moukden was made the seat of government by the Manchu sovereigns in 1631. In the *Middle Kingdom*, I find the following description: "The streets are wide, clean & the main business avenue lined with large, well-built shops, their counters, windows & other arrangements indicating a great trade...

"Everywhere marks of prosperity & security indicate an enterprising population & for its tidy look, industrious & courteous population, Moukden takes high rank among Chinese cities. Its population is estimated to be under 200,000, mostly Chinese."

This railway is but the entering wedge for the extension of such roads all over the empire. The opposition has been rigorous but the party of progress has triumphed. In this party may be ranked the Emperor & the great Viceroy, *Li Hung Chiang.*

Among other signs of progress may be mentioned the opening of a new government school at the Kiangnan Arsenal, in which pupils will be instructed in English, French, & Mathematics. The undertaking was expected to begin with forty-two pupils and nine teachers.

The cotton cloth mill at Wuchang, near Shanghai, opened with increased machinery, after the New Year's holidays. Six hundred looms now run day & night. This enterprise is also the work of the great Northern Viceroy. To him is also due the fleet of Merchant steamers & the establishment of a medical school. Lady *Li* is patroness of the medical school for women.

L. Moon

Tungchow, China
April 10, 1894
Dear Dr. Willingham,

At our last Mission meeting, Mrs. Hartwell was requested to open a school for girls. The need was considered so pressing that it was thought best for her to begin as soon as arrangements could be made here to receive the pupils. The cause for this seeming haste was that a number of children of our church members were about to be placed in the Presbyterian school in this city. Our members said if we would open a school, their daughters would, of course, attend it. Otherwise, they would be sent elsewhere.

Already, several children of our church members have been sent to Presbyterian schools & have thus been entirely lost to us. Not only this, but the pupil is used as an entering wedge to gain admission into the family & village from which she comes & thus our general work suffers seriously. These facts constituted the urgency of the case & demanded prompt action.

(2) There is a desire among our Christians for the education of their daughters. They are mostly poor & it is as much as they can do to provide the proper clothing for their girls, who must dress better at school than would be necessary at home. While the sons of Christians could attend heathen schools, if it were desirable, there are absolutely no schools for girls. It seems to be a part of our duty as missionaries to foster the idea of education for girls as well as boys. To ask the Chinese to establish their own schools for girls would be like telling a crawling child to walk. The walking time will come, but meanwhile, a wise mother will be patient & not force it before the child's strength is sufficient.

(3) The Mission, in establishing a school for boys, has admitted the principle that a duty rests upon us to give Christian education to the children of our Christians. To confine this to boys would be manifestly unjust.

(4) Another reason is that Christian daughters-in-law are in demand. A member of the present committee has been asked by non-Christian mothers to get them Christian daughters-in-law because, they said, they make better daughters-in-law. An educated Christian woman, entering a non-Christian family, ought to be an immense power for good. In China, all girls must marry. Is it not best to fit our girls for the widest usefulness in the sphere to which they must go?

(5) This leads us to our final reason which is that educated Christian women make better women, better wives, better mothers & better house-keepers than those who have no education. The apostle bids us "covet

earnestly the best gifts." We do covet these best gifts for our Christian girls. We have no wish to make foreigners of them. We are not planning to educate them out of the accustomed sphere of Chinese women. We desire to elevate & ennoble their home lives. We feel sure that the Board will grant this unanimous request of the Mission & will sanction the inception of the work without waiting to hear their decision.

By order of the Mission.
Laura G. Barton
Effie J. Sears Committee
L. Moon

Tungchow, P. O. Chefoo,
China
Jan. 22, 1895
Dear Dr. Willingham,

On my return from P'ingtu last Saturday, I found your letter of Nov. 26th awaiting me. My report for the year had been sent to Dr. Hartwell, who was asked by the Mission to write the general report. For that reason, I do not make any quarterly report now.

I spent about three weeks in the P'ingtu region & should have remained there all winter, but that I supposed I would be more needed here. As it has turned out, the storm of war burst over our city last week & most of our Christians have fled. The Japanese shelled the city on two successive days last week, the bombardment lasting only about half an hour each time. I reached home after dark on the second day of the attack. The U.S. man-of-war, "Yorktown," came up next day to take away such of the missionaries as cared to go. My first thought was to return immediately to P'ingtu, but further reflection made me think it best to remain here. I believe the attack here was only a feint to draw off attention from some other point. This city is a place of no consequence. Chinese troops will probably be rushed here to defend it & the Japs will strike a decisive blow elsewhere. The chief danger to us & to the natives has always been from the Chinese soldiers. My front wall was struck in the bombardment & part of it carried away by a shell & I also notice that the woodwork about my front door was injured.

I hear that the people are fearing a scarcity of food in case a large Chinese force comes.

I am very glad the women raised the promised sum for the debt & that they were hoping to do great things at X[mas]. I have always believed that if our

Southern Baptist women are fully aroused on missions, the men would follow, of course. "Complimentary to the men" you say? Well, it proved so in case of the Northern Presbyterians & why not with us?

With best wishes and cordial X^{ian} greetings,

Yrs. sincerely,

L. Moon.

Tungchow,

(P. O. Chefoo),

China,

April 2, 1895

Dear Dr. Willingham,

The quarter just passed has been full of intense excitement. It witnessed the bombardment of Tungchow & the fall of Wei-hai-wei. The Japanese paid us four visits & their vessels are still almost daily hovering around. For over two months business has been nearly at a standstill, but the city is now recovering from the depression & most of those who fled have returned. There is, however, much poverty & suffering. The price of silver has touched a low point & the cost of breadstuffs has advanced. During the height of the terror & confusion, direct mission work was almost out of the question. Simply to stand at one's post & try to inspire hope & cheerfulness into the terror-stricken people who could not fly, was about all that one could accomplish. Gradually, however, things changed for the better & a wide open door has been found for presenting the gospel to the people. Sympathy with them in their trouble & sorrows has been an "open sesame" to many hearts. For more than five weeks, regular services have been carried on in the church & Dr. Hartwell has preached with great power & tenderness to apparently deeply interested audiences. I have never seen anything like it before in Tungchow. I have been recently visiting daily in the city & have never before been received so cordially & at times even joyfully. There are often eager listeners & it is rare that I do not have opportunity to teach hymns & prayers. In general, the people were never in a more teachable spirit than now. Their reverses have taught them a beginning of humility & they have learned to look on missionaries as their true friends.

I am sorry to learn from your letter of Jan. 19 that there is no hope of early reinforcement. As soon as peace is declared, we hope for advance, & men & women should be here now preparing to take advantage of improved conditions for preaching the gospel. O that the Lord may open the hearts &

purses of our Baptist hosts that they may cheerfully respond to the growing demands of the work.

With Christian regards,

Yrs. sincerely,

L. Moon.

Tungchow, China,

P. O. Chefoo

Jan. 13, 1896

Dear Dr. Willingham,

I have the pleasure of sending you by this mail the Mission reports for last year. This includes General Report & various personal reports.

Spite of war, we had a good year. I am glad to say that our prospects are very cheering. It is time we were looking for a greater harvest in this field so long & faithfully worked. The Sunday School is growing hopefully. This is due largely to Miss Hartwell, whose class of boys & girls has now gone over a hundred. She has divided them into two classes now & for recitation rooms (classrooms) utilises the rooms formerly occupied by Miss Barton. The mission voted those premises to Miss Hartwell for her work. Some of the buildings are being used also for the girls' school, which has outgrown its former limits. Dr. Hartwell hopes to rent rooms adjourning his premises & so gave up to Miss Hartwell's use the rooms Miss Barton had. The place is too small & inconvenient for the residence of a family, but is admirably suited for Miss Hartwell's woman's work during the week & for her classes on Sunday. If the S.S. continues to grow, as we hope it will, such supplementary rooms will be absolutely necessary. The church is not large & thus outside classrooms are needed.

Of course, no one would dream of blaming the F. M. Board that reinforcements cannot be sent, but oh! we do so need them. Our present force cannot begin to over take the work clamoring to be done. More women are needed here, & two each for Hwanghien & Pingtu. Alas! whence is the money to come? We also sorely need another man & wife here. May the Lord send them in His own good time. Praying his blessing upon your arduous labors, I am

Yrs. sincerely,

L. Moon.

Jan. 21, 1896

As Dr. Hartwell has been very busy & also sick, he suggests that I do not wait for his personal report which he kindly offers to send to you direct. I therefore send the Gen. Report, with personal reports, except Dr. Hartwell's.

Yrs. sincerely,

L. Moon.

Tungchow, China

(P.O. Chefoo)

March 9, 1896

Dear Dr. Willingham,

It seems to me a duty to God & to the work here to write a few plain facts for the consideration of the Board. I have refrained for some time from urging our pressing need of reinforcement because aware of the heavy financial embarrassment. Times seem to be improving in America & our needs become more urgent as the work grows on our hands. Our first need is another man for Tungchow. Dr. Hartwell, while full of energy & enthusiasm, is carrying a burden too heavy for his strength. Our annual meeting, lasting eight days, has just closed. Dr. Hartwell conducted services twice a day, the native brethren taking the afternoon preaching. There ought to have been a missionary here whose especial business it should have been to instruct & train inquirers. Dr. Hartwell, active as he is, is only human. How can he prepare two sermons a day, meet the social duties connected with the presence of so many brethren from the country, & at the same time give the inquirers the personal teaching they need & ought to have? Formally, a very large share of this teaching was done by Mrs. Crawford, whose knowledge of the language was abundantly equal to the task. For a year or two, Mr. Bostick was here as pastor, with Dr. Crawford to do outside work. Now, Dr. Hartwell must do the work that used to be done by the three just mentioned. In addition to city preaching, he has charge of the Shangtswang church, which neither Dr. Crawford nor Mr. Bostick undertook. He also visits outstations to the East of the city, where we have Christians. The work is more than one man can do unless we could bid the sun stand still & so lengthen out the days. The physician here sent word to Dr. Hartwell to quit work & go to bed. Instead, on yesterday, he baptized at nine o'c'k, preached immediately afterward & conducted Sunday school in the afternoon. Two were baptized & there are several applicants for baptism, besides a number of inquirers. The work is broadening out in every direction & we have not the force of workers needed to meet the demands upon us.

I hope I shall be pardoned for calling attention to my own needs. I am trying to cover a country field once occupied by Mrs. Holmes, Mrs. Crawford & myself. It is a vast field, with several hundred towns & villages & calls come to me from many quarters. It is hard for people in America to understand how very long a time is required for a missionary to gain the confidence of the Chinese. A new missionary always labors under a strong disadvantage in this respect. As regards our country work in the region, I am now the only missionary here acquainted with the field &, what is of equal importance, long known by the people. Besides myself, Dr. Hartwell is the only old missionary & he has been away from China eighteen years. I have reflected much & sorrowfully on the fact that, if the Lord shalt call me from earth within a few years, there is no one here to take up the work I am trying to do. There ought to be women here preparing to aid in pushing the work during my life time (each independently in her own chosen field which I should hand over to her,) & to take over my share when I am gone. Three more single women for the Tungchow region would be none too many. I would not be understood as meaning we only need one more man here. I believe our minimum force at each station should be three men. Other missions keep many more at one station. I only mean to press very urgently that we ought to have, within a few months, just as early as possible, another man for this place.

Hoping the Board will consider favorably the subject of this letter, I remain

Yours for the work,

L. Moon

P.O. Chefoo,
China
April 6, 1896
Dear Dr. Willingham,

Your note with regard to $15.00 for school girl, "Virginia" I handed Mrs. Hartwell, as she has charge of the girls' school here.

My report for this quarter is necessarily brief, because, owing to sickness, I lost about one third of the time. In Jan. I visited four villages, spending the time, as usual, in teaching, day & night, those who came to me.

This village work is practically a Sunday School that lasts all day, every day, the pupils constantly changing in numbers, in quality & in character. Sometimes there is a learned teacher to be conversed with & even instructed, for the teachers are as ignorant of spiritual things as very young children. Sometimes one teaches a bright young girl & old grandmother, very stupid, from the same book. After dark, the school boys usually come & it is amazing how they will work to memorize hymns & prayers, after being all day in school.

In January I made visits in the city, as I was able. During Feb., I was unfit for work & remained quietly indoors. In Mar., I resumed city visiting & country work. The latter seems to me increasingly hopeful & I trust that this field so long hard & unfruitful will yet bring forth an abundant harvest to the glory of God.

I sympathize with you in the difficulties of the home work & pray for a blessing on your labors. With X^n regards,

Yrs. sincerely,

L. Moon

Tungchow, China,
(P. O. Chefoo)
July 8, 1896
Dear Dr. Willingham,

Thanks for your kind letters which have come duly to hand. The latest bearing date May 23rd, was rec'd on yesterday & served to remind me that my report for the past quarter should be sent you.

My time has been given almost exclusively to what is called country work, which means work in towns & villages, as distinguished from work in the cities. I have visited thirty-two villages during the quarter. The longest trip I have taken occupied nine days & was undertaken for the purpose of visiting a large town where some of our native brethren & sisters had begun a good work. I was delighted with the people & with the progress already made under the teaching of the native Christians. At other towns & villages, I have remained several days, according to the circumstances. One village seemed so hopeful that I rented rooms, at the rate of five thousand cash a year with the purpose of visiting it monthly. It once seemed very hopeful, but wicked men combined to break up the work, which was nearly abandoned for some ten years or more. Then it grew hopeful, the opposers having died off. Some faithful Christians, now we believe in glory, were shining lights there to the day of their death, in spite of the fierce & bitter opposition. To other villages, I have gone out only in the afternoons, or in the mornings from home. This work to me is very delightful, as it is done almost entirely in the open air, with the blue sky above, the lovely sea views constantly offering their charms to the eye as I go from place to place & the kindly country folk giving me pleasant & sometimes hardy greeting. There are boundless opportunities & possibilities in this country work & we do most sorely need more laborers.

I trust that oppressive strangling debt will be met & that all our over-tasked workers in China and other fields may have the joy of receiving reinforcements. How difficult *your task* is, we missionaries, absorbed in work, cannot fully realize, yet we do pray the Lord to substain & guide you. May the home part of the foreign work take a new impetus & may your heart be gladdened by many who shall "come up to the help of the Lord—to the help of the Lord against the mighty."

With X^{ian} regards,
Yrs. sincerely,
L. Moon.

Tungchow, China,
(P. O. Chefoo,)
June 12, 1897
Dear Dr. Willingham,

I was most glad & thankful to read on yesterday in the *Religious Herald* of May 6 that the debt had been reduced to thirteen thousand dollars. I trust it was "exterminated, annihilated" at Wilmington, in accordance with an editorial suggestion in the *Herald*.

About a year or more ago I wrote you of our great need here of another man & wife & also of more single women. You said that you would bring the matter before the F. M. Board whenever the financial situation should justify it. I know that the return of missionaries to their field should precede everything else & that the Pinnocks & McCloys are still waiting for funds. Still, I hope you will bear with me as I again call attention to our needs in Tungchow. Dr. Hartwell has never rallied from his long illness in 1894 & yet he has faithfully continued to do the work of two men. Dr. Seymour, his physician, said that he would give him three years to live, if there were not a change. The mission, therefore, urged him to go away & he gladly consented. He hoped to return in two months, tho the mission wisht him to rest three months. He has improved very slowly indeed. It is now well on in the 4th month & there is no prospect of a return earlier than in the latter part of July. We ought to have prompt reinforcement this fall. If the Lord spares Dr. Hartwell to us, he should have a colleague to share his burdens. He has aged very rapidly in the past three years. When he came to China, his hair & beard were iron gray. Now, they are white. He has lost his elastic step. The work & the burdens have been too heavy. If God should take him from us, a man should be here preparing to take his place. No other brother now on the field can be expected to give up his own prosperous work to come here to the hardest & most unproductive field we have. Miss Hartwell & I are working on here alone. Our Presbyterian brethren, Prof. Hayes & Mr. Irwin, have been very kind in preaching for us & we have a young licenticate who is a very good preacher. But we very sorely need another man here. I would also urge two more single women for Tungchow. Miss Hartwell is over burdened with three schools & has little time for country work. In connection with our Tungchow station, there are about thirty towns & villages to which lady missionaries should go & stay some days, at least twice a year. How can we do it? These villages & towns are some of them centers of itineration, giving us access to hundreds of other towns & villages. You see our heavy need then. Miss Hartwell has undertaken perhaps eight or nine of these central towns & village stations. The remainder press on me as a burden too heavy to be borne. I long to go, but it is a physical impossibility to reach so many & others are constantly opening. O that the people of God would rise to their opportunities! This city is open as never before. Ladies who could give their time to house-to-house visiting are needed. I think, too, that the way is opening for day schools, such as they have in Canton. O for a strong force here! How we do need new workers!

I have been sick with tonsilitis & unable to work for a while. The doctor has finally given me permission to go to the country. I have been visiting in the city without his permission.

With cordial regards & best wishes,

L. Moon.

Tungchow, China,
P. O. Chefoo,
July 1, 1897
Dear Dr. Willingham,

My report this quarter would not be satisfactory to myself if I were in fault. I have been kept from working, over a month, by a severe attack of tonsilitis. The doctor positively forbade my seeing Chinese at home, for a while, & for a long time, would not permit me to go to the country. I am now in full work. I have visited only nine villages this quarter. At one of them, I remained nine days, but during the latter part of my stay, was too ill to work. I didn't know I had tonsilitis. I came home & soon had my Chinese guest rooms full of people. Thirteen guests, including babies! They stayed various periods, from five days to more than a week. After that, or rather while they were here, I went to the doctor & he said I had "the popular disease—tonsilitis." It has been very slow in getting well.

I find everywhere great kindness from the people & a surprising readiness to listen. The women often ask me to "kiang" to them. This is the only word we have for "preaching" & is applied alike to the pulpit ministrations of the brethren & the informal talks the ladies make to women & children. Everywhere, children are ready to listen or to be taught. The work is boundless, the need of workers very great. I am now going out, almost daily, to villages near the city. It is a delight to speak to people so kind & ready to hear.

Do send us reinforcements as soon as possible. I greatly fear that Dr. Hartwell ought to go home. He has been away from here now about four months & is still far from well. He speaks of returning in August. I very greatly fear that the worries here will throw him into his old state of health & that he will succumb to the disease. I may explain that we have had a church trouble that greatly distrest Dr. Hartwell in his poor state of health.

Things have quieted down in the months he has been away. I fear a renewal on his return. Meantime, some of the brethren are working nobly. They energetically go to the country to preach & also push the church work. In that respect, I seem to see positive growth. The brethren feel their responsibility in the pastor's absence perhaps more than when he is here. Mr. Hayes, President of Tungchow College, has been exceedingly kind in preaching for us frequently. But, if Dr. Hartwell must go away to America for healing, we ought to have a resident brother to look after the work. Mr. Pruitt has to leave his own work to come over here for the communion. He is to be here next Saturday. Even if Dr. H. should not have to go away, he is not strong enough now to do two men's work. There should be a young man here to do the rough country work. Dr. H. goes to Shangtswang six times a year to administer the Lord's Supper; to villages out East, three times a year for the same purpose. Besides, he keeps up work regularly at *Ta Shin Tien.* There should be a colleague to take at least half the work off his shoulders.

I do trust that the F. M. Board will see its way to send us helpers. We (especially Dr. Hartwell) were bitterly disappointed that Mr. Chambers did not come here as we expected he would. We have not urged reinforcement during the heavy embarrassments of the Board. But now that the debt is paid, we hope, after all old missionaries have been sent to their fields, that our needs will be supplied. We need another doctor very badly for Hwanghien. The brethren & their families run a risk in having no physician there. We ought to have immediately two women (single) for Tungchow & two for P'ingtu.

Mr. Sears & I have been begging them for years. Think of thirty towns & villages connected with our Tungchow work & only Miss Hartwell & myself to visit them. Now, these thirty are centers for working other towns and villages, so that the whole now runs up into the hundreds. Miss Hartwell is now working in three schools & has little time for country work. I have city visiting in addition to country work. If you could send us *ten* single women, it would be none too many for the work before us. But we could make out with four. Oh that Southern Baptists would awake to their responsibilities & raise the amount you suggested, five hundred thousand dollars annually. Virginia could give fifty thousand a year, if she would only try.

This letter is intended only to give information to the Secy. & the F. M. Board & *not* for publication. I am sure that if Dr. Hartwell were strong & well, he could rise above the worries here. But his health has been simply desperate for many, many months. He is a man of the most delicate sensibilities. He will work till he drops & "make no moan." We ought not to stand by & see him die when a little money might save him. He wouldn't go without an assurance that he would be sent back as soon as well enough. It wouldn't cost a great deal for him & Mrs. H. to go over to San Francisco. They need not go east. Dr. Randle said, last spring, that he advised Dr. H. to try to tide over the summer here & go to San Francisco in Sept. Miss Hartwell says that if that advice had been followed, she thinks her father would not have been alive now. It is a very serious matter. Mrs. Hartwell has written to Miss H. saying that only a miracle can save him. It used to be that if he & Mrs. H. were away a few weeks, I missed them keenly & wanted them back. When they went in March, I was so glad to see them go, for his sake, that I didn't miss them at all. Now, though I miss them, I don't want Dr. H. to come back & fade & die before my eyes. I want the Board to invite him home to get well & to promise to send him back when he is well. He lost his health by coming to China & risking this climate, at the Board's request. He over-workt. I think the F. M. Board is morally responsible to do everything to save him. I need not say that I write without consulting Dr. H. He would not hear of my writing thus & I do it on my own responsibility. The F. M. Board would run no risk in inviting Dr. Hartwell to go to San Francisco. If he were well nothing could make him go. In any case, he would not go without the approval of the mission & they would not give it unless it were necessary.

With best wishes & many prayers for a blessing on your work, I am

Yrs. sincerely,

L. Moon.

Tungchow,
(P.O. Chefoo,)
Oct. 2, 1897
Dear Dr. Willingham,

Your kind letter of Aug. 18 was rec'd a week ago. I quite appreciate the difficulty of sending reinforcements & am sure it is right not to do so on borrowed money.

For the present, Mr. Pruitt has kindly consented to act as pastor, coming over occasionally from Hwanghien to preach for us & look after church matters. He was called by the church to this position & was requested to hold it until Dr. Hartwell's return. We have had very serious trouble in the church, growing mostly out of mis-management in the girls' school. We hope it is now settled & that we shall have peace. The offenders have been excluded from the church. During the quarter just ended, I have visited 41 different villages. In July & August I rested from active work about three weeks, doing, of course, what came unsought & teaching regularly my S. S. class of men.

You may be interested to know that the telegraph is now used to undermine Christianity. On yesterday, I rec'd a shamefully slanderous telegram attacking the character of a missionary. For this I had to pay a charge for turning it from the code in numbers into regular Chinese characters besides 100 cash for delivery. Of course, had I known the character of the telegram, I would have declined to receive it. I was in the country when it came, & a friend advanced the money. Returning to dinner, you may fancy my chagrin at having to pay out money for so shameful a piece of rascality. All I could do was to enclose the telegram to the brother whose character is assailed & express my indignation, & my hope that he may be able to ferret out the authors. It was signed by two names, whether true or false, I do not know.

Perhaps you may be interested in seeing an official telegraphic envelope. I enclose the one rec'd yesterday. The telegraph is under government control & the messages are sent in English or Chinese as preferred. Foreigners send in English mainly to secure accuracy.

This letter is not intended for publication as the reference to the girls' school might cause pain to Dr. Hartwell & there is no need to speak of the telegram, as it might be unpleasant to the brother attackt.

With best wishes for you in your arduous & often disheartening labors,

Yrs. sincerely,

L. Moon.

Note: A long time ago, Dr. Randle mentioned that the *F. M. Journal* was not sent him. I offered to mention the fact to you, as I felt sure it was an oversight, but have forgotten it until now.

Tungchow, China,
(P. O. Chefoo)
Apr. 18, 1898
Dear Dr. Willingham,

I was glad to receive your letter of March 5th. Our work continues to prosper. I had a delightful visit last week to one of our country stations. The Christians there seem to have taken on new life. I sometimes think that I will write a letter for publication bearing testimony to some of the beautiful Christian lives that I see or have seen among the natives.

It is so hard, just now, to get time to do what I wish in the writing line. I am giving five days a week to the country work. I go out on Tuesdays & return on Saturdays. I never knew the people to be in so receptive a-mood. Inquirers multiply. We hav had nine baptisms here this year, & expect other applicants at the next Communion season, which falls on the 1st Sunday in the 4th Chinese month. So far as I know the church is harmonious. All our difficulties seem happily surmounted. The schools are, with one exception, full to overflowing. The girl's school ought to have enlarged quarters. There is not room to receive the numerous applicants.

I feel very hopeful for all branches of our work. I must not worry you about reinforcement, but three ladies want to come & live & work with me. The work simply clamors to be done.

Miss Hartwell is kept in the city & so I only am left to look after the country work. There is plenty for four women to do among our country stations, & as there is only one to do it, you will know that much is left undone.

I do trust that the brethren will lift the burden of that awful debt from your shoulders. Believe me to be with sincere sympathy.

Yours for the work,

L. Moon.

Tungchow, China,
May 24, 1898
Dear Dr. Willingham,

It is always so pleasant to write good news that I feel like telling you how the Lord has blessed us. On last Sunday our regular Communion came around, & there were nine baptized. This makes eighteen who have been baptized here this year & there are others who will apply hereafter. Mr. Tsung, who brought eight applicants, said that if all had come there would have been twenty applicants. This brother is a voluntary worker this year. He was formerly supported by Chinese money, but as it is not forthcoming this year, he quietly remarkt that he did not work for money & goes on, if anything, with redoubled energy in his work. He told me today that his son had written, urging him not to stay at home, but to go everywhere preaching the Gospel. Among those baptized, were Mr. *Tsung's* daughter & two daughters-in-law & some connections by marriage. It is delightful to see our church growing in this natural way. The wives of two of our members were also baptized. There are many inquirers springing up in all directions, & the work is increasingly hopeful. Mr. Sears told me that he had thirty applicants for baptism, of whom twenty have been received.

I need not say that the heart of our pastor, Mr. Pruitt, has been made glad by such blessings as we have received. We are hopeful & happy in our work. Praying God's blessing upon you, I am

Yrs. sincerely,
L. Moon.

Tungchow, China
P. O. Chefoo,
June 30, 1898
Dear Dr. Willingham,

I have visited during this Quarter twenty different towns & villages. At many of them, I remained several days. At others, I have made but brief visits, going out after dinner & returning about sun-set. I hav had much to encourage in the work. The people are very friendly & more ready to listen to the gospel than I hav ever known them to be. In two places, there are, apparently, some genuine inquirers. I hav been pressingly invited to go to a new village to visit a family said to be very favorably disposed to Christianity & I hav promist to go. It is a source of sorrow that I cannot meet the numerous calls. I hav simply to decide what cases & places most urgently demand attention & to neglect many others to which I would gladly go, were I free to do so. We need *at least* three more single women here. Miss Hartwell is doing noble work in the school, but, thus far, this year has been unable to leave the city. There are about thirty towns & villages connected with the Tungchow station, that ought to hav visits of several days duration, at least twice a year. With our present force, this is simply impossible.

We are rejoiced at the good news from the Convention. To hav that awful debt rolled off, what a blessing.

With best wishes & earnest prayers for a blessing upon your labors,
Yrs. sincerely,
L. Moon.

Tungchow,
Shantung Province,
China
Oct. 5, 1898
Dear Dr. Willingham,

Your letter of Aug 26, permitting me to draw twenty-two dollars for my day school reacht me on yesterday. I hav sent it on to Mr. Pruitt. It will enable me to pay for benches & tables for the school, which hav been furnisht at my own expense. There is a small room-rent & also there is some expense for stationery. I hav advanced whatever was needed, intending to pay myself out of the amount allowed, if sufficient. The school gives me much pleasure. I see markt improvement in the children in behaviour & in their studies.

The books, thus far, are nearly all religious. I allow one native educational book for each pupil, but he must provide it. The religious books, I provide. They learn a hymn book by heart; read the "Peep of Day" & the more advanced are learning by heart Matthew's Gospel. You see, it is a Sunday school every day, with the advantage that you can hold your pupils all day & make them study, as you can't in the Sunday school. The children attend our Sunday school quite regularly, but I find it somewhat difficult to get a good attendance at church. This is partly due to the distance. I don't think I ought to require girls with small feet to take that long walk twice a day. The teacher is a woman with three small children & I can't think it right to ask her to come twice a day. She attends Sunday school regularly. She is a good & faithful teacher & I think the religious influence in the school is good. The children are taught to sing hymns. I expect to have Arithmetic & Geography taught next year, but the religious teaching wil always be dominant. All the children will be taught Old Testament History & the New Testament, as they grow older, if they stay in the school. I visit the school once a week & examine them on what they hav learned during the preceding week.

During the quarter just ended, I hav visited 65 different villages. My health has been so good that I found that I could dispense with my usual summer rest. The people are friendly & a few hav seemed to listen with genuine interest.

A letter received from Mr. Sears today tells of recent baptisms in Pingtu. He said that, thus far, there had been 62 baptisms. At the Association which meets in November, we will hav the largest number of baptisms reported in the history of the mission. The native brethren in Pingtu are pushing their educational work at their own expense. Our church school here has had many difficulties to contend with, owing to the starting of an opposition school & to the necessity of changing the teacher soon after the opening of school this year.

A young lady from Va. wishes to come out & work with me. We hav been in correspondence some years. I judge from her letters that she wil be a great acquisition. She thinks her own church would support her. We sorely need new workers here. It is utterly impossible to overtake what ought to be done & we are forced to neglect much work that we would gladly do. I understand that the Board can only do what the brethren & sisters provide funds for the doing. I wish some of them could come here & see the need as we see it. Then, I am sure, they would gladly provide the means to send out new workers. We hav a P.O. now at Tungchow & the address is given above.

With best wishes for your work,

Most cordially yours,

L. Moon.

Tungchow,
Shantung, Province,
China
Nov. 12, 1898
My dear Brother,

Yr. card of Sept. 15 reacht me two days ago. It would not be possible to get an article to you in time for the Jan. no. of the *Journal.* It is always best to allow three full months for a letter & reply. The very shortest time from here to Virginia is one month & it usually takes six weeks.

I hav just returned from Shangtswang where the Tunglai Association met. I think it was the best we hav had. One hundred baptisms were reported for the year; the best record, thus far, in the history of the N.C. Mission.

We are in sore need of more workers. "The harvest is plenteous, the labors are few."

With best wishes & earnest prayers for a blessing on your work,

I am

Yrs. sincerely,

L. Moon.

P. S. We hav now a P.O. here and the address will be hereafter as the head of this letter.

Tengchow, Shantung,
China, March 23, 1899.
Dear Dr. Willingham.

I think the F. M. Board ought to know the exact state of the force at Tengchow. Miss Hartwell has been ill for some weeks & is still unable to sit up for any length of time. She has been heavily over worked and is badly run down. Dr. Hartwell is returning, better this time, but not strong nor fit for full work. He is sure to over do and may relapse. Mrs. Hartwell is worn out with nursing him more than two long, weary years. Owing to her age & to head trouble, she never learned the language. She can teach English, but not Chinese, nor can she do any evangelistic work.

A member of the N.C. Mission wrote me not long ago. I hope we are not to have three broken down people in one family. It looks very much that way now & we, the mission, & the F. M. Board may as wel face the fact.

With cordial good wishes
Yours sincerely,
L. Moon.
Lottie Moon Collection, SBTS, Folder No. 8.

Tungchow, Shantung Province,
China,
June 2, 1899.
Dear Dr. Willingham,

Some two or three years ago, I wrote you of the need of two more single women here in Tungchow & you said in reply that when the finances of the F. M. Board should justify it, you would lay my request before the Board. I am aware that you have had a very hard struggle, yet I feel bound to keep you notified as to our needs. If you can send help I should rejoice & so, no doubt, would you, for I know you have the interests of the work at heart. When Miss Barton forsook us for Mr. Taylor, you directed Miss Hartwell to take her place. Miss Hartwell, before receiving your letter, had taken up work in two schools & felt unwilling to make a change. Besides, after Mrs. Hartwell left China she had to take the girls boarding school & to look after her youngest brother, Claude. The others went to Chefoo to school. Miss Hartwell was thus tied down in Tungchow.

We have a very large country work & one that bids fair to yield large returns if lookt after. But it can't be lookt after with our present force. I hoped that on Mrs. Hartwell's return, Miss Hartwell could take up country work. She consented two or three years ago to take a very promising field out east of Tungchow & had her time allowed, she would have workt it faithfully. But, she was fully occupied in the city. I took over Miss Barton's country work and have tried also to keep up my own work & also to go now and then to the field out east above mentioned. Of course, in trying to do this I have simply skimmed over the field. It is distressing, but there is no help for it. Four women ought to have charge of our Tungchow country work & four others ought to be sent later on for the work is always enlarging. Now, Miss Hartwell has been ill four months and there is not the slightest prospect of immediately recovery. I presume she has nervous prostration & no wonder. She has mothered and fathered four children besides her missionary work in three schools and various other things that she lookt after. She has had pneumonia, meningitis, congestion of the brains, besides a chronic trouble of some years standing. I fear she is an invalid for life, if life is spared. Our Presbyterian friends hav therefore done little country work in the region. Our mission has always done a great deal until the Gospel Mission parted from us. All our workers here have been based on the country. Our Christians are nearly all from the country. The Presbyterians have lately began to push the country work in this region. It is inevitable that they will gather the nuts of our labors of years if we have not the force to occupy the field. They are disposed to be fair now, as some of them were not years ago, but we can't say such a field is ours if we are unable to work it. Certainly, one woman can't hold a field that ought to have at the least four.

At present, I only am doing country work in the Tengchow station. I have been hindered just eight weeks, this springs through other peoples' necessities. Still, I have done what I could. Dr. Hartwell is much better than I ever expected to see him & he is prudent, I am glad to say. He preaches only once on Sunday and does not attend prayer meeting. He has steadily gained in health. Mrs. Hartwell's health is superb. Our good doctor is about to leave China on account of his wife & health. She has nervous prostration. Dr. Randle has consented to fill his place temporarily. Miss Snowgrass, also of the Pres. Mission, has nervous prostration & must go home if she gets well enough to travel. The Presbyterians keep so large a force in Shantung, about forty missionaries, that they are usually able to fill vacancies promptly by transfer from other stations, or new missionaries step in as in Mrs.

Seymour's case. I wish our people could realize that our Lord's last command is as binding as is the command to baptize.

   With best wishes
   Yours sincerely
   L. Moon.

Lottie Moon Collection, SBTS, Folder No. 8.

Tengchow, Shantung,
China Sept. 9, 1899.
Dear Dr. Willingham,
   Your letter of July 25th has been rec'd. I am cheered by your promise to do what you can to send new missionaries to Tengchow. They continue to be sorely needed. In all the twenty-six years I have been in China, the force here has never been so low as during this year. In the spring, for a month before Dr. Hartwell's return, I was compelled to lay aside mission work except on Sunday & devote myself to nursing Miss Hartwell. I had to be with her every other night. At present the situation continues as when I last wrote you. Dr. Hartwell preaches three times a month, & attends Sunday School without undertaking any work there. He is not able to attend the Wednesday night prayer meeting, nor to do any country work. Miss Hartwell improves slowly & has begun to creep out to church & S. S., but is unable to do any work. Her father told me on yesterday that she would have to go away. I have felt all the time that the best thing for her to do would be to go to America for a prolonged rest. This she is unwilling to do, but prefers to go to Macao. Half measures did not benefit Dr. Hartwell & were only a loss of time & money. I much doubt if the trip to Macao would effect a cure. It is now determined, so far as I know Lottie Hartwell has also been ill, is up & about, but rallies hardly at all. Both sisters suffer from head trouble. Dr. Neal told Miss Hartwell to try to write for ten or fifteen minutes a day. She is unable to do so. From this you may judge how serious the trouble is; neither can she read.
   If you send missionaries this fall, it would be well to advise them to bring plenty of warm under clothing. It is very cold here in winter & missionaries often suffer from cold the first winter. This is partly due to their not being properly clad. After Sept., one would need flannels at sea, except at

Honolulu where it is hot as summer in Nov., and where the people are dressed in white. Some passengers swelter in hot clothes because they are not aware of this fact. In packing one's steamer trunk, it would be well to put in summer clothing sufficient for a few days. I notice on the schedule that all steamers now call at Honolulu. I mean, all steamers from San Fran.

I keep at country work & find much to encourage me in its preserving prosecution. I shall rejoice when there are others younger & more energetic to share & push the work. I have waited long & longingly for their coming. I trust it will not be much longer that I must wait for co-workers.

With most earnest good wishes for your work.

Yrs. Sincerely,

L. Moon.

Lottie Moon Collection, SBTS, Folder No. 8

Tungchow, Shantung
China,
Nov. 13, 1899.
Rev. Dr. R. J. Willingham
Dear Dr. Willingham,

Please allow me to say that in the *F. M. Journal* the word Shantung is not spelt correctly. There should be no g in the first syllable. The word Shantung means East of the hills, but the work Shangtung means something different.

Miss Hazelton of Washington, D. C. has enclosed me a letter from you dated July 21, 1898, herself asking me to select a boy to be supported by her S. S. Class. She writes that her boys have agreed to contribute fifteen dollars this year for the support of such a pupil as I may select. I have thought of a boy that I would gladly see in school. His father, owing to poor crops has not been able to send him to Mr. Pruitt's school. He (?) goes now to a heathen school, but his mother teaches him Christian books at night. He is a bright boy & comes of Christian stock on his mother's side, grandparents & mother Christians, also sister & aunt.

As Mr. Pruitt's school is now constituted, several boys who ought to attend it are not able to do so. All boys are required to pay full board and non-Baptist boys must also pay a small tuition fee. Every year Mr. Pruitt has to make up a deficit out of his own pocket since the one hundred dollars granted by the board does not cover necessary expenses over & above what the boys pay. This year the deficit will be larger than heretofore because the head teacher demanded an increase of salary. It has occurred to me that a system of scholarships would be desirable from two standpoints. First, boys could come in on them who are not able to pay board and tuition. Second, Mr. Pruitt would be relieved of this annual drain on his private funds. I should be very glad if the Board would let me try in a quiet way to get half a dozen scholarships for the school. That is to say, if they approve of the proposition.

I now make that Miss Hazelton's class' contribution be regarded as a scholarship & be not included in the one hundred dollars granted Mr. Pruitt. I wrote Mr. Pruitt concerning it & he says in reply, "it would please us immensely to have such scholarships as you speak of." I suggested to him that the scholarships had better come through my hands to avoid charges of partiality on his part. If the Chinese thought that he had scholarships to bestow, some of them could resent his not giving them to their children. If they knew that the choice of pupils & bestowal of scholarships was in other hands, there would be no resentment against the managers of the school. I am glad to say that Dr. Hartwell seems himself again and is now in full work. It is very pleasant to have him & Mrs. H. back. The Sunday School was very cheering yesterday. Dr. H. began a large Bible class for the older church members & more advanced schoolboys. I hear that Miss Hartwell's head does not get well. Mr. Sears and I thought she ought to go to America for a prolonged rest.

With cordial regards and earnest prayers for your success, I am

Yrs. Sincerely

L. Moon.

P. S. Mr. Pruitt sent me a letter from you asking an article for the China No. of the *F. M. Journal.* The letter reached me Oct. 7th, the day you say the article must leave China, so of course I did not write.

Lottie Moon Collection, SBTS, Folder No. 8

Tengchow, Shantung,
China, Dec. 5, 1899.
My dear brother,

I have a fear that you will consider me troublesome, but we do so need workers here that I feel I ought to urge again & again, that they be sent. At present, Dr. Hartwell & myself are in full work. It should be remembered that he is considerably past sixty & that in about a year more I shall also be sixty years of age. It is not to be expected in the natural course of events that we can go on many years longer. It does seem that younger people ought to be here to learn the ins and outs of the work. I say the simple truth when I affirm that I am the only one now in the mission fully acquainted with the Tengchow field. All the others who know it have left the mission. There ought to be women here now whom I could introduce into the work. There are about thirty sub-stations connected with Tengchow.

Dr. Hartwell has resumed country work, but as pastor here, he cannot give much time to the country. For nearly six years the chief burden of the country work has fallen upon me. I have tried to do it faithfully, but it is utterly impossible for one woman to do the work of four women. I regard Miss Hartwell as indefinitely invalided. I have never waved in the belief that she should have been to America. She is not in Macao & has had two of her fearful nervous attacks. Possibly, she might get well at Clifton Springs in two years. Mrs. Hartwell, lovely in character & in person, since she does not know the language, cannot do evangelistic work. She is a blessing to us by her sweet spirit & she is useful in over looking the girl's school. Still, she is not able to work in the city or in the country. We are very thankful to have Mr. Owen here, but he is only one & we need several more. I know that you have calls like this from all our fields & that you long to answer them all. I think however that it should be remembered that Tengchow was left unmanned nearly two years, & that now the station has only two missionaries in full work. You promised me some years ago that when the finances of the Board should justify it, you would bring the matter before them. Later, you gave me hope of reinforcement this year. Pardon me, if I venture now to stir up your pure mind by way of remembrances.

I have been going to the country every week for some time and expect to make two trips more before settling down for the winter. So, I hope you won't think that it is laziness that makes me call for help. All the trips I can make will not overtake one-half the work, & maybe not one-fourth of what clamors to be done.

Yours for the Master,

L. Moon

Lottie Moon Collection, SBTS, Folder No. 8. Presumably sent to Dr. R. J. Willingham

Tengchow, Shantung
China,
Feb. 13, 1900.
Dear Dr. Willingham.

Your letter of Dec. 29 brings me joyful news & I thank you very heartily for your New Year's greeting. Nothing could be more to my taste. My only disappointment was that the Board appointed one instead of three. Miss Dutton & I can't begin to cope with the work now demanding to be done & it is always widening, broadening out indefinitely. Please don't think me unreasonable. I speak the words of truth and soberness. Tengchow should have not less than four families as the maximum force, say, three for minimum. To this, add four single women to do the hard, rough, country work that women with young children ought not to be expected to undertake. If the Board could give us such a force as that, we could not only hold our own, but could lengthen our cords & strengthen our stakes. One great difficulty is to get people at home to realize the immensity of our fields in actual square miles & the countless numbers living in said square miles. Take, for instance, a big town like Buh Ko where Mrs. Crawford workt so long, so faithfully, & so efficiently. A missionary might take that town as a centre and spend a lifetime working only it & the adjacent towns. Take Wu Shi Li Pu, to which I go constantly.

Were I free to settle there, the work there and in the neighboring towns & villages would more than engross all my time. Why, only about three or four miles away is a large town of probably 5000 inhabitants, which I can't get time even to touch. One fairly groans over the neglected possibilities.

In the expectation of an increase of pupils in my day school, I have been looking out new quarters. Rent, heretofore, has been at the rate of about fifty cts. a year. The room is too small & is overcrowded. I tried to find a place that would cost about five dollars a year, but have not succeeded. We ought to have quarters where the pupils could have a play yard. At present, they have none. If a suitable place should present itself, I shall rent. Otherwise, I may have to divide the school, which would necessitate another teacher. I have rooms on my place here that I could use if the school be divided. Perhaps you will say, "Where is the money to come from for this school enlargement?" If the Lord gives the enlargement, He surely will not withhold the funds. He will surely say to the brethren of the Board, since you have authorized that work, don't let it suffer. If however the Board hears no such voice, missionaries have a way of quietly supplying deficits out of their own pockets, whatever personal self-denial to economies may be needed in order to accomplish it.

I don't know that I made myself plain about those scholarship for which I askt. They are desired for the Hwanghien Boy's School. That School is on a wholly different basis from the Girls School here. In the latter, girls are boarded & taught at mission expenses. The Board allows G $400, a year. Scholarships in the Girl's School properly fall within that sum allowed & when a scholarship is desired, nothing is needed but to select a girl, already in school, & assign her. The boys already pay board & some of them pay tuition. All pay for books, stationery, & c. The one hundred allowed by the Board does not cover outside expenses. That is salary for two teachers, school cooks, wages & incidentals. The fact that Board is charged keeps a number of worthy boys out of school. I thought, if the Board would allow six scholarships, $15.00 x 6 = $90.00, that sum would not only pay the board and purchase the books of half a dozen boys, but would leave over a small balance to help pay teachers & cook & so relieve our Brother Pruitt of an annual deficit which grows larger as he has to pay more for his head teacher. The latter began at cash, 5000 a month. Now, things have changed so that he would only stay last year at 8000 cash a month without promising for any longer. The Presbyterians here had to run up two years to 12000 cash a month to keep one of their teachers. I may say in passing that these added prices affect only certain kinds of teachers. If a man knows English he can command large wages, large in Chinese eyes. If he knows the sciences he may procure as much as the ll lbs. 50 a month in wealthly Chinese families who want western sciences without western religion.

Please allow me, to repeat my cordial thanks for Miss Dutton. With Prayers for God's blessing on your work

Yrs. Sincerely

L. Moon.

Lottie Moon Collection, SBTS, Folder No. 8

Tengchow, Shantung,

China,

March 23, 1900

Rev. Dr. R. J. Willingham:-

My dear Brother,

I have already written you hearty thanks for the appointment of Miss Dutton, but since seeing her picture in the *F. M. Journal*, I feel like reiterating my thanks with emphasis. I am looking forward to her coming with much pleasure.

With regard to the scholarship I proposed, neither Mr. Pruitt nor I desire anything that would injure the general work. It was not at all Mr. Pruitt's plan, but mine, & it was suggested by the impossibility of selecting a pupil for Miss Hazelton's class, except under such conditions. The boys all pay their own board & those not from Baptist families pay tuition. It would not, therefore, be truthful to allow Miss Hazelton to think that her class was supporting a pupil under such conditions. In the girl's school it is quite different, as they pay nothing whatever. A friendly (?) sum, counted by the rules of the F. M. Board as part of the annual estimate, is entirely correct & truthful. I could not select a boy from my school because the Norfolk Freemason St. Sunbeams already give twenty-five dollars to that school. I saw no way therefore to comply with your request to select a boy for Miss Hazelton, but to suggest a scholarship. She sent me a letter from you, which she had held for over a year, telling her to ask me to select a pupil for her class. As I have explained above, I have not been able to do it. I was moved to suggest several scholarships because the Board had cut Mr. Pruitt so short in his estimate for his school that he has to provide for a deficit every year out of his own funds. I suppose he does not mention it & it seems right that someone else should.

Speaking of deficits, my day school will certainly fall short this year. The rooms are jammed to their utmost capacity, too much, I fear, for the health of the pupils. I have borrowed desks & benches for three months while seeking gradually to purchase second hand ones. Those now in use will have to be returned to Dr. Hartwell in June for the use of his Bible class.

When boys first come to school I use books printed here in Tungchow (hymn books and catechisms) and these cost very little. Later, I have to get books from Shanghai, Peep of Day, Old Test History, Pilgrims Progress & geographies & the cost is very heavy in comparison, besides, extremely heavy postage. One can't have a school without books. The twenty-five dollars gold exchanges for about 37,500 cash. I pay the teacher 36,000 cash a year. That leaves 1500 cash for stationery & nothing for rent or for books. This year has an intercalary month & the sum required for the teacher will be 39000 cash, which is more than the twenty-five dollars will bring, leaving nothing for benches, desks, books & stationery. The Chinese months are shorter than the Western months & so the time gradually comes around when we have to pay for an extra month. If I had proper rooms, the school could easily run up to forty or fifty pupils. There are some rooms I covet & had I the funds, I should buy them on my own account. They would do not only for the school, if it should grow to a hundred pupils, but would be a place for holding Sunday School in a wholly destitute part of the city where we used to have a church years ago. I have never been willing to abandon our hold on North St. where Baptists were first to establish themselves. The first Missionary to Tengchow, Dr. Hartwell, settled on North St. I lived there three years. Mr. Pruitt & Mr. Halcomb also lived there. I hope to see the day when we shall have missionaries again living on North St.

I am delighted to learn that there is a prospect of the appointment of more workers for North China. The first class men & women you have recently sent or appointed only make me long for more of the same kind. In this, I have scripture authority, for we are told to covet earnestly the best gifts. I admit that I have somewhat twisted the meaning, but the application is admissible, I think, that the F. M. Board is doing its very best.

I am sure that the secretary is indefatigable. I am equally certain (that) I greatly rejoice in the blessing of God upon the work at home. That His richest blessing may continue to rest upon the Secretaries in their arduous labors is my constant prayer.

Yrs. Sincerely,

L. Moon.

Lottie Moon Collection, SBTS, Folder No. 8

Tungchow,
Shantung,
China,
April 7, 1900
My dear Brother,

Miss Dutton reacht here last Tuesday, after a journey by land & by water which she describes as having been full of enjoyment. The most cordial welcome awaited her not only from our mission, but from the Presbyterian, also. We hav an exceptionally pleasant community here!

She (Miss Dutton) is all I could desire as a co-worker & I thank you heartily for sending her. Her coming, however, does not fill all long-standing vacancies. When I went to America in 1891, there were here at work or preparing for work, Mrs. Crawford, Miss Barton & Miss Thornton, now Mrs. Bostick. It was settled in Mission meeting that on my return from America, I should work in the Tungchow mission, instead of at Pingtu, where I had been working, while still keeping my home here. This would hav given two experienced workers, & two, nearly ready for full work, & it would hav fairly met the immediate needs of the country work connected with the Tungchow station. Ever since I hav known Tungchow, (now nearly 27 years), the country work has held the important place because the city was for many, many years hostile & its homes inaccessible. The schools & the churches were alike built up from the country. For several years prior to 1891, our schools were not in operation, owing to the decided opposition to that method of work on the part of some members of the Mission. After that element withdrew to help start the Gospel Mission, schools were resumed here & at Hwanghien. They met a felt necessity. Not only were boarding schools establisht but day schools had now become possible because the hatred & opposition in the city had largely passed away.

Miss Hartwell gave herself almost exclusively to work in the city. She had a day school, taught English in the church school, besides two or three private pupils in English, &, after the departure of her parents for America, took full charge of the girls' school, at the request of the mission.

Country work, which needed four women, had to depend on one & therefore could only be done in the most unsatisfactory way. Some places, previously workt for many years, have had to be abandoned. Miss Dutton has consented to take what used to be Mrs. Crawford's field. This is about one-fourth of our whole country work. If the Lord will, I shall try to do another fourth. This still leaves one-half unprovided for. To my mind, it is clear that we should hav two additional single women, about thirty years of age, or somewhat past that age. Younger women cannot wel stand the hardships of country work, nor hav they the experience of life that is desirable. Younger women might work with advantage in schools or in city visiting, especially in teaching small children.

I beg you, therefore, to consider our needs. There is room here, where I live, for two more ladies, without undue crowding. You would not, therefore, hav to provide them separate houses. I am earnestly hoping that the Convention in May wil order another advance. Our work has languisht for years, largely because our force is so very weak.

As I write, Miss Dutton, sitting near me, with a Chinese teacher is ringing the chime of the four tones used here. It is pleasant to hear. I think she wil acquire the language rapidly.

Praying the blessing of God upon your labors, I am

Yrs. sincerely,

L. Moon

Tungchow,
Shantung,
China,
May 16, 1900
Dear Dr. Willingham,

My school on North St. is much too crowded for health & for good order. The school has not only filled the original room, but has crowded into the only sleeping apartment in the small house where it is held. I was forced to refuse some pupils & was askt in two cases, to promise to take them next year. It seems to me that the F. M. Board ought to be willing to provide suitable quarters for a growing day school. It is in a part of the city where no missionaries reside now, but which was occupied by our mission for many years. I hav always opposed the giving up of the work on North St., the first inaugurated in Tungchow. I think the school could easily run up, in a few years, to a hundred pupils. This, of course, would necessitate more teachers & a suitable building. Good quarters could be bought & fitted up next door to the present narrow quarters, for about one hundred & fifty gold dollars. I think such an enterprise would pay because, in time, it might grow into a mission Sunday School.

The twenty-five dollars now allowed for the school wil not suffice to pay the teacher this year. The China months are shorter than ours. Finally, these omitted days mount up & we hav an extra month. It wil, therefore, take 39000 cash simply to pay the teacher. G. $25.00 about brings 37500 cash. So, you see, there is nothing left for books, stationery & additional school furniture. For one year (nearly) I ran the school myself, though I made no report of it to the F. M. Board. After that, the Sunbeam Society took it up, but I hav always been hampered for lack of sufficient funds. I hav already expended this year nearly three thousand cash for extra tables & benches & shall hav to pay a book bill in Shanghai. Postage on books is very heavy. Still, it is useless to hav a school unless one supplies suitable books. I want, as far as possible, to keep out the heathen classics and fill their place with religious books & suitable school books, such as Geographies, & Arithmetics, which are not taught in native schools.

We are rejoicing in the prospectiv addition of Miss Miller to our Mission. She is a noble & lovely woman about twenty-eight years of age & suitable in every way to Mr. Owen. God has greatly blessed him in giving him such a helpmeet.

We are hoping to hear very good news from the Convention.

Praying God's blessing upon the Board & especially upon the Secretaries, I am

Yrs. sincerely,

L. Moon.

Fukwoka, Japan

Sept. 24, 1900.

Rev. Dr. R. J. Willingham

Dear Dr. Willingham:-

When we left Chefoo it was because it was considered unsafe & the consul particularly desired that all Americans should leave Shantung. Each one who stayed added to his burdens. The English consul notified his nationals that Chefoo would not be protected. The anxiety about Trentsim was intense & but for Russian gallantry, the place [was] unsafe. I stayed on, however, until the brethren called a meeting to consider the propriety of buying arms to defend the place in case of attack. To an outsider like myself, it seemed wholly impossible that five or six men scattered in four different houses could defend the place against a rush of hundreds of boxers or local robbers. When the time came to talk seriously of buying arms it seemed to me the time had come to leave Shanghai. Some five weeks later the English and others landed troops there as the telegrams have told you, & then Shanghai was felt to be secure. When I was there in July there was a general feeling of insecurity that the city could not have been saved. Had the allies failed there, Chefoo would have been in imminent peril from Chinese soldiers and boxers. To my mind the only sensible thing for non-combatants was to go to a place of safety. At Chefoo, two forts commanded the foreign settlement. For protection, there was the local guard, a small volunteer force & there was usually about two gun (boats?) located in the harbor. In a sudden up rising there would have been great danger. When we were at Shanghai we were outside the city limits & most people considered this as a doubly dangerous time to be outside the city limits where our mission houses are. Besides, I felt that I should be risking my health to stay in Shanghai through the month of Sept. The mission houses are surrounded by rice fields full of water & are thus exposed to malaria. For two reasons, then, I thought it best to leave the danger from boxers or bandits & the danger of malarial fever.

I have gone into these particulars as I wish to make them the basis of a request to the F. M. Board to pay my traveling expenses from Chefoo to Japan & also to pay for house rent here. I came with Mr. & Mrs. Crocker & we took a Japanese house immediately at sixteen yens a month beginning Aug. 1st. Misses Kelly and Dutton had previously come over & were at Mr. McCollum's. I hope the F. M. Board will not consider my request unreasonable. We are now in a country that has adopted the gold basis & where missionary receive higher salaries than we receive in China. While we do not desire any increase of salary, it seems to me right to ask that the Board shall authorize our Mission treasurer, Dr. Hartwell, to refund the sums we have expended in coming to a place of safety, & also to pay our expenses when we return to China. Miss Dutton and I are now living together as we did in China. She joins me in the above request for payment of travelling expenses and house rent.

 Yrs. Sincerely
 L. Moon.
Lottie Moon Collection, SBTS, Folder No. 8.

Fukwoka, Japan,
Nov. 21, 1900.
Rev. Dr. R. J. Willingham:-
My dear Brother,

I hope you are assured that I will not (stay) in Japan longer than is necessary. I wrote Mr. Stephens not long ago about returning. In reply, he says, "Mr. Fowler requested me two or three times not go back yet. He said it might be a means of complicating matters making it inconvenient both for himself & the Chinese officials. Dr. Hartwell has gone to Tengchow, but will return by Dec. 3rd. Mr. Hayes has been there for some time. Mr. Fowler did not want either to go, nor did he give his consent for either. All seems peaceable enough now, but no one knows what day the trouble may start up again."

A North China *Daily News* rec'd on yesterday tells of very serious trouble between the Germans and the Chinese in Shantung. The letter in the *Daily News* is dated one day later than Mr. Stephens' letter. The situation is extremely grave & even if the Governor should continue his friendly policy, he may not be able to retain the people. The Germans seem greatly to blame in their harsh methods of repression. All the right in this trouble is not on the side of the foreigners I send the paper which contains the letter above mentioned. The worst of the situation is the certainty of violent persecution of the Christians in the interior. Thus far, though persecuted they have not been massacred to any very great extent. I very much dread to hear of terrible massacres at Weishien where the Presbyterians had a very flourishing work in the country. The trouble may extend to Pingtu, only two days journey away. But for the Germans, our province might have escaped the worst harms of war. They are very largely responsible for the attitude of the people towards foreigners.

With very cordial regards and best wishes for your work, I am

Yrs. sincerely.

L. Moon.

Lottie Moon Collection, SBTS, Folder No. 8.

Fukwoka, Japan
Dec. 31, 1900
Rev. Dr. R. J. Willingham:-
My dear Brother,

Your letter saying that the F. M. Board had agreed to pay my expenses to & from Japan, & also my house rent, was rec'd not long ago. I informed Miss Dutton that the same provision had been made for her, & I sent the letter to Dr. Hartwell. My stay here has been prolonged far beyond my original expectation. I confidently hoped to be settled again in Tungchow early in October. I kept myself in communication with the mission at Chefoo & have always held myself in readiness to return promptly when the way should be open to go to Tungchow. Miss Dutton wrote, I think it was in August, to inquire if the Consul was willing for her to return to Chefoo. He sent her word to remain in Japan. She returned to China about the 20th of this month &, I suppose, reacht Chefoo last week.

The house which Mr. Seasman placed at the service of the North China Mission (reserving a room for Dr. & Mrs. Crawford) has been constantly over crowded. When the members of our mission reacht there, the house was already occupied by ten Chefoo residents, who had been ordered from their endangered homes near the Chinese for what was supposed to be somewhat safer quarters in the foreign concession. Dr. & Mrs. Crawford were there at two different times, but only for a few days each time. Three sets of people were using one kitchen when I was there. Later, after some had left, the Lowes came & also a family of Swedish Baptists. The residents of Chefoo above mentioned have returned to their homes, or gone to America. So far as I know, only our own mission now occupy the house, but these number seventeen people. The house was built as a summer home for one family. It is on a high bluff just above the harbor and faces north. Mrs. Owen writes what I knew before that the house is bitter cold. I have a letter from Mrs. Hartwell dated Dec. 2, in which she says we can give you the room Miss Downing had last summer, but it cannot be heated except from opening the door into our room. She adds this would only do for a few days before we could be getting ready to go to Tungchow, but I think there is no hope of our going home this winter. Mrs. Owen remarkt in her letter that Mrs. Hartwell had the coldest room in the house, in spite of its having double windows and doors. It would be utter folly in me to leave the warm climate of Kiushiu where I have a good room with a stove, & go to the severe climate of Shantung to live in an exceptionally cold house & have to occupy a room that could not be heated. The dining room is the only room used in common. In summer we sat on the veranda or in the hall. I go into these particulars because I wish you to understand my reasons for still delaying in Japan. As to mission work in Chefoo, there would be none for me to do. Dr. Hartwell wrote me last fall of going to Tungchow because he thought it would be better than being idle in Chefoo. Had he decided to spend the winter in Tungchow as he once spoke of doing, it is probable that I should have joined him there, though it would have drawn down on me severe criticism & would have added to the Consul anxieties. Dr. Hartwell finally decided to remain in Chefoo this winter and this fact decided me to remain in Japan. Chefoo is crowded with refuges & will continue to be so for some time. I am hoping that after the China New Year's festivities are over & the people settle down to their usual avocations, we may all go back to country work.

I am very glad indeed to learn of the valuable reinforcement in store for the Hwanghien station. Couldn't you send out with the party that promised additional woman for Tungchow? Miss Dutton & I cannot overtake the work that will need to be done. Four single women for Tungchow is the smallest number that could meet the exigencies of the work, even supposing it should only remain where it was before. Missionaries all over China are expecting unprecedented growth in the work after an assured peace. It would be wise to prepare for such growth.

My stay in Japan has been very beneficial to my health. For six years and a half I had neither rest nor change & was feeling seriously in need of both. I hope to do better work when I go back because of my long rest. I have had the pleasure of meeting all the members of our Japan mission & I find them very lovable. On my way to Fukwoka last summer, I spent a delightful day with Mr. & Mrs. Walne. In Oct. I visited the hospitable home of Mr. & Mrs. Maynard & saw something of their good work in Korea. Recently, Mr. & Mrs. Clarke were in Fukwoka on their way to Kumamota where they have settled. They gave me a very kind invitation to visit them. I am under deep obligations to my good friends Mr. & Mrs. McCollum for increasing kindness during all my stay here. They confer their favors so graciously that they seem to convey the impression that it is they who are receiving the kindness.

It is my hope to leave here in Feb. & to reach Tungchow about March 12th. The China New Year falls about Feb. 20 & the holidays are over twenty days later. The rowdy element is always in evidence during the New Year holidays & I do not think it would be safe to go to Tungchow until they are over.

With best wishes for your work and with cordial regards, I am

Yours sincerely,

L. Moon.

Lottie Moon Collection, SBTS, Folder No. 8.

Fukwoka, Japan
Feb. 15, 1901.
Rev. Dr. R. J. Willingham
My dear Brother,

Mr. Owen has written asking me to send my report direct to you. I enclose it herewith. I also enclose a recent letter from Mrs. Owen which confirms what I have previously written of the overcrowded state of the house where most of our mission in North China are gathered. My latest news dated, Chefoo, Jan. 31, from Miss Dutton, is as follows: The missionaries from the interior are getting anxious to return. The gentlemen hope to go back the first of the New Year. Should Mr. Fowler be willing, Mr. Fowler has sent a petition to Peking requesting Mr. Conger to give his consent for the gentlemen to return. In this request it was thought best not to mention the ladies, less the petition would be refused. If the gentlemen are allowed to return, it will be time enough then to ask that the ladies return too. I have always planned to return to China as soon as the way should be open to go to Tengchow. As Mr. McCollum remarked not long ago, there is no beauty in setting gazing into vacancy & that is all I could now do at Chefoo. There is absolutely no work that I could find to do.

About a month ago I was invited to take some classes in a school just being opened under the auspices of the Commercial Club. They wished me to teach four hours a day for three months. As I was expecting to return to China early in March, I could only promise for six weeks & as I was teaching Mr. McCollum's boys, I could only give two hours a day. For this they pay me 255 yen a month, which I shall put to the account of the F. M. Board & hand over to the N. C. Mission after deducting jinrikisha hire. I took the classes chiefly with a view to doing something, however little, towards my own support. Of course, I hope to do some Christian work among the pupils. No obligation whatever has been made to my teaching the young men Christian truth & they do so need it. My heart yearns over them, bright, enthusiastic, gentle, courteous, lovable young fellows, in utter spiritual ignorance & darkness. The head of the school & the Japanese teacher of English, both come to me daily for private lessons in English for which they pay, though the sum is not large. The head of the school is a teacher of fencing in three government schools here in Fukwoka & I have been told is famous as a fencer all over Japan. He has been very kind and courteous to me at the school. He takes kindly all the religious instruction I have ventured to give him. I highly prize the opportunity to present religious truth to such a man in the quiet of my own home & with ample time to explain what may not be understood. This gentleman stipulated for a lesson of two hours on Saturdays. On other days I give him what time I can spare. The Japanese teacher of English is an evangelist in the Greek Church. He has much religious feeling but is very ignorant of the Bible. I have urged him to study it daily & he voluntarily promised to buy an English Bible & study it. Several young men come to me on Sundays to learn the New Testament. With most of them the object is not to get English, but to learn Christianity. One of them is a choice young man, a teacher here in Fukwoka. He is a member of my advanced class in English in the young Commercial School. Every evening these young men come to me to study English. He always begins with the New Test. It is really a daily Bible class. I do not charge them. Besides the New Test., they spend part of the time on an Eng. Reader. So, you see I am doing here my old work in China, teaching young men the New Testament.

Yours sincerely,
L. Moon.
Lottie Moon Collection, SBTS, Folder No. 8.

Fukwoka, Japan
Feb. 26, 1901.
Dear Dr. Willingham.

I wrote Mr. Stephens that if not providentially hundred, I should leave Nagasaki on March 1st by steamer going direct to Chefoo. I infer that the enclosed telegram is in response to that statement.

My Shanghai paper rec'd on Sunday has telegrams showing that war has recommenced in Manchuria & would most likely begin again in China. I have always believed that in the present, most barbarous state of affairs in China, the place for non-combatants, especially women, is out of that country. The men's papers, even in China, refrain from telling the nameless horrors perpetrated on helpless victims. One is willing to be shot or murdered outright, but [not] to be cut to pieces as was the wife of that Belgian engineer before her husband's eyes. The bravest would shudder to meet such a fate. The Chinese call it ling chi. It begins by cutting off the eye lids & so on piece meal, the whole body, by unutterable tortures. So you see, knowing these things before I left Tungchow, I determined to keep out of the reach of such savages & persuaded Miss Dutton to do the same. She, however, thought the war was ended & went back to be with her teacher.

Yrs. sincerely,
L. Moon.

Lottie Moon Collection, SBTS, Folder No. 8.

Tengchowfu, Shantung,
China, June 18, 1901
Dear Dr. Willingham,

If Dr. Evans should be appointed to North China, may I trouble you to forward the enclosed letter to Mrs. Evans, as I do not know her address? May I also venture to urge that prompt provision be made for at least additional missionary house in Tengchow? Mr. & Mrs. Owen are at Dr. Hartwell's & the house will be uncomfortably crowded when Miss Hartwell returns. None of our houses are large. If Dr. Evans should come here to live, as we very earnestly desire, still another house would be needed in the near future. It would be better that both houses should be foreign, for the sake of health & comfort. There are already several foreign houses here in the Presbyterian Mission & building two more would not shock the native mind.

I am very glad to report that Miss Dutton is taking hold of work energetically. She is taking as a specialty the establishing of day schools for girls & has already started one in the city with nine pupils. She went to the country on yesterday to consult about starting another. This morning, she interviewed the deacon of our church concerning a school (mixed) in his village. He appeared much delighted. In the country, the Christians will provide the building & Miss Dutton, the teacher. In the city, at present, she provides both. She has had a class in S.S. for sometime.

Now, I want to urge you to send that other woman promised over a year ago for Tengchow. Mr. Owen & Miss Dutton are taking up a long neglected field, once worked very faithfully, but of late years necessarily neglected for a lack of workers. Mr. Owen is brim full of energy & makes things go, whether in the city or country. He preached very well indeed last Sunday. It was the first time I had heard him & I was surprised at his command of the language & the freedom with which he spoke.

I don't know that you are aware of the fact that I am due a furlough one year from next fall. Such being the fact, another woman should be here just as soon as possible to get hold of the language so that she can take over my work while I am away. Miss Hartwell has her own country field & no one has been able to enter it in her absence. Our force is always lamentably inadequate to the needs of the work. We ought to have four families in Tengchow & not less than four single women. The English Baptists man their forces heavily & hav large results, usually about 400 baptisms annually. We have never had enough men & women in Shantung to meet the needs of one station & yet we hav three stations & voted last year, before we were driven out, to open two new stations. Oh! that Southern Baptists could realize their responsibilities!

I returned here in April & have made five country trips since.

Yrs. sincerely,

L. Moon.

Têngchowfu, Shantung,
China,
June 29, 1901
My dear Dr. Willingham,

My report for the quarter is due. I have made five trips to the country. The first was to Buk Ko, where the Christians gave me a most joyful welcome. They could hardly talk of anything but the fearful perils through which they passed during two months of last summer. Out of them all the Lord delivered them. They were full of thankfulness for this deliverance. At Wu Shi Li Pu, which I used to consider very hopeful the work seems to have gone backward. Poppy planting is much in evidence & I heard of many opium shops. Of course, they have been there all these years, but I have never before seen the poppy growing there, & women pressing out the juice. The women & girls came about me as usual, but the men, with whom I used to be on excellent terms, were conspicuously absent.

At *Mengchia*, considerable interest was manifested. I expect to go there again next week.

I teach as usual in the Sunday School, though my old class of boys & young men is scattered. I have a small class of young men none of whom can read.

We had a very pleasant Mission meeting this week at Hwanghien. We regretted very much the absence of our P'ingtu brethren, who are busy attending to indemnities & restoring their homes. They desire our deepest sympathy. Their burdens are heavy. I heard yesterday that a new society has sprung up in P'ingtu & Lai Yang, whose purpose is to resist the payment of indemnities. In Chihli, seven hundred villages have banded together for this purpose & have united their forces with the Boxers. The Imperial troops have been defeated & no one can foresee the end. We pray that the trouble may not extend to this part of the country. A Boxer proclamation was put up on Mr. Stephens' door recently saying that his house was to be burned. Mr. Stephens was absent at the time, but Mrs. Stephens took vigorous measures & the affair seems to have been nipped in the bud. The officials are sincerely anxious to keep down disturbances. If once they get beyond control, the scenes of last year will be repeated with added horrors.

I greatly enjoyed meeting Dr. & Mrs. Ayers. The Board made no mistake in appointing them, I feel assured.

We are rejoiced at the good report presented to the Convention & at the missionary spirit manifested at New Orleans. May the interest continue to grow. With best wishes,

Yrs. sincerely,

L. Moon.

Tengchowfu, Shantung
China,
July 27, 1901,
Rev. Dr. R. J. Willingham:-

The proposition of the Presbyterian Mission here to withdraw from Tengchow & leave it entirely to our Mission is so extravagant & so generous that I think our F. M. Board should have all possible information from us on the field before acting upon it. In going away they practically offer to make over to us all the good will they have gained through many long years, all the influence they can convey, & much of the prestige they have obtained by their fine college work. They only ask from our Board assurances that this field shall be really occupied. They offer to sell us at reasonable rates such buildings as an adequately increased force would imperatively need.

Because of its admirable location, we ought, by all means, to purchase their church. Our own church is quite off from all places of public resort. The Presbyterian church is so situated that it is in close proximity to the quarters occupied by students when they come up for their examinations. These examinations not only draw men from our own country for the district examination, but men from the countries for the Prefectural examinations. Students have to keep in hearing of the summons to the examinations, as these some times come very suddenly. If they are not on hand promptly, the consequences are very serious. The Presbyterian church is within hearing of such calls and therefore the students may attend it without apprehensions. On the other hand, our church is so far away from the students boarding places that few of them attend it. While the Presbyterians, during examinations, suspend their Sunday School and have preaching three times a day, we have so small an attendance of students that we do not need to make any change in our usual order of services. The attendance at the Presbyterian Sunday School grew so large that they were compelled to divide it. Their school for outsiders is made up largely of children from the neighborhood with others from a distance. It is to this school that we should fall heir, if we should buy their church. If we had it, we ought to have enough missionaries to keep up regular services every Sunday at both places.

To my mind, it would be wrong & unwise from all mistaken ideas of economy to fail to keep open a house where the gospel has been faithfully proclaimed for so many years. Rather than that such a calamity should happen, our Presbyterians friends would do well to stay and preach there themselves. We have been urging our F. M. Board for years to give us larger quarters for our Girls' school. The mortality of the pupils after returning to their homes has been fearful, it is probably due to the running down of their health at school on account of over crowding. The buildings for the Presbyterian school are ample and the grounds are large. A school of fifty girls could be accommodated with ease. We need quarters for at least that many. This school building is near enough to the Presbyterian church for the girls to attend there conveniently. It would be entirely too far away for them to attend services at our churches. There are enough churchgoers to justify Baptists in keeping up services at two places if the other mission withdraws.

I have touched upon the points which I thought likely that Dr. Hartwell might not mention. While we shall be very sorry to give up our Presbyterian friends & neighbors we yet realize that the greatest opportunity ever offered our Mission is before us & we earnestly desire that the F. M. Board & the Mission shall fully rise to the occasion.

With very cordial regards,

Yours sincerely

L. Moon.

Lottie Moon Collection, SBTS, Folder No. 9.

Tengchowfu,
Shantung,
China,
Sept. 18, 1901
Rev. Dr. R. J. Willingham:-
My dear Brother,

The news contained in your letter of Aug. 6th is very pleasing. We shall give the young lady assigned to Tengchow a hearty welcome. There is plenty of work for her to do. Miss Dutton kindly offers to give up one of her rooms for her use. This will crowd them both a little, but it will be only temporary.

Both our mission homes will be crowded about to their utmost capacity, but we look hopefully to the time when we shall have more houses.

I suppose the two young ladies will come out with Miss Hartwell. We are expecting Dr. Evans & family sometime in October. They are due in Shanghai in about ten days from this time. Dr. Ayers says that Dr. Evans can see all that Shanghai has to show in hospital work in two weeks. I shall therefore except them in the latter part of Oct. Our Association meets in Hwanghien on Oct. 31st & I think Dr. Evans would enjoy being present. Mission meeting follows the Association & some important questions come up for decision. Dr. Evans would enjoy hearing them discussed.

It is very gratifying that the Board has recently sent us such superior men. We want many more of the same sort. The Mission askt for two men to join Mr. Owen in country work in this region. Here let me say that Mr. Owen is most active & energetic. Still it is hardly possible for him to cover a fourth of our field & his heart goes out to the regions beyond. He is a choice spirit, & I believe will accomplish much for the Master. His wife is a very gifted worker & does well whatever she undertakes. We are greatly blessed in having such workers.

Our most imperative need in Tengchow just now is more men. With Miss Hartwell & the other young lady, we shall be reasonably well supplied, for the present with single women. We greatly need active, energetic young men like Mr. Owen for the country work. It is a hard, rough life & the only attraction it possesses is that it is the Master's work. All our churches have been built up largely or entirely from the country people. In all denominations the same is true. It is therefore wise policy to send out strong young men who will be ready to endure hardship for the gospel's sake. One hardly hears of Mr. Owen's return home before he is off somewhere else. He is now in the country. Next week, he starts out with Mrs. Owen for a long stay at Laichowfu. After their return, as soon as circumstances permit, they are intending to spend a month at one of the stations connected with Têngchow. Fancy how delightful it is to an old worker to see such energy & zeal exercised in a field so long neglected for lack of workers! If only you could send more such!

I want, too, to plead for P'ingtu. They have begged so long for two women for that important station. They also askt—the whole Mission asked—for men for that field, with a view to opening new stations. The Laichowfu station has been opened, but is not yet manned. Do send us more workers, & the plea is always for strong men & women, the very best that can be had. We want those who will be missed in their communities and home churches. Dr. Yates used to insist that men should be well educated & thoroughly prepared for their work. The longer one is on the field, the more one believes that the home churches ought to send their best and strongest men & women.

I follow your work with deep interest and earnest prayers. May the Lord bless you abundantly and give glorious success.

Yours sincerely,

L. Moon.

Tengchowfu, Shantung
China
Nov. 7, 1901
My dear Dr. Willingham,

I wish to lay before you a statement. At the Mission meeting in Hwanghien, after permission had been given Mr. Lowe to remove to Laichowfu I introduced the following preamble and resolution: -

"Whereas Tungchow & Hwanghien are already partially supplied with single ladies & whereas the North China Mission has formally asked for two ladies for Pingtu, be it

Resolved, That the F. M. Board be requested to assign to the Pingtu station the two ladies now under appointment for North China."

Mr. Stephens promptly seconded the motion. Dr. Hartwell very strongly opposed. The only reason he gave was that his daughter, Miss Anna, needs a coadjutor. Mr. Stephens immediately withdrew his second, giving as his reason that Dr. Hartwell's opposition was sufficient to make us drop the matter. Dr. Ayers said that referring the matter to the F. M. Board was "a farce," as had been proved by the Board's failure to send Dr. Evans to Hwanghien on request of the Mission, & that he would never again suggest to the Board where to send anyone. Besides, there had been some intimation that Miss Willeford would be sent to join Miss Thompson & we ought not to interfere.

Mr. Owen seconded my motion &, in a strong speech, urged that the ladies ought to go to Pingtu. He said that both were more needed in Pingtu than either one was needed in Tengchow or Hwanghien.

Mrs. Pruitt objected to the word "assign," I do not know why. I offered to amend the resolution by saying, "on consultation with the ladies." This was not accepted. Mr. Sears who, as moderator, had no vote, spoke strongly in favor of the resolution. He said that in Pingtu there are one hundred heads of families whose wives are heathen. Married ladies cannot do country work. Single women are needed at Pingtu to teach the wives & children of Christian men whose families are heathen. He said it was one of the saddest sights in the world to see a congregation made up wholly, or almost wholly of men. Then, there is Mrs. Lowe's school of girls, now numbering twelve; next year, there will be twenty. Who is to look after this school? He thanked me for bringing in the resolution, but said that if the brethren objected, they would manage somehow in Pingtu. The motion was lost by a small majority. I think several did not vote. Now, what I want to urge is that something be done & done promptly for Pingtu. I told Mr. Lowe, on yesterday that surely the South has two other women who might be found for Pingtu. The need is very great. The resolution of last year asking for one single lady for Tungchow, one for Hwanghien & two for Pingtu certainly was meant to lay as much stress on the needs of Pingtu as those of the other two stations.

Dr. Ayers said, let us all write privately to the Board & express our views. I say emphatically that I agree with Mr. Owen in his view of the relative needs of the three stations. Tungchow has three single women; Pingtu, none. Hwanghien has one single woman; Pingtu, none. As to overwhelming pressure of work, Tungchow & Hwanghien combined do not compare with Pingtu. Besides, *our* chief need now is two strong young men to join Mr. Owen in country work.

We had a most enjoyable meeting at Hwanghien. It was the first meeting at which the Pingtu missionaries could be present since last years' troubles & our dear friends, Mr. & Mrs. Pruitt, were also with us. The opening of Laichowfu filled some of us with enthusiasm. Even those who held back only did so because they thought the time had not come. Dr. Evans' presence added much to our pleasure. He is a very lovable brother & wherever he may finally decide to settle, our best wishes will go with him. Mr. Crocker writes that he hopes Dr. Evans will go to Yangchow but that if he comes here, they will rejoice with us. I wrote him today that I hoped Dr. Evans would go to Laichowfu, but that if he went to Yangchow, I should rejoice with them. Dr. Evans, Mr. Lowe & Mr. Owen went over to Hwanghien today. Dr. Evans told me he had decided to write & leave the question of his location to you.

Yrs. sincerely,

L. Moon.

Têngchowfu, Shantung,
China,
Nov. 26, 1901
Rev. Dr. R. J. Willingham:—
My dear Brother,

I have always held it to be a part of my duty to keep the Board fully informed of our needs. I know that they are always ready to meet our growing needs so far as the funds allow & duty to other parts of our great field permits.

Our mission laid hands on Dr. Hartwell for a general work which necessitates his absence from Têngchow for over a month at the present time. He is in P'ingtu teaching a class. Early next year, he will be obliged to go to Hwanghien to do the same special kind of work. The original plan was for the brethren from our three stations to come to Têngchow for united study. This looked beautiful in theory, but practically proved a failure. The brethren simply could not spare the time for the long journeys involved, to say nothing of the expense of travel. It was therefore decided that, since they could not come to Dr. Hartwell, he must go to them. Now, all this is very nice for the folks in P'ingtu & Hwanghien, but what about the work here in Têngchow? Mr. Owen, of course, puts his shoulder to the wheel, but however willing he may be, he can not do three men's work, nor be in two places at once. In consequence, while trying to fill Dr. Hartwell's place in the city & the country, his own very promising country work, on which he had set his heart, has to be left undone. He & Mr. Owen had promised to spend the 10th moon in *Shia Li Chia* in the neighborhood of which there is an immense field on which, in days gone by, much labor was expended by our mission. Mr. *Li*, being disappointed now, asked Mr. Owen to go in the first month of next China year. It happens that this is just the month for Dr. Hartwell's work in Hwanghien. The brethren are then at leisure. So, Mr. Owen will have to be tied down again & his country work go undone. I have been here now about twenty-eight years &, in all that time, up to within a few months, the country work has been by all odds *the* important work of the mission. All our churches have been filled almost entirely from the country. Now, Têngchow seems slightly awake to the fact that there are churches & religious teachers here. The city work is much more promising than ever before. The country work is no less promising now than in the past. In future, the two should be equally pressed. Now, who is to do it? It is clear that we ought to have immediately another man for Têngchow, & a second, as soon as possible. Then there are P'ingtu and Laichowfu. It is very distressing, our lack of adequate force for immediate pressing needs. I know you will do all you can to send us the help we ought to have.

With Christian salutations,

Yrs. sincerely,

L. Moon.

Tengchowfu, Shantung,

China,

Jan. 6, 1902

Rev. Dr. R. J. Willingham:—

My dear Brother,

There seems to be some mis-apprehension with regard to the question of salary agreed upon between the F. M. Board & the North China missionaries & Mr. Owen has asked me to write & state the facts. In the spring of 1894, there came a circular from the Board suggesting that our salaries be reduced to $450.00 with an allowance of fifty dollars for medical expenses. The question came up in our mission meeting held in Hwanghien in the summer, for the purpose of making out our estimates for the following year. I had prepared my estimate in advance & had put my salary down at five hundred dollars. I stated to the mission that I would consent to have the salary lowered to that amount, but that it would never be put at less than that with my consent. Dr. Randle strongly commended my position & this led to a discussion of the whole matter. The mission finally passed a vote saying that they would accept five hundred dollars salary for each person, making one thousand dollars for a family, exclusive of children. This, of course, cut us off from the proposed medical allowance. After returning home, I remember distinctly writing you & saying that I preferred to pay my own medical bills. I have never swerved from that position, but stand now where I stood in 1894. I think the fact that Dr. Randle and Mr. Sears both continued to draw salaries of one thousand each, conclusively proves that the F. M. Board accepted the proposition of the Mission to make the salaries as stated above. Dr. Hartwell's remembrance of the circumstances tallies with mine.

I know that the Central China Mission accepted the Board's proposition as to salary and medical allowance, for one of them stated to me a scruple of conscience on the subject. She wished to know if it was wrong to use that fifty dollars additional on a trip to Japan for the purpose of keeping her health. The North China Mission distinctly did not accept, but passed a resolution saying they "would accept" other terms. The F. M. Board has all these years since paid our salaries in accordance with that resolution.

These are the facts in the case & I have written them because I think they have been forgotten in the lapse of time.

With cordial Christian salutations,

Yours sincerely,

L. Moon.

Têngchowfu, Shantung,
China,
Feb. 4, 1902
Rev. Dr. R. J. Willingham:—
My dear Brother,

Your letter of Dec. 18th was rec'd last week. Mrs. Hartwell kindly read to me your letter to Dr. Hartwell regarding the two ladies. They had been flooded with letters at Shanghai urging them to go to P'ingtu. Mr. Sears had also written me a strong letter asking me to "help a friend & a work in need" & I have communicated to them the contents of his letter, with such comments as seemed desirable. They had heard from you before leaving America & seemed quite prepared to accept your suggestion that one should go to P'ingtu & one to Hwanghien. Miss Dutton has doubtless written you of her decision to remove to P'ingtu. Her purpose was heartily sanctioned not only by her own station, but by the Hwanghien people. Needless to say the P'ingtu missionaries welcomed her most cordially. Now, if both the other ladies should decide to go to P'ingtu, it would be none too many. I shall always maintain that a well-equipped station needs not less than four single women & four families. Of the latter, one man should be a physician. Do wake up the F. M. Board to see our needs! O if they could all be transported to Shantung just for a few days & could see for themselves! Then, right quickly would they say, "men & women for P'ingtu, a good strong reinforcement for Laichowfu, another family & two single women for Hwanghien, two more families & two more single women for Tungchow." I verily believe they would say so & would send them. Why is it that new missionaries are so deeply impressed with the need of more workers? Why is it that as soon as they get on the field their hearts are stirred within them & they write to beg for more laborers? It is that their eyes are opened to see the awful need as people in America can not perceive it. I think we old ones feel it more than the new comers. Southern Baptists were the first to enter Shantung; they were also the first to settle in Tungchow. Yet we have never at any time had an adequate force at any station. We have had in all Shantung until within very recent years, only about as many missionaries as the Presbyterians have had in Têngchow alone. Besides, they have had strongly equipped stations at Chefoo, Weihsien, Chinanfu, Ichowfu and Chiningjeo. Recently they have also started a station at Tsingtao, the German port. Their force in Shantung has numbered not far from fifty. Even now, we have only twenty! Do you wonder that their converts run up into the thousands while ours still lag in the hundreds? The English Baptists began on a small scale, but Mr. Jones waked them up & they poured missionaries into Shantung. They have had strong stations in Shantung and Shansi and their converts in Shantung went up into the thousands. They used to baptize about four hundred annually, I think, in this province. Do you wonder, when I see the need as I do that I continue to cry out for more workers? Why, the C. I. M. once sent in one year, over one hundred missionaries! Still, they go on adding to their numbers. Mission workers in Shantung are looking forward to a large ingathering this year. Who is to teach the new converts? Who are to evangelize the enormous masses hardly beginning to be moved? You should have heard the prayers that went up last Saturday evening in the station meeting for strong young men to go out into the country & build up churches, strong, earnest consecrated young men.

Praying God's richest blessing upon your work, I am

Yours sincerely,

L. Moon.

Têngchowfu, Shantung,
China,
April 1, 1902
Rev. Dr. R. J. Willingham:—
Dear Brother,

The month of January fell, this year, in the last moon of the China year. It is not good form to visit during the latter half, or even more, of that month. It was a good time to rest & to sweep away an accumulation of neglected letters. With the China New Year, which came in Feb., the real work of the year began. Visitors come to our houses & we go to see our Chinese friends & acquaintances. Early in March, the North St. school opened & it now has thirty-nine names on the roll. Of these, twenty-six are boys &, except three or four, they attend regularly.

The school is little more than a Sunday School running six days in the week. The advanced boys study the New Testament, committing it to memory; also Old Testament History and some hymn book which they commit to memory. Besides, they are allowed to study one Chinese Classic & are taught writing. The younger boys study catechism, a small hymn book & the "Peep of Day." They also are allowed one Chinese Classic.

The attendance of the girls is very irregular, but I am glad to have them come at all. They form a nucleus for a woman's prayer meeting on Wednesday afternoons. On Sunday mornings, the school house is used for preaching. On Sunday afternoons, the boys are required & the girls are invited to attend our Sunday School held at the church.

The grant of ten dollars for school room rent enabled me to procure a good building which could accommodate probably seventy or eighty children, with some alterations. I was obliged to put repairs on the inside of the house to make it usable. We still have only dirt floors. Some day, when money is available, I want brick floors. We shall soon need a second teacher. I promised the teacher that when the number goes up to forty, there shall be another teacher. In that case, I shall have to ask the Mission to second my request for an additional appropriation of about twenty dollars gold.

I think the school will run up largely, in the future. As it is only a day school, the expense is small. It gives me ready access to the homes of the children & besides some of the mothers attend prayer meeting & services on Sunday.

There are a few women whom I teach regularly either in their own homes, or when they come to visit me. They attend church with more or less regularity. One woman from the country has been baptized. She was taught from childhood by Mrs. Crawford & seems like an experienced Christian. She was extremely happy to be baptized. She has exercised a very fine influence in her husband's home. They are all now friendly to Christianity.

I have made but one country trip this year. That was to Buh Ko, where we have some earnest Christians. The work seemed absolutely prostrate there last year on account of the Boxer trouble of 1900. There has been a very great change for the better. One of the most hopeful signs is a self supporting English school taught by one of Mrs. Pruitt's former pupils. There are twenty young men & boys in attendance, of whom seven are boarders. They come from five different villages. Needless to say, they are brought under strong Christian influences.

Everything is bright & encouraging in our work, but as it broadens & expands we feel sorely the pressing need of more workers. I used to give five days a week to the country work & two to the city. Now, the city work is so exacting that I must devote four days in the week to it alone. What is to become of the country work, with only three days a week in which to do it? & yet there are always pressing calls to broaden the work. It ought to be deepened as well as broadened. One ought to spend weeks in the country work where now only days can be given. Would that our people could be aroused to see their duty & the present propitious time for winning this part of Shantung for the Master.

With most cordial good wishes & earnest prayers for the success of your labors, I am

Yrs. sincerely,

L. Moon.

Têngchowfu, Shantung,
China.
May 31, 1902
Rev. Dr. R. J. Willingham:—
Dear Brother,

In Nov. next my furlough is due according to the latest regulations of the F. M. Board. May I ask you to make application for me to the Board & let me know their decision? I should wish to leave here some time in Dec. & should probably reach America in Jan. 1903.

If the furlough is granted, kindly authorize the Mission Treasurer to draw for expenses of the journey.

Yrs. sincerely,

L. Moon.

Têngchowfu, Shantung,
China.
June 20, 1902
Rev. Dr. R. J. Willingham:—
Dear Brother,

Thank you for the copy of the annual report which you kindly sent me. I have read it with much interest. I am very glad to see the work in Africa prospering as never before. As to China, we hope for much better things this year than ever. Already, in Shantung, there have been over one hundred baptisms this year & there are still applicants for baptism & a good many inquirers. As to our own city, I have never known the people to be so friendly and accessible.

I think your son did a very wise thing when he persuaded that "excellent woman" "to go & assist him." Please present him my hearty congratulations. I don't think any one too good for Japan & so I congratulate the lady on going to that beautiful land. It seems to me the most attractive of all our mission fields. The people are most lovable.

Since your son has taken the "help meet" you intended to recommend for me I look to you confidently to replace her by some other "excellent woman." I am sure I shall not look in vain. We need so many new workers! P'ingtu and Laichowfu are crying out for men & women. Do send us all we need & then see if you we do not give a good account of ourselves. Here, we are severely hampered by the lack of an additional man especially for country work. It seems a pity that fields worked so many years by Baptists should pass into other hands because we lack workers. Dr. Hartwell must give a large amount of time to the training class and to preparation for it. This throws extra work in the city on Mr. Owen & so our promising country work has to be neglected. A man can not be in two places at once. I am aware that it is hard to get suitable men & I know that money is not always forthcoming to meet the many calls, yet I think the F. M. Board should always be kept informed of our immediate & pressing needs. I feel confident that there will be large advance this year both at home & abroad.

May the Lord bless you in the work you are doing so faithfully for Him.
Yrs. sincerely,
L. Moon.

Têngchowfu, Shantung,
China
Sept. 15, 1902
Rev. Dr. R. J. Willingham:—
My dear Brother,
Thank you heartily for your promptness in referring to the F. M. Board my request for a furlough, & also for the cordial way in which you make known their decision.

There is but one drawback to the pleasure of going & that is the very favorable opportunity here of giving the gospel to the people. I have never known such friendliness on the part of the people & my experience embraces nearly twenty-nine years. A few days ago, I had eighteen visitors at one time & some of them seemed eager to learn though they had never been here before.

More & more, people come here especially to be taught. A very intelligent woman was here two days ago & applied herself earnestly to learn. She reads very well, a rare accomplishment among Chinese women. A woman who was here on yesterday, when I was talking to her about Heaven, said sadly, "You can go to Heaven, but we Chinese who haven't learned the doctrine cannot go." Her son comes to my day school. This leads me to say that some of the boys have shown themselves real missionaries in teaching their own families. One has taught his grandmother; others have talked to their mothers & tried to influence them for Christianity.

It hardly seems possible to write a letter to you & not urge reinforcements for our North China Mission. It is a sorrow to me that when I go, the Mission House in which I live will be closed up. I had expected Miss Dutton to keep it open, but the needs of P'ingtu were on her heart & truly the workers there are very few. She had begun a good work here among the women & was especially successful in getting them to attend church. I hear that her efforts have added largely to the number of women attending church in P'ingtu.

Miss Hartwell is doing faithful & successful work, but, even if she were strong, she could only accomplish her own share of the general work. She is anxious for a co-adjutor & should have one as quickly as possible. Then, there is Miss Williford. Her parting injunction, the other day, was that when I go home, I should try to get workers for Laichowfu. Truly, that city needs & should have promptly not less than two more families & one more single woman. The minimum number should be not less than twelve workers to a station. As a maximum, I should say, an additional family & two more single women. Of the men, one should be a doctor. I speak with confidence, after long years of experience & observation. As a rule, small missions make a very slight impression on a heathen community. They are simply swallowed up. When there is an adequate force, they are always before the public, some preaching in the chapel, some itinerating, some in the dispensary, some visiting from house to house & some in schools. In short, the Mission becomes, as it ought to be, an all pervading force. Then, when once a native church is organized & set to work, the influence branches out in all directions. O that we should multiply such stations, not only in Shantung, but wherever our missionaries are working in Central & Southern China.

I trust there will be a great enlargement of the work at home this year & then we may hope for a larger force in China.

With very cordial regards,

Yrs. sincerely,

L. Moon.

111 Kirk Ave.,

Roanoke, Va.

Oct. 7, 1903

Dear Dr. Willingham,

It occurs to me that you ought to send an announcement of Mrs. Hartwell's death direct to her sister, Miss Rebecca Norris. I fear she might see it first in the papers & so receive a painful shock. I think she is the only remaining sister & Mrs. Hartwell was especially devoted to her.

Her address is

Miss Rebecca Norris,

Mitchell's, Culpepper Co.,

Va.

I hope you rec'd my letter this morning which gave the children's addresses.

I expect to be here until about Nov. 1st, when I shall go to Norfolk, to remain until the week before Christmas. My address there will be 414 Fairfax Ave.

Yours sincerely,

L. Moon.

San Francisco,

Cal.,

Feb. 24, 1904

Rev. Dr. R. J. Willingham:-

My dear Brother,

Our train was belated and did not reach here until nearly noon on Sunday. We arrived in a rain & has been raining ever since, but, on yesterday

I went to the office of the Pacific Steamship Co. & exchanged my order for a ticket to Shanghai. The agent said that I would have two room-mates as far as Honolulu & one on to Shanghai. The steamer has a full complement of passengers, as the Japanese steamer was taken off the line. The Japanese steamers are being fitted up with nine inch guns. Our steamer, the "China," is to take one million pounds of prepared beef for the Russians. This is to be delivered at Shanghai & there trans-shipped for Vladivostok. I shall be greatly surprised if the Japanese do not confiscate this beef. They claim that food and fuel are contraband of war.

I am at the Occidental Hotel, where I have stopped twice on former occasions. The rate for missionaries is two dollars a day. Before leaving China some one advised me strongly against going to the Menton Hotel, saying that it is in a very out of the way place & that if one goes there, one is not certain to find a room. The hotel is small & it has regular boarders. Transients may or may not get accommodated. The Occidental is admirably kept and a stranger is made to feel at home immediately. Kindness seems to be the law of the house. I have seen no where else such kind & attentive servants.

I want to thank you heartily for the satisfactory arrangements made for my trip to China. You have done everything I asked and more than was necessary. Now that my ticket reads to Shanghai, I do not need the extra fifty dollars I asked.

I have met with very kind and pleasant people in my journey across the continent. If the passengers on the steamer shall prove equally pleasant, I shall have an enjoyable trip across the water. With so very heavy a cargo, the ship can not but be very steady. I anticipate a very pleasant voyage.

The steamer is to leave on Friday at one P M.

With cordial good wishes, I am

Yours sincerely,

L. Moon.

Tengchowfu,
Shantung Province,
China,
April 26, 1904
Rev. Dr. R. J. Willingham:-
My dear Brother,

Your letter of March 16 was rec'd two days ago. I was not expecting the money earlier than Dec., but, of course, am pleased to receive it whenever it is sent.

As frequently happens in China, an unexpected difficulty has arisen regarding the purchase of the house now used as a school house. I thought it belonged to Mr. *Wu* & supposed he would sell it. Only within a few days have I come into possession of the facts. More than two years ago, Mr. *Wu* rented the property (the Chinese call it tein) for the sum of 45,000 cash. During three years the owner can redeem it at any time on repayment of the 45,000 cash. The real value of the property is 135,000 cash. If it is not redeemed within 3 years it becomes the property of the lessee at its full value, 135,000 cash. After that, it can only be redeemed at full value. Naturally Mr. *Wu* declines to sell. By holding it to the close of this China year, he will come into possession of property valued at 135,000 cash for the sum of 45,000 cash paid three years previously. Meantime he has been drawing rent at the rate of 12000 cash annually—a pretty good business transaction, I should say. He says he has spent 10,000 cash on repairs. He was having the roof repaired on yesterday.

He tells me that he holds what he calls the *Yuan shu.* As I understand, this is the title to the property given in the first place by the original owner to lessee No. 1. The real owner let the property (*tein*) with the rights to redeem it. He died in Manchuria and left a widow & one child. Under usual conditions, these will never return to claim the property; lessee No. 1 is too poor even to redeem it from Mr. *Wu* & the latter since he holds the *Yuan shu*, is the real owner, i.e., he will be at the close of the China year. He says he will not sell the property because the Chinese would accuse him of pretending to buy for himself & then selling to a foreigner. I suspect this is an evasion. I think he wishes to continue to rent the property to me, but as I have recently made some improvements at an advanced rent, I have told him that we will go on until the close of this year at the rate agreed upon & that afterwards, I will look out another house. I feel sure that he could not possibly get more rent than I pay from the Chinese. The original agreement was made between his wife & myself & has run on now over 2 years & we are in the 3rd moon of the 3rd year. He, all at once, discovers that I was entirely mistaken in the terms, that he rented me two rooms and I have been using 3!! all of which is news to me. I asked Him why he had let the "mistake" (?) go unquestioned up to this time, & reminded him that the property had cost him forty-five thousand cash & that, at the close of this year, he would have rec'd thirty-six thousand in rent from me. Besides this, all the improvements inside the buildings had been made by me, without any cost to him. Brick floors have been put in from time to time & *kongs* have been pulled down &, recently, a wall, to make the house suitable for school purposes. I had a wall pulled down which gave me the use of another very small room, thus throwing two rooms into one. I offered to pay a reasonable rent for this additional room, but he declined. Then, I offered to repair a hole in the roof instead, but this he also declined.

I shall try to find another place in the neighborhood. By waiting to purchase until the last month of the China year, the property can be bought to much better advantage, as I explained to Mrs. Whitehurst. The Chinese are usually up to their ears in debt & selling time comes in the last moon. Hence, property sold then is always put at a lower figure than at other times.

It is absolutely necessary to keep the school in the present neighborhood. Both teachers live over there & most of the pupils are drawn from that part of the city, or contiguous parts in the city, or the North suburb. It is a good strategic point not only for a day school, but for a Sunday School. We have had Sunday services there now for about two years. Two Sundays ago, I started a Sunday School in the school house. So, you see, besides a day school we may consider that the church here has a mission station on North St. Three of the brethren have been going there on Sundays and conduct the services. Work here is like work in cities in America. It is not wise to open all the schools in one part of the city & wholly neglect other places. Miss Hartwell has two day schools in this part of the city. I have one school, under two teachers, near North gate. The children are required to attend over there, in the morning & to come here to Sunday School in the afternoon. I believe I have now put you in possession of all the facts.

I wish instructions on one point. I expect Mr. *Wu* to make some final proposition at the close of the year. As he has the *Yuan shu*, I think it would be safe to buy from him, though, of course, I would not do this without the approval of the Committee on buying & building. This committee used to have three members, one in Tengchow, one in Hwanghien & one in Pingtu. Do you think that, if Mr. *Wu* should offer to sell & give the *Yuan shu* & the committee should approve that the property (I mean that north house) ought to be bought? I have made no inquiries about the other houses as yet. You know I did not originally suggest the purchase of Mr. *Wu*'s house as I felt sure we could rent it indefinitely at the old rate. This is Chinese custom. Once rent a house & you keep it until you choose to give it up, unless, of course, it is *tein*-ed and can be redeemed. The word for rent is *min*.

I am sorry so few people offer for mission work. It is their loss, for never was the work so full of interest & delight.

Yrs. sincerely

L. Moon.

Tengchowfu,

Shantung Province,

China,

May 10, 1904

Rev. Dr. R. J. Willingham:—

By an oversight, I suppose my North St. school was not provided for in the first quarter of 1904. Mr. Pruitt told me that he was directed to begin to draw appropriations for me on April 1. I had written to him before leaving America & asked him to pay Mrs. Mu's salary & the school house rent until my arrival In China, the teachers are paid monthly throughout the year, during vacations as well as when they are at work. They are engaged by the year, not by the school session. So, Mrs. Mu's salary for three months has not been provided for, nor has the school house rent. The appropriations asked for were, quarterly.

Teacher (woman)   G$6.25

School house rent   <u>2.50</u>

Total $8.75

I am short then, eight dollars & seventy five cts. out of the annual appropriation. It was all right to withhold the appropriation for the male teacher up to April 1, because he would not well be selected until I arrived. I have engaged one who is thus far most satisfactory. The school gives me very great pleasure. The spirit is very good among the pupils. Mrs. Owen had charge of the school until her departure for Pingtu. I suppose she paid the salary and house rent out of her own funds. I suppose she will send me the bill before mission meeting, or will present it at that time & I must meet it. Mr. Pruitt paid for the month of March out of private funds. As I had requested him to pay the money, of course, I have refunded it. How is it to be paid me? As well as what is due Mrs. Owen? It occurs to me that the whole bill might be met out of what is left over from my traveling expenses. I have not yet made out the account fully because I have mis-laid or lost the statement given me by the Shanghai Bank as to the value of U. S. Gold in Taels. I paid Tls. 22.50 (missionary rate) for my ticket from Shanghai to Chefoo. That amount is between fifteen and sixteen dollars in U. S. currency.

If I fail to find the statement, I will ask Mr. Pruitt for the rate & will send you on the itemized account. The balance is in the neighborhood of seventy-seven dollars. Shall I deduct from the balance the amount due for the North St. school in the first quarter?

There is another matter on which I should like to ask your opinion & that is with regard to the entertainment of Chinese guests, especially inquirers & applicants for baptism. The women come to Miss Hartwell & myself & the whole expense of their entertainment falls on us personally. It has been a heavy burden pecuniary for many years. I am no sooner in Tengchow then it begins anew. I am told that four women are to come this week to ask for baptism, accompanied by an elderly woman, five in all. It may usually be set down that each woman will bring from one to three children with her. I have entertained as many as thirteen women and children for days at a time in the past. Sometimes I have had women here a month at a time studying. They come as my guests. As I have said, this entertainment of inquirers & applicants for baptisms used to be a heavy burden. Now it is intolerable. The price of living has advanced. Recently, within ten days I have had seven Chinese guests, three of whom are to leave tomorrow. (The others left previously.) Before the week closes five more women (& probably a whole raft of children) are to be here. I simply cannot afford to go on that way any longer & yet I am forced to do it or seem lacking in hospitality. What would you advise?

Other missions, I believe, provide out of mission funds for the entertainment of inquirers. They have classes in the cities where missionaries live or the missionary goes to the country & holds classes, all being paid for out of mission funds. In addition to the advance in the cost of living, servants to hire, coolie hire & c. silver continues to drop down. I have sold two cheques of fifty taels each since reaching here. The first brought cash 49355. The second, nine days later, cash 48,883. I well remember when Tls. 50 used to bring over eighty thousand cash. I think you will see, then, that the question of entertainment of Chinese guests is growing to be a very serious one for some of us. Through Mr. Owen's efforts, Dr. Hartwell, as pastor, was relieved of the burden and the church assumed it. Miss Hartwell, Mr. Newton & I go on at our own expense &, as I have said, for me, the situation is intolerable. I ask again, what do you advise?

Hoping the F. M. Board has had a prosperous year & with all good wishes for your share of the work, I am

Yrs. sincerely,

L. Moon.

Tengchowfu, Shantung Province,
China, July 8, 1904.
Rev. Dr. R. J. Willingham
My dear Brother,
    The following is an itemized account of my expenses on the journey to
Tengchowfu from Crewe, Va.

Feb. 15, 1904.
To trunks to station	$.30
to ticket and extra baggage to Burkeville	$.20
dinner	1.00
Feb. 16, breakfast	$.75
Dinner	$.85
carriage to hotel	$.25
nights lodging	1.00
Feb. 17, carriage to train	$.25
breakfast	$.20
sleeper ticket to San Francisco	11.50
dinner	1.10
Feb. 18 breakfast	$.80
dinner	$.80
Feb. 20 breakfast	1.00
dinner	$.95
Feb. 21 breakfast	$.80

    Mr. Pruitt has gone to Shanghai now to attend a meeting of the
Publication Society. On his return I will hand him a cheque for the above
amount $54.84 & so close the business. It turned out that I did not need the
amount so generously provided for my journey, but there was a feeling of
security in being amply provided with funds & that conduces to one's
comfort. I had a delightful journey with many pleasant experiences by the
way.
    I am glad to report that the work here has never been so satisfactory to
me. Inquirers increase both in the city & in the country. We are sadly in need
of reinforcements here, as elsewhere. It was voted at the meeting in Laichow
that a man & wife & one single woman be asked for for Tengchow, it being
understood however, that Hwanghien was first to be supplied. Mr. & Mrs.

Stephens have been over burdened since Mr. & Mrs. Pruitt removed to this place & a single woman & a couple are needed in Hwanghien.

I have read with much interest the account in the *Index* of the fine meeting at Nashville. It seems to me the best of all & I hope great results.

With best wishes for the prosperity of your work, I am

Yrs. sincerely

L. Moon.

Tengchowfu,

Shantung Province,

China,

Sept. 22, 1904.

Rev. Dr. R. J. Willingham:-

My dear Brother,

I am happy to report that the title deed for the North St. property has been stamped by the proper Chinese official & is now in Mr. Pruitt's hands. As he is Treasurer of the Mission, the deed is in his name. The property cost Cash 450,000. The amount granted, G $375.00 bought Tls. 601.20. At present rates, somewhat over Tls. 400 go toward the purchase of the place. With the remainder of the money & with the materials that will come from pulling down some of the buildings, I hope I shall have plenty to put up a suitable building. This is to be for the older boys. The present school building is to be used for the girls & for smaller boys. We are trying to build up a Sunday School in connection with the day school. After Sunday School, a service is also held. Two of the Training School men go over on Sunday to aid in this work. This Sunday School comes in the morning & does not conflict with the Sunday School at the church, which comes in the afternoon. I teach a class in each school.

The North St. day school started out prosperously this year, but even before my return, small pox had broken out. In the spring, the epidemic was violent on North St. & in the Water City. It did not break up the school, but I was obliged to keep out of the school for several months those who had it. I feared they would bring the contagion in their clothes. One boy who had the disease in vacation is still kept out on that account. The teacher's child died of the disease, though she was not one of the pupils.

The most trying hindrance at the present comes from the extreme pressure of hard times. Our proximity to the scene of hostilities has greatly enhanced the cost of living. Parents who could formerly spare their children to go to school must now keep them out to help eke out a scanty subsistence. It is really pitiable. The poorest food, hu shi,[?] which is the staple food of even the middle class, used to cost from six to nine hundred cash a bushel; it has now run up to from twelve to seventeen hundred cash a bushel. Only very poor people used to depend on grass for fuel. Now those who were formerly decently comfortable have to send out their children to get grass. They dig it up by the roots, dry it in the sun & lay it away for the winter. It used to be three cash a catty; now it is ten cash (a catty is 1 1/3 lbs.). How the poor are to pull through this winter is a problem. There will be much want & suffering. Our region is dependent for the overflow of its population on Manchuria. Nearly every family has its representatives over there in times of peace. These send back money to help support those who stay at home. Now, the majority of those who should be in Manchuria earning money are idle at home, a tax on the dwindling resources of the family. Some are still abroad at Vladivistok or Port Arthur, unable to make remittances as before. The prospects are gloomy in the extreme.

A boy who used to be in the North St. school, an orphan, was turned out to sleep on the streets & beg. An old woman past seventy who once knew better days, has been sleeping on the street in a temple door, exposed to the wind and rain.

There are many other homeless ones. Those I have mentioned are people I have known for years.

Before receiving your letter of June 13, I asked the Mission to give me Twenty dollars for a class. I asked that a liberal view be taken of the use of the money, so that some of it might go to the entertainment of Christians & inquirers. No one objected to my having the money for a class, but Mr. Lowe said he could not vote for me to have the money if it was to be used in entertaining guests. He feared the precedent on his own field. I therefore did not press the matter & it remains in status quo. I think Mr. Lowe ought to take into consideration the difference of the fields. He is right on the midst of his work. People can easily attend his services & go home the same day. Here, we have never had any Christians in the near villages. The people of the near villages with us have been openly hostile or entirely indifferent. Until late years, with the breaking down of opposition in the city, our work was almost entirely in remote villages & towns. Those who come for communion, or for baptism, must stay at least two nights. Women invariably remain longer. They do not get away under three nights at the shortest in my expenses. Since Mrs. Crawford left, the country work has fallen largely on me & along with it the entertainment of women who come from villages when she works in this region.

I simply cannot afford to go on entertaining guests at my own expense, & yet the work cannot afford to have the entertaining stopped. Christians come to the Communion occasionally & people also come for baptism sometimes & they can't be left on the streets. Of course, the grant of Twenty Dollars for the class has made matters easier. If women need to come and remain a month for instruction, or less time as the case may be, I shall not have to supply their need out of personal funds. Still, if a dozen or more come up for communion or baptism, simply to remain a few days, I shall have still to entertain them.

I had a small class of five women in August, three of whom were from the country. They remained not quite three weeks. Of the three, two were baptized before going home and the other had been baptized in the spring. I am hoping to have another class in November to be composed of women from other villages than the two represented in the August class. It is delightful work. The class serves to attract women & girls, who like to come in & learn a little along with the women from the country.

I consulted with Miss Hartwell and tried to limit the expenses of the class to the same she allows for her school girls, 2000 cash apiece a month. This supplies good, but plain food.

Of course, guests have to be entertained on a different scale. It would seem niggardly to feed them as they live at home. The fact that they are guests entitles them to expect such entertaining as they would give to guests in their homes.

Recurring to your letter of June 13, I did not need $8.75 for the North St. expenses before mentioned, but only $3.74. This I deducted from what was left over from Travelling expenses, according to act. forwarded you. Mrs. Owen said there was nothing due her unless a small bill for charcoal & of that she was not certain. She would look at her book & let me know. That was in June & I have heard nothing from her. The accounts, then, for the first quarter are all settled, so far as I know. The allowance began with 2nd quarter. (April 1st.)

With Christian regards

Yrs. sincerely,

L. Moon.

Tengchowfu,
Shantung, China,
Nov. 14, 1904.
Rev. Dr. R. J. Willingham,
My dear Brother,

Mrs. Crawford has kindly sent me a copy of a letter written by her to Mrs. C. E. Kerr of Decatur, Ga.

In a note appended to the copy she says, ("N. B. The various points mentioned are in answer to the several questions asked by Mrs. Kerr who is much grieved by her sister's course"). Mrs. Crawford tells me that she has also sent you a copy of her letter to Mrs. Kerr. So far as I can gather, Mrs. Wilson has made some very grave charges against me & has cited Mrs. Crawford in evidence. Mrs. Crawford writes me as follows:–"*I never spoke a word to her on the* subject—have never seen her since 1882—and she intimates that some of our G. M. missionaries are trying to make of this a point against the Board—which is utterly without foundation. I cannot tell you how grieved I am at all this."

Before taking up Mrs. Crawford's communication to Mrs. Kerr in detail, I wish to express my surprise at the singular anachronism of the whole affair. A lady whom I have never seen brings charges; she calls as witness another lady whom she has not seen for over twenty years; this lady who is called to testify has not seen me in over ten years except once during a call in Chefoo, at the time of the Boxer trouble. Certainly, theological discussions would be far from our thoughts when we were fugitives for our lives! In the years since Mrs. Crawford left Tengchow, we have maintained a regular correspondence, but I think there has never been the faintest allusion to matters of theology. Mrs. Crawford's letter to Mrs. Kerr has an appearance of bringing matters nearer even date as she speaks of a conversation with Mrs. Kerr, on "Miss Moon's views," in Dec. 1900. It must be remembered, however, that it was then six years since I had seen her except as above, mentioned at Chefoo. She was leaving that night for Wei Hai Wei & I had just arrived from Tengchow.

Taking up the letter now in detail, Mrs. Crawford declares me guiltless of one charge. She says, however, "What she declined to teach in my catechism was the Mosaic account of the Creation of the world & the fall of man—I think nothing else."

With regard to this, I may say that Mrs. Crawford's catechism has been a part of the curriculum of the North St. school ever since its beginning. If any part of it is omitted in the teaching, I am unaware of the fact. When the children complete the book, they are examined in it from the first question to the last; nothing is omitted.

I do not use the book much in my work among the women simply because another book, *20 Hymns*, with prayers and the Ten Commandments has commended itself to my experience as the best to be used.

Mrs. Crawford is quite correct in her statement that I did not teach the first part of her catechism. I think this was for two or three years, say, 1882-85. I really have forgotten.

I quite fail to see what the views of the two gentlemen alluded to in Mrs. Crawford's letter have to do with me. One of them I have not met for twenty-seven years; the other for about seventeen.

I respectfully submit that, outside of Russia, a private letter to a personal friend would hardly be admitted by any Judge in a secular court as bearing on the case. I think it would be ruled out as irrelevant. The final count Mrs. Crawford herself indignantly repudiates.

In general, I may say that I have never taught contrary to the usual views of Southern Baptists. I am trying, in a very poor way, as I am aware, to lead the Chinese to the Lord Jesus. When they have accepted Him, I try to influence them to noble & useful lives for the dear Master's sake. Deeply conscious of weakness & failure, I yield to none in devotion to the Lord, who redeemed us with His own precious blood.

This letter will probably reach you about 2 weeks later than Mrs. Crawford's copy of her letter to Mrs. Kerr. I suppose you could write to me of Mrs. Wilson charges after getting in her evidence. This letter is meant as my reply to the charge as soon as soon as I have heard of them.

Yrs. sincerely

L. Moon.

Tengchowfu, Shantung,
China,
Jan. 21, 1905.
Rev. R. J. Willingham:-
Dear Brother,

Your letter of Dec. 9, with regard to a change of plan in employing native teachers, was rec'd on yesterday & has had my careful consideration. In compliance with your request for an expression of opinion, I am compelled to write somewhat at length, in order to do anything like adequate justice to the subject.

For acquiring the Chinese language, there are three essential points: one must learn the name of the character, its tone & its meaning. Where the initial sound is *p, t, or k*, one must also learn whether these letters are aspirated, or unaspirated. It must be remembered that, originally, the Chinese language was ideographic. Hence, the multiplicity of characters. Williams' dictionary, which is regarded as the standard, is said to contain twenty thousand distinct characters. Suppose a beginner learns accurately one hundred characters, name, tone, meaning & if necessary, whether aspirated or unaspirated. These hundred characters, which he has mastered, do not give any clue to the next one hundred. Thus, one might go on & learn a thousand characters, or even two thousand, which last if the right two thousand, would enable him to read the New Testament in Mandarin. How about the Old Testament? He must depend upon his teacher to give him the tone & name of all the new characters not found in the New Testament. He could depend on the dictionary, or on an English Bible, to get at the meaning, though, if he depended on the latter alone, his knowledge would be extremely inaccurate, on account of differences of idiom.

With regard to tones, some words differ here & at Hwanghien though the places are only about twenty-four miles apart. The Pingtu teachers will tell you that they have five tones; here, we have four. The punctuation of some classes of words there is so different from ours as almost to constitute a dialect. Further west, the diversity is so great as to be a different dialect. Mrs. Crawford, who had been in China more than forty years, on going to Taianfu, had to have a teacher & try to twist her tongue, as she expressed into the new & strange sounds of that region, yet T'aian is in Shantung. Miss Knight, who had lived in Pingtu five years, had the same experience on going west.

Perhaps one will say, "Why not depend on a dictionary to give these punctuations?" The dictionaries give the Peking sounds & tones, & the only way to get these locally is to have a local teacher.

The matter is immensely complicated by the fact that, in addition to Mandarin, which is both spoken & written in several providences, there is the *Wen li*, or Classical language, which all educated Chinese have at their tongues' end. They are drilled in it from childhood, say from fifteen to twenty years, more or less, until they complete their education, & then they go on learning it all their lives, if they intend to compete in the government examinations. A missionary who expects to associate with educated Chinese, should have a thorough acquaintance with the Classics; if he is to do educational or literary work, he must have much more than acquaintance with Wen li; he must be able to read & write it with ease. (When I say "write" I mean simply dictate to a Chinese teacher. Not one foreigner in two thousand, I should say, could write (*paint*) the Wen Li character to the extent necessary in literary work.)

If it takes Chinese students from fifteen to twenty years to get a working use of their own language, what of the foreigner? The missionary comes to China knowing English & most probably Greek, Latin & mostly Hebrew, also, one or more European languages and they are taught in American Colleges. These languages are all alphabetic & to know is an immense advantage in acquiring another. English & German are cognate; so are Italian, French, Spanish & Portuguese. Even Russian, which sounds to our ear barbarous, is alphabetic. To know Greek & Latin gives one a clue to the meaning of many words in English, or even in the study of the modern Continental languages.

Not one of these languages gives any help in studying Chinese. The Chinese language grew up in wholly (?) different fashion. It is not alphabetic. It was originally ideographic, each character being intended to be a picture of that object: If you have learned the alphabet of a European language, you can use a dictionary & found out the meaning of words, though your pronunciation may be execrable & would not be understood by a native of the country to which the language belongs.

You look at a Chinese character you never saw before & what is to guide you as to sound, tone & meaning? Of the forty characters, more or less, that go to make up the written language, what is the name of this particular character? Under which of the two hundred & fourteen radicals would you look for it? Was it made with one stroke of the paint brush, or with seventeen? Occasionally, one may guess the sound from one of the radicals of which a complete character is composed; another radical in a complex character might possibly very faintly hint at a distinct meaning. There are ten thousands of characters of which one could not guess the meaning by not looking at them, nor would he have the faintest idea how to call them. I have at command two good dictionaries, one containing over four thousand characters & the other said to contain twenty thousand. When my teacher has been busy teaching my woman helper & I did not like to interrupt him, I have spent hours searching both dictionaries for four characters which they simply did not have. I would go carefully over every character under various radicals of which the character composed & after all this useless waste of time there was no result. I should have to ask the teacher after all. Sometimes dictionaries give absolute meanings; in this case, one must, of course, depend on a teacher.

I have said that one may occasionally guess a sound or a distinct meaning from the radicals in a complex character, but there is still no hint of a tone. If you call the tone long, the word means something else. For example, I say hua, (first tone), it means flowers, dissipation, pleasure, in distinct vision. Hua two (superscripted) (second tone) to change; transformation. Hua three (subscripted) (third th tone) Stent's Dictionary give none, Hua four (superscripted), (four th tone,) language, speech, conversation. Thus, in the spoken language, one who does not know the tone, is liable to the most ridiculous blunders. Suppose one is teaching a class & called the tone wrong with the book before him, he will most likely have the mortification of seeing an amused smile on the faces of his class.

I have said above that occasionally one of the radicals in a character will give a faint hint of the meaning. I turn now, by way of illustration, quite at random, to radical ninety-six, niao, the character for binds; in Stent's Dictionary, I find twenty-nine characters given under this head with Peking tones & aspirates. The radical simply informs me that these twenty-nine characters represents something belonging to the feathered tribe; finding under the radical the English spelling, I must look up in the body of the dictionary, the word of which I desire to note the meaning. Take the 8-5 th radical, meaning water; under this, I find in Stent's Dictionary, one hundred seventy-eight characters, some of which have not the slightest connection with chui, water, as for example, ch'iu, to pray, to invite, to entreat, to seek; mo, a sandy desert, a careless manner. One might multiply these examples almost ad infinitum. If I don't know the tone of a word &, have no teacher to tell me, I am indeed at sea, for the dictionary is absolutely no help in tones & aspirates (unless, of course, if one lived in Peking, or its vicinity.) The books all refer you to the local teacher for pronunciation & tones.

As to the written character, the Chinese school boy, soon after entering school, begins to trace, with his paintbrush, over this paper, the characters prepared for him by his teacher. It is many years before he begins to paint the characters independently. One marvels at the deftness & the rapidity with which the Chinese teacher paints these complicated characters, some of which require as many as sixteen or seventeen strokes in the painting, but remember, he has been trained to the use of the brush since childhood. He has the Chinese trained eye for form (the heritage of thousands of years) & he has the marvelous Chinese trained memory (also a heritage from former generations). I do not know the statistics, but I doubt if one missionary in five hundred learns to write Chinese. (I mean the Mandarin) As to reading a Chinese letter, some could manage to get at the meaning if it were written in the *Chin Tze* (True character), but the Chinese teachers themselves stumble badly over the letters written in the *Tiao Tze* (Grass character,) yet many of the letters, & especially business letters, bank notes & c., are written in this indecipherable script.

I hear that the Presbyterian missionaries in Shantung are expected to pay for their teachers after two years. I also hear that they have men called "native assistant," who also act as their teachers. It does not matter in the least with me whether *Mr. Chiang* is called my teacher, or my native assistant. He is very useful in teaching Chinese women as well as in telling me what I need to know in taking up any new book in which I have to examine my pupils. For many years, he has looked after business matters for members of our station, such as aiding in buying, building, or repairing. Chinese masons & carpenters have to be looked after sharply, or they will slight their work & cheat in every way. Mr. Chiang saves valuable time in this way, to nearly every member of the Tengchow station. He has done this now for nearly thirty years. He formally was Dr. Crawford's teacher. (He was called a teacher; in point of fact, he was also a native assistant. He is the leading deacon in our church.) As to the proposed time limit: in point of fact, the higher the work one proposes to do, the more he needs a teacher. Dr. Hayes, a leading Chinese scholar, told me, one summer, that he was using four teachers. He was editing a newspaper & was also preparing important scientific works for the press. He had probably been in China fifteen years at the time to which I refer. I know that the gentlemen who were here once several months, working on the new mandarin version of the New Testament, each had his teacher. Some came from Peking, one from Kwei Chow Providence, one from Kiangsu & Dr. Mateer, author of very valuable books, then lived here. Not one of them could possibly have prosecuted their labors without a teacher.

It does not seem to me quite just to expect a missionary to pay for a teacher out of his salary. After mature consideration, our North China mission requested that their salaries be restored to the old figures in consideration of the increased rates of living. The F.M. Board declined to accede to their request. Now, it is proposed that the missionary pay annually, out of his reduced salary, the salary of a teacher. In some cases, this teacher is doing much more for the interest of the general work than he is doing for the individual missionary. I have been allowed forty dollars this year for repairs, roofing & c. & c. Am I to give us my work for the women & my care of the North St. schools to look after masons here? What about the work to be done to make the school premises on North St. what they ought to be? Am I to leave the work here, or to cease to go to the country, to look after carpenters, masons, whitewashers, & painters, & then get badly cheated in the bargain? That appears to me extremely poor economy. Year after year, my teacher has been helping someone. Sometimes, it was in repairs in the girls schools or in the many changes made there; sometimes, in helping Dr. Hartwell in building, or repairing; once, for nearly six months (or more), helping Mr. Owen while building his house. For years, he has collected the rents, or the interest, on the endowment for the church, & boys school. For many, many years, he looked after church guests, (men). Only the other day, he told me he was going to give this up on account of his eyes.

When I have classes, even small ones, my teacher is very helpful. He teaches women in one book, while I teach in another. In teaching the character to the women, it is almost like teaching each one separately. Their rate of progress is so very different.

In conclusion, I respectfully request the F. M. Board to continue to me the valuable assistance of Mr. Chiang. His salary would be the same whether he is called a "native assistant," or a "teacher." His work would, also, be the same.

With thanks for your cordial Christian greeting & the New Year's wishes, & wishing God's choices blessings upon your work & yourself

I am

Yrs. sincerely,

L. Moon.

Têngchowfu, China,
March 17, 1905
Rev. R. J. Willingham:—
My dear Brother,

Your kind letters of Dec. 21, 1904 & of Jan. 21, 1905 were received & read with much pleasure. Thank you heartily for both. I was very sorry to learn that Mrs. Calder Willingham was still in poor health. When I saw her in Nagasaki, it was hoped that the worse was over. I hope she is now better.

I am very glad to report that the Memorial School is prospering. The name of the 49th pupil was enrolled today & others are expected. The spirit of the children is fine. They are cheery, studious & docile. I am very happy over it all. Several large boys have come in. Then, there are some little fellows who hardly reach up to the desk when reciting. What can I do but pet them, those little ones? There are only five girls as yet. I have had to get a teacher for two hours a day to teach Arithmetic & Geography. The former is much in demand. Dr. Mateer's Arithmetic is meeting a great call[?]. The Chinese are eager for it. There is no study that broadens the Chinese mind more than Geography. It helps to knock the conceit out of a Chinaman to find out that, after all, China is the "Middle Kingdom" only in name. Mr. Newton told me to ask the Mission for money to pay this new teacher. It is only 2000 cash a month, that is, 24000 cash a year, say, about fifteen gold dollars. Shall I do that, or try to get the money out of some other part of this year's appropriation? What would you advise? I was obliged to have the new teacher. Boys have dropt off in the past & gone elsewhere, because the studies above mentioned, or rather, because Arithmetic was not taught in my school. The woman who had charge was overburdened & I don't think she knew Arithmetic herself. She is an admirable teacher for small children. The teacher in the advanced department is only able to teach purely Chinese studies, as also, of course, religious books. He does not know either Arithmetic or Geography. I told Mr. Newton I should get the teacher for Arithmetic even if I had to pay him myself. He replied, "Ask the Mission for the money." I have not yet done so as there is no hurry about it. I have advanced his first month's pay, 2000 cash & will pay the second month's in about three weeks hence.

I regret to report that there was not money wherewith to build. The Tls. Six hundred & one & some cts. did not go as far as I had hoped. The purchase money amounted to about four hundred & fifty taels. Then, Mr. Pruitt had to pay the U.S. Consul in Chefoo & a Chinese official fees of about forty-two Mex. Dollars. This was because there were two owners & two sets of deeds had to be stamped. A third part owner cropt up & her demand had to be met. Then, the middle-man had to be paid. Pulling down the old buildings cost fearfully. I am rejoiced that the buildings we still have are all that we need. Some have been fixed up in good style & the rooms are bright & sunny & fresh & clean as whitewash can make them. This, for the advanced school. There are two large rooms & a passage. One room serves also for Sunday School & preaching purposes. I am now having necessary repairs carried on both inside & out, on other parts of the premises. The building assigned the small school could easily accommodate thirty or forty pupils. That department now numbers 21. I think that in both houses I could seat probably a hundred pupils. So, you see, I have all I need. Best of all, the pulling down of the old buildings has given a big yard with plenty of air & sunshine. No wonder the children are so bright & happy. We are spending a lot on the street door. I thought it would cost 4000 cash. The carpenter's bill went over 20,000 cash & there were bricks and masons besides. When the door is finished, we shall have a nice looking entrance instead of the old shabby one. The old houses turned out to be built of wretched stones, with straw roofs of old date, only fit for burning. There were probably good stones enough to start a building & put it up two or three feet. I am not even sure of that. Finding that there would not be money to build, I have used some of it for desks & benches. I have strictly charged my teacher that we are not to go beyond the money we have in hand. I told him that it was provided by children & young ladies & that I would not ask them for anything additional.

When all the improvements & repairs are finisht, I will make out the account & send you. I am more than satisfied with what I have in the way of school accommodations. I am simply delighted with the facilities afforded me for carrying on the school work. With best wishes,

Yrs. sincerely,

L. Moon.

Têngchowfu, China,
June 29, 1905
Rev. R. J. Willingham:—
My dear Brother,

I have the pleasure of reporting a good half session of the Memorial School on North St. A better class of boys have come in this year, so we are not almost broken up by wheat harvest. Of course, we still have a great many poor boys who must go out to glean wheat & who, in the autumn, will have to dig up fuel for the winter. Still, in the advanced department more than half are above this necessity. I suppose that there are two reasons why the school is attracting boys of a better class than heretofore. (1) It is getting quite the fashion to wish to associate with foreigners. The officials & their wives have set the example & many are eager to follow it.

(2) Boys want a better education than the native schools, outside of government schools, can give them. The addition of Arithmetic has no doubt drawn in boys who would not otherwise have come.

The New Testament is & will remain the chief text book. The school is the joy of my heart. It is a delight to see the boys growing in character. Each boy feels that I am his friend & from the oldest to the youngest they come to me without hesitation. The Chinese ideal of the relation between pupil & teacher is of fear on the one side & severity on the other. The pupil must shrink away when his teacher appears. They have never dreamed that the law of life is love. My boys are growing up to be gentlemen, I hope, & perhaps, some day, they will be Christian gentlemen. I treat them with the same courtesy with which I should American or Japanese boys & they are not slow to respond.

I have enrolled about sixty boys & girls this year. In the primary department, the attendance is unsatisfactory. The girls are often kept out to work at home. From this department, too, the children go out largely to glean in the wheat field &, in the fall, they must dig up grass. I recognize the necessity and praise them for helping their parents. I should like, next year, to add a lace making department for the girls. There is a great demand among foreigners for hand-made lace. Some of it is beautiful, real Honeton lace. Three schools in Chefoo are thus supported. After the initial outlay the lace department would be self supporting & the girls would be taught books half of each day.

I have had much encouragement in woman's work, visiting in the city & in the West suburb. Some are truly interested.

I have made only one country trip. I found much interest in one especial village, *Sz Chia*. If I were three women (& still young) I might do something in the country. As it is, the country is perforce neglected.

I should have said that one of the school boys was baptized not long since.

We were rejoiced to know that the F. M. Board again reported, "No debt." May the "betterments" be provided.

Yrs. sincerely,

L. Moon.

Tengchowfu,

China,

Sept. 8, 1905.

Rev. Dr. R. J. Willingham:-

My dear Brother,

I was very glad to receive your letter of Aug. 3rd & to learn that you are trying to arrange for an additional force for Tengchow. Without an addition to our number, we should be heavily crippled in the work here. Mr. Newton is a hard & faithful worker, but one man can't keep the oversight of both city & country work. One department is bound to suffer. With four small children Mrs. Newton ought not to be expected to do much mission work. Practically, then, when the two families connected with the Training School leave Tengchow there will be only Mr. Newton & myself unless others come in the mean time. It ought to be remembered, too, that I am not equal to the rough country work that I used to do. I could formerly spend a month in the country more easily & comfortably than I can now spend a few days. Besides, the city work has so largely increased in hopefulness that I could give all my time to that with advantage. The day school also requires considerable time every week. So, you see, my hands are full. I have always thought that if I could be in three places at once, I might accomplish something. As it is, if one interest is pushed, two others suffer. If I am constantly in the country, the work of the city visiting & the school both suffer. If I confine myself to the city, there is no woman to work my district in the country, which is enormously large. Since Miss Barton left, I have been expected to work the fields she took over from Mrs. Crawford, in addition to my own already very large country district. The result has been that I was forced to abandon my field to the southeast where I used to visit & stay at about eight villages, twice a year, using these villages as a basis for working the surrounding country. I have a very large field out east, about 20 miles away. It is a beautiful region, full of towns & villages, but how can I more than touch the edges? The field used to be indisputably ours. Now, the Presbyterians are entering it. To the west there is Mrs. Crawford's large field, for which Mr. Newton and I are responsible.

The Presbyterians do not plan to reinforce Tengchow. Their F. M. Board & their Shantung Mission wish to abandon it. They never had any hold on the country about here. Their work was in schools & in city visiting. Their schools were filled mostly with pupils from the west. They are now massing their forces in the west. They said themselves that, when their schools should be withdrawn, their congregation here would be almost gone. So, they proposed to hand over the field to the Baptists. Two members of this Presbyterian station objected & have held on. They succeeded in getting a woman sent out last year for country work. She used to belong to the Weihien station. Now, that station demands her back & the Board upholds the demands. Their Board also spoke in a letter of Tengchow as an "out station." It seems that the idea of their Board & their mission is to "freeze out" those who persist in staying here. I mention all this to show that now is the time for Baptists to concentrate here & hold this immense territory.

Beginning with Pingtu, we hold all the country quite up to Tengchow. If the Presbyterians leave here, we hold beyond dispute all the region to the south & east; the latter more than half-way to Chefoo. Baptists have always worked this region. It is only of late years that the Presbyterians have done any country work in this region. Hence, they feel their hold to be so slight. I have heard that the station here has received a command from their Board to sell any property that it is desired to purchase. If that be true, new families coming to us would not need to build. The Presbyterians have here four dwelling houses. At present they occupy three of these. If we could have a strong force here, I think the effect would be admirable. I have known the field now for over thirty years & it has never seemed so hopeful as now. The people are not naturally religious as they are out west. It took more than twenty years to live down the hostility engendered by the Anglo-French war with China. Now, that hostility exists only to a limited extent. What we need now is many workers, missionary & natives.

If Miss Hartwell goes, she leaves the girl's school without a head. She also has two day schools in the city & one in the country. She has country work in Chauguen, but that she could keep up from Hwanghien. Her going will be a calamity for our situation & especially for the girls boarding school. Whatever she does, she does most admirably. Our loss would be Hwanghian's gain.

I am sorry to learn that Mrs. C. T. Willingham has not improved as much as you hoped. Please give her my love. I shall not soon forget the delightful visit I had in her home in Fukuoka. She & your son were both lovely in their hospitality. We have choice spirits in our Japan mission. I wish they could have a large reinforcement. Beautiful Japan! It is the land of my heart ever since I found refuge there in Boxer times. The people some how cast a glamour over one who lives among them with an open eye & heart. So, I feel under the spell & it abides.

What I have written about the situation at Tengchow is simply to give information. It is not intended for the public. With most cordial greetings,

Yours sincerely,

L. Moon.

PRIVATE

Tengchowfu,
China,
Nov. 2, 1905.
Rev. R. J. Willingham:-
My dear Brother,

In my letter I mentioned that the question of the withdrawal of the Presbyterian Mission from Tengchow was still pending. Next week, at their East Shantung Mission meeting, it is to be decided. The majority favor withdrawal; two are very anxious to get the station reinforced. The West Shantung Mission advises them to withdraw or re-enforce, with an emphasis on the withdrawal. Two people defeated the wishes of a large majority, some years ago, by cabling to their F. M. Board to hold on until they could be heard from. Had F. M. Board been then in a position to make some tangible offer to the New York Pres. Board, in very shame, they would have accepted.

It would be most advantageous for our work if these good friends of ours should withdraw. They would leave us in undisputed possession of a field that our mission has worked faithfully for nearly fifty years. While their missionaries were shut up in school rooms & doing no itinerating in this region, our mission not only pushed schools, after a fashion, but pushed *country* work very earnestly. Consequently, we got a lodgment from which we could not easily be ejected. Nevertheless, the Presbyterians have many well trained native workers & I have long anticipated that they would try to wrest from us our country work. This, of late years, they have been attempting.

I have been connected with this station so long that I perhaps feel a deeper interest in its success & prosperity than any one else. Though I may say that Mr. & Mrs. Pruitt feel very much as I do. At any rate, I could say, without fear of contradiction, that I am the only one left who really knows the Tengchow field, its history & its hopeful possibilities.

For this reason, among others, I venture to write & urge that, if the matter really comes to an offer to withdraw in our favor, the F. M. Board should look at the question on a broad-minded way. The matter of money should not be allowed to weigh a moment against the strategical & denominational advantages we should gain. Better pay, without question, a good price for such property as we could use to advantage than even stop to consult with over a reduction of price. Once, when the list was made out, I remember that the prices seemed to us perfectly reasonable. Property has now advanced & they would probably ask more.

Their former college property would be just the thing for a hospital & there is a good two story building which would suit for a doctor's home. I mention this especially because we are going to ask, at our Mission meeting next week, for a doctor for Tengchow. The Mission would not grant it last June because they feared that Dr. Seymore might not like it. Now, Dr. Seymore is ready cordially to invite a doctor to come here. He says it would leave him freer to do other than medical work. I think, then, that the Mission will not again refuse us & I do trust that the F. M. Board, as early as possible, put the Tengchow station on the same bases as Hwanghien, Laichow & Pingtu, in regard to medical work. These are all young stations as compared to Tengchow, yet they have enormous advantages that we still lack. One of the Presbyterian brethren is in communication with Mr. Newton on the proposed question of withdrawal. He said that the withdrawal was, nearer being accomplished than it had been for a long time, yet, he added that it might not take place. Hence, he wished profound secrecy so far as the Chinese are concerned.

Misses Jeter & Taylor reached here last week & their coming gave us great joy. They are to live with me. They have fitted up their rooms in a cozy & home-like manner & they both seem very happy. They have gone to Hwanghien today, where they will meet many Chinese delegates to the Teng Lai Association.

We were delighted to hear of the generosity of the Jackson Church. Surely the Spirit of God is working in the hearts of His people as never before. So many delightful surprises come to us that we are made very happy.

Praying God's richest blessing upon your work, I am

Yours sincerely,

L. Moon.

Tengchowfu, Shantung,
China,
Nov. 29, 1905.
Rev. Dr. R. J. Willingham:-
My dear Brother,

My last letter might as well as not have been left unwritten. The Presbyterians decided to remain in Tengchow. Their latest hinted wish was for union work on medical & educational lines. It would not be wise to go into union work with them in any line.

We are delighted with the young ladies you have sent us. They are hard at work on the language. I believe they will make superior workers.

They are diligent in attendance on Chinese services, which is always a good sign in a new missionary.

The Mission voted to ask for a doctor for Tengchow. We need one very much in order to be on an equality with our other stations, as well as with the other mission working here. All our people go to Dr. Seymore, which gives the Presbyterians an enormous advantage. Besides, they have a native woman doctor who gets into the best city families. Mr. Newton cannot possibly do the country work &, at the same time, be pastor of the Tengchow church. We sorely need another minister here to take on the other work after Dr. Hartwell goes. At present, he is pastor; Mr. Pruitt has the Sunday School, & Mr. Newton is pastor of a country church, besides doing both country & city work. He is indefatigable, but he is not a strong man physically & ought not to have too much put on him. He has now gone to Tsintsin & Mancuria by request of the Mission.

While the Canton Providence seems to be in a state of unrest here, we enjoy profound tranquillity. The high officials associate with missionaries on terms of equality all over our providence, so far as I know. Last week, we had three of the official ladies to a dinner served in Western style. They have invited us to a return dinner next Saturday. These ladies are always cordial & friendly.

I am rejoiced to learn from your letter of Oct. 21, of the ever increasing interest in Foreign Missions. I trust that added contributions mean strengthening old stations & opening new ones. A mission in Mancuria stirs the blood & kindles the imagination. I hope the F. M. Board will decide to open work there. With best wishes & earnest prayers for a blessing on your work,

Yrs. sincerely,
L. Moon.

Têngchowfu,
Shantung, China,
May 19, 1906
My dear Brother,

Thanks for your letter of Ap. 4, notifying the sending of Twenty Dollars by Mrs. Guy, Dendron, Va.

This money is for a boy named Li P'ei Ting. I assigned him a scholarship last year for general good behavior & for devotion to study. He belongs to the Memorial School out North St., which school is supported by the "Sunbeams" of the Freemason St. church, Norfolk, Va. With the consent of the station, I give scholarships as rewards for diligence and good behavior. To gain one, a pupil must have attended the school not less than three or four years & must have a good record in every respect. The first boy to gain a scholarship is now in the Hwanghien boys' school & Mr. Stephens has written highly of him. This boy wishes later to take a medical course. He is a Christian & is a kind, loveable boy, besides being bright in his studies. Li P'ei Ting lives here on my place & is constantly under my supervision. He attends the North St. school. My purpose is to send him later either to Hwanghien, or P'ingtu. I wish him to prepare to be a teacher. Our schools are graded. The day schools stand at the lowest point. Above these is the Hwanghien boy's school, next, the P'ingtu Academy & above the Normal School, also at P'ingtu. We expect the Academy to develop into the North China College, with Mr. Owen at its head.

I shall ask for another scholarship next year. I want one for a boy who has been in school already about five years & who has a good record. His parents have become Christians since he entered the school. I wish him also to prepare himself for a teacher. There is now a crying need for teachers & the demand will go on increasing.

We hope to hear glorious news from the Convention in Chattanooga. With most cordial good wishes

Yours sincerely,

L. Moon.

P. S. The Twenty Dollars is included in my appropriation for this year & I have been drawing it in monthly installments. I will write to Mrs. Guy & thank the boys & girls who raise the money.

Têngchowfu, China,
Dec. 18, 1906
Rev. Dr. R. J. Willingham:—
Dear Brother,

During the present quarter, in addition to my usual duties, I have had the oversight of the Girls' Boarding School. Under Miss Hartwell's wise administration, the discipline and the spiritual atmosphere of the school were such that even after her departure the school has seemed to run itself. The teachers have proved most trustworthy, & the matron is a beautiful Christian character. Even the school cook bears the impress of Miss Hartwell's faithful, prayerful training. A sweeter, lovelier, more docile set of girls I have never known anywhere. Under such circumstances, then, the care of the school has been far less exacting then I feared; it has really given a minimum of trouble. Yet, the time required to look after the school has necessarily been taken from other work. I have not been able to do the country work I had planned, & even the work in the city has been neglected. Miss Taylor is now kindly relieving me of some of the details of the school work. As she lives on the place, this is more convenient for her then it has been for me. The station has elected Miss Taylor to have permanent charge of the school, & she is to take the control after the China New Year. I shall than be able to return to work which I greatly prefer, that is, evangelistic work in the city and in the country.

The school on North St. has not prospered during this latter half session as I could have wished. The competition of the Government schools draws off the better class of pupils. Parents will send their boys where they get food and clothing free. Besides, by paying high salaries, the Government commands much better teachers than we can afford. Teachers in Government schools command salaries of about fifty taels a month. The very highest in our mission schools in Shantung is hardly ten taels a month, & in the day schools scarcely half of that. So, you see, even in the matter of good teachers, the competition is hopeless.

Some pupils withdrew from the North St. school because they were forced to go to work to help their parents. We began the school year in Feb., with about thirty-five pupils. We have now on the roll twenty-three names, but even these are not regular in attendance. In addition, eight pupils come in the afternoon to learn Arithmetic and Geography. Some live in the city and some come from the country. Most of them, though not all, attend the Anglo-Chinese school in the mornings.

The Sunday School, held in the North St. school-rooms, has had varying attendance during the year. Sometimes, it has been good. When there were rumors of trouble, the outside attendance fell almost to nothing. It is better now, but by no means what I could wish. The attendance depends somewhat, indeed I may say, very much, on the man in charge, of the school on Sunday mornings. A man locally popular naturally attracts his neighbors. An untried young man, who is a stranger, fails to hold the usual attendants.

With most cordial good wishes,
Yours sincerely,
L. Moon

Beginings in P'ingtu

About ten miles west of P'ingtu city, in a village called Säling, lives a man named Tan, who was head of a local branch of the Lao Tien Mên, Venerable Heaven Sect. It has been suggested that this sect is the representative of Nestorians, who flourished in China more than a thousand years ago. Their Ten Commandments read differently in some respects from ours, but this could easily be accounted for by the fact of oral transmission. The sect possesses few religious books, & only leaders would have access to them. They practice confession of sins. The penitent kneels in presence of the leader, while a stick of incense is burning, & makes confession. After the confession is ended, the leader pronounces absolution.

The worship takes place at night. This is due to the fear of persecution. It is considered extremely meritorious if one manifests no drowsiness during these meetings which often last nearly all night.

The sect believes in prayer. A few years before Mr. Tan came into connection with Christianity, his wife was ill, having consumption & her death seemed imminent. Her husband spent three days on his knees praying that she might be spared until their eldest daughter should be old enough to take charge of the younger brothers and sisters. This prayer was heard, & the mother was spared three years, just long enough for the eldest daughter to be able to assume the responsibility of looking after the younger children.

For many years, rumors of a new religion, brought by foreigners, had reached Säling. At length, a brother of the above mentioned Mr. Tan, in the prosecution of some small business, arrived at Hwanghien, & there he learned something of Christianity. Later, Rev. C. W. Pruitt, during a tour in the P'ingtu region, preached on the street in Säling. It was probably early in the following spring that three men came to P'ingtu city to seek an interview with a missionary sojourning there. The men were Mr. Tan, the leader of the Säling Venerable Heaven Sect, his brother & a teacher from the same village. The first-named could read very little & his brother not at all. A book of hymns & prayers was given to the leader & probably other books to the teacher. These men had come to invite the missionary to visit Säling. The invitation was accepted & a day appointed for going. On reaching Säling, it became manifest that here were people hungering for a bread of life, of which, as yet, they knew not. In the darkness, they were groping after light. The leader, with the help of his son, a school-boy, had nearly mastered the little book previously given him. Men, women & children were eager to be taught. At that time, the movement was confined mainly to the *Tans* & the *Yuans*, to which latter family belonged the teacher mentioned above. The Yuan family consisted of four generations & it would hardly be an exaggeration to say that from the oldest to the youngest all were interested in learning the new doctrine.

On this first visit, the missionary made only a brief stay. Feeling her inability to cope with the situation, she invited Mrs. Crawford to come from Tengchow & share in the work. The two went to Säling intending to remain about two days, but it proved impossible to tear themselves away, in less than a week, from a work of such absorbing interest. Many men came to Mrs. Crawford especially to question her about the new doctrine. On the first Sunday of our stay there, so rapidly had the people learned, that it was possible to hold a Christian service in the little room which served us as bed-room, kitchen, dining room & chapel. It was sweet to hear Christian hymns sung by those who, though they had just learned them, already entered into their spiritual meaning. The meeting was as quiet, orderly & reverential as if in a Christian church.

On a second visit to Säling, Mrs. Crawford was visited by Mr. Li, from a neighboring village. He is now the honored pastor of the Baptist churches in the P'ingtu region. At the time Mrs. Crawford first met him, he was a scholarly teacher probably under thirty years of age! He was a school-mate of Mr. Yuan & had become interested in Christianity though his influence. The self-propagating power of the Säling movement was remarkable. Men would go far & wide to look up their friends & tell them the good news of salvation. Another remarkable feature of the movement was the number of bright young women who became interested & who, in process of time, were hopefully converted. This is partially accounted for by the fact that some of them had belonged to the Venerable Heaven Sect & were accustomed to think on religious subjects. However, some of the most earnest young women had never belonged to this sect. One of these rises now before the mental vision, as she then was, handsome, clever, witty, fearless, full of life. It is with a pang, after all the intervening years, that one recalls her fate. She belonged to what was probably the leading family in the village. Her step-mother was violently opposed to Christianity. When, in spite of family opposition the young woman was baptized, the step-mother took a genuine Chinese revenge. She had absolute control of the girl's betrothal & gave her in marriage to a man beneath her in social standing. The family was poor, the house narrow, low-roofed & void of ventilation. No wonder that, in a year, or two, this young woman fell into a decline. Her husband, who was devoted to her, would have done anything to save her, but there was the inexorable mother-in-law. The food provided by the husband's kind thoughtfulness was appropriated to her own use by the mother-in-law. Within two or three years, this much-wronged victim of injustice & cruelty passed to the immediate presence of her Lord & Saviour. Scarcely less tragic was the experience of her younger sister who was practically disowned & cast out when she became a Christian. She died in Têngchow, far from home & family.

Of the young women, probably the most spirited spiritually-minded was a member of the Yuan family called "Tsang." On her baptism, she took the name "Martha," after Mrs. Crawford. The day she took her departure for her heathen home, when about to be married, was a very sad one for her Christian friends. They rose early & held a meeting for prayer in the bride's home. The brother who led in prayer broke down in uncontrollable sobbing. What could be expected but persecution & ill-treatment when she should refuse to worship the ancestors & should decline to kneel at the graves to which in accordance with local custom she would be taken? Yet, by her sweet & gentle tact she so won on her husband during their first interview that everything was granted to her wishes & no sinful compliance exacted from her. She, too, has passed to the presence of the Master whom she so faithfully loved & served.

By the summer of 1888 the inquirers at Säling had begun to hold regular services on Sundays & on one night in the week. They had heard that this was the Christian custom. It was probably in the autumn of 1889 that six applied for baptism. There was one very odd application. It was made by a heathen woman for her future daughter-in-law. She came into the room where Mr. Pruitt was examining "Tsang" for baptism. The latter was deeply moved & wept much. When Mr. Pruitt had finished examining her, this heathen woman, who was from another village, said she had come to ask baptism for her daughter-in-law who was crying because other people could be baptized & she could not. Of course, Mr. Pruitt gladly consented to examine her. Besides these two young women, "Tsang" & "Kai," four men were accepted for baptism. The scene of the baptism was strikingly beautiful. At the east end of the village was a small, placid pond. Around this pond gathered a crowd in the national dress of blue, giving vivid color to the setting of the picture. Nearby were the autumn fields & in the distance lay the azure hills. The crowd was quiet & orderly. After the baptism, the six, with Miss Knight, were constituted into the Säling church.

A few months later these peaceful scenes were exchanged for violent & bitter persecution. It began at the China New Year. A band of men, probably from neighboring villages, either in mere wantonness or with malicious purpose, personated the missionaries & burlesqued the baptisms. This was the signal for violence. Mr. Li was beaten cruelly by his own brothers & had to leave home. About forty men from Mr. Tan's native village, members of his own clan, came to his home, bound him hand & foot & slung him on a pole. In this ignominious position, they bore him through Säling amid the jeers of his heathen neighbors, who called to him mockingly to "pray to the Heavenly father to protect him."

He was taken to the ancestral temple, forced to kneel & commanded to worship. On his refusal, he was beaten. This occurred three times. He was confined to his "kong" (brick bed) for a month on account of the injuries received. The instigator of this outrage was a teacher of repute, a relative of the injured man. The persecution against Mr. Tan did not subside until some months later, after this teacher's return from Peking, whither he had gone for some purpose. While there he made inquiry as to the wisdom of his course & was advised to let the Christians alone, which he accordingly did. Some of the men engaged in the outrage came later, privately, to Mr. Tan & expressed their regrets for what they had done. Until the storm had blown over, he felt it best to leave Säling & he went into P'ingtu city to live temporarily. Here, he held services every Sunday for men & constantly taught all who came to him.

A young woman belonging to the Yuan family was married into a heathen family. Her husband threatened her life. On a visit to her mother, he said to the latter that his wife might come to visit her, provided she was not taught Christianity, otherwise he would not permit her to come. Mrs. Yuan replied: "It is for you to say whether or not she shall come, but whoever comes inside this door will be taught Christianity."

In 1894, a church was built in Säling without expense to the Foreign Mission Board. The Christians had previously worshipped in a private house.

L. Moon.
Têngchow, China
May 1, 1907

Chefoo, China,
July 25, 1907
Dear Dr. Willingham,

I write to bear testimony to the good work done by Miss Dutton, when in Tengchow. She lived with me from the time of her arrival until her removal to P'ingtu. She was a faithful & diligent student of the Chinese language. Within three months of her arrival, we were fugitives, & this, of necessity, broke up her studies for a time. From Japan, she sent for her books & tried to carry on her studies. In Dec., 1900, she returned to Chefoo, sent for her teacher, & spent the winter in study. In March, she returned to Tengchow, where she remained until the following winter. During that time, she was not only diligent in study, but also in city visiting. She told me that she had access to seventy families. This I consider a remarkable record. I have often said that, with the exception of Mr. Owen, she did more to build up our Sunday School in Tengchow than any missionary I have known. She also began two day schools, one in the city & one in the country. Those two schools are flourishing up to this day. The one in the country has become the centre of a good work, & men & women come in from that village to ask for baptism.

I think I can say truly that the Chinese like Miss Dutton. Though she has been away from Tengchow many years, she is still kindly remembered there.

I have written this letter at Miss Dutton's request. Personally, I should be glad to see her return to Tengchow. I think we need just the kind of work she can do, city visiting. Our working force is lamentably small, whether for city, or for the country.

With very cordial regards,
Yours sincerely,
L. Moon.

Têngchowfu, Shantung,
China.
May 16, 1908
Dear Dr. Willingham,

You are doubtless aware that, on Dr. Hartwell's departure from Hwanghien, Mr. Newton removed thither to take his place. I have recently read a statement that "the Board's rule requires at least two men in every centre." I was not aware that there was such a rule. I am, however, painfully aware of the fact that there is no man here to bear the burdens that rightly should fall on masculine shoulders. While our work in the city flourishes, we are simply not able to cope with both that & the country work. It is absolutely impossible for two women to keep a boarding & several day-schools running, receive visitors in their homes & carry on systematic city visiting, and at the same time press work in the country as it should be done.

There are unmistakable signs that the Presbyterians are preparing to take advantage of our present weakness & seize upon places where we have had undisputed rights for eight years or more. Our mission has always had the pre-eminence in the country work in this region & it is only in recent years that the Presbyterians have seemed to realize its importance. Now, they are trying to get their F. M. Board to provide a force equal to giving one missionary to every 25000 Chinese. Meantime, before this call is answered, they are beginning assert a right to enter our places because we have not the force necessary to keep the work going. Unless we are reinforced, we shall lose what has been conceded to be ours for at least thirty years. The situation is very serious & it is my duty to lay it before the Board.

Except on one Sunday in the month, the services are conducted by the Chinese brethren. We have a fairly good attendance in the morning & usually a very good Sunday School in the afternoon. If Miss Taylor & I were to let go the schools & the city visiting, & devote ourselves to country work, the inevitable result would be the retrogression of the schools & of the attendance on Sundays. The city visiting helps the church attendance.

When I returned to China more than four years ago, our work here seemed in the full tide of success. There were two strong, experienced men here & a younger man preparing for work. The Training School was then here. The latter having been removed, we lost, at one blow, four workers. If it were only the city work, I should hold my peace. With the natives, Miss Taylor & I could manage to hold our own. It is the country work that will slip from our hands if something is not done & done speedily.

Hoping to receive a favorable response,

I remain

Yours sincerely,

L. Moon.

Têngchowfu,
Shantung, China,
July 10, 1908
Dear Dr. Willingham,

My report for the second Quarter is a little delayed. The work of the Lord here has prospered. The schools have been growingly efficient, owing to good teachers. Our church & Sunday School services have been well attended. City work has been prosecuted; country work has been necessarily neglected. It is a physical impossibility to be in two places at one time.

I regret to say that Miss Taylor was taken down with small-pox in June, soon after her return from the Mission Meeting at Laichowfu. I had to lay down all work for about three weeks & devote myself to nursing her. Miss Jones kindly came & she has done the main part of the nursing. She undertook the whole, with the aid of a Chinese woman, about two weeks ago. This released me for work. I am now holding a woman's class. The teaching, however, is done mainly by two efficient Chinese sisters.

I have details of mission work to look after which take up more or less time.

I wish to suggest to the F. M. Board the imperative necessity of *requiring* attention to vaccination on the part of every candidate who receives appointment to China. Within my knowledge, three women sent out by our Board have contracted a disease. The first was Mrs. Bostick & she died. Her husband, I learned, had sent to Shanghai for vaccine matter, but before it came, Mrs. Bostick was gone.

The second case was Mrs. King, who came out as Miss Knight. She had a most unfortunate religious scruple with regard to being vaccinated. I think she had never been vaccinated. She probably took the disease traveling in a native boat. It was a case of malignant small-pox. She died in a few days.

Miss Taylor probably took the disease from placing a child on the mat who was broken out with small-pox. She had tried to be vaccinated, she said, four times in America, but it seems that she has some physical idiosyncrasy which prevents the vaccine from having its proper effect.

Besides the above cases, Mrs. Lewis, of the Presbyterian mission here, died of small-pox some years ago, within less than a year of her coming to China. It is supposed that she took the disease at church. We are constantly exposed to it, especially if we do country work. I earnestly ask that the F. M. Board shall take action in the matter & allow no one to come out who has not been recently vaccinated. This I ask, not only as a safe guard to new missionaries, but for the sake of those now on the field whose time &

strength are necessarily given to nursing those who contract the disease. A contagious disease can only be nursed by one or two people, & the tax on the strength is very heavy, not to speak of loss of time from mission work. Trusting that the F. M. Board will see the necessity of what I suggest,

I remain Yrs. sincerely,

L. Moon.

Têngchowfu,
Shantung, China,
Aug. 3, 1908
Dear Dr. Willingham,

The news contained in your letter of June 19th is very cheering. We will give the brother a royal welcome to our city by the sea. If he brings a fair lady with him, so much the better. Our Chinese Christians are much delighted at the appointment of this brother to Tengchow. His coming will give a new impulse to the work. Then, the promise of "more missionaries for Têngchow before long" is "as cold waters to a thirsty soul."

I have no doubt that Mr. Morgan has sent you a statement of the relative needs of our North China work. I was not present at the Laichow meeting, but have been assured by Dr. Pruitt & Mr. Sears that a family for Têngchow was put as the first need. I have always urged, as the minimum force, three men for each station. There should be one to take the pastorate, stay at his post & press city work. (Mr. Owen pressed city work grandly.) Then, there should be a man to do country work, along with the evangelists. Then, there should be a man to give his whole time to building up a first-class Academy. In addition, there should be not less than four single women to conduct a girls' boarding school & press city & country work & day-schools. The missions that accomplish most have heavily manned stations, as witness the English Baptists & the Northern Presbyterians. The latter, in Shantung & Chilili, now number ten thousand. The English Baptists in Shantung have about four thousand members.

I trust your son has now entirely recovered from his illness. May the Lord bless you in the great work committed to your hands.

Yours sincerely,

L. Moon.

Tengchowfu,
Shantung, China,
Sept. 5, 1908
Dear Dr. Willingham,

The news contained in your letter of July 30 has made me happy. I shall heartily welcome all recruits. The three promised, however, are not enough. We need a third man, as the work falls under three heads:—(a.) Pastorate (b.) Country work, with the evangelists. (c.) Head of an Academy.

We also need two women, one for city work & one for the country. My hands are tied by day-schools & city work. The station asked me, some time ago, to take all the city day-schools & I consented. Next year, I expect to open a day school about ten miles away. I wish to visit it at least once a week in order to examine the pupils. This will take my only leisure day, Saturday. So you see, with city visiting, I shall have all I can do. When I speak of "leisure day," I do not mean an idle day. I mean one day in the week to be spent at home. I usually have callers on that day. One young fellow asked me to teach him the Bible & I told him to come on Saturday afternoons. He is a member of my S.S. class in the English New Testament.

Miss Taylor's enforced absence in Japan leaves her boarding school to me for the present. It is much smaller than formerly because of the opening of girl's boarding schools in Chefoo & Hwanghien. All this is due to growth of the work at other stations, & we should rejoice in it.

With cordial good wishes & with prayers for your work,
Yours sincerely,
L. Moon.

Têngchowfu, Shantung,
China,
Sept. 16, 1908
Dear Dr. Willingham,

Your kind letter of Aug. 12 reacht me on yesterday. I opened it expecting to learn of the appointment of another man for Têngchow, & was disappointed to find that no such person had appeared.

As soon as I learned of Mr. King's appointment I wrote him, at Mr. Peyton Stephens' suggestion, inviting him to join the Têngchow station. I had a lengthy reply stating his reasons for feeling it to be his duty to remain for the present at T'ai an. It seems the Bosticks are sore pressed there by the Methodists & their aggressive methods, & for Mr. King to withdraw now would almost be to abandon the field to them. The Church of England people there are considerate and do not interfere with Baptist work. Not so the American Methodists. They seem to show scant courtesy in mission matters & to be consistently intruding where they ought not. So, for the present, at least, there is no probability of Mr. King's coming. His wife, also, is in most wretched health.

I think, then, that we will still have to look to the home-land for new workers. I by no means despair of suitable men being found.

Miss Taylor has been away nearly a month. As her eyes are in a bad condition, she writes few letters. I have not heard from her since she left, except indirectly, while she was in Chefoo. Her girls' boarding school is going on, but with only fifteen pupils. So far as I can see, the school is going on satisfactorily.

I shall be glad to have Miss Taylor back when her rest is over. She needed it & was right to get away from the Chinese. She planned to be gone two months. With cordial good wishes,

Yours sincerely,

L. Moon.

Sept. 16—Afternoon...

Miss Taylor writes from Unzen, Japan, that her eyes are somewhat better. She has to be extremely careful still in using them.

L. M.

Tengchowfu,

Shantung,

China,

Oct. 10, 1908

Dear Dr. Willingham,

During the Third Quarter, the work has gone on as usual. The day schools re-opened in August, after the summer vacation. They are all doing well. The teachers are faithful. The Girls' Boarding School re-opened on Sept. 2nd. It numbers seventeen. It lost heavily in pupils by the opening of the Hwanghien school; less heavily, to the Chefoo School. The station loss means mission progress. I hope that Miss Taylor will be able to build up our station school in time. She is now in Japan, having left here Aug. 20th. I do not know when she will return. She has not been able to do any mission work since the first week in June, when she was seized with smallpox. I am looking forward to Mr. Adams' coming with much pleasure. He can begin at once to attend church & Sunday School, & his presence will draw Chinese men. I regret to observe the falling off in the attendance of men. We used to have such large & orderly & attentive congregations. Now, we have not even a native city worker. All the evangelists go to the country. It is inevitable that the city work must suffer. I have done such city visiting as I have been able. With the oversight of four schools, time is lacking for much other work. I planned to go to the country. Just then, two school girls fell sick & I could not go. The fact is, I am afraid to go & leave the school with no one in authority in case of illness. So, country work has to be neglected. I am sorry, but can not help it. Country work has always been more fruitful than city work, so it seems all the more regrettable that there is no one to do it.

    With best wishes,
    Yours sincerely,
    L. Moon.

Tengchowfu, Shantung,
Jan. 12, 1909
Dear Dr. Willingham,

    I rec'd, on yesterday, the news of the death of my sister, Miss Eddie H. Moon. She died in Starke, Fla., on Nov. 19, 1908.

    Will you kindly notify the Treasurer of the Foreign Mission Board with respect to payment of the interest on Three Thousand Dollars, now invested by the Board? & oblige.

    Yours sincerely,
    L. Moon.

Têngchowfu, Shantung,
April 5, 1909
Dear Dr. Willingham,

    The schools opened auspiciously after the China New Year. Two schools were united, thus making only one boys' day school in the city. In the Girls' Day School the enrollment is seventeen, with an attendance of sixteen. The girls study with enthusiasm & the school is a delight to me. A few are children of Christians, but the majority are from heathen families.

    A day-school for boys has been opened at a country station called Mä Chia. The teacher is said to be "the best man in the village." The pupils number twelve. This school has to be conducted mainly on old lines, as the teacher has not a modern education. In the other schools, we have up-to-date teachers, though I have to insist on the Chinese Classics.

Our Sunday School continues to grow & flourish. Mr. Adams led in the singing of a hymn, on yesterday, & I need not say that he did it well. We have as Sunday School superintendent a very fine man, Mr. Keing. He is one who has made heavy pecuniary sacrifices in order to follow his conscience, having resigned a situation in a government school in Peking rather than teach on Sundays. He belongs to a leading Têngchow family & received his education in a Naval Academy in Teintsin. He had a narrow escape from the "Boxers" in the troublous times of 1900. Later, he was interpreter for the English forces during the "Boxer" war. Last year, he was offered a commission in the Chinese Navy, but declined.

The city visiting has gone on as usual during the quarter just ended. I have been most cordially received & have frequently found earnest hearers. A very pleasant feature of the work is the eagerness of girls & young women to be taught. Some girls are anxious to attend school, but are not permitted to go. They eagerly embrace the opportunity to learn at home.

We sorely need more workers here. With our present force, we cannot begin to overtake the constantly expanding work. We ought to have another woman for city visiting & country work, & one to take Miss Taylor's place in the Girls' Boarding School. Miss Taylor's eyes will not admit of her teaching, but she could do admirable work in the country, or in city visiting. The city is wide open to us as never before, but we have not the force to take advantage of the opportunity. Our work seems full of hope, but we ought to have speedily more workers. The station has asked, through Mr. King, for Misses Lide & Leggett. I trust they will be sent to Têngchow.

With cordial good wishes,

Yours sincerely,

L. Moon.

Tengchowfu,

Shantung,

China,

July 6, 1909

Dear Dr. Willingham,

I am glad to report that my two city schools have prospered during the last quarter. They closed last week for the summer vacation. The girls' day school is a joy to my heart. The girls are eager to learn & constant in attendance. There have been enrolled nineteen girls, but the average attendance is fifteen.

There is a country day school for boys that is also under my charge. It is taught by a good man who is a good teacher after the old order. The city schools have up-to-date teachers, & are conducted, as far as possible, on Western lines.

In the Memorial School there are young men, as well as boys. One teacher is employed for his whole time, & one for half his time. One teacher is a graduate of the Hwanghsien Academy; the other attended the Weihsien College & was within a few months of taking his degree, when his health failed.

For some years, the weak point in our Tengchow work has been the lack of a man to do higher educational work. We ought to have an Academy, which would be open to boarders. Our force is so extremely small that no man can be spared to do this necessary work. Mr. King has had the pastorate, & has done most faithful country work. He loves the country work & shrinks from no hardship in its prosecution. He would delight to give his time solely to that work. No man has time, or strength to do properly both the work of a pastor & of an evangelist. We hoped that Mr. Adams would eventually relieve Mr. King of the pastorate & allow him to follow his inclination to devote himself to country work. Mr. King's breakdown, however, leaves the station again without a responsible man. By the rule of the Board & of the Mission, no man must assume responsibility under two years, but must give himself to study of the Chinese language. Miss Taylor & I have insisted that Mr. Adams shall not allow himself to be drawn into responsibilities for which he is not ready, & which would break him down prematurely. He has consented, & the Chinese brethren will be notified to that effect. Miss Taylor & I will do our best. She is invaluable as a leader of Christian women. I regret exceedingly that the educational work has interfered with my evangelistic work, but there was no help for it. The station asked me to take charge of the educational work (except the Girls' Boarding School & one country school). There was no option, as we must hold the young. Still, there ought to be a man sent out as soon as possible to do educational work for the station.

Miss Taylor bids me say that she is well & happy.

I took it for granted that you would send the second quarter's annuity as the first, to my nephew, Mr. W. L. Andrews, in Roanoke, Va.

Please let the sum due in August go toward the debt of F.M. Board. Kindly acknowledge it not as from China, but under the Virginia contributions, under the word "Albemarle."

With very cordial good wishes,

L. Moon.

Tengchowfu, Shantung,
China
Oct. 16, 1909
Dear Dr. Willingham,

Mrs. King has shown me a letter from you in which you tell her of a resolution of the F. M. Board advising her to sever her connection with the Board on her return to the U.S.

I venture to offer some reasons for thinking such a course undesirable.

Mrs. King speaks Chinese very well indeed. This fact makes her a valuable asset in our work. A woman who knows the language & understands the people is on a vantage ground which it would take a new-comer many years to attain. The latter's blunders are not all in language. Would that they were! Sometimes in sheer ignorance, sometimes in careless contempt of the manners & customs of the people, new comers do incalculable harm. Mrs. King knows Chinese manners & modes of thought & she will never offend them by ruthless disregard of customs that are not wrong, but only different from ours.

Mrs. King is loved by our native sisters. In the short time she has been here, she has won their hearts. They could not understand why she should not return after a rest at home, which they must know that she needs after so many years in China.

Mrs. King has very winning ways with the Chinese. I remarked on this to Miss Taylor & her reply was "Mrs. King gives *herself* to the Chinese." Now, it is comparatively easy to give one's self to mission work, but it is not easy to give one's self to an alien people. Yet the latter is much better & truer work than the former. It includes the former & goes beyond it. It is the difference between the letter & the spirit.

Mrs. King is now doing a valuable & much needed work. To take her away from it would be to set it back. She is filling a gap which has long existed in our woman's work. She is out daily in the homes of the people. Tengchow is open as never before to woman's work. There are those who long to be taught in their homes. There are more invitations to visit than we can accept & follow up, as should be done. My time is necessarily much absorbed by my day-schools. Miss Taylor has charge of the Girls' Boarding School. It is time that we have three good Bible women. These women are cheered & helped in their work, if a missionary sister can go with them occasionally. Mrs. King is now the only member of the station who can give her whole time to city visiting.

The Wise Man said (Prov. XI, 24, "There is that scattereth, & increaseth yet more.") I am aware that it looks unwise to retain a woman on the field who has four young children. There is the added expense & there is the mistaken idea that the children must necessarily hamper the mother in mission work. In Mrs. King's case I fearlessly aver that the children are no hindrance. The older ones are in school at Hwanghien. The two little ones, so far from being a hindrance, are rather a help. The Chinese love children, & their presence in a mission home makes a bond of sympathy between their mother & the native women. Besides, the children have the care of a truly Chinese woman & do not in the least hinder their mother from going out.

I earnestly hope that the F. M. Board will reconsider their advice to Mrs. King &, instead of suggesting her resignation, will rather encourage her to go on in her good work. To my mind, it is putting on the scales a question of expense, on the one hand, & on the other efficiency, consecration, knowledge of the language, favor with the people & the sore need of a good worker here. I cannot but hope that these considerations will have weight.

With cordial regards,

L. Moon.

A Letter From Tengchow, China

One day last week Mrs. Turner and I, accompanied by a Chinese woman, went to visit a family. We were cordially received and after the usual chitchat, began to teach the girls and women who were willing to learn. We taught them hymns. Mrs. Turner had been learning "Jesus Loves Me," and, with a most commendable perseverance, she set herself to teach the chorus to the girls. They were so eager to learn that I suggested their coming to school. They wished very much to come, but there were apparent obstacles and I had no hope that they would be overcome. On the following day, soon after breakfast, two girls made their appearance, bringing the small hymnbooks given them the day before. They were eager to learn. They next day, Sunday, they were early at my home and brought the good news that they were to attend school. They sat at church with the day school girls and again took seats with them at Sunday school. On Monday morning they came, nicely dressed, to enter school. This runs the number in the day school up to eighteen. There was a time when such a day school of boys would have been considered a fine success. But girls! Who would have imagined such a thing in Tengchow, even three years ago? As our learned, colored brother, Jasper, remarked of the sun, so we may now say of Tengchow, "It do move."

On Thursday, after examining the girls, as usual, I was coming home and fell in with some nice looking school boys. We entered into conversation and I inquired if they studied Arithmetic. "No," they said, and I inquired about Geography, receiving also a negative reply. I told them that the girls studied both these subjects and added that they also studied the "National Readers." So it turns out that the mission school for girls is ahead of the native schools for boys. I don't mean that it is ahead of the government schools, but of private schools.

L. MOON.

Tengchow, China, Nov. 20, '09

Tengchowfu, Shantung,
China,
Jan. 29, 1910
Rev. Dr. R. J. Willingham:—
My dear Brother,

Mrs. King sent me the resolution of the F. M. Board, with regard to her. I write to say that I am much gratified that the Board has deferred a final decision until they can see & talk with Mrs. King. She is doing a very valuable work here in house to house visitation. Not only this, but she is helping Mrs. Turner to gain a knowledge as to how to do this work, as well as introducing her in Chinese homes.

Should it be decided that Mrs. King shall return to China, she should by all means be assigned to Tai An Fu, in case that station is turned over to the Board. The Chinese there could not understand why she did not stay there after Mrs. Crawford's death. They do not understand the difficulties in the way, & they thought she ought to stay with Miss Walker. This was when she went to Tai An hoping to see Mrs. Crawford once more.

Miss Walker, in her last letter to Mrs. King, said that Mr. Blalock had reacht Tai An. She said that he seemed very sad after she & Mr. Dawes had told him what they had planned to do. She did not write that they have made application to the Board, but Mrs. King thinks that they have done so. We are much pleased that Mr. Wade Bostick sent in his application, & only regret that his sister could not see her way to join him. Mrs. Blalock remains for the present in Shanghai, as she is not strong enough to undertake the journey into the interior. One feels very sorry for her in this seemingly hopeless struggle. Here is a man, Mr. Blalock, having to hold work in two or three provinces. Dr. Broadus' words to you seem peculiarly appropriate here,—"predestined failure."

If Tai An is handed over to us, we need a strong force there as soon as possible. Two other missions are working there, the Anglicans & the Northern Methodists. Mrs. Crawford has always kept me fully conversant with the work in that region. The Anglicans were truly kind & courteous in all mission matters, never meddling in any way with Baptist work. Not so the Methodists. They did not scruple to send their native workers into Baptist places. In spite of all this, a fine work has built up & is prospering, & Mr. King hoped to turn it over to the Board. Tai An is decidedly a strategic point located at the foot of Tai San, one of the sacred mountains. Many thousands of pilgrims go there every year. They used to be reckoned at a hundred thousand annually, but have now fallen off.

Our new missionaries keep full of enthusiasm in the study of the language. They also mingle with the people, make friends & use what they know of Chinese. Tengchow is very much blessed in having so many promising young missionaries.

With most cordial good wishes for the work in your hands, as well as yourself,

Yours sincerely,

L. Moon.

Tengchowfu, Shantung,
China,
June 8, 1910
Dear Dr. Willingham,

Miss Walker writes as follows under date May 29:—"You will be glad to hear, I believe, that Mrs. Blalock has consented to request Dr. Willingham to allow me to stay on at T'ai An.

"I feel *most* happy over it for I've a good hope that the Board will consent to it, as they did in Mr. King's case."

Miss Walker mentions with pleasure the arrival in T'ai An of some of our native workers from Chefoo. She says that the native brother is to settle at Tsining, though she thinks that Meng Yin would be better. I have an impression that Tsining is in a low region, & therefore probably malarial. The Presbyterians have a magnificent work there. I think that a good deal of Mrs. Herring's work went into their hands even while she lived there. It was a boast of the Presbyterians, Mrs. Crawford, told me that the Herrings were working for them. The Presbyterians had inquirers last year Tsining running up, I think, nearly to two thousand. They are a fine set of people, these Northern Presbyterians, faithful & successful workers. My good friend, Dr. Hayes, advised our Mission to take up work at Tsining. The Mission referred the decision of our location in the west to Mr. Sears & Mr. Dawes, that is, they advised this. I wish we might have a very strong station at once, wherever it is decided that the station shall be. Undermanned stations make slow progress. We need two good schools in our Western work.

Miss Walker expresses the hope that matters shall be settled this summer, so that they may not be handicapped in their fall work. The Board is to be congratulated on getting so superior a worker as Miss Walker. She is worthy to be classed with Mrs. Crawford, than which there could be no higher praise for a missionary.

I do hope she will be allowed to stay at T'ai An for the good of the work. Mrs. Blalock has consumption &, I am told, does no work. She may fall ill & take Mr. Blalock away again for years. I have heard that Mrs. G. P. Bostick has cancer. So there seems no prospect of the G. M. being able to hold even one station.

With most cordial regards & good wishes,

Yours sincerely,

L. Moon.

Tengchowfu, Shantung,
China,
July 6, 1910
My dear Brother,

The quarter recently closed has been spent in school work, city visiting & trips to the country. I visited eighteen villages in May & June. Miss Lide & I have an engagement to go out together twice a week, once for a visit in the city & once to some village. She is planning to take over a region of country once worked by Mrs. Crawford, but, of late years, necessarily much neglected. We visited Buh Ko recently & Miss Lide was joyously welcomed as Mrs. Crawford's successor. She plans to open a day school for girls in Buh

Ko which is the second largest town in our county. In Chao Swei, which is the largest, Mr. Adams has recently secured a fine chapel, & the work there is very promising. Mrs. Adams tells me that schools are desired there. The difficulty is to secure good Christian teachers.

Mrs. Adams & I have an agreement to go out together once a week. She has taken over one of my day schools for boys, & is delighted with that work. She tells me that the school has run up to twenty-nine pupils.

I have in the city two day schools for girls, numbering about thirty-one though the enrollment has been a little larger. The Memorial School on North St. closed this morning for the summer vacation after a prosperous session. The enrollment has been thirty-eight. More & more the young men & boys come from the better families. The school seems to be growing in popular favor.

I have not been able to pay proper attention to the boys' day school at Ma Chia. The pressure of other work, with rain just when I planned twice to go, has prevented my visiting the school. The pupils number fourteen.

I trust that your health is good & that your work is prospering. With most cordial good wishes,

Yours sincerely,

L. Moon.

Tengchowfu, Shantung,
China,
Oct. 15, 1910
Rev. Dr. R. J. Willingham:—
My dear Brother,

The writing of my report for the quarter is overdue, but there are so many interruptions that it is difficult to find time, especially as my eyes do not permit me to write at night. Work continued as usual during the summer, except that the schools were closed for vacation. During that time, I could do more city visiting. When the schools are in session, I can give but three afternoons a week to city visiting.

I am glad to report that the city work was never so encouraging. We ought to have a woman here to devote all her time to that work. Mrs. King did this & her work was very successful. Two women would be none too many to devote their whole time to city visiting. Those whose hands are tied by school duties cannot give a great deal of time to city visiting, or to country trips. Miss Lide & Mrs. Adams go out with me once a week, each. The wife of

Pastor Kao asked to go with me also, as she does not know many people, & I find her a most valuable worker. Of course, I knew before what an earnest, faithful woman she is, but I was never before associated with her in personal work. She is, withal, a very lovely woman. Fifty years or so ago, she was in Mrs. Hartwell's school on North St. That school supplied four of our present women workers, all of whom are now grandmothers!

My schools are flourishing. The North St. Memorial School has enrolled fifty this year. The quality of the pupils has steadily increased. We now have pupils from very well-to-do families. Three such have lately come in & are a joy to my heart. They are well dressed, well behaved & very diligent in study. Two of them had studied French in Paotingfu. I have one student who studied German in Tsingtau. He also is a fine student, though not as well dressed, or polished in manner as the other three. The Head teacher is a very valuable man. His discipline is firm, yet the boys & young men like him. The teacher of the small boys is a very fine character. He goes to the seminary next year. I passed over one boys' day school to Mrs. Adams. She is very much in love with it, & the boys seem fond of her.

My two schools for girls are a joy to me. It is delightful to see the diligence in study, good deportment & constant attendance of these girls, nearly all of whom come from non-Christian families. There is a very remarkable movement in Tengchow now towards the education of girls & the unbinding or non-binding of their feet. Along with this, there is a kind of groping-in-the-dark among the women for something better than they have,—which something is Christianity. Two women, each past sixty, have confessed lately, one that she is secretly a Christian, & another, only yesterday, that she & her grandson learned hymns & prayers at night with closed window lest the neighbors should laugh at them. The grandson goes to school & teaches his grandmother orally from a book Mrs. King gave him. And so the leaven works. Did it not do thus in the early days in Rome? Were not many ladies there Christians, in the days of Jerome, long before the men had accepted Christianity?

What surprises me is that men unfriendly to Christianity will send their daughters to Christian schools knowing that six days in the week they will be taught Christianity & take part in Christian worship. The girls are expected to attend church & the majority come. As to one or two who have stayed away from church, I have thought it best not to make an issue. They study Christian books daily. Two of my girls come from a family once official & wealthy. They must have an escort to & from school daily, & are addressed as *Ku niang* (Miss). They are gentle, modest, well dressed & very eager, diligent students. One dear little girl, very quiet, sweet & gentle, has a grandfather with a high literary degree & a father who also has a degree, though not so high. So you see, our schools are growing in favor with the better class. One school is in my front yard. The girls study aloud according to Chinese custom. Their childish voices are musical to me because they tell of a new China, especially for girls & women.

And so, our "labor is not vain in the Lord." Thanks be to his Holy Name. The joy of the work grows day by day.

We have a fine Sunday School. Mr. Adams' excellent singing & Mrs. Adams' music draw many. We are singing for half an hour before Sunday School & it draws many. The Chinese are eager to learn to sing.

I trust that your work is greatly prospering.

With cordial regards,

Yours sincerely,

L. Moon.

Tengchowfu,

Shantung,

China,

July 1, 1911

Dear Dr. Willingham,

As you doubtless know, in the early part of this year, we had here the Plague. Churches & schools had to be closed, or not opened. However, the visitation passed & early in March our schools re-opened. For a month or more, it did not seem wise to carry on city visiting for fear of coming on some unsuspected case of plague. For some months now, all kinds of work have been resumed.

I am happy to report that my schools are flourishing, both as regards the number of schools & the attendance. I have a school for boys & young men which has enrolled about forty-six. The students as a rule attend with regularity & the spirit of the school is good.

I have five schools for girls & one for women. These are day schools. Three of the day schools for girls are on my home place & the attendance is very good indeed. The three schools number about fifty pupils & the attendance is excellent. Parents like to send here because they feel that their daughters are safer. The girls study finely, some of them enthusiastically.

Only one school out of the seven has not done well & that is not a mission school, but a private enterprise that costs the Board nothing. One country school for boys I handed over to Mr. Turner at the beginning of the year this year. I passed over a boys' day school to Mrs. Adams & it has prospered under her care!

I find time three days in the week to do city visiting. Thus far, I have not been able to do any country work. Vacation is now at hand & possibly I may get out to some of the nearer villages then.

With very cordial regards,

Yrs. sincerely,

L. Moon.

Tengchowfu,
Shantung,
China,
July 12, 1911

Dear Dr. Willingham,

I do not know whose business it is to send me the annuity money & therefore I write to you to inquire. I have not received any of it this year.

I write now to say that if none has been sent since last November, I wish to contribute what was due in February & in May to foreign missions. There is only one condition attached & that is that my name shall not appear as the giver. The amount now due is seventy-five dollars ($75^{00}).

I feel deeply for you & the Board in the embarrassing debt that hangs over the work. My earnest daily prayer is that it may soon be removed.

With most cordial good wishes,

Yours sincerely,

L. Moon.

Tengchowfu, Shantung
China
Dec. 9, 1911

Rev. Dr. R. J. Willingham:

Dear Brother,

I am sorry to have to plead guilty to the charge brought against some missionaries of forgetting to make quarterly reports of work done.

My schools re-opened in August after a vacation of over a month. Two teachers in the girls' day schools were in hospital at Hwanghien & I had to do the best I could without them. I am glad that one day-school has begun to transfer pupils to our girls' boarding school. I should be glad if that were true of all my day schools.

Since the revolution began, some pupils have dropped out of the "Memorial School" & also out of two of the girls' day schools. They are afraid to attend. However, some of the girls are beginning to come back & in the "Memorial School" some new pupils have recently come in.

I am running a day school on my own account in the West Suburb & I am glad to say that it has lately taken on new life. It has run up to fifteen pupils recently & the general unrest does not seem to affect the school. Our Sunday School was gratifyingly large last Sunday.

In the present unsettled state of the country, it would be unwise to try to work in the rural districts & besides time is always lacking. More & more, the schools absorb my time. I manage to do some city visiting, but not nearly all that should be done. Mrs. Turner has been very faithful in that work, having taken over from me the work of visiting in the West Suburb. Mr. Turner plans to begin a day school for boys in the West Suburb next year. The school is to be in the small building now used as a chapel. The idea is to use it for a schoolroom during the week & a chapel on Sundays.

We are hoping to be allowed to remain quietly in our homes this winter. "An exile from home" has a doubly hard time in the bitter winter weather.

With most cordial regards,
Yours sincerely,
L. Moon.

Tengchowfu,
Shantung,
China,
Dec. 23, 1911
Rev. Dr. J. R. Willingham:
Dear Brother,

I am sorry to trouble you again about the annuity money, but as it fails to come, I am compelled to ask you to see that it is sent. When this reaches you, not only will the sum for November be due, but shortly, that for February. Will you kindly see that both are sent me?

In times of famine & revolution, one sometimes feels the need of money more than usually.

We have been kept in perfect peace thus far. I feel deeply thankful to be allowed to stay at home & prosecute the work when so many others have felt compelled to leave their posts. In the West, a few have been murdered. They belonged to a Swedish mission. Some French travelers have also been murdered & a few foreigners have been injured. These were all deeds of the lawless element, robbers & such like, but both the Revolutionaries & the Manchus try to protect foreigners & generally succeed. The Imperialist soldiers are guilty of atrocious cruelties.

With apologies for troubling you.

Yours sincerely,

L. Moon.

Tengchowfu, Shantung,
China
March 30, 1912
Dear Brother,

Please accept my thanks for the picture of your young folks that you so kindly sent me. I should think you would be proud of them. I suppose the one you call "Harris" is named for Prof. Harris formerly of Richmond College & the Seminary. The one who "expects to preach" will certainly preach Foreign Missions, or better still, perhaps he will follow his brother's good example & preach to the heathen. Miss Elizabeth & Miss Carrie will doubtless each make some good man happy when the right time comes, but how lonely you will be without them!

It is time for my Quarterly report. I am happy to say that I was not compelled by the war to leave home. Therefore schools were opened as usual after the China New Year. The North St. School is not quite so large as it was last year. This, I am sure, is due to the present unrest. Those who have come seem to be a nice lot of boys. There are a number of new ones this year. The latest report of number was twenty-six, but I think more were expected. There are five schools for girls. The number enrolled has run up to about seventy, but I am sorry to say that the attendance is not all that could be desired. This also is perhaps partly due to general unrest. We still have soldiers on guard at our city gates & are under military government. Some people keep their street gates bolted & few women sit outside as in normal times. Tengchow has accepted the revolution because there was no other course open. At heart, the people have always been Imperialists. I mean the real people of Tengchow. Some here from a distance are ardent revolutionaries, but they or their fathers are from other places. It has been necessary to walk warily so as not to alienate the real people. With one's sympathies all on the side of the revolution. This is not easy always. Still, neutrality is a duty on the part of a foreigner.

Our Sunday School is large & is growing continually.

I am doing some city visiting & as soon as the weather gets warmer, I plan to do a good deal of country work. My hands are now untied from teaching & I can go to the country.

With most cordial good wishes,

L. Moon.

Tengchowfu,
Shantung,
China,
July 1, 1912
My dear Brother,

My report for this quarter falls under three heads. I have had the superintendence of six schools. The numbers enrolled are large, but the attendance is not satisfactory. Girls will go off to visit their grandmothers right in the midst of the session. In one school, a good many have been sick, one with smallpox. Besides, in times of unrest, it does not seem wise to try to draw the reins too tight. Some girls always come; some, but seldom. Even with these drawbacks, the schools are a source of endless delight. The best of it is that the girls so often bring me new pupils, children I never saw or heard of until they are thus brought in.

I have steadily kept up city visiting trying to go four afternoons in the week. The reception is most cordial as a rule & some are very eager to learn.

I have made four trips to the country. In one large village, they told me that no one goes to the temple any longer. They do not believe in idols. The temple seems dropping to pieces. There is a small roadside shrine that seems to be kept in repair. I taught girls by day & boys at night. In a small village about ten miles away, girls & women learned most eagerly. I only went out for the day & they urged me to come & spend several days. This part of the field is wide open for the gospel.

With best wishes & most cordial regards,

L. Moon.

Tengchowfu,
Shantung,
China,
July 24, 1912
Rev. Dr. R. J. Willingham:
Dear Brother,

At a Station meeting on yesterday, the following resolution was passed unanimously:-

"Resolved: That we write the Board asking for the Misses Lide to be sent to Tengchow in case of their appointment."

At the Mission Meeting held in Chefoo in the early part of this year, the Mission asked for two single ladies for Tengchow. (See Minutes of the Meeting, page 23.)

We venture to suggest that in answer to this request of the Mission, the Misses Lide be sent us, in case of their appointment. The reasons for this especial request are as follows:-

1) These young ladies have expressed their wish to devote themselves to evangelistic work in the country. This is now the crying need of the Tengchow station. There is absolutely no one now in the station who can devote herself wholly to the work. Yet the country has always been our most productive field. The large majority of our church members have been from the country. It is true that we now have a Christian community in the city, but with few exceptions they came originally from the country. There have recently been ten baptisms. Of these, one was a woman from the country. Nine men were baptized last Sunday in C'hao Swei, the largest town in our county. These men came mostly from C'hao Swei, but one was from a neighboring town & another from a village not far distant.

Mrs. Adams has done faithful work in the country this spring & plans to do more in the coming autumn, but as the pastor's wife she has many duties in the city. Besides being the organist of our church & a teacher in the Sunday School, she has the superintendence of a boys' day school & is the natural leader of the women of our Tengchow church.

Mrs. Turner has taken up work in the West Suburb which largely fills her time. Besides, with little children to care for, she ought not to go to the country.

Miss Lide's duties as head of the Girls' Boarding School prevent her doing outside evangelistic work. She is not only the responsible head of the school, but she teaches several hours a day, besides being the matron of the school. In addition to all this, she has a large Sunday School class of outsiders. It ran up above eighty-one Sunday & is always very large.

My own work, schools & city visiting, usually holds me in the city though I have done a little country work this spring & hope to do some in the autumn.

I have gone into these details to show our destitution of workers for the country.

2) The country is open for work as never before. We should have two women who could habitually spend weeks at a time in the country. The work for the women should keep pace with that for the men. We should have women to give their whole time to evangelistic work & the building up of girls' schools in the country. They should not be tied down in the city, but should be free to spend the Sundays with the country people who so much need their help & guidance. It is almost impossible for one immersed in city work to tear herself away for even one Sunday from the clamorous calls upon her.

In the old days when the city was fast closed against us, Mrs. Crawford would spend a month at a time in one large town. It was the settled custom of all the women in the Tengchow station to give from two to three months of each spring & fall to country work. We would go out regularly on Tuesdays & return on Saturdays. Sometimes, of course, on distant tours, as to Shangtswang & elsewhere, we would be away a much longer time. Of late years, the city has become wide open for visiting, the school work has made ever increasing demands, & the country work has suffered in consequence.

Mr. Adams has been incessant in labors in the country. The baptisms last Sunday show how the Lord has blessed his work. He hopes to organize a church soon in the town where the baptisms took place. Who is to teach the women there? Mrs. Adams longs to go & plans to go, but one woman is not enough for such work. I suppose that C'hao Swei has not less than five thousand inhabitants. What can one woman, with exacting duties already as pastor's wife in a city church, do to meet this need?

In my own recent country work I have experienced the perplexities incidental to working alone. The Chinese girls who used to be extremely timid & shrinking are now wide-awake & alert. They are eager to be taught. The women listen gladly to oral teaching. The teaching best adapted to the two classes is very different. One or the other has to be neglected. In my recent experience in a town, during two visits, I gave the days mostly to the girls, allowing school boys to come in the evenings. I returned to that town on a third visit with the express purpose of devoting myself to visiting the women in their homes. What was the result? The girls came to my own lodging so persistently that I could not get away for the intended visits, and when the women came to me, I could give them but a divided attention. "These things ought not to be."

Two women should come out to work together. In Wu Shi Li Pei, the town above mentioned, with the exception of about ten families, the people have abandoned idolatry. They are at the parting of the ways. Who is to guide them in these days of doubt & hesitation? They have broken with the old & have not accepted the new. If there were no other work to be done, two women for these two towns, C'hao Swei & Wu Shi Li Pei, would be a good missionary investment. These towns are only three or four miles apart. Hundreds of villages are close to them, many within easy walking distance. The seed faithfully sown in past years ought to bring forth an abundant harvest. "The laborers are few."

On the West, we have work in the second largest town of our county. It was here that Mrs. Crawford labored so faithfully through long years. The Buh Ko church was largely the fruit of her labors. Mr. Turner has charge of that large field extending west until it meets the Hwanghien work & south almost indefinitely. Mr. Turner has been most cordially received in this field & he said that men eagerly purchased the Gospels declaring that they must make themselves acquainted with their contents now that a new era had come. What missionary woman is here to work this field? Not one.

We therefore for reasons already given very earnestly urge the Board to send us two women as soon as possible. In addition to the reason (No. 1) given for asking that the Misses Lide be sent to Tengchow in case of their appointment, there is a personal reason. In coming here, they would be coming to a second home. Miss Janie Lide's experience would help them over many a difficulty, while their work in the country would help to build up her school.

In accordance with the wish of the Station, I transmit the Resolution with the accompanying reasons, asking that this letter be read to the F. M. Board.

With cordial regards,
Yours sincerely,
L. Moon.

Tengchowfu,
 Shantung,
China,
Aug. 27, 1912
Rev. Dr. R. J. Willingham
Dear Brother,
 I have had it in mind for some time to write the F. M. Board on a subject which seems to me very important. At the meeting in Chefoo, February 26—March 2, the Mission made two requests for educational missionaries, in one asking the appointment of "one layman for school at Pingtu" & in the other suggesting "the foreign teaching force to be drawn from the laity as far as possible."
 I need not say that I am heartily in favor of cultured laymen being sent out to do this important work. There is, however, a fact with which the Board should be made acquainted. I have seen in print, & from trustworthy authority, I believe, a statement that many young men who come out to China to teach habitually indulge in the use of cigarettes. The objections to this are very serious. Dr. Wu Ting Fang, who is well known in the U.S., is the head of an "Anti-Cigarette Society." The Chinese in forming such a society show their conviction that the use of the cigarette is injurious and should be abandoned. For a Christian teacher, sent out by a Mission Board, to do habitually what well informed Chinese like Dr. Wu consider wrong, is, to say the least, not wise. The influence of a teacher in China far exceeds that of a pastor. There is simply no comparison between the two. What the teacher says is law to his pupils; what he does, is right in their eyes. I saw this fully illustrated here in Tengchow years ago in the Presbyterian Mission. Dr. Mateer was head of the Academy which grew into the College. No missionary wielded a stronger influence. The foreign pastor was quite secondary in comparison. To show the immense influence of Dr. Mateer, I will mention what he once told me. Their Shantung Presbytery grew very restive under what they considered foreign predominance, and there was a decided movement to draw off and form a wholly native Presbytery. Dr. Mateer told me that only his influence with his former pupils saved them from a disastrous split. I have no doubt that he spoke the truth. The first objection then to cigarette smoking on the part of a teacher is that it sets a bad example to the boys & young men of the school.
 The second objection is an economic one. Only a year or so ago, the Maritime Customs, I think it was under the heading of Imports, reported "Cigarettes, Taels Ten Million (Tls. 10,000,000)" in Manchuria alone. Think

of what China proper must pay on the same account. I seriously doubt if Thirty Million Taels could cover the bill. We know that China with its ever recurring famines is guilty of mad folly in thus wasting her resources. Is it right to encourage her young men is such folly? Should not a teacher of Political Economy, for instance, rather show the waste of national wealth in such habits of self-indulgence?

The third objection to sending out men who use cigarettes is the effect upon themselves. I once had a dearly beloved missionary friend who used cigars. From these, I have been told, he went on to cocaine. There comes in the awful danger.

I have written this letter from a profound sense of duty. It seems to me that before appointing young men for educational work, the Board should obtain positive evidence that the applicant does not use cigarettes. I would not say, "does not use tobacco," for Dr. Crawford used the mild Chinese tobacco, smoked in a pipe, & I could not affirm that it did him harm, or that it hurt his influence for good. The use of the cigarette is quite another matter.

Please bring this subject to the attention of the F. M. Board.

With cordial regards,

Yours sincerely,

L. Moon.

Excerptsof Moon's Letters
1894-1912

The second bi-monthly season for the administration of the Lord's Supper in the church here has just passed. We have been gratified by the attendance, & we are thankful for four additions to the church. Two of these came from *Buh ko*, & Dr. Hartwell paid a deserved tribute, in a talk to the church, to the zeal & devotion with which Mrs. Crawford had labored & prayed in that village during past years. "Her works do follow her." Miss Barton has taken up the work in the country from which Mrs. Crawford withdrew to go westward & is prosecuting it with a self-sacrificing devotion which is beyond all praise. She makes *Buh ko* a centre of work, & has faithful & efficient helpers in the Christians there.

Mr. Sears is expecting to baptize a number in connection with the work at Säling, in P'ingtu. I heard a man from P'ingtu say that there are about forty inquirers in that region. We are confident & hopeful but we feel deeply the need of more workers. I am simply appalled when I look at the hundreds of villages in my own field, east & south east of the city. It is not possible to reach them. When will the churches awake to their duty & send the men & women that ought to be here?

Moon to Willingham

May 7, 1894

I expect to begin country work in about two weeks. That has always heretofore been more hopeful than the city work. We long to see both prosper. We desire to see our church crowded with city people and country churches springing up all over the land. For this we labor and pray and wait.

Moon to Willingham

Published in the July 1894 *Foreign Mission Journal*

Your kind letter & also the circular with regard to salaries reached me while in Pingtu. For reasons given in my former letter, I am unwilling to place my salary below five hundred dollars. I may also mention; in addition, that the value of the tael in cash has steadly diminished. The average for the quarter, when I was at Pingtu, was 1393 cash. A good many years ago, I sold at over seventeen hundred cash per tael. For a long time, it was about sixteen hundred cash; then, it fell to fifteen hundred or so; now, if we get over fourteen hundred, we do well. I sold yesterday at 1410. Shanghai Taels 50 brought me cash 67299 here in Tungchow. The Shanghai tael weigh less than the Tungchow tael & the value in cash is dependent on weight. In former years, I often rec'd over 80,000 cash here for the Tls. 50 Shanghai. Thus you see that it is incorrect to say that in Shantung the purchasing power of the tael remains the same. Here the loss, in fifty taels, of over twelve thousand cash. Purchases are made usually not in taels, but in copper cash. We buy cash at a largely reduced value in the purchasing power of the silver tael. In addition, everything foreign has gone up in price. When I landed in Chefoo, I bought kerosene at (Mex.), $4.50 per case. Next time I ordered a case, the bill came for five dollars. A box of cuticura ointment for which I use to pay fifty cents in Virginia, comes to me with a bill calling $1.75 (Mex.), besides which I must pay for getting it from Shanghai. All of our coal, we pay for in

Chefoo & then pay freight to Tungchow. So, of all stores purchased in Chefoo. Coffee & butter have advanced in price. One house in Chefoo declines to publish prices owing to fluctuations in exchange. It may be safely said that prices continue to advance. Years ago, on comparing Chefoo prices for canned articles, I noticed they were about doubled, fifty cents in Chefoo for what could be procured in Shanghai for twenty-five. I don't know how Shanghai & Chefoo prices compare now.

Moon to Willingham
July 5, 1894

Though China is at war, we have been kept here in "perfect peace." I have a proclamation posted up at my street door, which was sent me by an official. One day, as I was passing out of one of the city gates, some soldiers cried out, "Beat the foreign devil." I took no notice, as I dislike to get into trouble with them. On my return that same day from the country, a child cried out, emboldened by the impunity of the soldiers, "Beat the foreign devil." I know that I ought not to put up with that, not only for my own sake, but also for the sake of my fellow missionaries. I therefore had my sedan chair sat down and went in pursuit of the child. I saw him fly from a certain door, which turned out to be an inn. I entered & called for his mother. It takes no time, in China, to collect a crowd. I was soon surrounded, & a number of soldiers were in the group. The child's mother was full of apologies. I stated that, in the morning, soldiers had called out "Beat the foreign devil," but that I had taken no notice, that I was unwilling to report them to the officials lest they should be very severely punished & that I had a proclamation at my street gate ensuring me protection. The crowd listened in silence & that is the only time I have had to assert my rights with the soldiers. They occasionally speak of me as "foreign devil" as I pass about, but one gets used to that & it's no use resenting it. Missionaries all over China have been notified by the Foreign Office to go on with their work as usual, that the Government would protect them. Surely it is God's hand, stretched out to shield His servants when a non-Christian government notifies Christian missionaries that they will be protected & requests them to go on with their work.

Moon to Willingham
October 29, 1894

"The close of the quarter reminds me that I should send you a report of work. I have been somewhat hindered by the unusually heavy rains, and also lately, by throat trouble and so have not accomplished all I hoped. I have, however, visited sixty-nine towns and villages. I am glad to report a very kindly reception on the part of the people, and a gratifying readiness to hear the Gospel. I distributed a good many books during these country trips and many are eager to obtain them. The primary purpose in visiting these towns and villages is to reach the women and children, but I have constant opportunities to talk with men and present them the truth of Christianity. I rarely fail to meet a respectful hearing. Besides visiting the villages and towns, I have continued to go to Chinese homes in the city, as I have had time."

Brethren and Sisters, what would she have done if the rain and poor throat had not hindered?

(Ed.)

Moon to Willingham

Published in the December 1895 *Foreign Mission Journal*

I sometimes think, "We faint, we die," here for lack or workers. Yet, if this long-continued trial shall bring us to closer dependence on God, it will not be in vain. I know it is not the fault of either the Secretary or the F. M. Board that we are left so long without reinforcement.

Moon to Willingham

October 15, 1896

Last year was, in some respects, one of the hardest in our history. The school trials are now over-past. The worst of them was their influence over the church members. While the latter were engaged in a struggle to get an unworthy person out of the school, religious interests languished. Now, after two exclusions from the church, we have peace & a return of prosperity. It seems to me that our prospects are brighter than for some years. We have been obliged to keep these matters from Dr. Hartwell, as, in his weak state of health he could not have borne them. This letter, therefore, is intended only for the Secretary & not for the public. I am sure you will be glad to know that our troubles are ended. After her exclusion from the church, the mission dismissed from the school the person whose mis-conduct had wrought such widespread mischief. As the charges on which she was excluded from the church could not have been proved in a law-court, we continued her salary up to the end of the China year, for fear of injustice. Her successor is paid 5000 cash a month instead of 15000. Miss Hartwell has charge of the school & is conducting it beautifully. There is much religious interest in the school. Our missionary society (Woman's) has money in hand for a Bible woman this year, if we decide to employ her by the year. Heretofore, we have employed her only for a set time, less than a year, & may continue this plan.

  Moon to Willingham
  January 18, 1898

If I might be allowed to express a preference, I should say that in general it would be advisable not to send out unmarried women under thirty years of age. They are then still young enough to learn the language and they ought to have gained a useful practical experience. Here in my home is room for three more women & thus no extra expense would be required in providing them with houses. Northern and Southern Baptists don't seem to realize the need of strongly manned stations. English Baptists and Presbyterians do. Look at the results. Their converts run up into the thousands in Shantung, which we who were the first to enter the province, have but about four hundred. Having sown sparingly, we reap sparingly. The fault is not the Board's & most certainly not the Secretary's, but lies also in the selfishness & stinginess of the churches. There is no reason why we should not have as large success as the others, except lack of workers. The Northern Presbyterians have about as many in Shantung as Southern Baptists have in all China. They have here in Tungchow about the number that we have in all Shantung.

  Moon to Willingham
  June 19, 1889
  Lottie Moon Collection, SBTS, Folder No. 8

As a rule, the work is increasingly encouraging. In general, I am received very kindly. The attitude of listeners seems changed in many places. In the old days it was impossible to keep people quiet long enough to get any good. Now there is great change for the better. They sometimes listen in almost absolute silence. School boys especially show a real desire to hear. I hope you will understand that the work is still in the stage of "seed-sowing." I hope a great harvest is being prepared, but it is not ripe yet. When it is, where are the reapers?

  Moon to Willingham
  September 30, 1899

Thank you for your readiness to offer help for entertainment of Chinese guests. It is possible that the plan of holding classes may be the solution of the difficulty. Instead of writing women to come as suits their convenience & remain at my expense. I shall set times for those to come who wish to study. It is really largely a distinction without a difference. Nearly all who come to visit give part of the time to study. The Laichow people might be embarrassed by my having help in entertaining. I am hoping to do more country work next year than I have done this year. That usually means a considerable increase in the number of visitors. Still I shall try to let none come except those who have a purpose & restrict them to times of holding classes. This does not mean, of course, that now & then I shall not entertain personal Chinese friends at my own expense.

As winter deepens, the poverty and want around us grows more acute. One admires the uncomplaining spirit in which the people meet these trials. They fall heavy on the respectable poor, who are half the time (I may say now, all the times,) on the verge of starvation. When the war is over, things will brighten.

Moon to Willingham
December 14, 1904

I hear that in P'ingtu, in order to erect the quarters absolutely necessary for the boys' boarding school, money has been borrowed, & that, to pay this debt & complete the buildings, fifteen hundred dollars are needed. The work in P'ingtu is growing with wonderful rapidity. The Normal School is to be established there & thus P'ingtu will become the feeder for our whole North China work. Since Mr. Owen took charge of the educational work there, the advancement in that department has been rapid. The grade of scholarship has been elevated & the tone of the school has been uplifted. Not only has the school been over-crowded—& many turned away,—but fine work has been elicited from the students. Their singing—quartetle singing—is said to be inspiring.

I have been in China over thirty years & in all that time I have seen the work hampered by narrow quarters, by lack of requisite facilities. It is only recently that the girls' boarding school here has had adequate quarters; only now, that at Hwanghien they have suitable buildings for the boys' boarding school. The boys crowding to P'ingtu are probably twice as many as go to Hwanghien. I most earnestly beg that the F. M. Board will provide the facilities needed for the boy's boarding school in P'ingtu. Not long ago, a fine young man, a teacher, came to see me. I had sent for him because I wished to engage a teacher for a school in the country. This young man felt that, instead of teaching, he ought to go to P'ingtu to study two years. His two younger brothers are already in the P'ingtu school. A new spirit is abroad in China. Young men want the Western sciences. Government schools give these & English, without Christianity. Ought we not to build up strong Christian schools & colleges for our Baptist Chinese? Japanese agnostics and Chinese Confucianists give tone[?] largely to government schools. The only hope I see is for us to build up strong denominational schools to leaven the educational world of China.

Moon to Willingham
January 9, 1906

My work goes on as usual. The school numbers thirty-six names, & but the attendance of some pupils is irregular. Some are always present. The discipline is satisfactory & the children do well in their studies. In the advanced department, there are seventeen boys. About a dozen learn Arithmetic & Geography. All learn the New Testament, or some Christian book. The same is true of the primary children of whom there are nineteen enrolled. Two children dropt out of school to attend a Government school just opened this year, and one young man left to go to work. I consider the school to be in a good condition, in the main. One boy was expelled by the new teacher. Probably both were to blame, so I got the boy admitted to the Anglo-Chinese school. But for these losses, the school would number forty, which is not bad when we consider the competition of government schools. These offer inducements in cash & promises of employment to successful students, in the civil service. Unfortunately, there is no religious freedom in government schools. I regret the fact that some church members send their children to these schools. It is deeply to be regretted as the children are compelled to worship Confucius.

Moon to Willingham
May 7, 1906. Published in the August 1906 *Foreign Mission Journal*

Our church has been blessed this year in receiving twenty-two for baptism. The people seem very friendly. Yet, it is certain that a secret society exists in Têngchow which is both anti-foreign & anti-Christian. It may, or may not, rise & give trouble. At present, I do not think we are in danger.

Moon to Willingham

May 7, 1906. Published in the August 1906 *Foreign Mission Journal*

Dear Dr. Willingham:

I recd today a letter from Miss Lottie Moon in which she relates conditions in Tengchowfu and other sections of China, which are surely very distressing. I am sure of course that you are also posted as to conditions. Before when the Plague was on the Missionaries I believe I went to Japan. I was very much in hopes that Miss Lottie had refugeed in this case, but she says not. From her letter, I judge that the condition in her city and section must be appalling. My reason for writing you is due to the fact that Miss Lottie is an Aunt of Mrs. Cofer's and a very dear one; we of course realize the danger she is exposed to, even though she remains isolated as much as possible, and if she can get away, we are very desirous of having her return to America. She was here something over 8 years ago, and I believe it is nearly time for the usual furlough. In view of this and the conditions prevailing there, I thought if you would cable her granting a furlough at this time, that we might induce her to come on, provided she would be permitted to come. Kindly let me hear from you by return mail, as we wish to cable her also, and I trust that it can be so arranged that she can come on now if she will and if she can. She does not allude in any way to returning to America, but we would like to insist on it if she can come.

Awaiting your reply with interest.

Yours very sincerely,

J. H. Cofer to R. J. Willingham

March 8, 1911

THE LOTTIE MOON

CORRESPONDENCE

IV. FAMILY AND FRIENDS

"And a Christ-like spirit ev'rywhere be found ..."

LETTERS TO FAMILY AND FRIENDS

Lottie Moon's letters to her family and friends offer their readers intimate glimpses of this dedicated missionary's personal life. Among other things, they articulate Moon's genuine sense of adventure and her love of travel. They also express the tenderest feelings of a woman who cherished her closest relationships, especially those with her family.

While each letter addressed to her various family members and friends reveals interesting facets of Moon's personality, the letter dated March 24, 1911 is particularly poignant. This letter has come to be known as "The Hunger Letter" because it discusses a famine that was slowly destroying her province. Moon loved her neighbors and this vivid account of their plight demonstrates that her feelings for them transcended mere pity. Her empathy for the Chinese people proves that she no longer viewed them as "heathen Chinamen," but rather as her friends.

No date (June 21, 1870)
Dear Brother John.

The worst, no, the *best* has come. Mother went home to God today about two oclock. We bury her Saturday. She spoke of Sister often—said "my affection for Orianna is unchanged." She said "all of my children are dear & sweet to me."

She died peacefully & happily. For about three days there was no pain. The last moments were of course sad, but I think I can never fear death after seeing her triumph over it. I wish dear Sister could have seen her. We told her we would all meet her in the many mansions. How happy she is now with the husband & children gone before! She said to me on yesterday, "Lottie, my darling, don't cry for me. I want not a tear at my grave to be shed." Then added, "You must rejoice with me." I will write more fully soon. My precious sisters & brother bear it with Christian resignation. I do so sympathize with dear Sister. Tell her this with my love, Mother said, "Peace, live at peace among yourselves." She meant her children.

I am too exhausted to write more.

Yours,

Lottie

Lottie Moon Collection, SBTS, Folder No. 1, transcribed from a handwritten copy. The letter has a headline that reads, "Copy of letter from Miss Lottie Moon to her brother-in-law, Dr. John B. Andrews telling of her mother's death." As indicated, this copy reads "no date." The date, June 21, 1870, was added parenthetically.

Cartersville, Ga.,
July 10, 1871
Rev. Dr. J. B. Taylor:
Dear Sir,

My sister & I propose to write in the support of one of Mrs. Crawford's Chinese pupils. My sister, Miss Eddie Moon, has been in correspondence with Mrs. Crawford, & she has assigned to us Wun Kwé Fun. She says it will take $45.00 in gold yearly. Of this I propose to pay one third, & my sister promises to procure the rest. Would seventeen ($17.00) dollars in greenbacks cover $15.00 in gold? I propose to send you a postal order as soon as I hear from you.

Yours respectfully,
Lotte Moon

Address
Miss Lotte Moon
Cartersville,
Georgia.

On Board Steamer
"Costa Rica"
Sept. 30, 1873
My dear Sister -

We rose very early this morning to see one of the wonders of this lovely island sea through which we have been passing since night before last. It is raining continuously but we took umbrellas and stayed in the front of the steamer until the point of interest was passed. At this point the land comes so close together on either side that you can plainly distinguish the foliage crowning the hillslopes with the naked eye. It is said that but one steamer can pass at a time, so narrow is the strait. Navigation is very dangerous just there and we lay by four hours last night so as to avoid passing it in the dark. I utterly despair of giving you even a faint idea of the beauties of Japan. The islands rise up in bold bluff or sloping hills & these are covered with verdure almost to the water's edge. Junipers & pines seem to be the usual growth. Many of the hills are beautifully terraced. We had a very merry day at Yokohama. I went ashore with some Northern missionaries and was to join my own party at the hotel. The party with which I landed had a different destination. We went first to the Pacific office where the gentlemen were to procure tickets for berths on the Shanghai steamer. After transacting this and other business, we decided to take one of the Japanese conveyances instead of walking. I say one, but I mean one apiece. These conveyances are made like baby carriages only they are large enough to hold a grown person. They are drawn by natives & it is wonderful how fast they will carry you. They are cheap enough—ten cents an hour. On emerging from the office we were deafened by the clamour of the owners of these carriages. Heedless of all, my friend, Mr. A. pushed forward to the carriage he had selected for me & I followed in spite of the efforts made to induce me to take others. At last, I was fairly in the carriage, but it required some time & skill to extricate it from the crowd of vehicles around. At length, however, this was happily effected and I moved off in style followed by Mr. & Mrs. Holt in similar conveyances. Two men laid claim to the carriage into which he stepped and of course there was a difficulty which Mr. A. succeeded in stopping only with vigorous application of his umbrella to one of the contestants. This threw him behind & I saw him no more that day until we met on board the steamer about sunset & laughingly recounted our respective adventures. Meantime however, (we ?) moved in gallantly in a line, my carriage heading the procession. All at once we came to a halt & I saw little Mr. Holt standing in the street and making frantic efforts to give directions to our natives; but of course as neither knew the language of the other he failed to be understood. It was ludicrous to the last degree—"Yonder comes a *man*," exclaimed Mr. H. at last, laying such stress on the word that you might have thought men were scarce commodities in Japan. In fact it was a white face that drew forth the exclamation. The stranger very politely gave directions as requested & my friends went one way & I the other. I was immensely amused to think of the figure I cut-all alone in a baby carriage, drawn by a man who couldn't understand a word I should say.

It has been delightful to meet people in various places who knew Eddie. They seem to admire her so much.

Lottie Moon Collection, SBTS, Folder No. 2, transcribed from an incomplete, handwritten copy. The letter has a headline that reads, "Copy of letter from Miss Lottie Moon to her sister."

Tung Chow
Oct. 11, 1875
My dear Mr. Hartwell,

You are perhaps aware of the changes directed by the Board. Among other things, they proposed that Mr. Crawford should buy the property on North Street. This he was not willing to do. The natural inference from this proposition was that you do not propose to return very soon to Tung Chow. *Hoping to preserve* this valuable property for the Board, as well as for yourself whenever you do return, my sister and I decided to move into it. We have done so with the express understanding that *it is yours whenever you desire to occupy it again.* Should circumstances arise to prevent your return it might be desirable for us to purchase the property instead of building. It is certainly very convenient, in admirable preservation and well adapted for carrying on a girls' school. The ladies of GA & VA have nearly raised the amount necessary to build. If you do not return would you advise us to buy your place, or to build? I should be glad of your opinion on the subject. The native pastor continues to have the use of the chapel. *I am most happy to aid him or his members in any way in my power.*

I find here a good deal of medicine, some vinegar, porter & a few other things. If the medicine is your private property, I should like to purchase it. If it belongs to the Mission I suppose there will be no objection to my using it for the Chinese. I suppose the vinegar & porter is yours? There are also a Chinese table, two chairs & a few other things. If you desire I will make a list & send you & if you will kindly fix the price I will send an order on the Board for the Money.

We are in much anxiety & suspense on account of the threatened Anglo Chinese War. Rumors fly thick & fast. One week war seems imminent (?). The next we hear is China has conceded every demand; the following week comes a contradiction of this, and so we feel thoroughly unsettled.

Our community is as usual. My Sister & Sanchum are on a visit to Loong Shin. Mr. & Mrs. Crossitte await the issue of events before going to Lsi Nau Soo. Mr. and Mrs. Mateer are in Shanghai. We expect Mrs. Capp about November.

We had a visit of a week from Dr. Yates. He is looking remarkably well, and his voice is much better since that attack of(?) cholera.

Please give my love to Mrs. Hartwell. I should be sincerely glad to hear of her restoration to health.

With kindest regards, I remain

Yours truly

L. Moon.

Shanghai, Oct. 9, 1878

We sailed from San Francisco as we expected about noon, Sept. 1st. The sun was shining brightly and the waters of the bay sparkled brightly in its beams. The passengers gathered in the rear of the vessel and many looked mournfully at the land they were leaving. Some had friends on the wharf waving them farewell. Others saw in fancy, the dear ones to whom they had already said farewell, or cast their thoughts forward to the land which was to be their future home. The bay is large and very beautiful. It is said that all the navies of all the world could be gathered there & find room. The shores on either side are noted for their loveliness. As we were passing out and getting our last view of land, the gong sounded for lunch. Very prosaically & as it turned out, very unwisely for me I chose the lunch in preference to the beauties of nature. I felt rather queer about the head & made my escape from the table as soon as possible & in five minutes or less, I was the sickest mortal I ever saw—not to die. From that time forth I had no rest. Other people were sick a little, or much and got well, but during the whole twenty-five days I scarcely escaped sea-sickness more than a day or two. It was very mortifying and annoying. Other people could enjoy themselves—as for me I simply existed. (*A marginal note for the last three sentences of this paragraph reads: "Note—exaggeration of course." Ed.*)

Our dinner hour was six. The number of courses seemed endless. The steward would strike a bell for the dishes to be uncovered. No matter what you wanted you had to wait for it till the regular time came. Dinner was a perfect nuisance from my point of view, though there were some people who seemed to eat of every course and to drink wine in proportion.

We had various amusements on board. The gentlemen played quoits or practiced feats of gymnastics. For those who liked quieter games there were cards, chess, and anagrams. The surgeon of the vessel who is quite a literary character, treated us to a very interesting letter on Shylock, & interspersed it with the readings from the play in which the Jew (?) appears. One gentleman favored us with California stories, and another gave an account of a dangerous voyage he had made under a drunken captain.

Another night an Egyptian mummy was on exhibition and a lecture was delivered on the subject. The mummy had been bought for the enormous sum of 37 _ cents. By the processes of modern science he had been revived to some extent, and [?] could understand what was said to him, & could even respond by a wink. The lecturer proved this by asking various questions as to the mummy's past, inquiring if he had walked about the streets of Thebes three thousand years ago & c. A wink gave satisfactory evidence that the mummy understood and responded. The lecturer then proceeded to state that he hoped in time that the mummy would speak. He would now try to make him do so. He uplifted an enormous iron ring which so startled the mummy that he sprang up with a terrific shriek and in endeavoring to get away dragged off the tablecloth and revealed our young friend from Boston. Of course, that part was a failure because the design was for him to vanish under the table.

We had one little gale which scared some of the passengers. I was too sick to more than lift my head & there really was no danger. We were driven out of our course about a day and hence did not arrive in Yokohama until Sept. 25th. Land never appeared so beautiful to my eye. As it was late, we determined to remain on board the steamer that night, and devote the next day to seeing Yokohama. The following morning dawned rather unpropitiously with a drizzling rain which threatened to interfere seriously with the contemplated expedition. Nothing daunted, however, we resolved to persevere, & soon after breakfast we entered the boat which was to take us ashore. Eight of us were to disembark, & when on land were to divide into parties of five and three as our destinations were different. The boats could carry but four so I embarked with the party of three arranging to meet my own party at the Grand Hotel. We landed and the first objects demanding attention were the jin-rikshaw, a mode of conveyance peculiar to Japan. They are made like baby carriages, only they are large enough to hold grown people. They serve the same purpose as street cars in America and are cheaper. The usual price is ten cents an hour. The men who own and drive these carriages are miserable specimens of humanity. They are wretchedly clad, and doubtless their fare is of the poorest, but I noticed they seemed light hearted enough when standing in groups laughing and jesting while waiting a demand for their services. Declining their assistance, we walked on to the Pacific Office where the gentlemen wished to secure berths for the Steamer to Shanghai. In front of the office was gathered a number of carriages and the owners were chatting gaily & keeping a sharp look out for a job.

The friends with whom I had come ashore were going by invitation to pass the day with a resident missionary, while I was to join my own party at the hotel. As we emerged from the Pacific Office and it became known that we wanted carriages, a clamor arose that would have done credit to the hackmen of San Francisco. I don't know what act of desperation I should have committed had I been along, but with heroic fortitude my friend, Mr. A forced his way to the carriage he had selected for me & I stepped in and was born off. Mr. Atkinson himself was not so fortunate. Two men laid claims to the carriage in which he seated himself and he only ended the difficulty which arose by a vigorous application of his umbrella. This necessarily caused a delay & I saw no more of my good friend until we met on board the "Costa Rica" about sunset and we recounted to each other the adventures of the day. There were still three of us together & we met in a line, my carriage leading the way. Soon it became evident that our men did not know where we wanted to go, & as they were unacquainted with English & we with Japanese the case looked ridiculous enough. The first thing I knew we were at a stand still, & Mr. Holt had leaped from his carriage and was making frantic efforts to explain the way we wished to go. At last a welcome object hove in view. "Yonder is a *man*," Mr. Holt exclaimed as if the newcomer were the only being in Yokohama who could lay claim to that title. In fact it was a white face & this gave promise of relief from our perplexity. The stranger very politely responded to Mr. H's request for assistance, & directed the men respectively to No. 39 & to the Grand Hotel. Imagine one lone woman born rapidly through the streets of this foreign city in a baby carriage & convulsed with laughter at the novelty of the position & the ludicrousness of the morning's incidents, & you have a pretty good idea of the situation. The carriage halted in front of a large building which I took to be the Hotel though there was no sign to indicate the fact. Entering, I beheld Japanese servants enough, but could not make myself understood. I appealed to the first white man I saw, & soon found the friends of whom I was in search.

We then hired jin-rickshaws and spent about three hours viewing the city. We visited a number of native shops & made a few purchases. In a silk store, I saw very handsome dressing gowns for gentlemen, wadded and quilted, for eight dollars. If I had been only going to America instead of in the opposite direction I should have been tempted to make a large collection of rare and beautiful objects. Some of these were astonishingly cheap. These were in what they call the *curio* stores & consisted of lacquered ware, boxes inlaid with mother-of-pearl, faus, & c, & c. I priced a box, a perfect gem & it was only $1.25. The shape was hexagon. On opening it three smaller boxes appeared, diamond shaped, & just filling the larger box. The workmanship was exquisite. One of our party in Nagasaki, bought a large & beautiful workbox inlaid with mother-of-pearl for $2.50. Such a box would cost six or eight dollars in America.

We left Yokohama on Friday & reached Kobe sometime Saturday night. Here some friends who had traveled with us from San Francisco were to leave us. They had been sent out to strengthen the mission at that place. They introduced us to missionaries already settled there & they took us at once to their hearts and homes. We attended service in the morning at the Union Church. It was conducted by Mr. Burnside,(?) a clergyman of the Church of England—then visiting at Kobe. We heard the English service for the first time, & I am sure I responded heartily to the prayer for the Queen & Royal family. In the afternoon, we heard a sermon in Japanese but I will not tell of that as you will find it in the *Herald* provided I can get time to write.

We had a most delightful day ashore, & returned to our ship by moonlight. Next day we found Mrs. Burnside & family on board, returning to their home in Nagasaki. They were very cordial and sociable, & insisted that we should spend a day with them, an invitation we were well repaid for accepting. Mr. B took us all over the native city, showing us various temples, shrines, & other objects of interest. We had barely time to get on board after dinner. Various courses, conversation & c & c, lengthened that meal out nearly two hours. The English are quite ceremonious. They assign each person a seat, placing the gentlemen beside the hostess & the ladies on each side of the host. Yesterday, I attended a dinner where the hostess directed each gentleman what lady to take in to dinner.

We left Nagasaki with light hearts, confident of reaching Shanghai in 48 hours. Our own party had been increased (?) & enlivened by Mr. Helm who came up from China especially to meet us. He is very sociable & full of fun. Better than this his whole heart is in his work and he seems to delight in preaching the gospel. About ten oclock that night, Wednesday, Oct. 1st, the wind, which had been favorable before increased to a perfect gale. The vessel rocked from side to side, shifting the wares, every few minutes there was a crash in the dining-room of crockery & glass. In the cabins we were tossed about even when lying down. The next day matters grew darker. The hurricane deck was partly swept away & it was feared that the whole deck must go. In that case cabin passengers would have been compelled to go below. Our gentlemen, Mr. Painter, & Mr. Helm, stationed themselves in readiness to help us, & at night "camped out" as they called it, almost at our cabin doors. The rudder of the vessel was broken, and it seemed almost certain that we must go down. We were driven helplessly back in the course we had traversed at first.

You will want to know how we felt, this facing what seemed almost inevitable death. The Captain & officers did their duty nobly. Without any thought of themselves they bent every energy to the guidance of the shattered ship. The surgeon & one other buoyed themselves up with bottle after bottle. Our own party spoke & felt calmly of the coming end. If it was God's will, surely it was well. As I watched the mad waste of waters, howling as if eager to engulf us, I think I should scarcely have been surprised to see a Divine Form walking upon them, so sweetly I in my inmost soul the consoling words: "It is I: be not afraid."

Towards ten oclock the second night the storm began to abate. The Capt. decided to steer for some island not far off. Next day, however, he decided to return to Nagasaki, & so, Friday night, about nine, we steamed quietly into its beautiful harbor. We fired no gun to announce our approach, but our hearts were full of gratitude for this wonderful deliverance.

The gentlemen went ashore next morning but we ladies were too exhausted. In the evening, however we accepted an invitation to play croquet at the house of Mr. Street of the Dutch Reformed Church. On Sunday we heard Mr. Burnside again in his own beautiful church. It is small, but perfect in every respect, stained glass windows, comfortable seats, nice matting,(?) good organ, first rate choir, and five preachers. It was indeed sweet to be in the house of God, after having expected to be the prey of devouring waters.

We left that evening for Shanghai, had a smooth & pleasant trip & reached here Oct. 7th. Mr. & Mrs. Crawford, & Dr. & Mrs. Yates came on board to welcome me. I am delighted with them, & also found a letter of welcome inviting me to dinner for Thursday. One of the callers wanted Mr. & Mrs. Crawford & myself for dinner Wednesday so you see there is no lack of hospitality in China.

I know you will be delighted to hear the high esteem Eddie has established. People speak of her in terms of enthusiastic praise. She has been in charge of three schools, her own, Mrs. Crawford's & Mrs. Holmes. Mrs. Holmes was on a tour in the country, but has probably returned ere this. Eddie is likewise superintending the building of additional rooms to Mrs. Crawford's house, & has under her eight carpenters and masons. So you see the dear child is a woman of business. Mrs. Yates says the gentlemen here, married & single were up in arms, very indignant that a "pretty young thing" should be hired at Tengchow. They abused the Crawfords for it, & said if Eddie must be a missionary let her be stationed here where she could see something, that she would die or go crazy at Tung Chow. Mrs. Crawford said she has shown wonderful good sense in her power of adapting herself to circumstances, & that she hears [?] off the palm for quickness in acquiring the language. She said that E. speaks it with remarkable ease & fluency & very much like the Chinese.

It is almost impossible to snatch time for letter-writing, there are so many engagements to be met. I therefore send a joint letter & beg *some one* from each place to answer at once.

I am invited with the Crawfords to dine with a bachelor who has a wide-spread reputation as a first rate house keeper. We called there yesterday to see some friends who came over with us from San Francisco. The house was in beautiful order, well furnished & c. Public gossip has it that Miss E. Moon was invited to preside there permanently but declined the honor. Of course, I give the report for what it is worth. E. has never mentioned it in her letters. So you see we have gossip here as well as in America.

With very much love to all,

L. Moon.

Lottie Moon Collection, SBTS, Folder No. 2, transcribed from a handwritten copy. This letter has a headline that reads, "Copy of letter from Miss L. Moon to various relatives."

Tungchow, China.
April 29, 1881
My dear Sister—

I have really forgotten when I wrote to you last, & I have not had a letter from you since I left America. But I know your duties are manifold, & it is almost impossible for you to find time to write. I had a letter from Jimmie about a year & a half ago, I should think. He said you all were going to Texas & you would start in a very short time. So I thought it useless to answer his letter until I should hear again & get your P. O. address.

About myself there is nothing especial to tell. I *plod along in the old way.* I have a small boarding school of some 15 girls, more or less. Like all other schools, I suppose, there are things pleasant & things disagreeable. I take most pleasure in the little ones of the school, the youngest of whom is about five years old. She is a very merry happy little creature, fat and rosy, & laughs & sings nearly all day long. I think she is rather proud of having a book & going to school. Of course, I do not allow her to be confined. Your boys would be vastly amazed to see her take a pointer, & try to point out the provinces on the map of China. It often sets me to laughing to see her. Of course she learns only a very little bit of Geography in this way, but still she learns something. Her father is a hopeless invalid and her mother works out. I was askt to take the child and consented not knowing what a little thing she was. She was a poor injured looking creature in very poor health. But good fun (?) and kind treatment have worked wonders. It is astonishing how she can sing. I am quite surprised sometimes to hear her singing hymn after hymn she has picked up, hearing the other girls sing.

I have not gone to the country very much this spring for various reasons. *It is a very hard life, & wears upon one's health. I have now quite a dread to go out on a country tour. The dirt and discomfort & fatigue are very trying on one's nerves.*

We had a mild winter, but it has been followed by a cold and disagreeable spring. Every thing is very backward. I grow [?] flowers which are the only things I try to cultivate. I have no garden, & depend upon the Chinese market & the kindness of my friends for vegetables. I would rather, of course, have a garden, tho' I get on very well without. I had a visit of several weeks (?) last summer from my friend Miss Safford of whom you have often heard me speak. I hoped she would come again this summer, but from what she has written me lately, I fear she cannot come.

Mrs. Holmes has come in & wants *me to go with her to the sea. The walk is a pleasant one, & I wish your boys could take it with me. My girls have had holiday today, & took a lunch with them to the sea-side. I think I'll go out & see what has become of them.*

Love to all,
Very affty,
L. Moon.

Lottie Moon Collection, SBTS, Folder No. 4, transcribed from an incomplete, handwritten copy. This letter has a heading which reads, "Letter from Miss Lotte Moon to her sister, Mrs. Andrews."

Tungchow,
Dec. 8, 1884
My dear Mrs. Holmes,

Your letter of July 24th was rec'd sometime since. After mature consideration added to the experience of the present year now closing, I do not feel any inclination to resume the school. The delightful sense of freedom from care is not to be easily given up. Perhaps it is selfish, that I do not want ever again to bear the heavy burdens of a boarding school. If such work must be done, I prefer that younger hands should take hold & push it. I wish to carry the gospel without money inducement to as many as I can reach. I cannot do both school & country work so as to satisfy my own conscience. If I have a school I must devote to it my whole time & strength or it seems to me inefficient. I don't mean this as criticizing those who think & work differently, but we must all plan & judge for ourselves. As between school & evangelistic work, being free to choose, I elect to do the later. Had the school gone on without the distressing disease that broke out, & had there not been such determined hostility here to my plans & wishes, I should doubtless have elected to push the school. But all that is in the past & henceforth I regard my work in the school line as ended.

You will have heard of our sad loss in the death of Mrs. Pruitt . . . very unselfish & was holy consecrated to the work. Mr. Pruitt remains for the present at North St. & suspects to have the Joyners' live with him. We heard on yesterday of their arrival in Shanghai & hope they will be here, with the Davaults, this week or soon after. The later are to live at Dr. Crawford's. The Halcombs are living at Mrs. Shaw's place. They seem very happy. She has progressed in the language, in ten months, about as much as people do in two or three. Yet she is publisht in Ky. & S.C. as having made more rapid progress than anyone ever did before! She studied pretty well at first, but got interested in other things, as Eng. Lit., courting, getting married, housekeeping & c.—& now a (unreadable).

Presbytery is in session & the Chefoo brethren are here—also Mrs. Corbett & the children. The later are much grown.

Mrs. Pruitt's long illness kept me from my usual amount of country work. I made but two trips, the last of which lasted about three weeks. I was at *Chiang Eng ju's* and home, west of *Whanghien.* The Presbyterians are much up there with the Baptists & the situation was rather embarrassing.

The new mission at Whien is to be open next year probably. There has been a desperate effort to keep the foreigners out, but it seems to have broken down. Dr. Crawford has worked the affair with most admirable tack & skill through the higher officials here.

With much love

Yours,

L. Moon.

P'ingtu, China,
Jan. 9, 1889
My dear Miss Armstrong,

I write to thank the Executive Committee for the hearty response they have made to my appeal for more workers for P'ingtu. I urge that the new missionaries be sent out immediately. I am holding on, after more than eleven years of work, at considerable risk of permanent injury to health. Yet I must not leave until others are here to take over the work. After the new missionaries arrive, there must be preparation on their part & delay on mine. Therefore, the sooner they come, the better. Please listen to no suggestion of delay. The two should be in Tungchow in June at the latest. Then they could come out with me in the autumn to P'ingtu & make acquaintance with their field. Write me in advance when they will arrive, so that I can arrange to have them met, or meet them in Chefoo.

A two years' supply of clothing is all they need bring. They should have abundance of heavy flannel underclothing. The climate of Shantung is colder in winter than it is in the same latitude in America. I suggest that they bring sheets, pillow cases, blankets &c.

Please say to the new missionaries that they are coming to a life of hardship, responsibility & constant self denial. They must live, the greater part of the time, in Chinese houses, in close contact with the people. They will be alone in the interior & will need to be strong & courageous. If "the joy of the Lord" be "their strength," the blessedness of the work will more than compensate for its hardships. Let them come "rejoicing to suffer" for the sake of that Lord & Master who freely gave his life for them.

Hoping soon to welcome them to the field,

Yours for the work,

L. Moon

P.O.,
Chefoo

Private

P'ingtu, Feb. 11, 1889
Rev. T. P. Bell:
My dear Brother,

I suppose I ought to confess with shame the fact that for more than a year—is it so long?—your request for a "bright little tract" has remained unheeded. The truth is that little word "bright" frightened me from the effort. You can not possibly conceive the dulness of my surroundings & the general mental stupidity that supervenes. So I must beg you to forgive my failure to write the tract. The promised tract about Mexico did not reach me.

I am looking very anxiously for the reinforcement that is to release me from duty here. Staying is not wise on my part, yet the demands of the work are such as to force me to stay on.

While I think about it, I wish to suggest that no missionaries, hereafter, be allowed to reach Shantung in cold weather. Some think that the foundation of Mr. Davault's illness was laid on the trip from Chefoo in the middle of December. Not long ago, a new arrival of the Pres. Mission in Chenanfu died of consumption in six weeks, the disease having been contracted in journeying to her station. People at home have no conception of the hardships of travel in North China during winter. It is hard on all, but means *death* to those whose lungs are weak. Above all, don't let anyone come to P'ingtu who has the slightest tendency to lung trouble or scrofula. The natives die here chiefly of consumption & of course the climate is harder on foreigners than on natives.

Hoping to have good news soon of reinforcement this spring,

Yours sincerely,

L. Moon

P.S. Please send specimen copies of *F. Journal* to enclosed addresses.

Tungchow, June 30, 1891

My dear bro. Bell:

In accordance with the suggestion in your letter to brother Bostick of Ap. 24, he has talked over with me the matters therein discussed. I desire to add my cordial testimony to what he has written you with regard to Dr. Crawford's friendly sentiments toward the board. I do not doubt the facts you state as the harm done by some of his utterances while in America in 1885. Yet I think many allowances are to be made for the effect of the sharp disappointment involved in the failure to achieve the fixed purpose of his life,—the revolutionizing of mission policy—& in the necessity to accept defeat. Whatever may have been the case then, I am convinced that all feelings of resentment have long ago subsided & that Dr. C. is a sincere friend of our Board. For the Board collectively & for each individual, I believe that he entertains no feeling but of cordial good will & Christian love. That he differs from some members, or it may be from all members of the Board, on certain questions of mission policy, & that he propagates those views as occasion may arise, is only to say that he exercises his rights as a man. I say this the more freely because I have always steadily opposed him whenever I saw in him any disposition to impose his views upon any other mission or upon individuals of our own mission who were not ready to accept them. I believed that he was injuring a good cause by injudicious advocacy.

There is another point upon which I think light may be thrown & that is with regard to Dr. C.'s failure to write to the Board. I believe it has arisen simply & solely from the fact that, aside from his missionary work which he prosecutes with admirable zeal & earnestness, Dr. C. is intensely interested in questions, psychological, sociological, archaeological, which absorb all his spare time & thought. Mission work demands tension of mind & body. One turns away to seek relaxation in things absolutely foreign to work so exhausting. It requires, therefore, considerable effort of will to write missionary letters. We must not forget that at Dr. C.'s advanced age such efforts become more & more difficult. You would naturally say that Mrs. C. has refused to write for the organ of the Board on a certain explicit ground stated in a letter to yourself. To this I can only reply that, such is & has always been the nature of women that they resent fancied or real slights to their loved ones more than the latter would resent them for themselves. I repeat emphatically that I do not believe Dr. C. entertains any but brotherly & kind feelings towards each member of the Board. After his last return from America, he told me that he had given up all thought of trying to set people to rights according to his own notions. I believe that he is honestly acting on that resolve & that his heart is full of love towards the Board & every member of the Mission.

I think you are entirely correct in saying that there are "elements of mighty power for good" in bro. Bostick. He is a man of boundless energy & he has thrown himself heartily into the work whether of preaching to Christians or evangelizing the heathen. I sometimes fear that he makes himself burden-bearer to too many people—he is always doing kindnesses.

As regards the general principles on which we desire to conduct our work, the members of the Mission are in hearty accord. Without having the slightest desire to urge those views upon others, my study of the New Testament leads me more & more to feel that the Christian life is one of self denial & that we must lead our converts by example & precept to endure hardships for the sake of the gospel. I do not think this ideal is best attained by bearing their pecuniary burdens for them in building their churches & establishing schools, but by waiting patiently for the development that time will bring. I do not mean that I would refuse to aid native Christian schools or to subscribe to build churches, or that I should fail to open my home or my purse to a persecuted brother or to one in any distress, but I should do it exactly as if I were in America, privately, & not out of public funds.

With very cordial regards,
Yours sincerely,
L. Moon.

Tungchowfu Shantung
(P. O. Box Chefoo.)
China
January 16, 1892.
My dear Cary,

I had been thinking that, when I could command the time, I should write your mother, but last night the U. S. mail brought me your welcome letter, so full of pleasant news about Nell and other dear ones. I am glad the wedding went off so pleasantly to all concerned and that Nell is settled comfortably in her own home. You will miss her for a long time, but after awhile the old order of things will give place to the new and you will grow accustomed to living and planning without her. Then, too, she will often go back to her old home and you will go to visit her. You said nothing of your intended visit north. Is that given up?

I am very sorry to learn of the sad affliction that has befallen the Hills. The suddenness of the blow only makes it harder to bear. If you should see any of the family, please express my sincere sympathy.

I left San Francisco on the day intended and was glad to find several friends aboard the steamer. One was Mrs. Yates of Shanghai, to whom I am much attached. Another was her lovely daughter, Mrs. Seaman and a third was Miss Wight, a Presbyterian missionary belonging to my part of China. On the 7th day out, we reached the Sandwich Islands. I went ashore that afternoon and walked about the streets of Honolulu. There was a singular mixture of tropical surroundings in foliage, flowers and native people and Western houses and white people. The native women dress in mother-Hubbard wrappers not belted in and look exceedingly slouchy and comfortable. Some of the men dress well in European style, especially the young men. Chinese were abundant and seemed prosperous. The natives were evidently being pushed to the wall by the whites and the Chinese. The Provisional Government was in full power, but I hear it has since been set aside by Cleveland. I hope so. I was indignant, as I walked about the queen's palace, to see an armed man on guard and to see a squad of men marching about the beautiful grounds. The queen had been sent to a private house in the city. Only one native was allowed a share in the government. The people wanted their queen back. I was told by a native. Many natives speak English.

I never care to see the Sandwich Islands again. The scenery is beautiful but the climate was very hot and mosquitoes plentiful. How they did swarm that night we were in the harbor! Japan was as beautiful and far more comfortable. The scenery of the Inland Sea is beautiful beyond description. We halted at Kobe and Nagasaki, going ashore at each. At Yokohama, we spent several enjoyable days while waiting for our steamer. We had a good run to Shanghai, where I took two meals ashore with friends, and then another good run to Chefoo. I was caught in a snow storm between Chefoo and Tungchow and took three days to make a journey usually made in a day and a half. I had a cordial welcome from friends both native and foreign. I am not yet settled because I have not yet procured a cook. Meantime, I spend my days at home, but go, for meals and to sleep, to the house of my friend, Miss Barton. She is kindness itself and I am very comfortable at her house, but it would be more convenient to be at home. My friend, Miss Knight, has written that she wants to come and work here with me in the spring and then have me return with her to Pingtu. I am very devoted to her and have gladly written to accept her proffered visit and to promise to return with her to Pingtu.

My love to your mother and the boys and keep a good share for yourself. You must not drop me as you did before, but continue to write. Much love to your Auntie and Uncle Jim and all the family. I mean to write to some of them, when I can get the time. I think often of many dear ones to whom I would gladly write, but I have a large correspondence connected with the mission work and it is a good deal behindhand just now. I am writing almost daily several letters to try to bring up arrears, after which I hope not to be so pressed in that line. The last two or three months in America I allowed such letters to accumulate, owing to pressure of other matters and now I have to make up for that neglect.

With much love,
Cousin Lottie

Lottie Moon Collection, SBTS, Folder No.7, transcribed from a copy.

P. O. Chefoo
China
Nov. 7, 1895
My dear Luther—

By last U. S. mail I had the pleasure of receiving your letter of Sept. 19th and also the photo of our unknown grand niece—"Lennie Lucille"—I thank you for both. I should like to see the little maiden and am sure I should find her bright and interesting. She must be a great joy to you and her mother. I should greatly enjoy a share in your quiet life for a few days. I certainly honor people who "practice self denial" & discharge their obligations. If all would do that the world would contain many more happy people. My life in one sense is also a quiet one. That is, I live alone, & except on special occasions, entertain very little. One such special occasion has lately occurred in the meeting of our Association with our church here, & at the same time, in the meeting of a Presbytery in our city. I had a family of five with me during the Asso. They were here only from Saturday until Tuesday. Besides these Americans, I had seven Chinese guests. I have separate apartments for Chinese and foreigners and they do not eat together. Then there were members of the Chinese brethren calling to pay their respects, so that I had a busy & fatiguing experience. I have also had members of the Presbytery to dine with me several times. Our Asso. was a gratifying success. Two new churches were admitted, & in general the zeal & enthusiasm of the members were admirable. There have been more accessions to the churches than in any previous time of their history. Among the subjects discussed were foot-binding & education. Some of the younger men have developed a strong opposition to foot-binding, but the older men were significantly silent. Their conscience tells them that the custom is wrong, but they think it bad manners probably to talk publicly on the subject. One young man in opening of his address said that he had once felt horrified at the thought of discussing the question publicly, but his conscience forbade his remaining silent. An exhaustive paper was read on education; the writer urging that each church have a school. He was followed by a foreigner who urged that every child in any family should be educated. The Chinese custom is to pick out one and send him to school, leaving the others in partial or complete ignorance. Of course well-to-do people generally sent all their sons to school, more or less.

I suppose you have seen in the papers the account of the awful massacre at Kuchwing (?) in August, & also of the earlier riots in Lychow (?). Here everything has been quiet since the Japanese left us. The people are more friendly than I ever knew them to be before. There is a Mohammedan rebellion out west of which we have varying accounts. Thus far, China has managed to survive foreign wars & internal [?] commotions, and probably this rebellion will be put down as others have been. To my thinking, Russia is the most formidable power that China has yet been brought into contact with, & yet she turns from Japan, her natural ally to cast herself headlong into the arms of Russia. I believe she will rue the day when it is too late. Missionaries naturally do not want Russia to acquire Chinese territory because she tolerates none but her own "orthodox" propagating of the gospel. Japan on the other hand is very friendly and liberal toward Protestant Christianity.

Lottie Moon Collection, SBTS, Folder No. 7, transcribed from an incomplete, handwritten copy.

Tungchow, China,
P. O. Chefoo,
June 22, 1897.
My dear Cary,
    I shall be interrupted presently by a clerk coming in from the shop which I do most of my dealing; but I will begin a letter. It is the custom here for women not to go to the shops. The goods are brought to our houses. Of course, that is not half so interesting as to go to a well stocked place and see lots of lovely new goods displayed temptingly on the counter. Probably one buys a good deal less, being not exposed to temptation. I suppose clothes are the smallest of my expenses. I wear the Chinese dress in modified form and that costs less than the Western. There are no expensive bonnets or boots. For three-fourths of the year, my shoes cost less than 80cts. apiece (800 cash). In winter I wear boots that cost a little over a dollar. They are made by a Chinese woman. They are not real Chinese shoes, but a modification, or rather, a foreign cloth slipper (shoe, I mean) and boot. They are very comfortable. So far as Chinese dress goes, I wear the very large, long, loose, flowing sacque, as we used to call them in my young days. They "cover a multitude of faults." Owing to that fact, I have worn my old skirts since my return from America and am now having my first one made in about 3 _ yrs. Don't you think that pretty economical? I am the only one here who wears

the Chinese dress under all circumstances. Several wear it when they go out among the natives, but not at home or usually among foreigners. I find it too troublesome and too expensive to wear the foreign dress. Besides, as a chief reason, one gets nearer to the people, I think, when wearing the Chinese dress.

I have been quite over-run with masons for about a week and they are still here. Some of my many roofs got out of order and I am having some parts changed from thatched roofs to tiled. The straw roof is vexatious as the birds pick it to pieces and so it does not last. The tile roof is lasting. I have also three whitewashers here at work in my Chinese guest rooms. In all, there are seven workmen. I hope they will get done some day this week. Last week, a thief came over my wall at night, broke into the kitchen and carried off between four and five thousand cash. Part belonged to the cook, but most of it was mine. One of the masons was suspected, but there was no proof. Evidently the thief climbed over by aid of an overhanging tree. I had the tree well trimmed and a foreign door, with foreign lock exchanged for the Chinese door and lock of the kitchen. Heretofore, my house has remained unlockt at night, and windows all up. I trusted to the security of the street doors, not thinking of any one's climbing over the wall. I suppose the low, overhanging limbs of the tree were tempting. Once climb up on the wall, get into the tree and come down "just as easy." I had sharp pointed glass on top of the wall and then inside is a frame for flowers. I didn't think how easy a thief could climb over these by means of the tree. He knocked off the glass, got a foothold on the wall, swung himself by a limb into the tree, came over the wall, down into the yard–and I slept.

L M

Lottie Moon Collection, SBTS, Folder No. 7, transcribed from an incomplete copy.

Tungchow, China-
April 28, 1899
My dear Luther-

Your very welcome letter of Feb. 26 reached me a few days ago and gave me much pleasure. I had been thinking that I would write to you though you were owing me a letter. I thank dear little Lennie for stirring you up to write. I wish I could see her and know her and her sister and brother while they are growing up. One misses a good deal in losing the childhood of the young people among ones relatives, and I am especially fond of children. Even among the Chinese, I have the reputation of being a lover of children.

I rec'd the invitations to the boys' weddings—no—only to Bryants,—and I ought to have written my congratulations long ago. I am glad they are both happily married. Owen sent me his photograph while he was in Col. but no letter. I wrote thanking him, but had no reply.

I am very sorry to know that Mrs. Andrews is in such a poor state of health. Minnie mentioned it in one of her letters, but thought she might be better. Minnie has been a very good correspondent since I left America, & has kept me posted in family news. She is a noble unselfish character. Mammie is not so good a correspondent as she was before her marriage. Herbert has written me once, & they sent me their photographs at Xmas. Though I had never seen him, I am very partial to Herbert, as Mammie has told me so much about him. Herbert's cousin is one of my correspondents & she has written me very sweet and pleasant things about Mammie. Herbert & Mammie live in the family of this cousin's father & mother. This lady, Mrs. Whitehurst, has an infant class in one of the Norfolk Baptist Churches (S.S.) and they support a day school here in Tungchow.

I have been kept closely at home all this spring owing to the sickness of some members of the mission. One of them has now gone to America. The other is still ill. She has been confined to her bed for nearly three months. For a short time I was up with her every other night. Some of her family who have been long absent have returned and this relieves me from responsibility.

Yesterday I went out to the country and greatly enjoyed it. I visited three villages. They are two or three miles from the city & within a stone's throw of each other. In the first village, I sat in my sedan chair & talked to the people. In the second village it was much better for a woman askt me to go in, & after dinner I had a quiet time talking to several women. My hostess especially seemed very favorably disposed to Christianity. She has an opium smoking husband who is in Manchuria. With an aged mother-in-law and 2 children to support she has a hard time. This is not a rare case. The no-account men go to Manchuria as a last resort and leave helpless families behind. The energetic men go, make money and send it to their families.

You probably know from telegrams what goes on in China, as we here learn what goes on in Europe and America. Our province is supposed to be mostly in the German sphere of influence. There has been much disorder in the interior, as well as violent persecution of Catholics, & Presbyterians.

Some of the former were murdered with aggravated cruelty. Of the latter, the Christians in eight villages were rendered homeless. Some Germans were attacked with intent to kill. They defended themselves & killed or wounded some of their assailants afterwards making their escape to the coast, where they were rec'd on board a German man-of-war. All foreigners would say, I suppose, that Germany did right to send soldiers to the disturbed district. The partition of China seems only a matter of time.

Please give Lennie the enclosed card. It reads "Moo La Dee—(Lottie Moon)"—The Chinese put the cart before the horse in writing or calling our names.

With much love to all,
Your aff. Aunt,
L. Moon.

Lottie Moon Collection, SBTS, Folder No. 8, transcribed from a handwritten copy. This letter has a headline that reads, "Copy of a letter from Miss Moon to her nephew, W.L. Andrews."

Tengchow
Shantung,
China, June 28, 1900
My dear Luther,

I have heard with sorrow of the death of your father and of Mrs. Andrews. It seems a mercy that they were taken together. She was helpless and dependent in body and he seemed to be dependent on her in other ways. What disposition has been made of the children?

Long ere this reaches you, you will have seen from telegrams the desperate state of affairs in the North. Thus far, there has been no outbreaks here and the people seem friendly. Emissaries of the "big sword society" have been here recently trying to persuade the people to join them, but so far as we can ascertain without success. The people answer, "We have our small trade," they don't want things upset. They also have said, "We like the foreigners here, they seem a clever sort of people. Why are the foreigners at other places so bad when they are good here?" Our relations with the people here have been very friendly since the Japanese War. They lookt to us then for protection & help & their leading men askt that we should not leave.

Since then they have been increasingly friendly. If there should be trouble, it will most likely come from outsiders.

I go on with my work as usual. I go out to some neighboring village nearly every day. As we go about the streets as usual China is not the slightest token of hostility.

We had our mission meeting last week. Two brethren were present (one a Swede) from Kiaochow and Pingtu. They had left their wives and children at Pingtu where there were no other foreigners. On the morning of their departure from here, news came of persecution of native Christians at Laichowfu, which lies on the direct road to Pingtu and is only distant from Pingtu City 100 li (about 4 miles). The brethren were much troubled. I urged them to go a different, but more circuitous route. The objection was they were on bicycles. I said they had better walk all the way than run the risk of being killed & leaving their families helpless at Pingtu. The trouble has been all along that the foreign Ministers at Peking did not realize the actual facts of the situation. The consul at Chefoo fully understood the state of affairs but Conger overruled him. Mr. Fowler, the consul, consults the missionaries, who, being scattered all over Shangtung, know the real situation. From here & elsewhere remonstrance after remonstrance went to the minister through Mr. Fowler. The latter was powerless because the minister just out from America thought he knew better than old missionaries of thirty or forty years standing. The foreign ministers were sadly hoodwinkt. They persuaded themselves that the troubles were anti-Christian solely, while missionaries & many others equally well informed, knew that they were anti-foreign. Some recent letter writer in the *Daily News* "expressed the wish that the Boxers would throw a brick or two at the sacred head of a Minister." Now the ministers are in as great a danger themselves as were missionaries in the interior of Shangtung last winter. It seems like retribution. If the energetic measures not being taken because Ministers are in danger had been taken last winter when missionaries were exposed to torture and massacre, Ministers would be in security in Peking instead of having troops sent in hot haste to prevent them being massacred. Shangtung missionaries have known that the Gov't at Peking was behind the Boxers and was actually restraining local officials from dealing severely with them. The Ministers do not seem to have suspected the astute old Empress—Dowager of treachery. Until she is suppressed, we can have no settled peace in China.

I hope you are well & prospering in your affairs & better still your soul is prospering. May the Lord be gracious to you all. I sent a book to your Aunt Eddie which was to go to you later. Please accept with my love. It is the biography of *David Hill, Missionary & Saint*. I think you will enjoy reading it. Much love to Mary & the children & also to Bryant & Isaac and their wives & to Jim & the other boys when you write.

    Yr aff. Aunt

    L. Moon

Shanghai,

China, July 17, 1900

My dear Luther,

    Your letter was rec'd aboard the Chinese Man-of-War the "Hai Chi" but, as it was wrapt up in a package was not read until I was on the "Yorktown." Opening the package, I was delighted to have a home letter. We left Tengchow on account of rumors of the "boxers." I was on the Hai Chi several days & was treated by the Commodore & other officers with the greatest kindness & curiosity. I spent one night on the Yorktown and went down next day to Chefoo. There, I felt very unsafe and the consul was anxious for all non-combatants to leave. We therefore took the first available steamer and reacht here a week ago yesterday. Our friends, the Bryans, found us next day and brought us out to their pleasant home. We eat with them (Miss Dutton & I) & sleep in another mission house. No one can say whether Shanghai is safe. Miss Dutton expects to leave for Japan this week. Steamers are crowded with people leaving and it is somewhat difficult to get passage. Some say there is nothing to fear, that even if there were a rising it could be quelled. I suppose the quiet of Shanghai depends largely on news from the North. A succession of victories there would tend to quiet all China.

    The Chinese uprising government is sending (or has sent) a tissue of falsehood to the Chinese ministers in foreign countries. It is lies from beginning to end. The "Boxer" trouble was most industriously fomented from Peking. The Shangtung missionaries knew it & protested to the American minister, but all the foreign ministers at Peking were blinded by the artful Empress-Dowager & her advisors. They have probably paid the price of their lack of foresight by their lives. Here, at Shanghai, the people saw clearly the dangers but foreigners in Peking were strangely blind. The telegram on yesterday tells of an awful massacre sparing neither age nor sex. We are hoping the China question will be not made political. It involves the lives & the property of American citizens & the honor of the U.S. It is shameful that Americans must look to friendly power for protection. However I must say that in North China, or rather Shantung, the U.S. consul, Mr. Fowler, has been fully awake, since the murder of Mr. Brooke last Dec., to the perils of the situation. It is thanks to him & him alone that Americans, British, and the French have been rescued from massacre. He pledged his own money & chartered a steamer repeatedly (at $300 a day) to bring away those who were in danger.

If things seem very threatening here, I shall try to go to Japan. There does not seem the least probability that we can return to our post in a long time. Some of the mission are still in Chefoo. Some have probably gone direct to Japan. We fear that the American Board missionaries in the North (except four) have been all massacred. There were also Northern Methodist, Presbyterians & etc.

Please give much love to all.

Always affy your

Aunt Lottie

Tengchowfu,
Shangtung,
China.
May 22, 1901

My dear Mrs. Clarke:

Since my pleasant visit to you in April, I have often thought of you & of your good husband & have wished to write you, but as I did not know your exact address, I feared that a letter might fail to reach you. I ascertained your address from one of your letters published in the *Index*. Upon doing so, I wrote to Shanghai to have a book sent to Mr. Clarke & have secured notice that it was forwarded. I hope you will accept it & will enjoy reading it. The book to which I refer is *David Hill, Missionary & Saint.* It is one of my favorite biographies.

I have had a letter recently from Mr. Pruitt in which he makes mention of your mother's special kindness, which, he says, is for your sake. He spoke of how well she is looking. Mrs. Pruitt had started to the convention at Valdosta, intending to stop at two towns on the way & Mr. Pruitt was to set out the day after he wrote. They expect to start for China in Oct., that is, to sail in Oct. I believe Miss Hartwell plans to return about the same time.

Things are as quiet here as if there had never been any upheaval here last year. In point of fact, though the "Boxers" were extremely threatening, there was no actual outbreak in this region & this has made the return of foreigners easier & more pleasant. There are no bitter memories of bloodshed or of property destroyed. My friends are mostly in the country & they have given me a very cordial welcome back. I have made three trips to the country since my return & plan to make three more, after which the wheat harvest will be at hand & the country people will be too busy to desire visitors. We have just had our accustomed Communion and I have had a few guests from the country, but they have all returned to their homes. Our Communion seasons occur once in two months, the most largely attended being in the first China month when the members are mostly at leisure. The very large majority of our members are country people. In all our forty years in Tengchow, we have made no perceptible impression on the city. They agreed in the very beginning to ostracize the hated foreigners & only of late years has this determination relaxed a little. Of course, the events of last year brought out some of the old hostility. Mr. Owen has been trying to rent a house for a chapel, but people who wish to rent refuse when they find the purpose for which a house is wanted. One man said he feared the neighbors would rise & tear up the property if it were rented for a chapel.

Mr. & Mrs. Blalock of the "Gospel Mission" are here for the summer & perhaps longer. They are just setting up housekeeping. Mrs. Hartwell, Mrs. Owen & I have had the pleasure of furnishing their rooms & I think they are comfortable. I think one of the Presbyterian ladies also sent some articles of furniture to add to their comfort. They had their own cooking utensils & some table ware. Mr. Blalock's health is poor & the baby, a beautiful child, is suffering much from lack of nourishment. The little fellow is always hungry & is starving in the midst of plenty. It is very sad. They feed him but he assimilates almost nothing. They are trying to get a wet nurse. One presented herself on yesterday who fulfilled all the requirements. The only trouble was she was already engaged in a Mandarin family. Her own child, it seems, was dead. She said that if Mrs. Blalock would promise her more money than she was now getting, she would tell a lie to her present employer, go home & come thence to Mrs. B., or perhaps she would simply say she was going home & come direct to Mrs. Blalock. Of course, the negotiation stopped there. Meantime, the poor little baby is starving. He is only five months old.

This reminds me of your bright little fellow. How is he? & how is Mr. Clarke? & how are you? Do take a little time & write me about yourself and your belongings. How is your house progressing? & your work? especially your Sunday School.

Please give my very cordial regards to Mr. Clarke. I hope he will remember his promise to visit China someday.

All the members of our station are well and cheerful. The Hwanghien people are at their posts. Dr. Ayers & Mr. Stephens were in Tengchow last week, but I was in the country & failed to see them. I cannot tell you about the Pingtu missionaries. They are so far away that we do not see them & seldom hear from them. They are still at Kiao Chow. Mr. Fowler, our consul, forbids ladies going further into the interior than Hwanghien. He considers the prospect as anything but hopeful.

Hoping to hear from you, I am

Affy yours,

L. Moon.

Tengchowfu, Shantung
China, June 28,
1901.
My dear Mrs. Clarke,

I was very glad to receive your letter & thank you very much for the photograph which reached me by a recent mail. It is a capital picture of yourself & baby. He is looking very well & you look not only well, but happy. Miss Dutton was delighted with the picture.

I hope you will be able to see the Pruitts as they pass through Nagasaki. It would be very pleasant for you to see those who have so lately been in your old home. Then, too, I think that S.B.C. missionaries working in Japan and China would get mutual benefit by knowing each other. Mr. Pruitt is one of the best "all around" missionaries that we have. Mrs. Pruitt has been a successful worker in her school for boys & keeps up a good influence over them after they go out into the world. I trust that you and Mr. Clarke will make that promised visit to China. The whole mission would give you a most cordial welcome. I think you would be interested to see the resemblances & the differences in the work as carried on in Japan & China.

I returned on yesterday from Hwanghien where we have just held our biennial mission meeting. We much regretted that the Pingtu brethren were unable to be present. They are very busy setting up indemnities & getting their homes in order. Not only was Mr. Sears' house looted, but even the floors were torn up. Mrs. Sears has had the great sorrow of the death of her father, which occurred shortly before she left America.

In Hwanghien I had the great pleasure of being the guest of Dr. & Mrs. Ayers. They are lovely Southern people with a charming family. Four boys are with them & they left two daughters & one son at home. This seems to me wonderful consecration. Dr. Ayers is full of energy & decidedly a man of affairs. He showed himself a leader & in medical matters we cheerfully voted as seemed contrary to our interests in Tengchow. We had been hoping for Dr. Evans, but Dr. Ayers wishes him to go to Hwanghien & be associated with himself in hospital work & we acquiesced in his request. The resolution asked for Dr. Evans or some other physician. Dr. Ayers thought the Board would give us only one more physician for North China & he believed he ought to be sent to Hwanghien. There is already a good Presbyterian doctor here. It seemed a question whether it was better to have two doctors of different denominations here, or two of the same at Hwanghien. That, however, was not the deciding factor. Dr. Ayers thought there ought to be two at Hwanghien, so that he himself might do a large country work in addition to hospital work.

We decided to ask the F. M. Board to send us two more men for the Tengchow station, to join Mr. Owen in country work. The force here is wholly inadequate. Over a year ago, an additional single woman was promised for this station. So you see, we are hoping for two more families & one single woman for Tengchow & another family for Hwanghien. We askt a year ago for two families for the Pingtu region and the brethren there have long been calling for two single women. Besides, Miss Thompson wants to set up housekeeping & have another lady to join her. In all, then, we are hoping for fourteen new laborers. The Convention instructed the F.M. Board to send out twenty-five new women this year. It does not seem likely that we shall get fourteen out of twenty-five, but Dr. Tupper once said to me, "The more you ask for, the more you will get" & Dr. Willingham said or wrote to Dr. Ayers that missionaries, in letters to their friends at home, should emphasize the need of more workers. We are hoping that a new era is dawning on China & we want to get abreast of the most advanced column of workers.

I am very glad your class of girls is growing & trust that you may have many additions to it & that many may become deeply & savingly interested. I hope Mr. Clarke's work is also growing in interest & power.

Please remember me very kindly to Mr. & Mrs. Gato.

I shall rejoice to hear that your house is completed & that you have moved in. I do not like to think of you as being in the hot, close rooms you are now occupying.

Mrs. Blalock has succeeded in getting a wet nurse for her baby & the child is a little better. If he can only be pulled through the hot months, July, Aug., & Sept., I hope he will come out all right. He is now six months old.

Mr. Owen and Mr. Blalock think of starting out to Pingtu next week. Mr. Owen wants to go out & show his sympathy with the brethren there in their many trials & difficulties.

With very cordial regards to Mr. Clarke & much love to yourself

Sincerely yours

L. Moon

Tengchowfu, Shantung,

China,

July 25, 1901.

My dear Russell,

The missive that came over the waters telling of the important event of "June Twenty-Sixth," reacht me a short time ago and deserves more than a word of thanks. I send you my very hearty congratulations on an event which will, no doubt, make the happiness of your life. I have had from Minnie only the most pleasing accounts of your wife. I trust that you both will be greatly blessed in your union and that you may be spared to each other down to old age. Give my love and very cordial greetings to my new cousin. I shall hope to make her acquaintance in person, at some future time. It is possible that I may be in America toward the close of next year. My furlough is due at that time.

I returned here, as you may have heard from Minnie, about the middle of April. Shantung is apparently as quiet as it ever was. The people are kind and friendly. Yet everything depends, humanly speaking, on the life of one man. If our governor should die, or should be removed, the province would be in a blaze in a few weeks. His mother died over a month ago and according to Chinese custom he should go into retirement for a period of 27 months. Immediately in a district out west, the "boxers" began to drill and they declared that they would exterminate all Christians in that region. Last year, they killed one hundred and twenty. The Governor was ordered not to go into retirement for the usual period but to mourn in his Yamen (Court of

Law) for one hundred days according to Manchu custom. His substitute was ordered to consult him on all matters of importance. The Governor then remains in power. As soon as the "boxers" began again, he sent out cavalry to suppress them. He is said to have the best troops in China. They are well fed and clothed and are promptly paid. Hence, they are contented and obey orders. They are drilled in Western style. The "boxer" movement is not dead, but it no longer has government help and therefore is not to be greatly feared.

I am going on with mission work as usual. Unless prevented, I usually go out to some village in the afternoon. This afternoon, I am detained by having some work done by a painter. He finished the floor of the veranda this morning, but now he is working on the door of my store room and I do not like to go away and leave it unwatched. So I sit where I can see what he is doing. The masons, carpenters and painters have made a good job of putting down a new floor to the veranda. It was shocking when I returned home and it was no use to try patching it up as before. The floor had to be wholly renewed. It looks very nice now and I shall enjoy it as soon as it is dry. It is drying rapidly as the weather is hot. We are having a fearful drought. I never saw anything approaching it in all my life. The sky looks strange at times. In the evening, beautiful pink clouds stretch from the sun set almost to the east. In the early morning, the whole sky is yellow. I suppose these effects are due to the extreme dryness of the atmosphere. The crops are withering to death in the fields. We had a rain night before last and while usually such a rain would do good the ground was previously so dry that nothing can be done without more rain. It is good that the drought is local and mainly confined to the region adjacent to the coast. In Central China the rains have been so heavy as to cause floods and it was feared the Yang-tz-keang would break its bounds. If it should the destruction of life and property would be fearful.

When you see your mother and family, give them much love. Also, to cousin Fannie, Canetta, John and Nellie. With much love to yourself,

Cousin Lotte

Lottie Moon Collection, SBTS, Folder No. 9, transcribed from a copy.

Tengchowfu, Shantung
China
Feb. 7, 1902
Dear Mrs. Clarke,

In the delightful freedom of the days preceding the China New Year, I have an opportunity, much prized, for uninterrupted letter writing. For two or three weeks before New Year it is decidedly "bad form" to make visits. Schools are dismissed & personal teachers go home. It is the missionary's winter holiday. Tomorrow will begin the Chinese holidays & we shall be receiving callers. On the third day, the women call. Then follow some two weeks of feasting & jollity, after which the city settles down to its usual humdrum existence. Tengchow is a very quiet city.

Schools open about the 21st of the month. Our annual meeting takes place on the first Sunday after the 20th. We usually have a larger attendance of men and some women come. It is then that work is laid out for the coming year. This meeting is only for the Tengchow church, the majority of whose members live in the country. For the churches in general we have an association which meets in November. The church in Kiaochow, under the care of the Swedish Baptists, joined our association last year, so we have now nine churches. Our work seems very encouraging. Here, we have very satisfactory congregations on Sundays & an attendance of about sixty at Wednesday night prayer meetings.

Our S.S. has been divided & we have one for adults at 2:30 p.m. & one for children at 3:30. Mr. Owen is superintendent of both. He is incessant in his activities. During last month, there were eight baptisms & two applicants were put off. In Pingtu, the brethren refused to baptize any more during this China year, because they were afraid that motives were not right in all cases. It is getting popular, you see, to join the church in some parts of China. In Central China scores have to be rejected. Men will even offer bribes to the native assistants to get their help in joining some church. The wisdom of the serpent is surely needed now in China.

You will be glad to know that Mrs. Blalock's baby is doing well. He is a lovely child & I am very fond of him.

Misses Hartwell, Pettigrew & Willeford arrived here last week. Miss W. will probably go to Pingtu to take charge of the girls' school, though it is not yet settled. Miss Pettigrew seems undecided as between Hwanghien & Laichowfu. Their destination is left to themselves & to the N.C. Mission.

I see your published letters now and then & read them with much interest. I am so glad you are encouraged in your work. Since my long stay in Japan, I feel an intense interest in the progress of the work there.

Please present most cordial greetings to Mr. Clarke. With much love to yourself

Yours sincerely,

L. Moon

Tengchowfu, Shantung
China
February 13, 1902
My dear Cousins,

A fall of snow last night gives me leisure this morning for a letter to you. I am hoping for an uninterrupted chat with you. China New Year came in on last Saturday. On the first and second of the year, the men and boys go out calling on their friends. On the third day, the women and girls go out visiting. This has seemed a more than usually happy season to the Chinese. Probably, it is largely by contrast with last year when the political situation was by no means reassuring. Then, too, there really seems to be greater material prosperity than there was two years ago. We were then over-run with beggars, who had fled from a region of famine. It was piteous to hear their cries nearly all day for help. Now, I rarely give to beggars oftener than once or twice a week and they do not cry out, but watch for me and ask help quietly at the street door. It is a great relief.

The Emperor returned to Peking last month and this gives assurance to the people of settled peace. The mission work goes bravely on. We are very much encouraged. Tengchow has always been a very hard place, but now shows decided signs of softening. We have many invitations to visit and the people come freely about us. At Pingtu, there were so many wishing to be baptized that the Missionaries there decided to accept no more candidates during that China year. This seems strange, but it was because they feared that many wished to enter the church from wrong motives. Out in Pingtu, during the Boxer troubles, the Mission houses, chapel and dispensary were torn to pieces and contents looted. In considerably less than a year, the Missionaries were back there and indemnities had to be paid for all loses. The missionaries wisely insisted that the indemnity should come only from the guilty parties. This pleased people in general. The Mandarins were very friendly with the Missionaries and invited them to feasts. So, you see, the Missionaries and the Christians were now on the top wave and many wished to come into the church on that account. The Missionaries felt that it would not hurt the true, sincere ones to wait awhile, and time would help to test the false. We had the pleasure recently of welcoming back a former worker, Miss Hartwell, and two new ones came with her. One of them is Miss Pettigrew from Farmville, Va. The other is from Texas. We are much pleased with them both. They will probably not remain permanently in Tengchow, but go, one to Hwanghien and one to Pingtu. Miss Dutton, who formerly lived with me, felt a sudden call, which she believed to be from above, to remove to Pingtu. She left here over three weeks ago and is comfortably settled in Pingtu and was trying to change her dialect, when she wrote. It will, perhaps, take two or three months to make the change.

I had expected the new Missionaries to be with me while they remained in Tengchow, but before Miss Dutton left my good friend, Mr. Owen, asked for her quarters.

Just here, two boys have walked in uninvited. I stopped them at the sitting room door and instructed them that they are always to knock at the outer door before coming in. I told them that was the foreign custom. They were here twice on yesterday, besides coming on previous days and I really hoped the snow would keep them at home today. They came to say that their mother is coming to visit me this afternoon. I dined with them day before yesterday. On yesterday, a Chinese woman dined with me. I do not enjoy Chinese food and drinking tea does not suit me, but social intercourse is one way of winning the people.

One of these boys is very jerky in his manners,—perhaps I might better call it nervous. He can't keep still. Both are looking on as I write and interrupt not a little.

As I was saying, Mr. Owen wanted certain rooms, so I handed them and several others over to him and the day after Miss Dutton left the Owens were comfortably settled here. They have long wished to keep house, but, until now, had no opportunity. Mr. Owen has bought property south of me. He will pull down some of the houses and rebuild. I suppose he will get into his own home probably by June or July. The Owens are very pleasant neighbors and I like to have them near. As they came here, Misses Pettigrew and Willeford went to Dr. Hartwell's to live. There was really no suitable place there for them to study in, and the one important thing for them now is to get the language. I felt sorry too for Mrs. Hartwell to have her house so crowded. I therefore offered the ladies the use of my study and dining room and they gladly accepted. They come over at nine o'clock, but return to Dr. Hartwell's for dinner. Then they are here again in the afternoon. They are very quiet and I hardly know they are on the place. As I live alone, it is pleasant to have them coming in.

I hope you will write again. Your letters are always welcome. With much love to you both,

I am

Your affectionate cousin,

L. Moon

Lottie Moon Collection, SBTS, Folder No. 9, transcribed from a copy.

Tengchowfu, Shantung,
China.
March 18, 1902.
My dear Cary,

I was very glad to have your letter of January 25th. I am very sorry for you and John in your loneliness. You are blessed in having Nell and the children to stay with you so much. Nothing brightens a house so much as a child.

It is very good in you to want me with you when I go to Virginia and I assure you that your invitation is very attractive. Nothing seems to me so alluring as an old Virginia country home such as yours. I shall be very glad to visit you, but I can not now say at what time. I am hoping to be in Virginia in the latter part of December, but can not make any definite plans. The work here is developing with such a rush that I don't know how I can get away. I never saw such a change.

From being the hardest, coldest and most indifferent of people, the inhabitants of Tengchow have become most cordially kind and friendly. I have lived on this street, where I now reside, about twenty years and my nearest neighbors seem absolutely oblivious of my existence. They were altogether too respectable to associate with "foreign devils."

Now, they seek me and invite me to their houses. Of course, some still hate us, but as I go about the city numbers of people, especially children, speak to me most kindly, by name. I have not the remotest idea who they are. My day school has run up to thirty-five children, 23 boys and 12 girls, with probability of increase. We have begun a woman's prayer meeting in the school house on Wednesday afternoons and have begun services for men, women and children on Sundays.

But for my brother's poor health, I should, without hesitation, defer my return to America for a year longer, but it seems that I ought to go for his sake, as soon as my time limit expires.

By the way, will you ask the Scottsville Sunday School to gather up all their old cards and send me, unless they are sending them to some one else? I need about one hundred and twenty a month. Please ask Mr. Daniel to speak to the Hardware and other Sunday Schools and ask them to send me Sunday School picture cards. I need them as rewards once a week when I examine the children in my day school. This school is really a Sunday School six days in the week. The books studied are almost wholly religious. On Sundays, the children attend Sunday School in the afternoon at our Church, which is near my home. I am busy on Sundays from after breakfast until about sun set. Fancy how glad I am when the darkness settles down and I can rest. I am not only teaching and attending services in church and school house, but also have people here between times.

There have been twenty-two baptisms this year and there are other applicants for baptism and many inquirers.

With much love to yourself and to John, I am

Very affy. yr. cousin,

L. Moon.

Lottie Moon Collection, SBTS, Folder No. 9, transcribed from a copy.

Tingchowfu, Shantung.

China.

May 26, 1906.

My dear Cary,

I had not quite finished visiting the above when a woman and girl walked in. I supposed they had come for a visit, but they had merely called in, on the way elsewhere and they soon took their leave. I am writing inside, at my desk; on the porch are two Chinese women, one of whom is teaching, the other. A child is rolling a tin can, to his (?) own amusement and without serious annoyance to other people. He is more like Western children than any Chinese child I ever met. He is very natural in his ways and is not in the least afraid of foreigners. I like to have the little fellow around. He came with his mother on Thursday. I had not seen her for twenty years and had not the remotest idea who she was. She said she had longed to see me and so, had come. She used to be in my school when a girl about twelve years old. She was in school about two years and has forgotten some and remembers some that she learned.

About four years ago, her husband had small-pox and lost his eye-sight, so the burden of the family has fallen on her. I feel very sorry for her and am glad for her to have a rest from household and farm (?) cares for a few days. She will be here about eight days longer. She studies diligently and is trying now to master a little book called *Twenty Hymns*. I want her also to learn a part of the "Peek of Day" while she is here. Her father-in-law, a man past seventy, brought her here. He said he would like to learn about Christianity, but that those who go to his village to preach stay so short a time that he cannot hear them, being away at his farm work, and that he has not time to stay in the city to learn. He said he worshipped Heaven. He has a kind, pleasant face and I felt sorry for him. His second son is said to read Christian books, and to be favorable to the doctrine.

I was out in a village last Wednesday which I had not visited for more than twenty years. Going and returning the distance was about 28 miles, which I made in a sedan chair, with forbearers. I was pretty tired when I reached home. The country is very beautiful just now. The green wheat fields stretch in every direction. There are no fences to cut off the view. I found the people friendly. The woman I went to visit was not at home, so I was not invited into any house. I talked about two hours to the people, mostly women and children who gathered around. A good many school boys seemed pleased to have some hymn-books (*Twenty Hymns*) that I gave them. This little book has also prayers and the Ten Commandments. If I should go back there and find my friend at home, I think these boys and women and girls would probably come to see me and some might wish to be taught there in the city, there is an increasing desire to learn about Christianity. We have had over twenty baptisms here this year. There were twenty in the Hwanghien region last Sunday. The work seems to be growing, and prospering everywhere. Our mission is hoping to see Wanchuna [?] entered by Southern Baptists, next year.

Where Japanese and Russians had their death struggle, we hope to see the messengers of the Prince of Peace enter in.

The Scotch Presbyterians had a very fine work in Wanchuna, previous, to the Boxer troubles. Their converts suffered fearfully. They are still working in Wanchuna, but there is great room for more workers.

One of our number, Mr. Newton, went over to Wanchuna in the spring to look around and he is enthusiastic on the question of opening work there. Probably some member of our Shantung mission will volunteer to lead the workers who we hope will come from the U. S. for this purpose. Wanchuna is full of Shantung people. The Chinese colonists have pushed out the Wanchus largely by a peaceful conquest. Many Japanese are also in Wanchuna. It would be an interesting field for work and most likely it would prove a fruitful field.

I was much interested in what you wrote of the President as also in the clipping you enclosed. Give my special love to Elizabeth. I hope that Nell and all her family are well. I am sorry I have been so long in writing to you. I am subject to so many interruptions that it is hard to write a consecutive letter.

Much love to your Auntie. Please remind her that she owes me a letter and tell her that I should be glad to hear from her.

Miss Jeter lives with me at present. She is a beautiful character and is a very pleasant companion. She will probably leave me in August to set up housekeeping with Miss Taylor, who is to take the girls' boarding school. The necessities of the work require these changes.

Much love to John and to your own dear self, from

Your cousin,

L. Moon

Lottie Moon Collection, SBTS, Folder 11, transcribed from a copy.

Tengchowfu, Shantung,

China,

March 23, 1907.

My dear Annie,

I was glad to hear from you and through your letter from other members of the family.

My love to Jeanette. I wish I could see her sweet little girl, Mary Elizabeth. I hope Russell will have much success in his farm and his store.

I am so sorry to hear of Mrs. Gibson's sad affliction.

The famine has not extended to our part of China. It is mainly confined to Central China. It touches the southern border of Shantung. We have a good many beggars here now. I do not know whether they are all local beggars, or not. Last year, we had a remarkable immunity from beggars. The price of living is constantly going up. Last year, work was abundant and well paid and our region was prosperous. I hope it will be so again. A famine that covers an area as large as the state of New York and that affects three million people could not but raise the price of food-stuffs even in distant parts of the empire. Missionaries are engaged in distributing food, or money, in the famine region. The risk they run from famine fever and small-pox is not slight, but, no doubt, they have counted the cost and are ready to lay down their lives, as others have done in previous famines.

My life here is so much the same from day to day that there seems little to write about it. After breakfast, I study Chinese for a short time with my teacher. After that, for fours days in the afternoon [?], I must visit day-schools and examine the pupils, or hear them examined. In the afternoons of several days in the week, I go out to visit the Chinese with a Chinese Bible woman, who is supported by the Woman's Missionary Society of our church in Tengchow. On yesterday afternoon, we made three visits. The first family visited were not cordial. My companion Mrs. Kiang, talked to them awhile and then we went to see some people living in the same compound. They received us warmly and Mrs. Kiang taught the young woman hymns, while I talkt to the older woman. I told her of our Lord's birth, life, wonderful works, death, burial, resurrection and ascension. This took a good while. Then, we went to a place to which I had never been before. We entered a little yard, passed through a small house, then into another yard and so into the house for which our visit was intended. It was small and dark. A man smiled pleasantly as we entered. A woman and two girls sat on the kong (brick bed). We also sat on this kong and presently two other women came in. We talkt to them a good while. When I came home, the two girls followed me and I taught them part of a hymn. So closed the day's work.

Where I am accustomed to go regularly, I usually spend most of the time teaching hymns, prayers, religious books, or the New Testament. I prefer this, as it seems most useful, but, of course, we ought to extend the work, and when one goes to a new place there is not always an opportunity to do anything but tell the gospel story, or talk of the sin and folly of idolatry.

We recently had a meeting of two weeks at our church. Part of the time we had services three times a day. A good deal of interest was manifested and there are several applicants for baptism. They are mostly young men and boys and girls from our various schools.

The Presbyterians are holding special services this week, but I have not heard with what result.

Much love to Russell and the children and also to yourself.

Yr. aff. cousin,
L. Moon.

Lottie Moon Collection, SBTS, Folder No. 11, transcribed from a copy.

Têngchowfu, Shantung,
China,
May 29, 1907
Dear Dr. Smith,

I saw in a recent copy of the *F. M. Journal* that pictures of all missionaries would be given in future numbers. I therefore send you a copy of the latest photo I have had taken. I am in the middle of the group & Misses Pettigrew & Jeter are on either hand.

Please do not, under any circumstances, reprint an old photo taken in Atlanta about 1872. It was sent to Dr. Tupper without my knowledge, as it would have been against my wishes, had I known. It has been put twice into the *Journal*, the second time to my annoyance. I am sure you will not allow it to appear again.

With kind regards & best wishes,
Yours sincerely,
L. Moon.

Tengchowfu, Shantung,
China,
July 31, 1907.
My dear Mattie,

Your letter of June 6 reacht me while I was in Chefoo. After seeing Mr. Newton, I wrote to Dr. Willingham in accordance with your request. I hope that your cash will be settled satisfactorily & that you will return to Tengchow this year. There is abundance of work for you in both the city & the country. At present, the Tengchow station is very weak in numbers. Mr. Newton has been elected to succeed Dr. Pruitt in the Training School. He has decided to stay here until someone can be found to take his place. No one is in sight for the post. If Mr. Vingren returns, he will settle in Tsing Tao. We are hoping for reinforcements this year.

Just now, I am the only member of our station in Tengchow. Miss Taylor is at the "New Missy. Home" in Chefoo. This home is kept by Mr. Stooke, who use to be head of the old home. Mrs. Oxner & Miss Jeter are also boarding there. So are the Pruitts. The Hartwells have the upstairs of the old Boone house. Dr. Ayers & family were to take the lower rooms. He has, however, been ill & the new general consensus of opinion in the mission seems to be that he must go to Japan for us and change, as Dr. Stooke has suggested. Dr. Ayers & family were to leave Hwanghien for Chefoo on yesterday. Miss Pettigrew would be with them. Miss Taylor was waiting to consult Dr. Ayers before returning home. The Newtons have Miss Mills' little house near the sea. Mr. Newton was not at all well.

I am expecting to hold a class soon. I have sent for some to come on next Saturday & must send messengers to others. I expect to keep the class about three weeks. I want them to learn to read, as far as possible. Mrs. Tai helps me in this sort of work. She was in Miss Williford's Training School during the Spring term, but is not willing to return. She is earnest, but younger than is desirable for a woman helper.

Miss Taylor has the Girls' boarding school & has done very well indeed as it head. She speaks the language well & is gifted in many ways.

The work seems to progress steadily in all the stations.

Hoping to see you soon, I remain, With love,

Yrs. sincerely,

L. Moon.

Tengchowfu, Shantung

China

August 30, 1907

My dear Cary,

Your nice chatty letter of July 1st gave me much pleasure, as your letters always do. How you must have enjoyed the Reunion of the Confederate veterans. It is not probable that there will ever again be just such a one so largely attended. I read an account of it in the *Religious Herald*.

It must have been very pleasant, too, to have your father's cousin, Dr. Tompkins, in your home. The Snowdon family and their relatives must have greatly enjoyed this family re-union. I am so glad for Lucy and Kate that they could see their brother once more in the flesh. No one writes me of Mattie Hall. I suppose she still lives with Belle and that she also enjoyed being with her long absent brother again. Fifty-two years in Mission seems almost a life time. I suppose Dr. Tompkins went out quite young and became identified with the people.

As I wrote the above, I heard a knock at the door. A visitor from the country called and made a rather prolonged stay. He has now gone and I may resume my letter. Probably, the next interruption will be the call to dinner. After dinner, I take a rest and then go out to visit some Chinese homes.

I had a pleasant stay in Chefoo during a part of July. I went down on a steamer. There were eight in the party, quite an unprecedented number for the small cost steamer. The run takes about four and one-half hours. There is a beautiful coast, and we are never out of sight of land. The day we went, it was like sailing on a quiet lake. We sat on deck and read or talked. When I returned, I was the only passenger (save Chinese). We had some fog and were a little behind time. The officers kindly lent me reading matter, and so fast did the time fly that I was surprised when told that we were in ten miles of Tengchow. Pretty soon we were there.

Since coming home, I have taught some women from the country. Some of them were here more than three weeks; others stayed a shorter time. I was kept very closely confined at home. The weather was abnormally hot, and mosquitoes were plentiful. However, some of the women and girls learned very well. The last of them left this week, and my life resumes its usual course. I superintend day-schools (3) and visit Chinese women in order to teach them and the children, so far as they are willing to learn.

Just now, Miss Taylor is with me. Her house is undergoing extensive repairs and alterations.

L.M. (penciled)

Lottie Moon Collection, SBTS, Folder No. 11, transcribed from an incomplete, typewritten copy.

Tengchowfu, Shantung,
China
Jan. 3, 1908.
Dear Miss Shepherd,

Your letter reached me a few days ago & has given me pleasure. I hope that, ere now, your coveted relief has come and that you are again free.

Nothing seems harder than uncongenial work, especially if it takes up time that ought to be spent in preparing for one's legitimate tasks.

Here we have had our trials, but of a different kind. I am accustomed to say that I am not disheartened by anything that comes from the Lord. It is when men rise up against me that I feel unsafe.

In the summer we had a visitation of cholera & there were many deaths. Later there was an epidemic of meningitis, which is supposed to be contagious. One missionary (Presbyterian) was very ill for a time. Before meningitis was over, the bubonic plague made its appearance. Every foreigner left the city for a time & some are still away. I went to Hwanghien & remained not quite three weeks. All the missionary schools were disbanded. My three day schools are again running, though with diminished numbers. Still teachers & pupils are doing excellent work & I enjoy examining the children. I give a part of five days during the week to these schools & on Sunday I attend two Sunday Schools. I have not yet resumed city visiting. I have an accumulated correspondence & spend the brief afternoons in writing unless interrupted by callers. The days will soon be longer & I can then do more. However, we shall have our annual cessation from work in about three weeks more. The schools all close for China New Year. In the first half month of the old year, it is not considered "good form" to visit, so we missionaries get the only holiday in the year that we can have at home. Last summer, I went to Chefoo for a holiday, or rather, I went because a friend so insisted that it would have been churlish to refuse. I aim to take a rest on Saturdays but do not always succeed in doing so.

It is predicted that the plague will return with the warm weather. I hope not. I am laying my plans for next China year as if there were no such thing as the plague.

I was in Dallas for two or three days. I was in Dr. Walne's family. He has since died. I have very pleasant memories of the visit. I was much impressed by Dr. Truett's S. S. Church, though I did not meet him. He was in Louisville, Ky., in a meeting.

Have you entirely abandoned all intention of engaging in the foreign missionary work? I cannot tell you where the Bostick children are. Mr. Bostick is, I suppose, married again. I saw an invitation to the wedding.

I wonder if you are kin to the Shepherds of Nelson Co.? My dearest niece is a daughter of Dr. Shepherd, now deceased, who was from near Faber's, Nelson Co. My niece now lives in Norfolk & has five sweet little girls. She has a half sister, Victoria, who lives in Washington. Dr. Shepherd's second wife was a Miss Pope. If the family is not the same as yours, I fear these details may only bore you.

You did not tell me whence to address my letter, so I send it a venture, to Columbia. If you are not there, it will doubtless be forwarded.

May the Master's blessings be with you wherever you are.

Sincerely Yours,

L. Moon.

Tengchowfu
Shantung, China
April 14, 1908
My dear Cary:

I have about an hour that I can call my own, provided no one comes in. I have to go later to see the mother of a pupil who has been playing truant. Complaints to mothers do not always break up that fault. Sooner or later a boy of that class, the truant–class, drops out of school, as a general rule, though not always. I am glad to say that my three day-schools are all prospering. They are a source of much pleasure to me. In one of them, I teach English in the mornings. This involves a daily walk about half way across the city. I dare say the walk is good for me, otherwise I could hardly keep as strong and vigorous as I do. After dinner I rest awhile, and start out again usually about three o'ck. Two afternoons, I have to give to examining two different schools. On three afternoons, I go out visiting.

Miss Taylor has a boarding school for girls, which is also prospering. She is now in the country, so I am the only one left here in our mission. Our force here is reduced to two now, Miss Taylor, and myself. We have not been in the least discouraged by that fact, but go on hopefully and cheerfully in new work. There is a good Sunday school. The native christians have a mind to work and some of them seem to feel their responsibility.

The Presbyterians are better off for workers than we are. Just now, they have two men and two women. One of the latter has charge of a girls' boarding school. I went to see her yesterday and found her not very well. She is a widow, with an only child who is at school in Chefoo. The mother lives alone and feels very keenly the separation from her little daughter. She could have a place as teacher in the school to which her daughter goes, but she feels that duty requires her to stay here. I feel sorry for her. She looks on the verge of a break-down. The Easter holiday is close at hand so she will have her daughter with her for a few days.

One of the men here has left his family in Chefoo. His wife is afraid of the plague. We had, last year, an epidemic of plague which carried off about two hundred of the natives. Previous to the plague there was an epidemic of meningitis which was fatal to many. One missionary had it severely, but recovered. When the plague came, all foreigners left the city. I was away about three weeks. I was forced to get home again. This year there have been a few sporadic cases of what Dr. Seymour calls "septic plague."

It is usually fatal in twenty-four hours. The Chinese tell me that there is now no plague in the city. Most of the few foreigners now there have been inoculated. I have not been. If the plague returns as an epidemic, I may be inoculated. Inoculation is no longer regarded as dangerous. There are two objections to it. The one is that it avails only for six months; the other is, that it is very expensive. The Chinese are charged only a dollar (American) for inoculation. If too poor to pay they would be inoculated free. (The Mandarin gave one hundred Mexican dollars to purchase serum.) I should have to pay twelve dollars Mexican, that is, about six dollars U. S. money. Of course, I should not hesitate on account of the cost, if it seemed necessary.

The India people are realizing the value of inoculation and, it is said are coming forward voluntarily to submit to it. The English are hoping to stamp out the plague in India in this way. It is said that, within a few years, five million people have fallen victims to the plague in India. How is it that Moylin is with her mother? I thought she lived in S. C. My love to your Auntie and to Moylin.

I congratulate you on the prospect of a new pastor. May he prove very useful and very successful in building up the work at Scottsville and in the region round about.

My love to Mrs. Hill. Miss Bessie is an occasional and valued correspondent. Some of her little folks help to support a boy they have selected. He is a dear, good boy from the country and was here on my place. He is one of the sweetest children I know, and is bright withal. As to dear little Elizabeth, I am convinced that no one is too young to love and serve the Lord, who so loved little children.

My love to John, and also to Nellie when you see her, or write to her.

By time I get on my wraps, I ought to be off for that visit above mentioned.

With much love,
Cousin Lottie

P. S. Mrs. Wang and I made our visit. The mother said that her son had been sick. Mrs. Wang taught the mother and others who came in. I mean that she read to them and talked to them. I taught two girls who were anxious to learn, and sang with them. As we were leaving, the two girls wanted to come home with me. They have just left. I taught them from the catechism while they were here.

Lottie Moon Collection, SBTS, Folder No. 11, transcribed from a typewritten copy.

Tungchowfu, Shantung China
June 29, 1909
My dear Luther—
Lack of time keeps my unanswered letters piled up, but today, your last letter is on top, & shall have attention. I have a whole afternoon at my disposal.
We have had a very severe drought & the crops are a failure. Failure of the wheat crop means such suffering. All grains have advanced greatly in price. Some people are ready enough to believe the drought was caused by foreigners. The first mutterings of discontent that reached our ears was heard last week. A house adjacent to me is a mission compound took fire. The fire was communicated to all old straw roofed buildings on our property. The men on the street cried out. "It is the devil's house," "we will not help put out the fire! The Heavenly Grandfather is punishing them." Pretty soon it became known that the fire originated on Chinese property & then the crowd rushed to help. Of course, the Christians went to help on the mission compound. The Mandarin also promptly sent men to help us. The flames were readily extinguished. My good friend, Mr. Adams, who was at dinner with me when news of the fire came, went promptly to the rescue. After working manfully(?) on the mission property, when the fire was extinguished, he went over to the neighbors to help pass the buckets. He was greatly amused by the primitive methods of the Chinese. On the mission compound the loss was slight. The house was very old and was to be pulled down in the fall. The family who lived on the place were away in Chefoo. The next evidence of hostility is the very free use of a term that is forbidden by treaty to be applied to foreigners. Miss Taylor and I, in passing about

heard the children crying: "Devil woman!" Even in worse times, I had never heard that term used on our street.

On last Saturday as I stood outside my street door I heard some children cry repeatedly—Devil old woman. I was stirred into indignation & expressed my opinion in most unmistakable terms of such treatment of one who had been a neighbor so long.

On Sunday most of the street doors were closed between here & church, & I had nothing to complain of. In the afternoon, however, Miss T. was passing a house in another section at the remote end of the street & she heard twice—(just here the words are worn out of paper so faded as to be indistinguishable) –

I remembered that in passing that same place I had heard these words in passing. On Monday morning on my way to school I called to see the man who lives there. I knocked long, but was finally admitted. The door was opened by a polite, nice looking man and I was invited into _____ the apartment. I told the gentlemen that I had some reason to visit him, & called his attention to the treaty. The offenders were not his children, it seems, but children of his neighbor. He was very nice & kind & I think there will be nothing more to disturb us at present.

Lottie Moon Collection, SBTS, Folder No. 12, transcribed from an incomplete handwritten copy. The handwritten copy dates the letter in 1889 but that date has been scratched out and replaced with 1909.

Têngchowfu, Shantung, China,
May 18, 1910
My dear Sister,

I was pleased to receive your letter of March 30th. It reacht me about the first of May. With three societies, I should say that your church is much in earnest in foreign missions. It seems natural to hear of a Miss Harris & a Mrs. Willis as leaders in this good work. Then, too, your niece, Mrs. Dorsey, is teaching the boys lessons of unselfish interest in the salvation of those they are not likely ever to see. How happy you must be in all this!

Here we are happy in seeing our work prosper as never before. Têngchow used to be hostile to foreigners & the people have been very hard to know. Now the people are very friendly. We have large congregations on Sunday mornings & our Sunday school in the afternoon is constantly growing. It seems that the matter of seating those who come will be a problem confronting us ere long. Our fellow missionaries, the Presbyterians, are talking of enlarging their church to meet the crowds who go there. On one Sunday, forty could not get in.

Last year I was very pleased to have one day school for girls. Now I have two. On yesterday, a lady sent to say that her two granddaughters had asked to be allowed to attend my school. I sent word that I should be very glad to have them come with another girl to enter school, attended by two servants. Girls in their position do not go out alone.

Mrs. Turner is about to open another school for girls in another part of the city. So you see, the idea of educating girls is rapidly growing in favor.

I have a school for boys here in the city & also one in the country. I teach in the former, but for lack of time have not been able yet to visit the other this year. Christian schools are growing in favor & are being rapidly extended both in cities & in villages. In P'ingtu, our Mission has about eight hundred pupils in the various schools. Of these, probably over two hundred are girls. What surprises me is that men will send their daughters where they know they will be taught Christianity every day.

Têngchow is wide open for Woman's Work, & I have much joy in visiting & teaching women & girls in their homes. Besides now that warmer weather has come, I go out to the villages to take the gospel to the people. Miss Lide & I have been most kindly received where we have recently gone.

With most cordial regards & good wishes,

Yours sincerely,

L. Moon.

Tengchowfu, Shantung,
China,
July 9, 1910.
My dear Cary,

Your bright, chatty letters are interesting reading, and it seems strange that I am long in answering them. I am, however, away from home a good part of each day, and on Saturday, my so-called "rest Day," I am subject to many interruptions.

My schools are now closed for the summer vacation. In the boys' day school, we were busy with examinations on the mornings of four days. I was much gratified with the progress the boys have made. The class of boys is constantly improving; they come from much better homes, regarded from a social standpoint. The school began in a kitchen some twelve years ago and expanded into the adjoining bedroom. Some of the pupils were little above beggary. Slowly others began to come. The "Boxer" outbreak broke it up for awhile. Later, the Norfolk Sunbeams, Freemason St. Church, raised money to purchase good school property. Unsatisfactory teachers injured the school. Now, we have had excellent teachers, Christian men, and the school has flourished. The enrolment reached nearly forty.

But my pet schools are for the girls. One has been going on many years and is flourishing in numbers and in constant attendance and enthusiastic devotion to study. Chinese girls are eager for an education.

Two or three months ago, I started a school for girls on my home place. To my surprise, girls from my street have attended it. My surprise was due to the fact that nearly all the people of this street have been coldly indifferent, (secretly hostile, I suppose) to foreigners. There are some sweet and pretty children in this school. Two come from so good a family that a servant has to escort them to school and on their return home. They are daintily sweet and have beautiful manners. All this shows the breaking down of prejudice. As to my city visiting, more homes are open to me than I have time to visit. Now that vacation has come, I hope to do more evangelistic work both in the city and in the country. I have visited twenty villages this spring and enjoyed it. I prefer evangelistic work, but necessity knows no law and I was forced into school work. I lately passed over a boys' day school to Mrs. Adams. They are little fellows and are sweet and attractive. Mrs. Adams is very found of them.

I have a day school for boys in the country. Both of my efforts to visit them this year have failed on account of rain. We are now in the midst of the rainy season. A heavy thunder storm came up about daylight and it has rained nearly ever since. The roof of my front porch has tumbled in; happily no one was hurt. The sun is now keeping out in a sort of shame faced way, as if he wasn't quite sure of being wanted. In point of fact, when we get too much sun and no rain the ignorant people blame the foreigners and become hostile. This year, timely rains saved the wheat crop. Now, the regular old fashioned rainy season seems to have returned, after some years of capricious dallying. Right glad are we not to be subject to blame for what we can't help. In a part of Hunan, a famine exists on account of excess of rain. A river broke its dykes and destroyed a promising rice crop. Last year, their rice crop was short for lack of rain, with much suffering in consequence.

I cannot give you the information you wisht. I once heard my mother say that the Bapt. church used to meet in her home, but I cannot tell for how long. At one time, it was reduced to a very few members, on account of the acceptance by many of Mr. Alexander Campbell's views. A gentlemen, then a Presbyterian, earnestly warned my mother against being led astray. Later on, he accepted Mr. Campbell's views. My father was originally a Presbyterian. His pastor gave him a book on baptism to confirm him in the Presbyterian view, with the result that its reading made him a Baptist. He was a deacon in the Scottsville Bapt. church up to the time of his death. As a child, I attended that church regularly, and remember the pew in which we always sat. Later, owing to distance (nine miles) my mother moved her membership to Hardware, which was only about four miles from our home. Dr. Long was at one time pastor of both churches. He was a fine pastor, a cultured gentlemen and a lovable man.

I suppose dinner is nearly ready, so I must close. I have as a guest in the house a Chinese lady. She eats some food such as I do (chickens and fish and some vegetables) but neither milk nor butter. Strange to say, she eschews tea also. She is my adopted sister. The dainty little girls mentioned above come from her home and are called her granddaughters, but are really no kin to her. They live in a very handsome compound.

Much love to all, John, Nell, Elizabeth, your Aunty, Moylin and Cary.

Don't forget a big lot of love for yourself from your

Cousin Lottie.

Please give my love to Mrs. Hill, Mrs. Fox, Mrs. Bell and her sisters.

L. Moon.

Lottie Moon Collection, SBTS, Folder No. 12, transcribed from a typewritten copy.

Tengchorofu, Shantang
China
March 6, 1911.
My dear Cary,

I have just read over your nice chatty letter and enjoyed it for the second time. No, I never heard Dr. Hatcher at an association, but I read about everything that I see from his pen. His freshness is wonderful.

It seemed like old times to read about Hollins, where I was at school more than fifty years ago. I do not remember Tkill Mt. of which you speak. There used to be a Tinker's Mt. on which the school girls liked to go roving on a holiday.

I have never visited the Orphanages. Here we have been afflicted by a visitation of the Plagues. Some hundreds of years ago, it swept over Europe and was called the "Black Death." There are said to be ten kinds of plagues and it is asserted that the Black Death is the worst of all. One hundred pr. cent die of this who take the disease. It has ravaged some parts of Manchuria frightfully. Some time ago there had been 7000 deaths at Hasbin. Some physicians have nobly laid down their lives in the effort to combat the disease at Hasbin and Mukden. It has raged at Chefoo. Just now, I hear, no ships are allowed to come here from Chefoo. The Chinese say that there is no plague here now. For a month, Dr. Seymour advised us to quarantine ourselves, since the Chinese took no precautions. About a week ago, the doctor relaxed the quarantine and I have re-opened three of my day schools. I am delaying one because the teacher would have to pass a door where plague might possibly have entered. About twelve days have elapsed and no case has occurred there, so I hope it was a false alarm. The house in question is just back of Miss Taylor's Girls' Boarding School. She dismissed the school for the China New Year's holidays and has not dared to re-open it. The girls from the Presbyterian boarding school were sent home on the alarms of the plague and I hear that the school will not re-open until next fall. The risk is too fearful. In one family, all were swept away except two children; and also the doctor, a woman who sent to help and a friend of the family took the disease and died; in all ten persons. The disease attacked the lungs. The patient spits blood and a yellow sputum; the lungs break up, the face turns black and the patient dies. The disease germs seem to be losing power here. I have only heard of two cases recently. They occurred last week. I very much hope that the outbreak here is over. Some of our station, however, take a different view and are still in quarantine.

I was inoculated some time in February. That is said to be some protection. The disease has appeared at all our stations in North China. It seems that there have been fewer deaths here than at some of the other stations. Our only protection is to quarantine ourselves. Churches and schools are all closed for the time and all Mission work ceases.

It was very lonely during the quarantine. No one was admitted except the foreigners and these dared not leave their homes often. New Year is usually a time of jollity with the Chinese, but I did not admit a single caller.

The Chinese did not seem to pay any attention to the plague, but went on with their usual New Year's fun.

The Japanese deal effectually with the plague and stamp it out immediately. My love to all your Auntie's family; also to John and Nellie not forgetting Elizabeth.

Believe me to be

Very affectionately your Cousin,

L. Moon

P.S. I forgot to say that my furlough is due in 1913. Should I live so long I shall hope to see you.

L.M.

Lottie Moon Collection, SBTS, Folder No.13, transcribed from a typewritten copy.

Tengchowfu, Shantung

Mar. 24, 1911

My dear Luther,

I am enclosing you the official statements about the famine in Central China. Will you not speak to the pastor of your church & ask him to obtain a contribution to help these poor sufferers? The details are heart rending as we get them from Pochow where our missionary, Mr. Bostick, is stationed. He & a Catholic priest are charged with the distribution of grain. Of course, others go to their help.

A man from the country going into Pochow on China New Year to make calls counted thirteen corpses, people dead of hunger. Two men, who in the distribution had received a little grain for their families, were found dead on the road with their bags of grain beside them; they had perished of starvation. Mothers are eager to give away their children, but no one wants them, children roam the streets with none to care for them. A woman went to beg a little help which was given & on her return found that her mother had hanged herself. One cent U.S. money a day up to the next harvest will save a life.

There was a famine here some three or four years ago which was fearful, but this surpasses in horrors anything I have ever known. Unless help comes & that speedily, from one to three million men women & children must perish from hunger. How can we bear to sit down to our bountiful tables & know of such things and & not bestir ourselves to help? I hope you know that missionaries not only give their money but also give their lives to help the famine stricken. Hardly ever did I know of a famine that did not claim its victim among missionaries & doctors also who are not missionaries. It is the famine fever that carries off these noble workers. In the famine three or four years ago, two doctors fell victims, one a missionary & one the port doctor. Another missionary lost his health for years on account of his fight with the famine. He contracted a disease called sprue. The last appeal I rec'd from Miss Bostick said, "for the sake of God & humanity send all the help you can." She & her brother and his wife are standing nobly amid all the awful horrors that rend their hearts daily.

I earnestly entreat that you will do all you can to help get contributions.

The Plague in Tengchow has ceased but Chefoo is still on the infected list. Foreigners dare not travel either overland or by steamer. Indeed, the steamers have about stopped calling here as the boatmen refused to go off & help land passengers & freight. They had at least learned the danger.

With love to all

Aunt Lottie

Tengchowfu, Shantung,

China,

May 2, 1912

My dear Mattie,

I was glad to receive your letter of March 14th & would have answered immediately as you requested but I was out of ten cts. stamps. No stamps could be bought here & I had to send to Chefoo to get some. China is now a republic & they will not print any more dragon stamps. Still, it will take time to get out new stamps. The dragon flag has gone forever & with it must go the stamps.

We have been very greatly blessed in being able to remain quietly in our homes. Before the Revolutionaries came, they sent a proclamation to be posted up commanding protection of all foreigners & also of churches. The provisional President, Dr. Sun, is a noble Christian man. He resigned in favor of President Ywan because he believed that the latter could do more for China. It was a grand thing to do & has resulted in good. President Ywan is a very able man. In Boxer days, he was governor of Shantung & kept the province in peace.

In Feb., I went to Hwanghsien, twenty miles distant, to help take care of the wounded. I found I was not needed for that, as many local Red Cross workers were there, but some of our Christians wished me to remain because they said my presence would re-assure the Christian women. I was glad to be of service in that way. Later, members of the Hwanghsien station returned (two, the day after my arrival,) & I came home, having been absent ten days. During the last day or two at Hwanghsien, incessant fighting was going on, day & night. On the morning of my departure, Mr. Hartwell sent a message to the Republican commander in the city asking him not to fire at the time I should start & telling him that I was a member of the Red Cross Society. So, I got away in safety. Mr. Daniel would insist on escorting me some miles to the river & on his return was in danger from bullets. That very day the Republicans had to withdraw & retreated to Tengchow. I heard that their ammunition failed. The Imperialists were guilty of frightful atrocities. They butchered men who were queueless & looted the shops. Hwanghsien was a wealthy city & suffered accordingly. We confidently expected fighting here & a few of our foreign community left & went to Chefoo. An American man-of-war came up to see about us & offered us free passage to Chefoo. Most of us were unwilling to go & thought it best to share the dangers of the bombardment expected. Happily it did not take place. The Republicans moved on to Hwanghsien & recaptured it, the Imperialists retreating westward loaded with booty. Neither Imperialists nor Republicans interfere with foreigners, or foreign property.

My schools re-opened in March & have greatly prospered. I have now the superintendence of seven schools, all but one for girls. This is most delightful. A few years ago, even one girls' day school was considered good, but now the girls are growing very anxious for an education. I love them more than I can tell you & delight in having them on my home place. The people were never before so kind & friendly. The Tengchow people have always been very conservative & naturally they are Imperialists.

I have tried to be careful not to offend them, though naturally all my sympathies are with the Republicans. The chief difficulty for the government now is to get money. I trust President Ywan will be able to negotiate loans. Just now, the local authority has issued notes, but it seems there is no specie back of them. The city people use these notes, but the country people refuse them. I accept them from my banker for use in the city, but demand the old style of bank notes for country use.

My furlough is due in April, 1913, but I do not expect to leave so early as that. A member of our station, Miss Taylor, is now in the U. S. & I planned not to leave until her return. She expected to be back about June, 1913. The latest news was that she was in a sanitarium & had just undergone a very serious operation. Her doctor was hopeful.

I am looking forward to seeing your mother & all the family. I wish I could have seen your father again. I have lately come across a daguerreotype of him as a little chap hardly two years old. I think it was that picture your grandmother wanted & I could not find it. Not long ago, I came across it unexpectedly. I wish to take it to your mother.

I congratulate you on your success as a business woman.

With love to all,

Yr. aff. Aunt Lottie.

Tengchowfu, Shantung,
China,
June 13, 1912.
My dear Cary,

Your chatty and interesting letter deserved an earlier reply, but I have been short of stamps. Some time ago, I sent to the P. O. to buy stamps and they had none. This rather alarmed me as my stock of nearly all kinds was nearly exhausted. I sent to Chefoo and got a Mexican dollar's worth and they were nearly used up when I learned to my great joy that the P. O. here had obtained a new supply of stamps. We are fortunate in having had perfect peace here throughout all the troubles. There was severe fighting at Hwanghsien and I was there during a part of it. The day I returned home the revolutionaries were compelled to retire on Tengchow. I heard that their ammunition fell short. The Imperialist troops entered Hwanghsien and were guilty of brutal atrocities. They killed men whose queues had been cut. Most of our Christian men there had cut their queues, but the presence of the Missionaries saved them. Had no Missionaries been there, I suppose they would have been massacred. Both sides in the beginning adopted the policy of protecting foreigners of all nations so there has been no cause of fear except from lawless banditti, or from stray shots while the fighting was going on. We fully expected Tengchow to be bombarded, but were happily mistaken. The Imperialists looted wealthy Hwanghsien and then went west laden with booty. It will take long years for Hwanghsien to recover from the losses suffered, not to speak of the men who were foully murdered. Someone counted fourteen dead bodies in one pile.

All this is now ended and the Republic is an established fact. Strange to say, Tengchow people are extremely conservative and they remain Imperialist at heart. I have tried to be strictly neutral though my sympathies are all with the revolutionaries. There are a good many soldiers here still. They are from the south and seem to be a fine manly lot. They behave admirably and the city has about returned to its normal aspect. At first, Tengchow had the appearance of a conquered city and all business was at a standstill. Of course, there was much suffering among the poor.

The China New Year came late and after the holidays were over my schools were reopened. This was in March. I shall therefore run them on a little later than usual in July. The schools have done very well, much better than I expected in such troublous times. I have some very sweet little girls in school. They are well dressed and well behaved. Some of course, are poor and untidy, but I reject none on that account. It is not their fault that they are poor. It is a very pretty sight to see them at play on my front porch and in the yard during recess. Their bright colors in dress make a pretty picture. The mothers seem to like to send their children here. One of them said that they felt that they were safe here. They feel sure that their girls will be carefully watched over. The children love to come because they have a happy time studying and at play.

Besides the schools on my place, I have four elsewhere. Of these I do not see so much, I am sorry to say. I visit three of them once a week to examine them. The school for young men and boys is now thrown entirely on the Chinese teachers. Until this year, I used to give a part of five days in the week to teaching in it. I am glad to be relieved of this duty and to have found a young man to take my place. This gives me more time for evangelistic work and releases me for country trips. I have made several trips recently, three or four days duration each and one of only one day's duration. The whole country seems wide open for the preaching of the gospel.

You ask about my return to the United States next year. I have not yet set the time. It depends somewhat on Miss Taylor's return. When she left, she spoke of getting back about the first of next June. She has undergone a very serious operation, but is reported as making a good recovery. I don't know whether this will delay her return or not. She would naturally wish some time at home after being so long in hospital.

I shall be only too glad to make you a visit. Annie wrote me about seeing Jim who visited them on his way to Richmond. Annie had never seen him before and she spoke of him in high terms. She especially referred to his not being afraid to stand for the right. It did my heart good to read such words. Jim is one of my especial favorites. Certainly that was an honor bestowed on Luther and I am glad to believe that he deserved it.

Please give much love to John. I shall be glad to see you and him again. I should like my visit to you to be when you and he are alone so that I can see more of you than if you have a house full of guests.

I am looking forward to seeing my dear Sister Maggie, as well as many other loved ones.

With much love,

Your cousin,

L. Moon.

Lottie Moon Collection, SBTS, Folder No. 13, transcribed from a typewritten copy.

Tengchowfu, Shantung,

China,

Aug. 10, 1912

My dear Mattie,

I was very pleased to receive your letter of July 7th enclosing two photographs. I suppose you failed to put in Clara's picture of which you wrote. I never saw your father after he was about six years old. His mother brought him to Virginia twice. The first time, they remained, I think, over a year. The second visit was shorter. She sent me a picture of him as a youth & I also have a daguerreotype of him as a child about two years old. Your grandmother wrote asking me for a picture after your father's death. I sent the first picture above mentioned, not being able to find the other at that time. Recently I came upon it & am saving it to take to your mother. Being in a case, it would be troublesome to send by post. One half the case is gone.

You do not look well & strong in your photograph. I fear you work too hard & have too much responsibility. What is your chum's name? She looks full of fun & as if she enjoys life.

I am very pleased with my nephew's face, but do not admire what he holds in his hands. Tell him to imitate a Chinese teacher with whom I have dealings. I do not allow smoking on my school premises & forbade this teacher smoking there. I told him to go elsewhere for his smokes. About a month later, I renewed the subject & found that he had given up smoking altogether. It is pity your brother does not do the same. I had a dear friend who smoked cigars. From that he went on to cocaine. He thought that neither hurt him. Finally, he was asked to resign his position, later fell ill & died, leaving a large family almost destitute.

I am glad you had the trip to Dardanelle. I used to hear your mother talk about the place. I wish the old home in V^a were still in the family & that you might go visit it, but it long ago passed into the hands of strangers.

I expect to go to the U. S. some time next year, not earlier than July, I think. I promised to wait Miss Taylor's return & she expected to be back about June. My schools close about July 6th & after that I shall feel free to go if Miss Taylor has come. She has been in hospital for an operation & was expected to die, but is now out of hospital. Of course, no one knows how soon she will be permitted by the doctor to return. We expected two new young ladies out this fall, but the F. M. Board is in debt & they must wait a year. This makes it all the more important for me to stay at my post.

We are in the midst of the rainy season for which I am glad for two reasons. The first is that it is good for the crops. The second is that I am not liable to interruption today.

We had no trouble in Tengchow during the war, but I fear some disturbance later on. It will not affect foreigners, however. It is the opposition to cutting off the queue. Edicts are posted up commanding its removal by a certain time. One month is allowed to shop-keepers; three months to coolies. On yesterday, a former pupil of mine, a young teacher, called, accompanied by his younger brother & a nephew, a child. All were queueless. The young man seemed in high spirits, In general, however, the men are very unwilling to cut their queues. Some months ago, the shop-keepers held a meeting & agreed to employ no one who cut off his queue. Now, the order comes from Peking to cut off their own queues. In Chefoo, the shops were closed I do not know how long because the shop-keepers did not wish their queues forcibly removed. I have been told that the country people will rebel if compulsion is attempted. This would be very unwise because they have no arms, while the soldiers here are well armed.

I have never felt so safe in China as under the Revolutionary government. They are thoroughly friendly to foreigners. I am delighted that the Manchu oppression is ended. Sad to say, the Tengchow people are mostly Imperialists, so I have had to be very careful about expressing myself on the other side lest I should injure my influence over those among whom I dwell. The soldiers are mostly from Shanghai, I think, but some from the province north of us.

Give my love to your mother & brothers & sister. Please thank your brother for his picture & tell him that I prize it highly.

Hoping to hear from you again.

I am, with love,

Your Aunt,

L. Moon.

P. S.

I enclose my visiting card. It reads

Mu Lä Dee,

Moon Lottie

P. S. 2nd

After sealing this letter, I found Clara's picture on the bureau! I suppose I dropped it when I opened your letter & that my servant picked it up this morning when she cleaned the room. Please thank Clara for the picture.

V. EPILOGUE

"Let us not grow weary in the work of love..."

EPILOGUE

Lottie Moon's last weeks in this world were a marked contrast to the rest of her life and career in China. She apparently began experiencing serious health problems in the fall of 1912, probably because she was giving her food to her neighbors. Her medical problems became increasingly serious and in October fellow missionary Jessie Pettigrew informed Dr. James Gaston that Moon was not in control of her faculties. Meanwhile, The Foreign Mission Board was preparing to bring her back to America. Miss Cynthia Miller, a nurse by training, went to China to fetch the frail and rapidly deteriorating Moon, but it was too late. On Christmas Eve, 1912 Lottie Moon died in Kobe, Japan. Her body was cremated and returned to her family for final interment in Crewe, Virginia.

As Southern Baptists continue to carry Christianity throughout the world, Lottie Moon remains an enduring symbol of love, sacrifice and dedication. She left a comfortable life in America for a life of privation and boldly invited others to do the same. Since the first Christmas offering in 1888, Southern Baptists have given some $2 billion dollars for international missionary endeavors in her name. Without doubt, this woman continues to enchant hearts and inspire imaginations.

Yet, surely there must be more to Lottie Moon than her marketing value for the annual Christmas offering. She literally gave her life in service to her God and deserves to be remembered as more than a mere symbol. Moon's life and work are urgent reminders that while missionary work seeks to bring the Divine to humanity, it is nonetheless a very "human" endeavor. Missionaries attempt to touch people as individuals rather than pursue statistical glory. Moon learned this lesson by living, and ultimately dying, among the people she wanted to reach. May her legacy outstrip superficial symbols and be one of loving commitment to her God and the people she felt called to serve.

Hwang Hien, Oct. 28, 1912

Dear Dr. Gaston:–

On last Thursday I received letters from Mrs. Turner and Miss Lide asking me to come to TengChow Fu to see Miss Moon who had been quite depressed for the past two weeks and a sore had developed back of her ear, which she insisted was only a boil. I went over on Friday and was much surprised to find the condition she was in. She did not know I had been sent for so knew nothing of my coming and at first did not seem to recognize me. She was very thin and face had quite a drawn expression. When I asked what was the matter she said; "It's my mind, troubles in my mind." Then she began to tell me what awful sins she had committed, how she had given away until she had impoverished herself until she was almost a pauper, while by actual count Miss Lide tells me she has money to her credit in the bank. Arrangements had been made a few days previous for her to move over to Miss Lide's to live but when the time came it almost broke her heart to leave the old place, so as her cook and all had been dismissed her meals were being sent by Mrs. Turner. She told me [?] she had made a fool of herself and had no face ever to see any of her friends again. It was all so strange for Miss Moon to talk in this way and it seemed to be the best thing to get her away from her present surroundings and see if a change of scenes and circumstances would not help. When I suggested that she come home with me she hesitated because of the cost and only when I told her I would bring her in my shenitsi and send her back did she consent to come.

The sore on her neck I think is a carbuncle. But it is not painful except when dressing though it is breaking down quite extensively. The opening is now about the size of a twenty cent piece but the inside cavity is much more extensive and a lot of affected tissue.

She says she rests well but can not sleep. A few nights before it begun to discharge she was sleepless from pain but she does not suffer at all with that now. Her mind at times seems (?) to be a perfect blank. She will sit all morning with her hands folded and perhaps doze a little, for instance her mail came in yesterday and her papers have lain unopened. I am quite at a loss to know what to do. A Dr. ought to see her I think. Dr. Seymour was away for a month else I would not have dared bring her over here even though a change seemed imminent.

I have been using carbolized solution and peroxide in cleansing the neck and carbolic ointment and am giving her Potas Bromide. I consulted Dr. Chii and he approved of this. She does not eat very well. I'm quite anxious to know if I am doing the right things. She is old and feeble and I hesitate in assuming the responsibility in her case. Will you please give me some advice? I would be glad if you could see her but use your own judgement about coming. She isn't in bed and does not complain but it seems to me she needs medical attention. There are times when she will talk quite intelligently on some subjects but not often.

I am writing you her condition without her knowledge and should you feel it best for you to come to see her, just come on, or if not please give me some advice. Thanking you in advance for your kindness.

My love to Mrs. Gaston please. I trust she is gaining her strength back these beautiful fall days.

Yours sincerely,
Jessie L. Pettigrew.

Lottie Moon Collection, Southern Baptist Historical Library and Archives, Nashville, Tennessee.

December 5, 1912
Mr. I. M. Andrews
Roanoke, Virginia
Dear Sir:

Your letter to Dr. Willingham has been referred to me in his absence. The cable message with reference to Miss Lottie Moon came last Sunday, stating that her mind was seriously impaired, and that it would be necessary for her to come home immediately. She is accompanied by Miss Cynthia Miller, one of our missionaries who is a trained nurse. She will reach San Francisco on January 13th, 1913. Dr. Willingham will be back tomorrow or next day, and he will write you immediately about arrangements for meeting her. We are greatly distressed over the sad news. She has been a heroic worker. Dr. T. W. Ayers, one of our missionaries who is at home, and who knew her while in North China, says—"She is one woman who will have her crown covered with stars. She is one of the most unselfish saints God ever made. I am so glad to say this of her while she lives." I write this to show you how the missionaries feel about her. We do not know the cause of her deranged mental condition. It is entirely possible I think that the ocean voyage and rest may do much to restore her health, though, of course, everything depends on the cause of the trouble.

Sincerely yours,
W. H. Smith

Dear Sir:

I am in receipt of information through Dr. S. B. Moon of your City stating that you had received a cablegram saying that aunt Lottie Moon of China had lost her mind and she would possibly reach San Francisco, California, on January 13th, 1913. I have communicated this information to her niece, Mrs. J. Herbert Coffer of Norfolk, Virginia, and also telegraphed my brother, W. L. Andrews, who is now in that part of the State to call upon and consult with her regarding the meeting of aunt Lottie Moon and on the return home of my brother on the 7th inst. we will write you as to which of her nephews will go for her. Kindly write me by return mail the full particulars in the matter and as to just what proportion of the expense your Board proposes to bear of cost of trip to and from San Francisco.

Very truly,

I. M. Andrews to R.J. Willingham, December 4, 1912.

Dear Doctor:

I am in receipt of yours of yesterday's date, and note with much regret the condition of Miss Lottie Moon. I have interviewed today Mr. George A. Pope, one of the leading managers of the Sheppard & Enoch Pratt Hospital, and am glad to advise that the Institution will receive Miss Moon on her arrival here, as a probationary patient at least, the terms and conditions to be adjusted later, but which will be reasonable under the circumstances. To save trouble, Mr. Pope suggests that, if Miss Moon is sufficiently herself to sign the application herewith enclosed, and marked #1, she do so prior to her arrival at the Hospital. In event of her mental condition not being such as to enable her to do this, then it will require the signature of two physicians. The contract also on the enclosed paper could doubtless be arranged after Miss Moon's actual presence at the Hospital, if it be deemed best to send her here. I presume you are aware that the Hospital is one of the best, if not the best, in the country. I am pleased to advise that the operation of Brother Tyler was successful, in that his life was preserved, with the hope of his living for awhile longer. How long this may be, however, cannot yet be forecast, but the Doctors hope for a year at least. It is a very sad case, and one hard to understand, if our faith did not teach that whatever happens is for the best.

Yours sincerely,

Joshua Levering to R. J. Willingham, January 9, 1913.

My dear Brother:-

Your kind favor received and appreciated.

Dr. Moon, a cousin of Miss Lottie Moon here, has arranged for her to be put, at least temporarily, in a sanitarium for nervous trouble, close to this city. It may be that after a little, we will accept the kind offer of the hospital there. I certainly appreciate your kindness in this matter.

I am to be in Washington tomorrow and Sunday. I thought of running over to Baltimore tomorrow afternoon to see Brother Tyler, but I hardly think I could see him. I will stop in Washington City with Brother J. J. Darlington.

With best wishes,

Yours fraternally,

R. J. Willingham to Joshua Levering, January 10, 1913.

Dear Sister:-

Your kind favor received and appreciated. We are expecting Miss Moon to land in San Francisco today. I suppose that you have heard that her mind has become impaired. I hope that by the time she arrives, she will be better. Dr. Bryan has gone out to San Francisco to meet her. Miss Miller expected to come across the ocean with her.

I enclose to you one of schedules of the sailings of the boats from San Francisco. You notice that some of these boats do not go to Shanghai, but land instead at Manila in the Philippines. The Nippon Maru, which is an intermediate boat, sails Feb. 21st. How would it do for us to buy a ticket for you to Nagasaki, and then let you buy from there across to Tengchow or Chefoo?

I enclose to you home salary for January. Our Board does not meet for several weeks. When the brethren meet, I can ask them to extend your home allowance. Perhaps by that time you can decide definitely as to the boat on which you wish to go.

I take it for granted that your physician there will give you a certificate as to your health being good. Perhaps it would be best for you to get this, so that I can show it to the Board.

With best wishes,

Yours fraternally,

R. J. Willingham to Ida Taylor, January 13, 1913.

Dec. 14, 1912

Dear Dr. Willingham,

I want to begin a letter tonight to send you when I arrive in America. Don't know what I'll have to write, but will just write when I have time. Dr. Hearn is going down with us to Shanghai. Miss Moon is exceedingly weak and refuses to eat anything and it doesn't seem that she could last long going on that way, but sometimes she has attacks which seem to give her super-natural strength. This makes my home-going sad and yet I count it a privilege to be able to minister to dear Miss Moon, even this little. I was much disappointed when I found that her condition was going to hurry me off to America this winter. I did want to get in one more good winter's work in China before going home but the Father's hand guides still, and I am willing to following for He has never made a mistake and lead (?) me wrong yet. When I have made mistakes it was when I failed to submit to His leading. Last winter while I had to be away from my work I thought, and I think all the mission agreed with me, that I should go home then, so that I might the sooner be ready to return after the war was over, but I didn't want to go against the Father's will, so I asked Him to manifest His will to me through the Board's answer, and I feel sure that He did, and I have seen since several reasons why it was far better for me not to go then, and this is one very important reason I think, that I should be here now to go with Miss Moon and thus keep any other worker from losing the time from the work to go and take her.

I know you have heard many missionaries experience as to how it feels to be going back home after being out seven years, but you haven't had mine, and so here comes another for you. It is a feeling of joy and sorrow, combined with hopes and fears, smiles and tears. Something altogether indescribable! At one moment I find myself looking forward to getting back home again, then as my thoughts wander on still in the future to getting back to my home in China again...

Jan. 5th, 1913

Now Dr. Willingham since passing over all these days of sorrow, giving up Miss Moon and then passing through some quite severe storms, this morning I have been glancing over what I wrote you between Tsingtan and Shanghai, and I came near deciding to throw it all overboard, ...

Dr. Pruitt or someone in the mission will no doubt write you fully about Miss Moon's illness and why she was sent home, but I suppose it falls to my lot to try to tell you something of the last few days of her stay on earth and of her leaving me at Kobe Japan to go home to be with Jesus. This has made my home-going a sad one, and yet I know it is so much better for her that I should endeavor not to be depressed over it. It grieves us to give her up; one whom we loved and esteemed so highly, not only for her work's sake but also for her own dear self's sake. She was gradually growing weaker when we left Tsingtan with her, but after we got to Shanghai she failed more rapidly until by the time for us to sail she had grown so weak that we questioned the advisability of starting with her. But finally decided to come on as tickets were already bought and passage arranged for but instead of improving she steadily became weaker until her poor tired suffering body fell asleep and her soul went to be with her Lord.

It was on Wednesday evening Dec. the eighteenth that the most decided change came over her as her body became weaker her mind seemed to become clearer and that night at ten o'clock when I was giving her some of the grape juice she relished so much, she said, "Where did this grape juice come from?" and when I told her that Dr. Hearn had bought it for her, she said, "Oh, Dr. Hearn is a good man. Will you tell me why it is that Christian people are so good?" I told her that I thought it was because Christ sent His Holy Spirit to live in their hearts. Then she said, "Why don't you pray for Him to come and fill my heart." I said, "I have been praying this very day Miss Moon that He would come and give you the peace and comfort which He alone can give." And she looked up at me smiling and said, "You have? Well He has come, Jesus is right here now." Then she said, "Would you pray now that He will fill my Heart and stay with me, for when Jesus comes in He drives out all evil, you know." I then prayed with her, she joining in the prayer occasionally and when we had finished she repeated the first verse of "Jesus loves me" this I know and asked me if I knew it, and I said, "Yes, many is the time you have taught that to the Chinese haven't you?" and she said, "Yes …but if we want Him to stay with us we must trust Him mustn't we?" Then (she) asked me to sing "Simply trusting every day" and I sang it for her, and she said, "Ah, but that is a sweet old song!" Then she would say over and over, "We are weak but He is strong." From that time her mind seemed better, though at times she was unconscious until the day she passed away she seemed to understand everything but couldn't speak. When spoken to she gave signs that she understood and kept pointing upwards and all the night before Christmas Eve she would look around and smile and work her lips as though trying to speak, then with great effort she would raise her hands and put her fists together as the Chinese do to greet anyone and act as though she were greeting someone. Christmas Eve at one o'clock in the afternoon she fell asleep just before we sailed from Kobe.

After consulting the captain and surgeon of the ship we concluded the best thing to do was to have her remains cremated in Yokahama and with the physician's certificate and the undertaker's cremation certificate I would have less trouble getting her body through. We discussed burying her at Sea, but the captain of the ship advised very strongly against that. He said that they only buried friendless people at Sea as a rule unless they had some contagious disease, and he said, "It wouldn't be any credit to the cause of missionaries to do it I am sure." So I had to decide it just as if she were my own loved one as none of her loved ones were here. I hope the Board will not disapprove of what I did for I did what I felt to be best under all the circumstances. Another thing against burying at Sea was that we were out there in the shallow Sea where they said it was not advisable to bury anyone, and the ship was not willing to carry her remains any further without being either embalmed or cremated and they were not sure that I could get her body through then without trouble if only embalmed, so as the cremation seemed to be the safest and also the cheapest I had it done and thus can carry her remains right along in the cabin with me.

Well I'm nearing San Francisco now. I shall close this long epistle. I'm ashamed to send it as it is, but haven't time now to change it, and though it may be tedious for you it explains some things I wanted to explain to you and hope you will bear with me this time.

I will send you my account of expenses of the trip after I get home.

The ship's officers and crew have been exceedingly kind and considerate through all my troubles which naturally gave them considerable trouble too. They not only did what was their duty to do but the many additional little kindnesses to cheer and help me. Truly the Father prepared their hearts that through them the Holy Comforter might work.

Yours in His service,
Cynthia Adaline Miller

Dear Sister:-

I have just gotten a telegram from San Francisco from Dr. Bryan. He sends word that Miss Lottie Moon died in Kobe. Her body was cremated at Yokohama, and the remains have been expressed to me here. I suppose they will arrive here in Richmond about next Sunday or Monday. I have notified

Dr. Moon of this city. I suppose her relatives will wish to take charge of the remains on arrival. If I can serve you in any way, call on me.

    With best wishes,

    Yours fraternally,

    R. J. Willingham to Mrs. Isaac Moon, January 15, 1913.

Jan. 20, 1913.

Miss Cynthia Miller,

Pickton, Texas.

Dear Sister:-

    Your favor of Jan. 14th has been received and I have just read it. I thank you for writing to me so fully and giving me the information in reference to the school, and also to our dear Sister, Miss Lottie Moon. I had heard from Dr. Bryan by wire and we have been looking for the remains of Miss Lottie to come by express, but so far I have not heard anything from the package which Dr. Bryan sent from San Francisco. I suppose it will be here tomorrow.

    I do not know just where you are at this time, so I am writing this letter in order that it may be forwarded to you in case any letter comes from you in the next few days. I leave tomorrow for a trip down South. Do not expect to return until next week.

    Please go to some place now where you can be quiet and rest. May the Lord watch over and bless you.

    Yours fraternally,

    R. J. Willingham

Tengchowfu, Shantung

China.

Via Chefoo

April 18, 1913

Mrs. Mathi Moon,

Paris Texas,

Dear friend:

    I am enclosing to you a letter which came recently addressed to the late Miss Moon. You no doubt know ere this that our dear friend and faithful Co-laborer passed to her reward last December.

Miss Moon took sick early in the fall of last year. In the latter part of October she was afflicted with a severe carbuncle on the back of the neck.

As our Tengchowfu Station has no foreign physician (the Presbyterian physician located here was not at home at the time), we sent to the nearest Station, which is twenty miles away, and secured a foreign nurse, who came and took Miss Moon to their hospital at Hwanghien.

Later Dr. Gaston of Laichowfu took Miss Moon to his hospital and there she was cared for by our mission doctors and nurse until Nov. 25th when she was taken to Tsingtao Hospital, where she with Miss Miller waited a few days and then started for America.

On Dec. 24 while the steamer was anchored at Kobe Japan, Miss Moon passed away. The remains were cremated in Japan and the urn containing the ashes was taken to Virginia for burial.

We all loved Miss Moon very much. She was one of the best missionaries in this part of China.

We miss her very much and I am sure that those of you who were looking forward to her visit in the U. S. are deeply disappointed with not seeing her again.

You have our sympathy in this loss.

On last October fourth Miss Moon made her will making me the Executor of her estate.

I have just been to Chefoo to see the American Consul with whom was deposited the will.

The Consul has authorized me to sell the property left by Miss Moon and attend to other matters pertaining to the estate.

Last January I wrote to Mrs. Margaret Moon of Crewe, Va. who is the beneficiary of the estate. As yet I have no word from Mrs. Moon.

The Consul orders me to wait two weeks longer for a reply. Should you care to write to the Consul you can address Mr. Julian H. Arnold, American Consul, Chefoo, China, Shantung. If I can answer further questions I shall be glad to do so.

Seeing your name and request on the enclosed envelope I have taken the liberty to write you this short letter.

If I can serve you in any way in these matters please let me know. I shall always be glad to do any thing for the relatives of Miss Lottie Moon. She was exceedingly kind and helpful to me as a new missionary.

When I came to China four and one half years ago Miss Moon was here in Tengchowfu alone. She took me in and provided my meals for nearly one year when I began housekeeping. But that was nothing strange or unusual for Miss Moon. She was kind and loving to all.

The poor people of Tengchowfu, of whom there are many, miss the aid which was so generously given them by Miss Moon.

Frequently we hear people, heathen people, speak of this and all have a good word of praise for Miss Moon.

She truly lived for the Chinese. Hoping this will reach you in due course I am

Sincerely,
W. W. Adams

W. W. Adams,
Tengchowfu, Shantung,
China
Via Chefoo

IN MEMORIAM—LOTTIE MOON.

(*Long missionary in China, dying in Japan, the ashes of her body were brought to America and interred at Crewe, VA., January 29, 1913.*)

Bettie Fowlkes.

And thou art come! And this is all they bring me of my friend
From 'cross the sea—sea, broad and world—embracing as the heart I love!
Ounces of paltry dust robbed by keen flame of all its comeliness—life's hue,
Fair lines of form, a lingering light in quench'd orbs—eyes that I knew,
Eloquent of love and aims, unmeasured.

Here 'neath earth's sod place we today some ashes, refuse of mortal change.
Can hence come body spiritual, immune from change, from incorruption?
From this dry dust, by flame expelled, o'er Japan's main rose vapors
Invisible—perchance o'er China's bosom soared to fall as loving rain,
Or, floating far to native land, blend with their kindred dust.

The "body spiritual"! Who, on grave gazing or sealed urn hath gazed,
Nor challenged sacred paradox? But who hath found what matter is or spirit?
Whether by nature or degree refined—their laws diverse? Say we, vain,
Man's philosophy that would explain an alchemy divine!

He who could this life and soul with matter blend can purge it of corruption
E'en as the soul of sin. But this we know, what master so employeth life
As with life's Truth, its pupils, to inspire, doth do a work immortal;
For "things not seen" shall live and live eternal.

Sleep well, loved worker, then; rich is thy gain.
Rest safe, dear ashes here; thy friends are near:
One with her arms so empty that, with fear,
Heart trembling, whisp'reth, "Shall we meet again?"

Washington, D. C.
From the *Religious Herald*
February 13, 1913

INDEX